D1220103

THEATERS OF CONVERSION

Theaters of Conversion

Religious Architecture and Indian Artisans in Colonial Mexico

Samuel Y. Edgerton
with photographs by Jorge Pérez de Lara

drawings by Mark Van Stone, James E. Ivey, and the author

University of New Mexico Press
Albuquerque

First edition

Library of Congress Cataloging-in-Publication Data

Edgerton, Samuel Y.

Theaters of conversion : religious architecture and Indian artisans in colonial Mexico / Samuel Y. Edgerton ; with photographs by Jorge Pérez de Lara ; drawings by Mark Van Stone, James E. Ivey, and the author.

p. cm.

ISBN 0-8263-2256-5

1. Christian art and symbolism—Modern period, 1500—Mexico.

2. Church architecture—Mexico.

3. Missionaries—Mexico—History.

I. Pérez de Lara, Jorge. II. Title.

N7914.A1 E34 2001

704.9'482'0972—dc21 00-011870

The following photographs taken by Mr. Pérez de Lara and the author are of monuments belonging to the Mexican cultural patrimony under the custody of INAH: I.1, I.2, I.4, 1.1, 1.2, 1.3, 1.4, 1.6, 1.7, 2.3, 2.4, 2.6, 2.7, 2.9, 2.10, 2.11, 2.12, 2.13, 2.14, 2.15, 2.16, 2.17, 2.18, 2.19, 2.27, 2.28, 2.30, 3.1, 4.1, 4.2, 4.7., 5.2., 5.3, 5.4, 5.6, 5.7, 5.8, 5.9, 5.10, 5.11, 5.12, 5.15, 5.16, 5.19, 6.2, 6.3, 6.4, 6.5, 6.6, 7.12, 7.13, 7.14, 7.16, 7.17, 7.18, 7.19, 7.20, 7.21, 7.22, 7.23, 7.24, 7.25, 7.26, 7.27, 8.1, 8.3, 8.4, 8.20.

All photographs and drawings not otherwise credited are the work of the author.

Printed in Hong Kong

To the inspiration and memory of

Linda Schele (1942–1998)

CONTENTS

PREFACE AND ACKNOWLEDGMENTS

My reason for writing this book was prompted by two decisive instances. The first occurred in December 1987, when, after returning from Italy where I was finishing a book about the relationship of art and science in the European Renaissance, my wife, Dottie, and I were invited to spend the Christmas holidays with our daughter, Perky, and her husband, Brian Meunier, both enjoying a sabbatical year in Oaxaca, Mexico. We had never in our lives been so far south of the United States before and possessed not the foggiest notion of Mexico's unique indigenous culture let alone her rich Hispanic heritage. One day during our visit, however, we were taken on a tour of Monte Albán, that ancient Zapotec/Mixtec acropolis just outside Oaxaca city. I knew nothing about it beforehand and was totally unprepared aesthetically as well as culturally for what we were about to experience.

I have not forgotten my amazement upon first setting eyes on those splendid ruins, magically enhanced at that moment by dramatic clouds sweeping up behind the stark gray-green masonry. I was awestruck and realized right then and there that I would have to know why anyone would want to construct such mighty monuments. I immediately went down to the library in Oaxaca, checked out Joseph Whitecotton's book *The Zapotecs: Princes, Priests, and Peasants* and read it overnight. A few days later, we returned to the States, and I quickly followed up by reading Michael Coe's two popular paperbacks, *Mexico* and *The Maya,* both just out in revised editions. From *The Maya,* I learned further about the extraordinary recent advancement in the decipherment of the heretofore inscrutable Maya hieroglyphics. With reaffirmed excitement I sought out and joined the Pre-Columbian Society at the University of Pennsylvania Museum in Philadelphia, where a study group reviewing the latest translations of Maya inscriptions was being conducted by hieroglyphic expert Ben Leaf. For the next several years, I dutifully commuted to Philadelphia on the second Saturday of every month to attend Ben's seminar. Along with Ben, I met and befriended fellow glyph mavens John Harris and Lloyd Anderson, who have over the years aroused more new ideas in my head than they will ever realize until they read this book. Ben Leaf prompted me to join another hieroglyphic workshop led by the charismatic Linda Schele, perhaps the most brilliant Maya scholar of the twentieth century. Every year in March, a colloquium convenes in her name at the University of Texas, Austin, to which linguists, epigraphers, and iconographers, amateur as well as professional, come from all over the world to catch up on the newest pre-Columbian revelations. After attending several of these workshops during the early 1990s, I became fast friends with Linda. Thanks to Mary Dell Lucas and her Far Horizons Archaeological and Cultural Trips, Linda and I paired together on a number of excursions to ancient Maya sites in eastern Mexico and Guatemala. During one of these in 1993, on a day that turned out to be the determining moment leading to the inception of this book, we were touring the Tzotzil Maya town of Chamula in the state of Chiapas, Mexico. Stopping before the community church in the center of the town, we began to discuss this most remarkable example of mixed Hispanic Christian and preconquest religious iconography. Linda, of course, quickly recognized the traditional Maya motifs openly displayed on this supposedly Christian edifice, but I was just as quick to point out the equally overt attempts by the local Maya artisans to inculcate European Renaissance-style illusionism in their otherwise native expressions. Right then, Linda turned to me with this admonishment: why didn't I, with all my background in Italian Renaissance art history, take upon myself the task of unraveling the politics and aesthetics of this peculiar Indian-Spanish promiscuity?

And so entered the bee into my bonnet. From that moment on I understood the direction of the next step in my scholarly life. This book is the result of Linda's prod that day. I only pray that she, who tragically died of cancer in April 1998, would have approved of my ultimate interpretation, which deviated somewhat from her anticipation. In any case, I have dedicated the book to Linda Schele in fond memory of that decisive inspiration.

My book also owes much to the influence of the burgeoning Internet, especially to so-called listserves where professional and amateur scholars share knowledge almost instantaneously in universal and borderless cyberspace. I speak specifically about four list-serve networks to which I subscribe, code-named AZTLAN, POST1492, NAHUAT-L, and SPANBORD, the fellow "listeros" of which all specialize in various matters of pre-Columbian history and Spanish colonial civilization in America. Indeed, I am indebted to so many people whose faces I have never seen even as I am exposed to their wide-ranging arguments and ideas. Of particular profit have been my many email exchanges with Claire Farago who first intrigued me about the indigenous Pueblo cultures of New Mexico; with Robert Carlsen concerning the survival of preconquest religious processional rituals among the modern Maya; with John "Fritz" Schwaller and Joe Campbell about the nuances of the Aztec Nahuatl language; with Bruce Rogers about *cenotes* and caves in the Yucatán; with Father Stafford Poole about the Virgin of Guadalupe; and with Larry Feldman, ever a gold mine of knowledge concerning colonial archives in both Spain and America. Fortunately, I was able finally to meet a few of my Internet correspondents in person, opening not only new friendships but also initiating active, face-to-face scholarly cooperation. With Richard Perry, Dottie and I spent a pleasant and useful week in the Yucatán, confronting and discussing the unique colonial churches there; with Bernard "Bunny" Fontana, we examined the beautiful eighteenth-century Franciscan church of San Xavier del Bac in Tucson, Arizona, to the restoration of which Bunny has contributed so much. I hope he will forgive me for excluding this fantastic monument on grounds of being outside the time and space limits of my present project. Bunny's thoughts and ideas about native Pueblo and Hispanic life in the early southwestern United States have nevertheless been basic to my own understanding. With U.S. National Park historian and archaeologist James "Jake" Ivey, Jorge Pérez de Lara and I spent two days studying the ruins of seventeenth-century colonial churches in New Mexico. Jake's on-site archaeological discoveries provide the scientific evidence underpinning my own hypotheses in chapter 11. Jake also generously allowed me to reproduce his architectural drawings as illustrations of structures he has personally excavated and reconstructed; some of these drawings have not been published elsewhere.

Last but hardly least of my debts to the Internet was via AZTLAN, where I first made the acquaintance of Jorge Pérez de Lara, my photographer partner and boon traveling companion in three photo-making expeditions to both Mexico and New Mexico. Through the mediation again of Linda Schele, Jorge and I first met in Austin, Texas, and there, over a Tex-Mex dinner of tacos and cervezas, made our pact to produce this book. Because of his high professional reputation in Mexico, Jorge was able to make an arrangement with the Instituto Nacional de Antropologia e Historia, known as INAH, the official government guardian of Mexico's cultural patrimony, who graciously gave us permission to photograph all relevant monuments under its supervision. For this privilege, we owe special thanks to

Adriana Konzevik for her indispensable intercession. In New Mexico, Jorge and I owe thanks to Gov. Harry Early of the Pueblo of Laguna and Lt. Gov. Laurence Lucero of Isleta Pueblo for permission to take photographs of the still-active, handsome early churches on their respective reservations.

I am likewise indebted to Barry Kiracofe for inviting me to accompany him on field trips to the Mixteca Alta in Oaxaca to see the *conventos* of Coixtlahuaca and Teposcolula on which he had just completed a doctoral dissertation, and to Logan Wagner for putting me up for a week in the Yucatán in order to observe his Earthwatch architectural team survey and document sixteenth-century colonial church sites.

It would not have been possible, of course, to make all these field trips and take all these beautiful photographs without financial support from interested patrons. I am especially grateful to Dean of the Williams College Faculty D. L. Smith and his appropriate committees for underwriting a major portion of these expenses by way of the Faculty Research Fund, the Art Department Powers Fund, and Dean Smith's own special discretionary financial sources.

I would need an extra dozen pages to explain the various and often charming circumstances of my exchanges with not only my wife, Dottie, but so many fellow scholars who offered, sometimes unknowingly and inadvertently, valuable information that helped shape my developing arguments. With regret that more about them cannot here be said, I list their names in alphabetical order, and admonish the reader to remember that many of the thoughts published in the succeeding chapters are beholden to the following. Indeed, I say to Dana Asbury, Gauvin Bailey, Karen Bassie-Sweet, Lynette Bosch, Michael Brown, Louise Burkhart, Lino Cabeza Gelabert, Edward Calnek, Allen Christenson, Flora Clancy, Amy Elder, Antonia Foias, Dody M. Fugate, Carmen Garcia-Pimentel, Brant Gardner, Joachim Garriga Riera, Anne R. Gibbons, Gary Gossen, Frank Hale, Dawn Hall, Ed Hanna, George Hand, Nicholas Hopkins, E. J. Johnson, J. B. Johnson, Lars Jones, Kathryn Josserand, John Justeson, Cecelia Klein, Peter Low, Linda Manning-Schwartz, Sidney Markman, Michael Mathes, Annette McLeod, Penny Morrill, Barbara Mundy, Francis Oakley, Charles Parkhurst, Naomi Pasachoff, Jeanette Favrot Peterson, Richard Phillips, William Pierson, Anson Piper, John Pohl, Michel Quinon, Eloise Quiñones Keber, Peter Selverstone, Melissa Tandysh, John Wasson, Pauline Moffitt Watts, Susan Verdi Webster, Andrew Weeks, and Robert Volz, thank you, and admit that this book could not have been realized without the collective input of your individual encouragement and nuggets of knowledge.

ILLUSTRATIONS

INTRODUCTION

CHAPTER 1

CHAPTER 2

CHAPTER 3

CHAPTER 4

CHAPTER 5

CHAPTER 6

CHAPTER 7

CHAPTER 8

CHAPTER 9

CHAPTER 10

CHAPTER 11

You said
that our gods are not true gods.
New words are these
that you speak;
because of them we are disturbed,
because of them we are troubled.
For our ancestors
before us, who lived upon the earth,
were unaccustomed to speak thus.
From them we have inherited
our pattern of life
which in truth did they hold;
in reverence they held,
they honored our gods.
They taught us
all their rules of worship,
all their ways of honoring the gods.
Thus before them, do we prostrate ourselves;
in their names we bleed ourselves;
our oaths we keep,
incense we burn,
and sacrifices we offer.
. . . .
And now, are we
to destroy
the ancient order of life?

Aztec chiefs to the first twelve Franciscan friars

Then, over the centuries, without much obvious surface change, a rapprochement took place in many spheres, often leading to forms that cannot be securely attributed to either original parent culture, but that were accepted all along as familiar to both. Even when the end result looked more Hispanic than indigenous, the Nahua [Indians], without second thoughts and with good reason, regarded the concept, pattern, or institution as their own.

James Lockhart, Nahuas after the Conquest

Introduction

ART AS A TOOL OF CHRISTIAN CONVERSION

This book is not about the aesthetics or stylistic origins of the European art introduced to the New World by the Christian missionaries (although many surviving examples are beautiful by any standard, as is evident in the accompanying photographs by Jorge Pérez de Lara). Nor will I be looking to reveal any heretofore undiscovered preconquest Indian motifs for their own sake, inadvertently or subversively disguised under Christian veneer—a subject already amply pursued by others.[1] Rather, my purpose here is to illustrate how the promiscuous mixture of Spanish

Gothic and plateresque, Mudéjar, Italian and Flemish Renaissance, and baroque motifs in the architecture, painting, and sculpture brought over by the Europeans (and initially so strange-looking to the indigenous natives) was deployed by the mendicant missionaries in Mexico during the sixteenth century, and in New Mexico during the early seventeenth, in such a creative, indeed theatrical way that native audiences reacted favorably both to the novelty of the style and to its Christian subject matter. This also occurred at the same time in South America, especially in Peru under similar colonial domination, yet it was engineered under a quite different strategy that has yet to be fully studied and compared.[2] I offer here an examination only of what happened in southwestern North America during the first 175 years of the Spanish conquest, in hopes of inspiring more comparative investigations of Catholic conversion efforts by friar missionaries in other lands occupied by the Spanish in that extraordinary era of Western colonial expansion.[3]

Another issue that is purposely side-stepped here is whether the word "syncretism" is applicable to the process I am about to demonstrate. As much as possible I have tried to avoid using this currently controversial term because it implies an interchange of ideas among equals, and surely the conquered Indians were not "equal" to the Spanish in terms of raw military and political power.[4] Instead, I have coined another phrase, "expedient selection," to describe the way the mendicant missionaries used the visual arts for conversion purposes. What the friars seem to have done most often was to choose from the vast store of European artistic motifs and Christian stories just those that would evoke in Indian eyes reassuring resemblances to certain indigenous preconquest concepts.[5] While this collusion between friars and Indian artisans (sometimes bordering on the heretical) was never documented in the contemporary written records, testimony exists all the same, still manifest in the extant fabric of the artifacts themselves.

Whatever the morality of Spanish cultural coercion, many if not most of the Indian artisans in postconquest Mexico became willing participants in the assimilation and dissemination of these European-style visual aids, inadvertent contributors to the great international cross-cultural process that Thomas Kaufmann has called the "diffusion of the Italianate," the spread of Renaissance and baroque art forms from Italy across the Alps and throughout the world during the sixteenth and seventeenth centuries.[6] This was a negotiated accommodation on the part of the American natives just as in transalpine Europe and even Asia. In truth, Spain herself was barely adjusting to the exciting novelty of Italian Renaissance art (much of it sieved through her dynastic consort Flanders) while at the same time she was transmitting her own syncretized version to the New World. In the chapters following, I show that the mostly anonymous Indian masons, sculptors, and painters working in this imported style not only grew expert in its techniques and conventions but also created their own regional version, a kind of "Indian Renaissance," as it were, that flourished in the Christian missions of Mexico from the 1550s until about 1600 and then revived in New Mexico where it endured for yet another two centuries.

This book aims furthermore to supplement

James Lockhart's interpretation of how Christianity established itself among the Indians.[7] My special evidence, however, will not depend on transcribed texts so much as on extant examples of sixteenth- and early seventeenth-century architecture, painting, and sculpture mostly done by natives trained by Spanish and Flemish artisans. What is demonstrated is that this new style, no matter how alien or harshly imposed at first, nonetheless successfully evoked in the Indians a profound and sincere feeling of "divine presence" (however one may want to define "divine" in terms of native spiritual beliefs) just as numinous as their own traditional language of forms. Hans Belting has documented the history of this phenomenon in Christian art from late antiquity to the Renaissance (see his *Likenesses and Presences*[8]). He adds that since the western European Enlightenment, scholars, especially art historians, have tended to dismiss the "miracle-working" power of images as a quaint *retardataire* superstition left over from the Middle Ages, no longer accepted as a legitimate inspiration for making art. The Virgin of Guadalupe, claimed to have been miraculously painted and now enshrined in a grand temple in Mexico City, for instance, has never been taken seriously by art historians, even though her icon is visited by hundreds of believing pilgrims every day, and reproductions hang in more homes and public buildings in Latin America than any other pictorial image. I only wish Belting had gone on in his excellent book to discuss the phenomenon of "divine presence" in the arts of non-European civilizations, because he could easily have demonstrated how all humankind seems universally predisposed to sense this power, no matter how crafted into a particular cultural likeness or style.

I am intrigued that the remarkable persistence of Christianity among all indigenous peoples of Hispanic America, in spite of the cruelties and indignities heaped upon them under three centuries of colonial rule, is due in large measure to the probability that they too sensed "divine presence" in the European-style churches and religious imagery the missionaries introduced. Whether the architectural and artistic examples I discuss here were just extraordinary coincidences or, as I hope to convince, often negotiated by friars and Indians together in the field, will be up to readers to decide. In any case, many of these monuments not only still exist but also are actively venerated by native American Indians to this day.

To claim, as some have, that the Indians only "accepted" Christianity because it was so thoroughly drubbed into them under Spanish occupation, is a demeaning rationale. It implies in fact that the Indians were a servile people. Such an argument denies the Indians yet another vital trait of universal human nature. No peoples anywhere in the world have ever accepted for so long an ideology inflicted upon them against their natural survival instincts—witness the internal collapse of Russian communism, plus the trashing of its secular icons after only seventy years of totalitarian imposition. By the same token, the late medieval version of Roman Catholicism brought to the New World by the Spanish would never have endured had it not struck a profound and sympathetic chord in the inherent psychic predisposition of Native American people.

While it is well documented that the friars were certain their art would have this effect, what was never recorded, unfortunately, is the Indians' immediate reaction to the novel European style. Considering what we now know of preconquest indigenous religious rituals, and what we now know about the universal psychological perception and reception of visual images—what E. H. Gombrich many years ago identified as the "beholder's share"—I believe we are in position, even without written documents, to make some educated assumptions based on the visual forms of the monuments themselves.[9] Just as the Spaniards viewed and comprehended the novelties of the New World according to familiar European historical and ideological models, so the Indians too viewed and comprehended European artistic innovations by trying to associate them with their own familiar autochthonous traditions.

Whether or not the forceful imposition of Christianity upon the subjected Indians had negative material and political consequences, one must still accept the obvious truth that the essentials of both the foreign religion and its expressive visual forms have adhered; even after the native peoples succeeded in throwing off the yoke of European colonialism; even after later civil wars in which religious tradition of any sort was challenged by the "enlightened" forces of Western secular materialism. This book attempts to show some of the reasons why.

What must have been the first questions the friars posed to themselves as they landed in the New World? What sort of didactic "visual aids" and what sort of teaching arena would they need to expedite their conversion strategies? Being so few in number (this problem would remain always crucial in both Mexico and New Mexico), the friars had to come up quickly with a practical plan dependent first and foremost on the availability of materials and the quality of native artisans. No doubt these European latter-day apostles were aware of a famous letter sent by Pope Gregory I to another friar-missionary, Abbot Mellitus, then proselytizing in still-pagan seventh-century Britain:

> The temples in that nation ought not to be destroyed; but let the idols that are in them be destroyed; let holy water be made and sprinkled on the said temples, let altars be erected, and relics placed. For if these temples are well built, it is requisite that they be converted from the worship of devils to the service of the true God; that the nation, seeing that their temples are not destroyed, may remove error from their hearts, and knowing and adoring the true God, may they more familiarly resort to the places to which they have been accustomed. . . . For there is no doubt that it is impossible to efface everything at once from their obdurate minds; because he who endeavors to ascend to the highest place, rises by degrees or steps, and not by leaps.[10]

The difficulty for the friars' applying Pope Gregory's advice to the similar situation in the Americas, however, was that the temples of the New World, even though soundly built of solid masonry, did lack one architectural feature essential to the presentation and preservation of the mystery of the Christian Mass, namely the technical means for spanning and enclosing a broad interior space, with openings specially placed to focus natural light for theatrical effect. How the friars and

Indians worked together to solve this matter is the express concern of later chapters.

In any case, an appropriate architectural plan and visual aids strategy was, surprisingly, agreed upon by the friars as early as the 1530s and followed more or less uniformly for the rest of the century by all three of the competing mendicant orders in Mexico. The architectural structures most famously built by the Franciscans, Dominicans, and Augustinians in accordance with this strategy are referred to as *conventos* (monasteries), although they were much more than mere monastic residences. The arrangement of contiguous parts in these structures was unique to Mexico proper and, though having some influence on the missionary architecture of South America during the same period, remained sufficiently different to suggest that their original formation had been conditioned by local, preconquest traditions quite other than those in the lower continent. Many modern Americans, especially of Anglo-Protestant heritage, persuasion, or both, have tended to dismiss these Roman Catholic structures in Mexico as pretentious palaces built for decadent priests by sullen Indian slaves.

Fig. I.1 Convento of Nuestra Señora, Izamal, Yucatán, looking southeast. Photograph by Jorge Pérez de Lara.

Fig. I.2
Detail of relief sculpture with artist's signature from the western facade of the convento church of Santa María Magdalena, Cuitzeo, Michoacán. Photograph by Jorge Pérez de Lara.

Their striking monumentality even by European standards (fig. I.1) is often disparagingly contrasted with the smaller scale and modesty of the churches and meetinghouses erected in the English colonies. The truth of the matter, however, is that these seemingly grandiose Mexican buildings were quite spare in both decoration and creature comforts, and staffed by no more than four or five resident friars each. The vast extra space was for the thousands of neighborhood Indians who crowded inside both to learn the tenets of the Catholic faith and to be protected from exploitation by the greedy Spanish lay-settlers [*encomenderos*] who really did abuse the Indians as slaves.[11] Only in the conventos were the Indians safeguarded and benevolently cared for, albeit under suffocating if well-meaning paternalistic authority. Some four hundred such complexes were eventually constructed in various population centers across New Spain before 1600, an ample testament to the artistic cooperation of at least a large contingent of native craftspeople in the service of the new religion, however forcefully it may have been imposed.

Essential to my argument in the following chapters is the fact that until the 1570s when recurrent, virulent smallpox epidemics had wiped out more than 75 percent of the innocent indigenous peoples, the number of all European immigrants in Mesoamerica, including conquistadors, missionaries, and lay-settlers, was proportionally minuscule (probably less than one-tenth of 1 percent in relation to the huge aboriginal population). Because of this paucity of Europeans, especially those with trade skills, the missionaries had to depend on Indian craftspeople to build and decorate their new Christian edifices.[12] Since the majority of the monuments discussed here were actually built after midcentury (usually replacing cruder pole-and-thatch temporary structures), it is probably true that most of these native workers were second- and even third-generation converted Christians—already loyal parishioners who, as Lockhart has pointed out, took pride in the upkeep of their new religious centers.[13] The natives not only did all the architectural construction but also painted and sculpted most of the decor, much of it still visible today—and in one very rare instance, on the handsomely sculpted plateresque facade of the Augustinian church at Cuitzeo, Michoacán, the decorative element was not only signed by an indigenous artist but framed in a pretentiously Renaissance-style Latin-inscribed cartouche: *F. Io. Metl me fecit* [F. Johannes Metl made me] (fig. I.2). *Metl* is the Nahuatl word for "maguey plant," and only a native Indian would have carried such a surname.[14] Unfortunately, the contribution of such largely unknown native artisans has yet to be recognized, even though their artisanry was as original and inspired as that of their pre-Columbian ancestors who built the pyramid temples that so attract the admiration of modern tourists.

Figure I.3 is of a similar plaque on the facade of the mission church at Acolman near Mexico City, this time showing the hieroglyphic place-name of the preconquest aboriginal community. The image shows a truncated right arm with streams of blood flowing flowerlike from the shoulder and refers to an Aztec story of creation when the native primordial deities plucked the first human being from Lake Texcoco and carried him by the arm to this sacred place where the Augustinians subsequently built their mission.[15] How remarkable that the supposedly uncompromising Christian friars would allow such a blatantly "pagan" reference to be exhibited on the front of their holy church! In fact, the display of preconquest place-signs as emblems decorating the facades of local convento buildings seems to have been generally encouraged by the missionary friars throughout New Spain during the sixteenth century, like "union labels" signifying that these buildings were regarded as community centers by and for the native townspeople.[16]

On an outside wall of the monumental Dominican mission at Cuilapan near Oaxaca city, one can still see a stone plaque on which is carved a pair of dates in the native Mixtec calendric style, apparently celebrating a sacred cycle of thirteen years that Indian workers devoted to building this handsome structure (fig. I.4). Sculpted by a skilled Mixtec artist, it displays the full hieroglyphic insignia for a set of separated year-, month-, and day-signs: "10 Reed 11 Serpent 6 Reed" on one side, and "10 Flint 11 Death" on the other (in the Christian calendar corresponding to August 5 and August 13, 1555, on the left, and either August 19, 1568, or January 4, 1569, on the right).[17] This lapidary commemoration, again placed with the friars' encouragement, was intended for Mixtec eyes; for the benefit of Europeans who only understood Western Christian calendrics, the numerals "1555" were crudely inserted in the Mixtec inscription.

There was considerable diversity among the various Indian communities themselves, presenting a correspondingly diverse set of challenges to the friars trying to adapt their conversion tactics. The vast geographic region conquered by Spain between the Isthmus of Panama to the south and the great desert of northern Mexico has been termed "Mesoamerica" by anthropologists to distinguish the general ethnicity of its collective inhabitants from those of South America and northern North America (fig. I.5), but it was by no means uniform either in languages or religious customs.[18]

Aztec Mexico was only a piece of the whole "New Spain" in which the mendicant friars wandered to proselytize during the sixteenth through eighteenth centuries. The name "Mexico" in fact derives from "Mexica," the true Nahuatl-language name for the Aztec people. By 1521 the Aztecs (for convenience sake, I continue to use that term) had only managed to dominate the central portion of Mesoamerica, albeit an area almost the same geographical size as Spain itself with three times the population.

Fig. I.3 Detail of relief sculpture of place glyph from the western facade of the convento church of San Agustín, Acolman, Mexico.

Nahuatl, the lingua franca of the Aztec empire, gave particular cultural cohesion to the dense habitation in the region around the Aztec capital, Tenochtitlan (now Mexico City), the core of the old empire comprising the present-day states of Mexico, Puebla, Morelos, eastern Guerrero, northern Oaxaca, western Veracruz and Hidalgo.[19] Here the missionary friars first set up their headquarters in the years just after Cortés's conquest. The former Aztec nobility was permitted by the new rulers to continue to exercise their old privileges on a local level, which in turn allowed the friars to take advantage of established political networks to expedite Christian proselytization.

The Indians of Nahuatl-speaking but independent Tlaxcala, which had remained an island of resistance in the geographical midst of the empire long before the Spanish invasion, not only supplied thousands of troops to Cortés (crucially tipping the military balance in his favor) but also were being converted to Christianity even before the official missionary friars arrived. Indeed, the Christianized Tlaxcalans continued to serve as elite janissaries in the Spanish colonial army, somewhat as native Gurkhas in India did for the British. Tlaxcalan troops accom-

Fig. I.4
Detail of relief sculpture of date plaque from the north sanctuary wall of the basilica, convento of Santiago, Cuilapan, Oaxaca. Photograph by Jorge Pérez de Lara.

panied Pedro de Alvarado in his conquest of Maya Guatemala in 1524 and took part in later Spanish *entradas* into Florida, New Mexico, and Arizona. Tlaxcalans became colonial settlers themselves in the conquered Spanish territories.

In the Mesoamerican hinterland north and south of Tenochtitlan lived many other native cultures speaking different tongues and practicing a variety of religious beliefs. The sparsely populated and arid northern frontier of the Aztec empire had always been threatened by uncontrolled Indian "barbarians," whom the sophisticated Nahua disparagingly termed "Chichimeca."[20] Actually, the Chichimecs consisted of many tribes of relatively simple agriculturalists and nomadic hunter-gatherers, but also included the Hopi, Zuni, and other more urbanized societies living in masonry houses in present-day New Mexico and Arizona. The friars would only penetrate these disparate and stubbornly resistant so-called Pueblo communities in the early seventeenth century.

Between the Chichimecs and the sophisticated native civilizations in central Mesoamerica were buffer nations of Tarascan and Otomí Indians, inhabiting what are now the Mexican states of Jalisco, Michoacán, Guanajuato, Querétaro, and Hidalgo. These likewise linguistically distinct peoples lived cheek by jowl with the northern Chichimecs with whom they were continually at war, thus serving as frontier police shielding the now Spanish-occupied Aztec territories. The friars found it expeditious to encourage this Tarascan and Otomí military tradition, leading to some fascinating if totally unorthodox Christian iconography

Fig. I.5 Distribution of Indian nations in sixteenth-century Mesoamerica. Drawing by Mark Van Stone, typography by Melissa Tandysh.

such as the mission church at Ixmiquilpan in northern Hidalgo (see chap. 6).

To the southeast of the fertile Mesoamerican central *altiplano* lay the arid moonlike mountains of the present-day state of Oaxaca, inhabited by the Zapotecs and Mixtecs, again speaking totally different languages. Like the Aztecs, these peoples were consummate artisans, masters of monumental masonry architecture and handsome painting. They also rivaled the Maya in the use of writing, arithmetic, and astronomically related calendrics. Indeed it was the Mixtec who gave the calendar and rebus-style writing to the Aztecs. Politically, however, Mixtecs and Zapotecs were separated into tiny lineage-led village kingdoms, constantly bickering with one another and thus falling easy early prey for Aztec conquest. The Aztecs treated them brutally and even attempted to eradicate the native Oaxacan languages. When Cortés arrived, the Mixtecs and Zapotecs succumbed peacefully to Spanish rule as the lesser of two evils. Their subsequent conversion also came about in relative peace, although because of traditional isolation in autonomous villages, preconquest "idolatry" persisted, blending into a colorful "folk Christianity" practiced in the region to this day.

Farther to the east of Mixtec and Zapotec Oaxaca, in the present Mexican states of Chiapas, Tabasco, Campeche, Yucatán, and Quintana Roo (the latter three conjoined in the Yucatán peninsula), and the adjacent independent nations of Central America dwelled and still dwell the Maya. Some five hundred years before the Spanish invasion, their glorious Classical civilization, once centered in the Petén rainforest of Guatemala, Belize, and Honduras had already collapsed. The Postclassic Maya, now divided into at least twenty-eight separate language groups, resided in the mountainous highlands that surrounded their former jungle paradise. Though never again reviving the stunning qualities of architecture, sculpture, and painting for which the Classic period is justly renowned, they still lived in handsome masonry-built cities, and in the Yucatán, still produced painted codices written in their remarkable syllabic hieroglyphic script. The treasured Dresden Codex, now in the Saxon State Library, Dresden, Germany, is one of only four Postclassic examples that have survived, revealing that the Maya still kept track of their extraordinary dual calendar and continued to study astronomical patterns, with the ability even to predict eclipse cycles.

Nonetheless, and in spite of their continuing cultural sophistication, the Maya at the time of the Spanish arrival were also split into arch-rival linguistic communities ruled by autocratic lineages, and thus were easy victims for the imminent Spanish conquest. First the highland Guatemala Maya (K'iche, Tzu'tujil, and Kakchiquel speakers) fell to Pedro de Alvarado after 1524; next the lowland Yucatán Maya (Yucatec speakers) after 1545, to the Montejo clan. The Franciscans then carried on a unique church-building campaign in the Yucatán, presenting a special paradigm case (see chap. 3). Conversion of the highland Maya in Guatemala and Chiapas was largely ceded to the Dominicans, who in this region were less organized, or less vigilant perhaps, since the Maya under their guidance managed to substantially modify enforced Christianization, preserving indigenous customs more obviously than any other of the conquered native peoples in Mesoamerica.

O Mexico, that such mountains should encircle and crown you! With reason will your fame now spread because in you shines forth the Faith and the Gospel of Jesus Christ. You, previously the mistress of sin, are now the teacher of truth. You, formerly in darkness and obscurity, now give forth the splendor of Christian doctrine and civilization. Your submission to the most unconquered Caesar, Don Carlos [Emperor Charles V], does you greater honor and glory than the tyrannical sway that in other times you sought to impose upon all. Then you were a Babylon, full of confusion and wickedness; now you are another Jerusalem, the mother of provinces and kingdoms. . . . At one time, on the authority of the Prince of Darkness, you were eager to challenge, capture and sacrifice men and women and to offer their blood to the demon on cards and on bits of paper; today, with pious prayers and holy sacrifices, you adore and profess the Lord of lords. O Mexico! If you would raise your eyes to the mountains that encircle you, you would see more good angels aiding and defending you than the former demons who stood against you in order to plunge you into sins and errors.

Fray Toribio Motolinía, Historia de los Indios de la Nueva Españaz

Chapter 1

THE MILLENNIUM OF THE MENDICANT FRIARS

Was ever a statement like the one on the facing page more quaintly out of tune with the ecumenical sentiments of North Americans in this dawning century of universal human rights? Could one ever believe that the pious missionary who wrote this was just as sensitive to the dignity and privileges of the indigenous Indians as any liberal humanitarian today? I answer emphatically yes, adding further that the first mendicant friars who came to the Americas after Columbus's "discovery" were the sixteenth-century equivalent of the twentieth-century Peace Corps.

Just as in our present secular humanist age when benevolent Western volunteers go forth in the non-Western world to help the indigenous inhabitants become economically prosperous, physically healthy (i.e., scientifically up to date with the West), and conscious of their human rights, so in an earlier more spiritual age, the European missionary friars, as compassionate regarding the oppressed poor as any of today's practitioners of liberation theology, believed (with just as much sincerity) that the highest and most inalienable human right—more important than the right to life itself—was the salvation of one's soul, and that the highest form of altruism, even to the sacrificing of one's own life to achieve it, was to confer that ultimate right upon the Indians who had not yet received the word of Jesus.

In this chapter I examine the historical circumstances and religious mood in late medieval Europe that may help explain what motivated the mendicants, not all of whom were Spanish, to come to the Americas in the first place and willingly suffer unimaginable hardships and deprivations, such as trekking in bare feet through steaming jungle and over icy mountains with little sustenance and no weapons except absolute Christian faith and obsession with their holy duty to save the Indians' souls. The primary historical records of the sixteenth-century missionary religious orders are vast, containing so much material about the life and times of the friars (among whom, as in any group of more than eleven human beings including the original Apostles, there has to be at least one bad apple), it has been relatively easy for critics to find instances of hypocrisy and malevolence. Contrariwise, because so few documents exist by Indians (and there is no record of a preconquest Indian Bartolomé de Las Casas condemning the atrocities of his own people), it has been all too easy to assume the native side as always virtuous.

Notwithstanding, there is abundant confirmation from both sides that the majority of mendicants serving in Mexico during the sixteenth century, including the writer of the manifesto of this chapter's epigraph, were as concerned about the welfare of the Indians as the outspoken Las Casas, even if they did not indulge in hyperbolic public condemnations. In truth, the missionary friars in their own self-effacing way were in the forefront of all Renaissance Europeans, Catholic or Protestant, in protecting the indigenous peoples of the Americas from exploitation by greedy European fortune seekers. Here, for example is how Fray Juan de Zumárraga, Franciscan and first archbishop of Mexico (1528–48), responded to Spanish encomenderos who warned him against mingling with "the evil-smelling Indians":

> You are the ones who give out an evil smell according to my way of thinking, and you are the ones who are repulsive and disgusting to us, because you seek only vain frivolities and because you lead soft lives just as though you were not Christians. These poor Indians have a heavenly smell to me; they comfort me and give me health, for they exemplify for me that harshness of life and penitence which I must espouse if I am to be saved.[1]

The Catholic mendicant, or "regular" friars following the monastic rule (Latin, *regula*), belonged to just three international and autonomous orders operating in the Americas from the first decades of the Spanish conquest: Franciscans, Dominicans, and Augustinians. The Jesuits, a largely Counter-Reformation order founded in 1540, did not enter Mesoamerica until late in the sixteenth century, after the general architectural and visual aids programs of the mendicant friars had already been well established. The regulars are also to be distinguished from the "secular," or non-order, clergy of priests, monsignors, and bishops who made up the hierarchy of the official Spanish church. The Spanish crown under increasing Counter-Reformation pressure became more and more uneasy concerning the uninhibited freedom (and potential heresy) of the mendicant missionaries and in the 1550s began to shift control of the converted Indians away from the friars to the seculars, who were to organize the natives into orderly parishes and dioceses under the inquisitorial eye of the mother church in Spain. Indeed, by the end of the sixteenth century, except for the far frontier wilds of the Spanish empire in the Americas, the mendicant friars in Mexico were all but marginalized and isolated within their spacious convents, holding out with a few loyal Indian converts in a last apotheosis of artistic and theatrical creativity.

Anyone wishing to form a fair-minded understanding of the motivations and operations of the original mendicants' mission to the Americas must begin by reading Robert Ricard's *Spiritual Conquest of Mexico,* first published in French in 1933 and available in English since 1966. While Ricard was thoroughly convinced of the moral righteousness of Christian conversion and patronizingly viewed the Indians as "childlike," he also provided equal and ample documentation of the friars' egregious if only occasional excesses and moral lapses, as well as their more usual generous and constructive enterprises. For instance, he minced no words in condemning the sixteenth-century church for not allowing the Indians to become priests or members of the clerical orders. While his title, *Spiritual Conquest,* may still be displeasing to some non-Christian readers, Ricard's overall scholarship remains unchallenged—although it should be said that his sources were all European. There is little information here about the religious beliefs and rituals of the indigenous Indians before conversion.

Concerning the religious temperament of late medieval Europe that motivated mendicant friars like Zumárraga to come to America in the first place, John Leddy Phelan's brief *Millennial Kingdom of the Franciscans in the New World* paints a vivid picture of the eschatological millenarianism rampant among the Christian faithful just before the year 1500, when many believed that the Second Coming and Last Judgment were imminent, and that the discovery of America was God's sign that mankind's redemption could come only through conversion of the last of the world's heathens. Disagreeing with Phelan's thesis that the friars were so apocalyptically obsessed, Edwin Edward Sylvest Jr. in his *Motifs of Franciscan Mission Theory in Sixteenth Century New Spain,* argues instead that the Franciscans were much more practical and even political in their motivations and dealings with the Indians. Sylvest also supplies an excellent summary of the training and indoctrination of the Franciscan friars on the eve of their mission to the Americas.

For background concerning internal church

politics in Europe, the mounting reformist movements culminating in the controversial writings of Erasmus and the intense debates going on in the Vatican concerning the nature of God, whether transcendent or imminent in the affairs of man, see Francis Oakley's *Western Church in the Later Middle Ages*.[2] Regarding lay piety and "cult of saints" in the small towns of late medieval Spain and how both orthodox bishops and reformist mendicants viewed this as recidivist polytheism (just as they were suspicious of "syncretism" among the American Indians), read William Christian's *Local Religion in Sixteenth-Century Spain*. The ecclesiastical controversies in Europe described by these authors significantly affected the style and substance of the friars' evangelizing in the New World. Fernando Cervantes in *The Devil in the New World* presents an excellent parallel study of how these matters touched the Indians as they struggled to comprehend the confusing incongruities of the new religion, particularly the dualistic concept of God versus Devil, a notion initially at odds with the traditional native belief in a universe of alternatives rather than polarities.

Unfortunately for the reader limited to English, most of the primary documents of the friars' activities so far remain untranslated. Among the earliest and most useful for the purposes of this book are the writings of Franciscan Fray Toribio de Benavente Motolinía, especially his *Historia de los Indios de la Nueva España* composed between 1536 and 1541, and *Memoriales* finished around 1549.[3] An English translation of the *Historia* (but not the *Memoriales*) plus an excellent introduction to his life and writings has been provided by Francis Borgia Steck.[4] Fray Geronimo de Mendieta's *Historia eclesiastica indiana*, written about 1595, is also fundamental, but as yet untranslated except for an analysis with excerpts by Phelan, and an abbreviated anthology by Felix Jay.[5] Two other sixteenth-century Franciscan treatises essential to this study are the doctrinal *Rhetorica Christiana* of Fray Diego Valadés published in 1579 and the chronicle *Tratado y docto de las grandezas de la Nueva España* of 1588 by Fray Antonio de Ciudad Real, documenting the journey of inspection he and the newly appointed commissary general of the order, Fray Alonso Ponce, undertook through Mexico during the 1580s.[6] An abridged English translation of only the Yucatán portion of Ciudad Real's chronicle was published by Ernest Noyes in 1932. Also very useful but only published in Spanish are the seventeenth-century Francican treatises by Juan de Torquemada (1615), Diego López de Cogolludo (1688), and Agustín de Vetancurt (1697–98).[7] Cogolludo provides a detailed history of the evangelization of the Yucatán, while Torquemada and Vetancurt follow the Franciscans even into New Mexico where the Friars Minor began to evangelize the Indian pueblos at the turn of the 1600s. Specific to the New Mexican entrada, furthermore, is Fray Alonso de Benavides's *Memorial* of 1620, which has been translated into English.

The most important of all the mendicant friars as far as this book is concerned, Franciscan Pedro de Gante, has left but a half dozen brief letters barely outlining his strategies for instructing the Indians. Almost everything about this seminal figure must be gleaned from various secondhand references in the above-mentioned documents.[8]

From the Domi
Bartolomé de Las
voluminous writin
World Indians als
accounts helpful f
religious life durin
1530s. Later Dom
Dávila Padilla an
from the retrospe
seventeenth centu
1674 respectively
of missionary act
Oaxaca. Likewis
Augustinian mis
algo were mostl
including Fraile
Diego Basalenq
ten as late as 17
Americana The
the last glory d
especially the C
of the rich con

My book al
nary ethnogra
Bernardino de
Dominican Fr
both of whom
native surviv
preconquest
scribing from
these friars n
know about
customs of t
subsumation
Curiously, n
icans worki
America sought similarly to record the customs of the magnificent Inca civilization of
Peru, with the result that we now know far

its once intricate and unique precon-
eligion.
ertheless, twentieth-century critics have
to be dismissive of all Mexican friar
clers as self-serving and glorifying their
issionizing without sympathetic consid-
of native customs or resistance. To be
he friars were addressing European
lic audiences whom they hoped to
ss with their conversion successes and
gain further political and financial sup-
At the same time the friars may have
painting an overly rosy picture of Indian
siasm for Christianity, however, they
just as often and for the same reason
ng out mention of the methods they used
e field to gain the Indians' confidence in
irst place. These methods were frequently
rthodox, bordering on the heretical. If the
s in the field dared reveal in their reports
often they sidestepped official doctrine in
er to win over reluctant souls, the Holy See
Rome, as it suspected during the Council of
nt (1547–63), would have been horrified.
n this vein, some reference should be made
the touchy matter of the Spanish Inquisition
Mexico. Although having nothing to do with
topic of this book, it is relevant because the
ue so often comes up whenever any aspect of
e friars' contribution to indigenous culture is
sessed. Two books in English provide a bal-
nced overview, both by Richard E. Greenleaf:
e first, *Zumárraga and the Mexican Inquis-*
ion, 1536–1543, the second, *The Mexican*
nquisition of the Sixteenth-Century.[9] Suffice
ere to say that throughout the sixteenth century unconverted Indians were excluded from
any jurisdiction by the official Holy Office of
the Inquisition. Moreover, regarding already

converted Indians who were subject to the Inquisition, judgments of apostasy and heresy were far less frequent than those against deviant Spanish colonists (the Inquisition in Mexico as in Spain was always more obsessed with rooting out suspected Lutherans and exposing relapsed Jewish *conversos*). In all Mexico during the sixteenth century, only a single Indian suffered capital punishment by way of the notorious *auto-da-fé*.[10]

The worst instances of inquisitional harshness in Mexico occurred in the Yucatán under the supervision of Fray Diego de Landa (1524–79) between 1562 and 1565, resulting in the unintended deaths of a number of alleged Indian apostates under torture to extract their confessions. Landa's draconian methods, especially his infamous burning of Maya books, have always been difficult to understand, especially since he had a record of staunchly defending the Indians against lay-settler exploitation. Furthermore, Landa wrote a priceless account of indigenous Maya religious rites that is still the basic ethnographic study of preconquest civilization in the Yucatán including an "alphabet" that has since been recognized as the Rosetta Stone for deciphering Maya hieroglyphics (see bibliography for the English translation of Landa's writings by Alfred Tozzer). Inga Clendinnen has attempted to diagnose Landa's curious behavior as a case of Freudian schizophrenia. David Timmer, on the other hand, has suggested that Landa acted quite rationally within the contextual logic of sixteenth-century millenarianism.[11]

Even as Hernán Cortés (1485–1547) was laying siege to the Aztec capital at Tenochtitlan in 1521, the Franciscan friars, at the urging of the conquistador himself (who preferred the humility and dedication of the regular orders to the bureaucracy of the secular clergy), were preparing for their epochal mission to bring Christianity to the heathen Indios of the newly revealed continent, which many Europeans still thought to be at the farther end of Asia (sometimes called "India" on contemporaneous Ptolemaic maps).

In April of that year, still four months before the fall of the Aztec empire, Pope Leo X, a Medici, issued his bull *Alias felicis* authorizing the Franciscans to commence Christian proselytization. Two friars were immediately dispatched to make contact with Cortés's chaplains in the field. When Leo died the following December, Adrian VI, his Netherlands-born successor (the last non-Italian pope before Polish John-Paul II in 1978) and former tutor of Holy Roman Emperor Charles V, quickly endorsed the Franciscans' mandate with the bull *Exponi nobis fecisti*. Three more friars were sent from Spain on the first of May 1523, arriving in Mexico City four months later. Under direct commission by the emperor, their job was to check out the lay of the new land in preparation for a full-blown mission to follow.[12] These three were not Spanish nationals but Flemish, the most interesting of whom was Peeter van der Moere of Ghent (1486–1572), relative of the emperor and friend of the new Dutch Pope (fig. 1.1). He was highly educated in the *artes liberales,* especially the Quadrivium arts of music and geometry (under geometry were included the new Renaissance art-sciences of shadow-casting and linear perspective), and like the Pope and his other contemporaneous fellow countryman, the great Dutch humanist Desiderius Erasmus, a religious fundamentalist. Better known by his Spanish name Pedro de

Gante, Fray Pedro (although he was only a lay brother) may also have been asked to devise an architectural master plan for the future monastic establishments.

On January 25, 1524, the Feast of the Conversion of Saint Paul, the official Franciscan missionaries embarked for the New World. They landed that May near present-day Veracruz and then walked barefoot for five weeks over the mountains to Tenochtitlan (renamed Mexico City by Cortés and rebuilt as the capital of New Spain) more than four hundred kilometers distant. These were the epochal "twelve," ten ordained priests and two brothers under the leadership of the ascetic Fray Martin de Valencia, a man whom many believed was the avatar of Saint Francis himself.[13] Their number was a deliberate allusion to Jesus' apostles whose original Pentecostal mandate the Pope as Vicar of Christ now passed on to the Franciscans. Moreover, in New Spain they should also found a unique "Indian Republic" like Saint Augustine's "City of God," wherein a purer, more fundamentalist Christianity would be preached as in the "primitive church" of the original New Testament twelve.

Fray Martin and the others had previously served in the special Franciscan province of San Gabriel in Extremadura in western Spain where friars were trained to convert the Moors after the Reconquista. This was the same barren area where Cortés and his fellow conquistadors were born and raised, and where the siren call to escape the bleakness of that spartan landscape and seek exotic adventure elsewhere was especially resonant. The names and reductive "portraits" of all twelve of these apostolic Franciscans are recorded in a charming mural (ca. 1570) still to be seen in the early Franciscan convent of San Miguel at Huejotzingo, Puebla (fig. 1.2), one of the first four to be established in New Spain. Among the kneeling brothers, Fray Martin is indicated just to the left of the cross, and second behind him is Fray Toribio de Benavente, called "Motolinía."

The twelve Franciscan missionaries to the New World were selected on the basis of their unwavering commitment to Saint Francis's vow of poverty. Saint Francis (1181 or 1182–1226)

Fig. 1.1 Fray Pedro de Gante, sixteenth century. Portrait in the Museo Nacional de Historia, Mexico City.

Fig. 1.2 The first twelve Franciscan apostles. Mural in the convento of San Miguel, Huejotzingo, Puebla. Photograph by Jorge Pérez de Lara.

was the son of a wealthy merchant in the small hill town of Assisi in central Italy (Umbria) who abjured his father's riches and sought to live with a few like-minded, ascetic companions, including a woman who later became Saint Claire, in total rejection of worldly goods and pleasures. Some fifty years after the Franciscans first arrived in Mexico, Fray Geronimo de Mendieta recounted that when Fray Toribio and the others passed through Tlaxcala on their way to Tenochtitlan, the Indians, observing the wretched, ragged appearance of Fray Toribio, were heard to murmur, *"motolinía!" Motolinía* is a Nahuatl reflexive verb phrase literally meaning, "he inflicts suffering on himself." Taking this to be a Franciscan compliment (Mendieta translated it *pobre,* or "poor"), Fray Toribio decided to call himself "Motolinía" thereafter.[14]

The Indians were indeed much impressed by the Franciscans' gaunt, ethereal appearance. The *Chronicles of Michoacán* record that when the Tarascan Indians of that region first encountered the Friars Minor, they were amazed that the Franciscans dressed so poorly and differently (in tattered and patched cassocks dyed brown or gray) from other Spaniards.[15] The Indians thought the emaciated friars to be dead men walking in shrouds who returned to the nether world as skeletons to sleep with their women at night.[16] The Indians were even more impressed when they witnessed the mighty Cortés abasing himself before the barefoot mendicants as they arrived in the Mexican capital. First Cortés lay his cloak before Fray Martin de Valencia just as was done for Jesus when he entered Jerusalem on the first Palm Sunday (and also for Saint Francis as depicted in the Assisi frescoes; see fig. 7.2) and then falling to his knees and kissing the friar's hands.[17]

Fray Martin himself was such a hermit that he chose to live in a "cave which is in a hill of almost pyramidal shape" outside Amecameca not far from Tlalmanalco.[18] As the Franciscan was certainly aware, this cave had been especially sacred to the Indians who believed it an abode of indigenous supernatural powers. When it was reported that the friar was mystically elevated in the air while praying and that he conversed with apparitions of Christian saints in this cave, the Indians, according to the early seventeenth-century Indian historian Chimalpahin, were awestruck.[19] After Fray Martin died in 1534, his body was displayed in an open tomb in the convent church of San Luis Obispo at Tlalmanalco. Within a few years nearly all Fray Martin's remains had been stolen by pilgrims. The Indians were so upset they secreted the rest of Fray Martin's relics in the Amecameca cave, which then took on greater reverence than ever.[20] Local Indian cacique Quetzalmacatzin even ordered a church built on the site, today known as Sacromonte and still visited by thousands of native worshipers.

Fray Motolinía is best known for having written the earliest extant eye-witness accounts of the Franciscan mission, covering events between the 1530s and 1550s, the crucial formative years during which the Indians were learning the new style of arts and crafts they would practice so well in the missionary conventos. By the time of his death in about 1569, the Franciscan enterprise in New Spain had grown from the half dozen or so friars already here when the twelve arrived in 1524, to nearly four hundred, with some ninety monastic establishments in central Mexico alone. George Kubler calculated that at least seventy-five were already in existence by 1550.[21] By 1590, according to Mendieta, the Friars Minor had planted some two hundred conventos encircling the capital and radiating outward more than six hundred kilometers into the present Mexican states of Hidalgo, Michoacán, Guanajuato, and Jalisco to the north and west, and Yucatán and Guatemala to the east and south. In addition more than a thousand satellite chapels were in the Indian villages.[22]

By 1535 the Spanish government deemed the new territory safe enough for the first appointed viceroy, Antonio de Mendoza, to assume his duties. For their crucial help in bringing about this state of pacification, the Franciscans were rewarded by being allowed to set up their own independent ecclesiastical authority, to be known as the Province of Santo Evangelio in Mexico City. As John McAndrew observed: "By the end of the century the monasteries were so thickly strewn through [New Spain] that one could travel its length without ever having to sleep in anything but a Franciscan house."[23] By this time too, the number of Franciscan friars missionizing in Mesoamerica had increased to nearly a thousand.[24]

Pope Clement VII, who succeeded Adrian after the latter's death in September 1523, was an Italian and a Medici from Florence with family ties to the Dominican order. He encouraged the black-and-white robed brothers to organize their own counterpart twelve to evangelize in America. Saint Dominic (ca. 1170–1221), the founder of the order, was born and raised in Spain. During his peregrinations to Rome to win support for his order, he met and became a close friend of Saint Francis. The Dominicans, however, emphasized active preaching rather than hermitic asceticism and were regarded as the most intellectual of the mendicant orders (Saint Thomas Aquinas, Saint Albertus Magnus, and Saint Antonine of Florence were all Dominicans). The Dominicans also believed that the holy rosary had been miraculously bestowed upon their founder. Pope Leo X gave official approbation to saying the rosary in 1520, and its recital thus became one of the most important religious practices the order wished to teach the Indians in America.

In 1526 the first Dominican dozen was duly dispatched to Mexico. Disaster struck, however, as five of the friars died within a few weeks after arrival. Four others, gravely ill, then returned to Spain. Only three managed to limp into the Mexican capital. By default, Fray Domingo de Betanzos, a friend of Franciscan Martín de Valencia, became the leader of these diminished Dominican apostles, and not until 1528 did enough replacements arrive to fulfill the sacred number and allow for a serious campaign of evangelization to begin. By 1532 the Dominicans had swelled to almost thirty, but it was already too late to compete with the Franciscans in the comfortable countryside around Mexico City (although they did found a few important houses such as the grand monastery at Tepotzlán, Morelos). Instead, they decided to direct their major effort to the south and east, especially in the Zapoteca-Mixteca region of Oaxaca, which the Franciscans had abandoned, and also into the indigenous Maya territory of Chiapas and western Guatemala. By 1596 the Dominicans numbered more than four hundred friars resident in ninety houses, several of which are some of the finest architectural masterpieces from sixteenth-century Mexico.[25] On the piers flanking the western portico of their great convent church at Yanhuitlán, Oaxaca, relief images of seated dogs with sticks in their mouths (symbolizing obedience to their master) still remind entering worshipers of the

Fig. 1.3 Detail of relief sculpture showing a "dog of the Lord" [*Domini canis*]. Western facade of the convento church of Santo Domingo, Yanhuitlán, Oaxaca. Photograph by Jorge Pérez de Lara.

Fig. 1.4
The first seven Augustinian friars in Mexico. Mural in the portería of the convento of San Nicolás de Tolentino, Actopan, Hidalgo. Photograph by Jorge Pérez de Lara.

old Latin pun on the order's name: *Domini canes* [dogs of the Lord] (fig. 1.3).

The third order joining the Mexican mission was the Augustinian. Seven was the sacred number chosen to designate this friar contingent, which arrived in 1533 under the leadership of the learned Francisco de la Cruz. The Augustinians were actually one of the earliest of the great monastic orders founded in Western Christendom. Conceived originally as a brotherhood of hermits in Egypt during the fifth century, they then dispersed to isolated hermitages in Europe after the Vandal invasions. In the thirteenth century Pope Alexander IV urged the order to take up a more active life as mendicant wanderers in the countryside. Thus in 1533 when the Augustinians betook their mission across the ocean to New Spain they comprehended the call as a providential return to a "Thebaid" wilderness.[26] In their new American retreats, the Augustinians often depicted themselves as wilderness pilgrims, as, for instance, on the wall of the *portería* [vestibule] of their friary at Actopan, Hidalgo, in a charming mural showing the black-robed seven wading ashore and falling on their knees before Jesus Christ crucified on a tropical palm tree (fig. 1.4). The Augustinians rapidly increased in number during the ensuing years (now in the pontificate of Counter-Reformation Pope Paul III) until by the end of the century, some four hundred black-robed friars were occupying seventy-six new conventos, which quickly gained the reputation of being the most sumptuous in Mesoamerica.[27]

Even though late in getting their mission underway, the Augustinians managed to build houses close to the capital city in what should have been Franciscan territory, such as at Acolman and Malinalco. Nevertheless, they, like the Dominicans, directed their major evangelizing into the hinterland, this time toward the north and west into what are now the states of Hidalgo, Michoacán, Guanajuato, and Jalisco where lived the Tarascan and Otomí Indians who were never quite absorbed into the Nahua cultures of the central Mexican highlands. This was the "barbarian frontier" even during pre-Columbian times, separating the Tarascan and Otomí kingdoms as well as the Aztec-Mexica empire from the savage Chichimeca far to the north.

In spite of the obvious competition and rivalry of the three orders, all shared a millenarian belief in the imminence of the biblically prophesied Apocalypse, with more or less the same vehemence as their near-contemporary the fiery Dominican Fra Girolamo Savonarola of Florence, Italy.[28] The great moral issue that so stirred Savonarola, and provoked such guilt in the minds of thoughtful Christians everywhere at that time, was the spreading evil of *avaritia,* the deadly sin of material greed that seemed to be corrupting mercantile Europe at the end of the fifteenth century.[29] Many devout, especially among the Franciscan and Dominican Orders, were convinced that the human race was threatened with damnation on the very eve of the Last Judgment. In about 1495–1500 the Italian artist Sandro Botticelli, much moved by Savonarola's apocalyptic preaching, painted a picture of Christ crucified before the city of Florence. Behind the crucifix, a giant black cloud filled with falling, fiery torches moves ominously toward the city from Jesus' left, while an angel beats an animal identified as Florence's lion symbol. At Jesus' right, shields bearing the sign of the cross fly in the sky, while Mary Magdalene hugs the cross, begging the Savior to forgive errant mankind (fig. 1.5).

Fig. 1.5 Sandro Botticelli, *Crucifixion with Penitent Magdalen and an Angel,* ca. 1500. Courtesy of the Fogg Art Museum, Harvard University Art Museums, Gift of the Friends of the Fogg Museum of Art Fund.

By a remarkable coincidence, in the year 1492 just eight years before the half-millennial year 1500 when many like Botticelli expected the Apocalypse would finally be revealed, two extraordinary events happened that seemed to prove that God's hand was indeed at that moment imminent in the world. First, Christian armies under Ferdinand and Isabella of Spain captured Granada from the Moors, the last heathen stronghold in western Europe, and second, Christopher Columbus in the name of the same Spanish sovereigns discovered a western sea route to what he and most others at the time believed was "the eastern end of Asia," not only the fabled land "of all spices and gems" but also the place of the original terrestrial paradise where God created the first parents of the human race.

The friars were quick to read signs of God's about-to-unfold prophecy in these events. Even the Latin etymology of Columbus's first name, *Christum ferens*, or Christ bearing, had providential meaning (as Columbus himself insisted) that the Christian religion be spread westward and that Spain be God's anointed agent.[30] The friars thus saw themselves as frontline soldiers in this cosmic psychomachy, as Pentecostal apostles of the Second Coming with the divinely mandated mission of bringing Christ to the furthest "Indies," the inhabitants of which were thought to be the last heathen descendants of Adam and Eve not yet exposed to the holy word.[31] It was God's intent that the unconverted portions of the tripartite world be evangelized before the Last Judgment and salvation of Christendom. The image of Saint Christopher in his characteristic pose as Christ-bearer became one of the most frequent subjects painted and sculpted in the churches of sixteenth-century Spain and her overseas dominions. Figure 1.6 illustrates an especially poignant example still preserved in the stair hall of the Santo Domingo Yanhuitlán convento in the Oaxacan Mixteca Alta. The giant saint is depicted here with young Jesus on his shoulder, stepping out of the sea onto the American shore. Notice also the decorative joined double-curl device in the border around the image. This is a common Mixtec symbol often shown in the native codices similarly indicating the borders or foundations of holy objects or spaces.[32]

By the same token, the mendicants admired the evident innocence and humility of the indigenous pagans who were to be their catechumens. Indeed, the friars were reminded of the original Christian community in Rome at the time of Peter and Paul.[33] The Indians' poverty was also a natural virtue just as Saint Francis had preached.[34] These new native converts, the friars maintained, must be shielded from exposure to the pride and avarice of the venal encomenderos flocking to Mexico in search of material wealth. One idea surely in the reclusive minds of the friars as they contemplated what sort of architectural form their proposed arenas for Indian conversion should take was that it be an earthly replica of the "celestial Jerusalem" as Saint John of Patmos envisioned in Revelation, and fifteenth- and sixteenth-century Spanish and Flemish artists painted, as in *St. John Writing the Book of the Apocalypse* by Martin de Vos, now in the Museo Nacional del Virreinato, Tepozotlán, Mexico (see fig. 1.7). The similarity of the artist's image of the apostle's vision to the actual convent plan conceived in Mexico could hardly have escaped the friars. They frequently referred to their mission enterprise as creating an "Indian Jerusalem" where Indians and friars could live apart from the corrupt world and together achieve moral perfection.[35]

Fig. 1.6 *Saint Christopher Carrying Christ across the Sea.* Mural in the stair hall of the convento of Santo Domingo, Yanhuitlán, Oaxaca. Photograph by Jorge Pérez de Lara.

Even before America and its strange heathen inhabitants were discovered, the Spanish church had realized the need for knowledge of foreign languages in order that her missionaries be better prepared to communicate the Christian Gospel to the world. Already in the late fifteenth century, their Most Catholic Majesties Ferdinand and Isabella, in order to implement the policy of converting the Moors and Jews still living in the liberated provinces of the Iberian peninsula after the Reconquista, gave permission to Franciscan cardinal Francisco Jiménez de Cisneros (1436–1517), confessor to the queen, to organize a program of study at the new university of Alcalá in Andalusia. Students and future missionaries would read the ancient authors, not in the usual badly translated Latin but in their original languages such as Greek, Hebrew, Arabic, and Syriac. Jiménez's educational reform has often been cited as the beginning of the Renaissance humanistic movement in Spain, but its emphasis, unlike in more secular-minded Italy, was strictly on religious texts and their potential revelations of God's master plan for mankind at genesis.[36]

Many of the friars, especially Franciscans trained in Jiménez's methods, quickly became fluent in Nahuatl, Yucatec Maya, and several more of the hundreds of distinct languages spoken in the various American Indian communities, even compiling dictionaries and grammars: for example, Fray Maturino Gilberti's *Vocabulario en lengua de Mechuacan* published in Mexico City in 1559, Fray Alonso de Molina's dictionary of the Nahuatl language likewise printed in Mexico city in 1571, and the so-called Motul dictionary of Yucatec Maya originally assembled in the late 1570s, possibly by Fray Antonio de Ciudad Real. Other diligent friars like Bernardino de Sahagún, Diego de Landa, and Diego Durán went so far as to gather and catalog information from elder Indians about preconquest religious rites and social customs. These early field investigators are now recognized as cornerstone founders of the modern science of anthropology. The original intention of their remarkable ethnographic studies, however, was not for objective science but rather to allow fellow missionaries to identify recidivist paganism disguised under Christian veneer.

Furthermore, the Franciscans were quite aware of the indigenous hieroglyphic systems of writing. Diego de Landa, for instance, recorded what he thought was the "alphabet" of the Yucatec Maya. He pronounced the sounds of Spanish letters to his Maya informant and then recorded the latter's drawing of the Maya grapheme, only it turned out that a gross linguistic misunderstanding was taking place between the two men. What Landa assumed to be letter-sound transformations in fact were syllabic sounds. The Maya did not write with letters but rather phonetic logographs, and Landa's respondent simply answered, not by indicating a letter but a syllabic phoneme. This error in understanding was not discovered until the twentieth century, but when it was, Landa's "alphabet" suddenly provided the Rosetta Stone to the decipherment of the heretofore inscrutable Maya script.[37]

The Franciscans were not only interested in Indian hieroglyphics but also invented a hieroglyphic system of their own based on the preconquest rebus-style script of the Aztecs and Mixtecs. The friars' intention was that the Indians would be more receptive to the

Fig. 1.7 Martin de Vos, *Saint John of Patmos Writing the Apocalypse*, late sixteenth century. Museo Nacional del Virreinato, Tepotzotlán, Mexico.

Christian catechism if communicated in a writing form made up of ideographic pictures and symbols. This system came to be known as "Testerian hieroglyphics," after a French Franciscan with the Hispanicized name Fray Jacobo de Testera. He arrived in Mexico in 1529 and, according to Mendieta, invented this method because he could not learn to preach in Nahuatl.[38] Whether Mendieta's story is true or not, Testerian hieroglyphics did lend themselves easily to Nahuatl phonetics, and in fact may reflect that some friars were aware, long before the discovery by modern epigraphers, that even Mesoamerican "rebus writing" contained phonetic as well as ideographic components. In any case, the Testerian system became quite popular as a teaching instrument in the missions of all three of the mendicant orders, even as late as the nineteenth century. Some forty-two manuscript and printed copies have survived in various museums and collections in Europe and America.[39]

A wonderful example of a Testerian hieroglyphic rendition of the Lord's Prayer for Nahuatl speakers is illustrated in figure 1.8. It is part of a seventeenth-century manuscript now in the British Library known as Egerton 2898 (nothing to do with the name of the present author). The whole of this extensive work is beautifully drawn and colored, probably the most elaborate of all known Testerian manuscripts. It is signed by one Dom. Locas Matheo Escriuano, no doubt the friar-painter who inscribed a date that looks like "1614," probably copied from another perhaps earlier prototype. No further information is given as to exactly where in Nahua Mexico this manuscript was executed.[40]

All the pictographic forms in this prayer are drawn in a crude but quaint Westernized folk art style, to be "read" from left to right starting at the top register left. The first glyph group shows an outlined form of a tonsured friar with a pendant cross and next to him a halolike pair of concentric circles with a frontal face in the center. This represents "Our Father who art in heaven." Next, a rectangle inscribed with the Latin letters INRI [*Iesus Nazarenus, Rex Iudaeorum,* translated as Jesus of Nazareth, King of the Jews] framed by a display of radiating lines, a convention that in every culture

Fig. 1.8 Lord's Prayer in Testerian hieroglyphics with Nahuatl translation, dated "1[6]14," [signed "Dom. Locas Matheo Escriuano"]. MS Egerton 2898, fol. 1b, British Library. By permission of the British Library, London.

indicates brilliance, sacredness, or both, here signifies "hallowed be thy name." Next, a figure of a man pointing up to another pair of concentric circles with a crown and scepter in the center means "thy kingdom come, thy will be done."[41] Above each pictographic expression, Fray Locas translated into Latin script the equivalent Nahuatl words.

Christian Duverger has explained that a number of the Westernized pictograms in Egerton 2898 were also deliberate Nahuatl-language rebuses, for instance the grapheme showing a human hand that appears intermittently five times. The Nahuatl stem-word for "hand" is *ma,* but the same sound, "ma-," is the syntactic prefix to Nahuatl imperative clauses. Hence, the hand-sign is really a phonetic signifier introducing all the imperative expressions of the prayer. Returning to the top register at the far right, a "hand" prefaces a figure of a friar smelling a flower beside an image of the world as an orb with a cross on top and flowers blooming inside. It has been suggested that this glyph group represents a special Nahuatl flourish not found in the regular Western version of the prayer, to be glossed as, "on earth the Father smells the flower; let flowers multiply in the Christian universe." Next, in the register below to the far left is an image of a friar distributing bread, hence, "give us this day our daily bread." Then to the right, another "hand" precedes a glyph group representing "forgive us our trespasses"; another in the third register below left indicates "lead us not into temptation"; and again to the far right, a "hand" before "but deliver us from evil." Finally, the last "hand" at the end of the bottom register closes the prayer with "Amen—make it happen!"

An even cleverer grapheme based on Nahuatl homophones is the symbol for what appears to be a stepped altar with a cross on top as in the second lower register on the left. The Nahuatl word for such an architectural form is *momoztli,* but a similar sounding word, *momoztlaeh,* means "every day."[42] What the original scribe did was simply to have the former symbol serve as a phonetic indicator of the latter meaning, even depicting two "altars" to accentuate that bread be given every day, every day! A later scribe wrote "*momoztlaye*" in Latin letters above the "altars" to emphasize this phonetic substitution.[43]

Like Savonarola's attempted return to fundamentalism in Italy, Cardinal Jiménez's revision of the church in Spain was part of a changing mood sweeping all Western Christendom as the sixteenth century dawned. Not only Pedro de Gante but also all the Franciscan missionaries in the New World hearkened to Jiménez's call, pledging absolute imitation of Christ's own life, hence their designation "Observants." Not only material wealth must be denied but also sensual pleasures of the body. Juan de Zumárraga, first bishop of Mexico, was said to have carried a pouch filled with gritty ashes to sprinkle on his food lest he enjoy its taste.

The most eloquent voice of this pan-European reform movement was that of Desiderius Erasmus. In his prolific and widely circulated writings, the Dutch humanist lashed out at the ostentation of the indolent self-indulgent religious orders, particularly their obsession with external ceremonies and lack of attention to Christ's self-abasing inner piety and moral example. In spite of the suspicion in some quarters that Erasmus was a

…ny
…nía,
…porters.
…wned
…gram-
…re's
…deas in
…Vasco
…sec-
…al
…r
(…
f…
h…
…n
se…
ak…
sh…
Sp…ith
the…
thei…
sixte…
into…
ancie…
manu…
doned…
Spain…
Byzant…
the fifte…
into Lat…
ied for h…
The theo…
the closer…
tions in th…
myths wer…
messages. I…
be true as s…
humanism…g the
Middle Ages invented.

It was at just this critical time, moreover, that Europeans "discovered" the American Indians. While many of the newly examined classical sources did bear the seeds of "modern" science and intellectual enlightenment, others posed questions that seem preposterous to us today. Some even suggested that the unprecedented humanlike Indians might still be creatures of lower status in God's design, thus deliberately created without immortal souls.[47] For all Christians during the sixteenth century, possession of soul was the singular feature separating true humans from all other living creatures in the great chain of being. Natural philosophers constantly argued about what substance the soul was formed of and where in the body it was located.

The ever-curious Leonardo da Vinci (1452–1519) looked for it anatomically and believed he found it in the front of the brain just behind the eyes, "the window of the soul" as he put it. While dissecting a cadaver, Leonardo made a series of beautiful section drawings of the human skull in which he revealed not only its true osteological structure but also its proportionate "architecture" (fig. 1.9). The point of perpendicular intersection of the geometric lines in his drawing at *d*, Leonardo claimed, was the place of "common sense" in the brain (see fig. 9.1) and, therefore, he advocated, must also be the locus of the soul.[48] What we have here in Leonardo's remarkably modern-looking scientific exercise is, ironically, a vivid example of what the sixteenth-century Renaissance was all about: "modernistic" technology still vainly trying to verify medieval "natural law."

And so in the sixteenth century it was imperative according to then-accepted natural law that the Indians of America be examined for

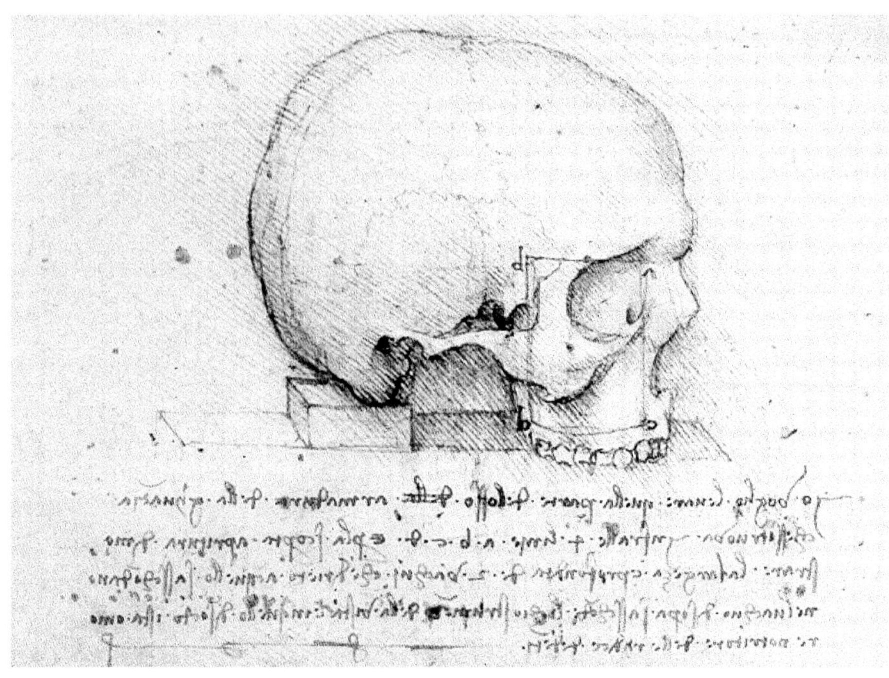

Fig. 1.9 Leonardo da Vinci, *Human Skull*, anatomical drawing, ca. 1485. Windsor Castle, Royal Library. By permission of Her Majesty Queen Elizabeth II.

possession of souls. If Indians had no souls, then they were surely a species like beasts of burden. But if they had souls, then they were not only humans but also subject to the Pope, God's anointed shepherd of all humanity and, by the same natural law, obliged to save their souls from eternal damnation.

For much of the sixteenth century, argument over this conundrum raged among philosophers and churchmen all over Europe, each side citing Scripture and Scholastic doctrine supporting one or the other opinion. Even though Pope Paul III tried to settle the issue in 1537 with his bull *Sublimis Deus* in which he declared that Indians did in fact possess souls and thus were subject to Christian conversion, powerful opposition persisted, especially in the erudite declamations of the learned and much respected Aristotelian scholar Fray Juan Gines de Sepúlveda (1490–1573). It was against the latter's nearly convincing arguments that Fray Bartolomé de Las Casas took up his own persuasive pen, but not really to pose modern-style humanitarian arguments. Rather, Las Casas, still very much a thinker of his own time, sought to prove that Sepúlveda was misinterpreting Scripture and the various Peripatetic and Patristic sources accepted as explaining the bases of natural law. Las Casas harbored not the slightest doubt that the Indians must be Christianized, but only by persuasion not physical force.[49]

Here then is the crux of the problem in trying to sympathize with the mission of the Spanish Catholic church in the New World. While natural law certainly meant to sixteenth-century thinkers like Las Casas and Sepúlveda that God had set an absolute standard for the practice of morality and the dispensation of justice in the world, and that man himself was endowed at genesis with the "right" to choose between good and evil, this had little to do with what we today assume to be "human rights." The latter indeed are the result of a slow evolution in the history of natural law that was not focused in the modern sense until the eighteenth century. If Thomas Aquinas in the Middle Ages had taken for granted that natural law descended from God down through the anointed hierarchies of heaven and earth and should be applied to secular man according to the teachings of the universal church, Thomas Jefferson reversed the origin and redefined the content of natural law to include "unalienable Rights" inherent in secular man himself. These, of course, were inscribed in the American Declaration of Independence, a document that doesn't even invoke the sanction of the Christian Savior. (Jefferson reductively referred to the Creator as "Nature's God," subtly redefining Aquinas's "God of Nature" as a subordinate demiurge.)

Ius and *lex*, two Latin words that in antiquity and the Middle Ages were synonyms for natural law, had by Jefferson's time split into two distinct meanings: "natural rights" on the one hand and "imposed law" on the other. From here, it was but a short step to our modern-day notion that not only are human rights self-evident and universal but also one dare not limit or presume even to grant such rights in the name of divine authority.

The above, of course, is an oversimplified résumé of a complex religious, legal, and philosophical shift having taken place, sometimes almost imperceptibly, in Western thought from the thirteenth through the eighteenth century that now expands almost exponentially into our present "postmodern" era. Yet even as we wish that the European exploiters of the New World had possessed some appreciation of "natural" human rights, it is necessary for the purposes of this book to recognize that the great majority of sixteenth-century Christians, few of whom were as legal-minded as Bartolomé de Las Casas, would not, and probably could not, have been as precocious.[50]

Finally, even if one accepts that the conversion efforts of Spanish friars were undertaken within the acceptable sixteenth-century standards of natural law and should not be judged according to the secularized human-rights standards of today (the "political theology" of the twenty-first century as some have predicted), what of the Indians' individual and cultural rights within their own non-Western and non-Christian moral paradigm? This is the question that is mulled in the following chapters, but only in relation to the evidence that the Renaissance artistic conventions introduced by the friars for didactic religious purposes became so thoroughly appropriated and so indistinguishably integrated into indigenous cultural expressions that most Indians now living do not realize that they were ever foreign.

Who has built so many churches and monasteries as the friars possess in this New Spain if not the Indians themselves with their own hands and sweat, and with the same will and cheerfulness that they build their own houses . . . even pleading with the friars that they be allowed to make [the churches] grand?

Fray Geronimo de Mendieta, Historia eclesiástica indiana

Chapter 2

THE CROSS AND THE TREE

The Christian Convento as Indian Cosmos

While the primary purpose of this book is to celebrate the indigenous contribution to the Christianized visual arts in what used to be called New Spain, I have also a second agenda and that is to convince fellow Anglo-cultured North Americans to visit and see for themselves the magnificence of these masterpieces of accommodation between foreign Spanish and native Indian artisanry.

Right here on our own continent hardly four-hours' flying time from any major airport in the United States (less than to Europe), one can witness the most monumental yet unheralded building

Fig. 2.1 Locations of Mexican conventos and other localities mentioned in this book. Drawing by Mark Van Stone, typography by Melissa Tandysh.

Fig. 2.2 Looking south toward the convento church of Santo Domingo, Yanhuitlán, Oaxaca, set in the arid landscape of the Mixteca Alta.

and decoration program ever conceived and carried out in so short a period in so large an area anywhere on earth. Between 1530 and 1600, a span of barely seven decades, nearly four hundred large mission complexes, or conventos, plus more than a thousand smaller satellite churches [*visitas*] were constructed and decorated with paintings and sculptural reliefs by skilled native artisans in Mesoamerica, a land greater in area and aboriginal population than Renaissance Spain, Flanders, and Italy combined.

These conventos and visitas were all built at the behest of the Franciscan, Dominican, and Augustinian friars for the purpose of providing appropriate settings wherein to teach Christian doctrine to the millions of Indians suddenly under Spanish rule after the conquest of the Aztec empire in 1521. More than a hundred of the original Mexican conventos and an untallied number of visitas, all dating from the sixteenth century, still stand and continue to function as community churches to this day (fig. 2.1). Many are gloriously sited. The fabled panoramas of European cathedrals such as Chartres in France or Durham in England surely have their counterparts in Mexico: the splendid vista, for example, of the Dominican convento of San Domingo Yanhuitlán, Oaxaca, set in a striking landscape that looks like it was painted by Piero della Francesca (fig. 2.2).

While well documented by scholars (mainly Mexican) writing in Spanish,[1] such a wealth of sixteenth-century architecture so near to and accessible from the United States has regrettably not attracted the attention of more art historians writing in English. The two most comprehensive books in our language were published decades ago, and little more has been printed since to supplement George Kubler's *Mexican Architecture of the Sixteenth Century* and John McAndrew's *Open Air Churches of Sixteenth-Century Mexico*. Both are exhaustively detailed, and one may sympathize with scholars trying to find much new to add. Both books are also formidable, demanding as they do a priori familiarity with some of the most backwater geography in Mexico. Furthermore the black-and-white photographs are small and grainy, offering readers little inducement to visit the sites and judge for themselves that these buildings are truly works of art.

On the other hand, there has been a discernible increase in interest in this sixteenth-century architecture during the last two decades, more or less in the wake of the rising fascination with the indigenous Indians of this continent, especially the ancient Aztecs and Maya of Mesoamerica. Elizabeth Wilder Weismann's beautifully illustrated *Art and Time in Mexico* has already aroused enough reader interest to be reprinted. Richard and Rosalind Perry's *Maya Missions*, followed by Richard Perry's *Mexico's Fortress Monasteries, More Maya Missions*, and *Blue Lakes and Silver Cities*, for the first time approach the subject region by region. Handsomely embellished with drawings by the author, these books are indispensable guides for anyone traveling to the relevant areas. Likewise in this regional vein is the thorough if less gracefully written *Architecture and Sculpture of Oaxaca* by Robert Mullen. Mullen's *Architecture and Its Sculpture in Viceregal Mexico*, published posthumously in 1997, is also an excellent general handbook.

Among the three Flemish Franciscans who came to Mexico in 1523, a year before the "twelve," was Peeter van der Moere of Ghent, whose Hispanicized name was Fray Pedro de Gante. A skilled musician, Fray Pedro seems to have been equally informed regarding the latest Flemish and Italian Renaissance styles of drawing and painting. Most important, Fray Pedro was a natural teacher determined to employ the visual, theatrical, and musical arts as didactic tools of Christian proselytization.[2]

In 1529 Fray Pedro founded a school in the new Christian chapel dedicated to San José de los Naturales (Saint Joseph of the Indigenous Natives) built adjacent to the Franciscan convento of Santiago de Tlatelolco, Mexico City, specifically for teaching music and Western-style arts and crafts to the sons of Indian lords, appropriate because in preconquest Mesoamerican society such skills were frequently indulged in by members of the elite class. All three mendicant orders encouraged this native tradition. The Franciscans set up other schools in the conventos at Mérida and Maní in the Yucatán, while the Augustinians established their own at Tiripetío, Michoacán.[3] One of the most decisive new architectural ideas the friars imparted to the Indians was how to build the keystone arch and vault, a technology

Fig. 2.3 Looking southeast toward the "basilica," the open chapel of the convento of Santiago, Cuilapan, Oaxaca. Photograph by Jorge Pérez de Lara.

heretofore quite unknown in the New World, with extraordinary implications for Indian conversion.[4]

In 1536 Fray Pedro took part in the founding of the first university and library of European books in the Americas, the Colegio de Santa Cruz, established in the old Aztec capital, Tenochtitlan, now renamed Mexico City. The idea was to expose elite Indian students to Latin arts and letters and to the Aristotelian *artes liberales* in preparation for their new role as colonial administrators.[5]

Many of the sixteenth-century books originally cataloged in the Colegio de Santa Cruz are still preserved in the Adolph Sutro Library, San Francisco, California, along with a number of other volumes circulating in Mexico at that time, which would likewise have been useful to Fray Pedro's teaching of the visual arts.[6] These latter include printed editions of Vitruvius and Sebastiano Serlio, Albrecht Dürer's treatise on fortifications, and the 1550 Cosimo Bartoli edition of Leon Battista Alberti's *De re aedificatoria*.[7] While few of the friars had any formal training in building construction, they would certainly have been interested in architectural books like these as they prepared to erect new churches in the hinterland. No doubt

Fig. 2.4 North facade of the convento church of San Juan Bautista, Coixtlahuaca, Oaxaca. Photograph by Jorge Pérez de Lara.

suggestive evidence that the facades of the Dominican buildings at Cuilapan and Coixtlahuaca, Oaxaca, were inspired by plates from Sebastiano Serlio (figs. 2.3 and 2.4).[8]

The original San José de los Naturales complex no longer stands. Its seminal, so-called open chapel was the first to be built in Mexico, and its general composition seems to have supplied the model thereafter for the distinctive convento layout adopted by all three orders evangelizing in Mesoamerica.[9] Unfortunately, no documentation exists concerning the designer, but it's quite likely that the guiding hand in the conception of this uniquely Mexican architectural idea was that of Fray Pedro de Gante.[10]

Similar to the conventional European medieval monastery, the Mexican convento complex established soon after 1524 consisted of standard friars' living quarters abutted to a church, along with other architectural features that were either adapted from European prototypes or especially invented in situ to serve the special demands of the Mexican mission (see fig. 2.5). There is no evidence of building plans ever having been

the friars made copies of some of the woodcuts and engravings, which they would then show to their Indian artisans. Architectural designs from such tomes did apparently pass from convento to convento, and there is imported from Europe. Like the pre-Columbian temple precinct, the sixteenth-century Mexican convento evolved into a uniquely Mesoamerican creation.

The church proper tended to remain the most conventional of all the convento buildings. Usually (but not always) it was single naved and covered with a plain masonry barrel vault.[11] There are several exceptions, however, as at Dominican Yanhuitlán, Oaxaca, with its ornate Gothic ribs, or Franciscan Tlaxcala with a ceiling not vaulted but trussed on wooden beams and inlaid with elaborate gilded geometric designs in the Moorish Mudéjar style (figs. 2.6, 2.7). Carpenters, skilled in the complex marquetry of Spanish-Moorish art, apparently were among the first artisans to migrate to the New World and become teachers of the Indians.

Convento exteriors tended also to be forbiddingly plain, especially the Franciscan, with massive walls thick to the point of looking like medieval castles, as at Dzidzantún in the Yucatán (fig. 2.8). The parapets were even studded with battlement-like merlons, giving rise to popular local legends that these buildings were designed as military fortresses to protect the Spanish colonists from native

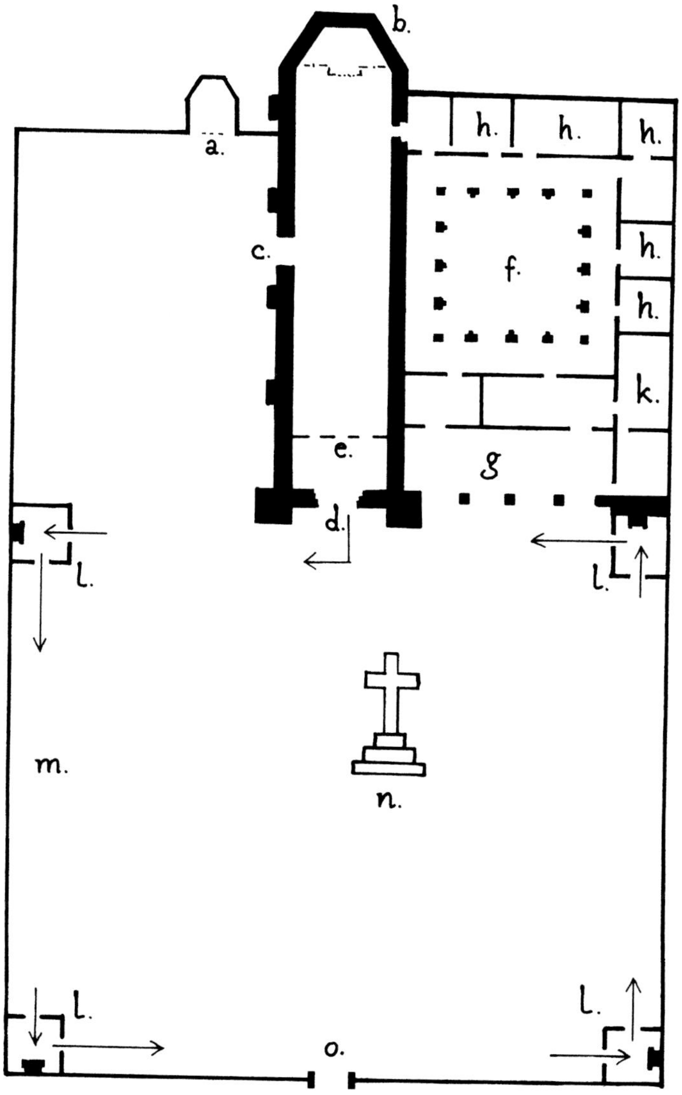

Fig. 2.5 Diagram of a prototypical Mexican convento, indicating its constituent parts and the conventional counterclockwise processional route around the patio: a, open chapel; b, apse with altar at east end of the church; c, north portal of the church; d, western entrance to the church; e, choir loft; f, cloister; g, portería; h, friars' cells; k, sala de profundis, or refectory; l, posas; m, walled patio; n, patio cross; o, western entrance to walled patio. Drawing by Mark Van Stone.

Fig. 2.6 Gothic-style nave vaulting in the convento church of Santo Domingo, Yanhuitlán, Oaxaca. Photograph by Jorge Pérez de Lara.

insurrections.[12] Convento church facades, on the other hand, did often aspire to more stylish ostentation, promiscuously mixing elements of Isabelline plateresque, Gothic, Mudéjar, and Italian Renaissance architectural details, and improvising these in such a way as to express local native individuality even within the general convento conformity. Especially fine examples of facade design are to be seen at Acolman, Mexico state, with its elegant plateresque-style entrance portal (this magnificent building is hardly ever visited even though within a few minutes' distance from the popular pyramids of Teotihuacan), and Yecapixtla, Morelos, with its splendid rose window (figs. 2.9, 2.10). Cuitzeo (fig. 2.11) is likewise impressive with its facade decor carved and signed by an Indian craftsman (see fig. I.2).[13] Cuitzeo is reached by a causeway across a beautiful, mirror-smooth, reed-rimmed, and bird-abundant lake that affects the modern viewer with something of the same emotion as felt by the Spanish conquistadors upon first setting eyes on the Aztecs' island capital Tenochtitlan in the midst of Lake Texcoco. That once-paradisiacal natural resource is now, tragically, almost completely obliterated, dried up, and buried under the sprawling detritus of Mexico City.

Perhaps the most exuberant masterpiece of sixteenth-century facade invention is to be seen

Fig. 2.7 Mudéjar-style nave ceiling in the convento church of the Asunción de Nuestra Señora, Tlaxcala. Photograph by Jorge Pérez de Lara.

Fig. 2.8 Southwest corner of the convento church of Saints Pedro y Pablo, Dzidzantún, Yucatán. Photograph by Jorge Pérez de Lara.

on the Augustinian convento church of San Pablo at Yuriria in Guanajuato, in the same lake region and only a few kilometers from Cuitzeo. The reliefs above the portal here were again executed by another (but unsigned) locally trained sculptor so carried away by the novelty of the imported style that he, perhaps deliberately, misinterpreted the classical cupids conventionally depicted as gamboling in such Renaissance floreate displays.[14] Instead, he reinvented them as contemporaneous Chichimec warriors (figs. 2.12, 2.13). The Yuriria convento in fact was built in part to serve as a bastion against these untamed Chichimecs who actually attacked the convento and damaged some of its sculptures with their favorite weapon, the bow and arrow. The glory of the Yuriria convento as well as the Chichimec danger to it are vividly described by Fray Matías de Escobar in his 1729 *Americana Thebaida* wherein he admiringly compares the church of San Pablo to the "most superb buildings in Italy" and even to the great Temple of Diana at Ephesus, one of the architectural wonders of the ancient Mediterranean world.[15]

Flanking and connected to the church was the friars' residence constructed around a one- or two-story open cloister in the traditional European mode, like that in the Franciscan convento of San Miguel Huejotzingo, Puebla (fig. 2.14).[16] The friary was usually entered through a broad portería, a kind of arcaded narthex that stretched across the facade and linked to the western facade of the church. It generally served as a shelter for Indian catechumens, sometimes even as a hospice for the indigent or sick. At Augustinian Charo, Michoacán, priests heard the Indians'

Fig. 2.9
West flank of the church and friary of the convento of San Agustín, Acolman. Photograph by Jorge Pérez de Lara.

Fig. 2.10 West facade of the convento church of San Juan Bautista, Yecapixtla, Morelos. Photograph by Jorge Pérez de Lara.

Fig. 2.11 Western flank of the convento church and portería of Santa María Magdalena, Cuitzeo, Michoacán. Photograph by Jorge Pérez de Lara.

confessions there, and at Cuitzeo, also Augustinian in Michoacán, it functioned as a porch, with an open chapel recessed in the facade proper (fig. 2.15). Here Mass was said to the Indians assembled in a large walled-around forecourt called by modern historians the *atrio,* or atrium. Frequently the portería was covered with didactic murals, like the grim *Last Judgment* painted on the end wall of the portería at Cuitzeo (fig. 2.16), intended as "visual aids" to the Indians' religious instruction.

The open chapel was another unique feature of the Mexican convento; it was for preaching to the large crowds of Indians who stood out of doors since they could not all fit inside the church. Hence, it came to be known as the *capilla de Indios*, or Indian chapel. Either abutting or slightly separated from the church, the open chapel when present took many forms and often received sophisticated architectural treatment, as in the handsomely trimmed and elevated example adjunct to the small Franciscan convento at Tlahuelilpa, Hidalgo, to the right of the church main portal (fig. 2.17). Most Mexican open chapels, however, were set at ground level (another raised-up exception is to be seen at Augustinian Acolman, between the main church portal and the portería in fig. 2.9).[17] Perhaps the most curious of all the open chapels in Mexico is the "basilica" constructed beside the Dominican convento of Santiago Cuilapan, Oaxaca (figs. 2.3, 2.18). Laid out along a rigid north-south axis thus perpendicular to the smaller unfinished church, which it completely dominates, this three-aisled rectangular structure is quite reminiscent of a pre-Christian Roman basilica, hence its modern nickname. Indeed, its long western flank is entirely arcaded and seems to have been intended as the principal facade before which the Indians gathered, standing both outside and inside the building in order to hear preaching from a still-extant raised pulpit on the east interior wall. While the entire building is presently without a roof of any sort, it may once have had a thatch or timber ramada covering the interior arcaded "nave."

In general, however, both the enclosed convento churches and their adjacent open chapels were oriented with the altars at the east end. Most of the convento edifices in Mexico were built directly on or near the foundations of preconquest temples from which building stones were often quarried and imbedded in the fabric of the new buildings. The convento at Izamal, Yucatán, is a famous example, and a fragment of preconquest sculpture depicting the prominent fang-tooth features of the Maya rain god Chac was deliberately set as a stepping stone in the threshold of the entrance portal as a symbol of the old religion having been vanquished by the new (fig. 2.19). This, of course, echoed an ancient practice during the conversion of pagan Rome when *spolia* from the old classical temples were promiscuously used as building material for the first Christian churches.

By the same token, the friars were quick to take advantage of that mysterious but natural phenomenon whereby a new shrine founded upon an earlier holy site osmotically assumes the latter's hallowedness even when the old cult has been supplanted. From the native Indian masons' point of view, placing visible chunks of their old temples in the walls of the new churches was not necessarily a desecration but a preservation of sacred material, reinvesting the succeeding shrine with the primordial sanctity of the old, as in the seventeenth-century church at Teotitlán del Valle, Oaxaca, where pieces of preconquest Zapotec sculpture with the figured sides conspicuously displayed can be seen imbedded on the facade (fig. 2.20). In fact, the local Mixtec parishioners are still collecting these fragments from an adjacent archaeological site. Whenever one is found, they implant it somewhere in the walls of their church complex.[18]

Actually, this practice follows an ancient indigenous tradition. Archaeologists excavating preconquest ruins in Mexico have frequently

Fig. 2.12 West facade of the convento church of San Agustín, Yuriria (formerly San Pablo), Guanajuato. Photograph by Jorge Pérez de Lara.

found evidence of what they call "termination rituals," whereby debris from early temples about to be rebuilt or replaced was carefully preserved under the replacing structures. The old buildings were thus "buried" just as reverently as the remains of deceased ancestors. An example can be seen today in the several restored and now exposed building stages of the Aztec Templo Mayor in Mexico City, where the Indians ritually interred statues and other remnants from each prior temple as they rebuilt and enveloped it with a subsequent "onion skin" enlargement.[19]

While the general ground plans of Mexican conventos were probably determined by the friars, few of whom possessed much more than a smattering of architectural or artistic skill, actual construction was carried out with considerable autonomy by trained Indian masons.[20] During the Middle Ages and early Renaissance, the notion of "architect" was not as we understand the term today. Planning new buildings by means of scale drawings was unheard of, not only in the native Americas but also in transalpine Europe until late in the sixteenth century. Actually, the medieval-Renaissance "architect," if that term be applicable at all, was more comparable to what today would be called a "general contractor," a working-class craftsman with some intuitive mechanical ability; only rarely was he a learned intellectual. Once the ground plan and general elevation of a new construction had been decided upon by the patron (sometimes with the aid of small three-dimensional wooden models), it was the responsibility of the "architect," as often as not a master mason, to make sure his fellow workmen built foundations and load-bearing walls strong enough to support whatever the form of the roof. Skilled and specialized Indians then did all the fashioning in between.

The heavy stonework of the Mexican conventos, as can be observed in a collapsed wall at Metztitlán, Hidalgo (fig. 2.21), is again less a reflection of European influence than of indigenous chinked mortar and rubble-fill masonry called in Spanish *rejoneado* and somewhat similar to ancient Roman *opus incertum*.[21] This is the same masonry technique that Indian laborers had always employed in the construction of their preconquest temples and pyramids.[22] Many Indians, of course, were already experienced masons.

Preconquest Mesoamerican construction teams were probably organized in much the same way as the masons' guilds during the great age of cathedral building in medieval Europe. In the Mixtec codices, the rebus symbol for "building a temple" shows two figures measuring with a rope (fig. 2.22), the same basic tool as would have been used for proportioning ground plans and projecting elevations by any master builder in the Old World.[23] Interestingly, one of the mendicant chronicles even mentions that Fray Toribio Motolinía himself "did the cords" [*hechó los cordeles*] in laying out the new convento in Puebla.[24] Standardized details like the framing of doors and windows were handled by specialized craftspersons who already knew how to make these things with no need for predrawn plans and little more direction than perhaps a template to insure design uniformity.[25] Adjusting these age-old cross-cultural construction techniques to the new European styles was what the Indians were taught in the schools set up by the friars in San José de los Naturales in Mexico City, Tiripetío in Michoacán, Maní in the Yucatán, and probably others elsewhere. No doubt, just as in Europe, trained artisans moved from site to site whenever and wherever their skills were needed. These native craftsmen not only did the structuring but also painted and sculpted most of the convento decor, much still visible today.[26] The friars were clearly in admiration and frequently remarked on the Indians' proficiency and quickness to learn and master European artistic styles and techniques, even surpassing their teachers.

Notwithstanding, critics of the "spiritual conquest" have taken the friars to task for coercing the Indians in the building of these massive, labor-intensive conventos. Yet long before the Spanish arrived, Indian peasants called *macehualli* in Nahuatl had been accustomed to donating their labor to the temples and other communal building projects at the dictates of their rulers. For the Indians, corvée labor in preconquest times was a ritualized activity, expected of everyone in order that the community remain in harmony with the supernatural forces that order the universe.[27] Participating in the building and upkeep of a sacred shrine offered the same assurances of moral and spiritual kinship with the cosmos as prayers and sacrifices. The friars were often amazed to find that even Indian *principales* would willingly perform menial tasks as expressions of their devotion. As Mendieta recorded:

> For their temples and everything consecrated to God, [the Indians] hold much reverence, and the elders, no matter how noble they might be, take pride in sweeping the churches, observing the custom of their ancestors who in sweeping the temples in heathen times showed their devotion (even the same lords) when they no longer had the power to go to war and fight. In the city of Toluca, the first lord who was baptized (to whom . . . [Cortés] gave his name, calling him Don Fernando Cortés, and who in his youth had been very valiant and brave) ended his days continuing to sweep the church as if he were a school boy.[28]

While the *repartimiento* laws of 1548 requiring the Indians to labor for the Spanish settlers were cruel and often abusively administered by the latter, the friars spoke out most vociferously in the natives' defense. Ironically, as Kubler has suggested, in those instances where the friars did altruistically pay wages to their workers, they unloosed another bond that tied the Indi-

Fig. 2.13 Detail of the Yuriria church's west facade showing a sculpted "Chichimec warrior" with bow and arrow. Photograph by Jorge Pérez de Lara.

Fig. 2.14 View into the cloister of the convento of San Miguel, Huejotzingo, Puebla. Photograph by Jorge Pérez de Lara.

ans to their ancient social system. One of the many new Renaissance ideas brought to the New World in the name of humanitarian reform was the notion of wage-labor, that workers be paid promptly according to the conditions of their hiring, their skill, the hazards of their work, and the needs of their families. The old medieval European habit (similar to the Indians') that local parishioners should build and tend their neighborhood church solely for the love of God was gradually giving way to the reformist concept that a person's physical work be disconnected from Christian duty. This new economic theory was especially championed by the Dominicans like recently canonized Saint Antonine of Florence and Fray Bartolomé de

Fig. 2.15 Looking east at the portería of the convento of Santa María Magdalena, Cuitzeo, Michoacán. Photograph by Jorge Pérez de Lara.

Las Casas.[29] While separation of church and state is now taken for granted in the litany of Western human rights, to the Indians of America during the sixteenth century it was a foreign and culturally deleterious idea.

The most distinctive and most significant "tool of conversion" feature of the prototypical Mexican convento was the immense courtyard, sometimes the size of a dozen tennis courts, extending from the front of the portería or the church and open chapel. Around its outer perimeter usually ran a crenelated wall, as at the Franciscan convento of San Gabriel Cholula, Puebla (fig. 2.23). While the convento courtyard is today usually referred to as an atrium and called *atrio* after the Spanish equivalent, the sixteenth-century friars tended to call the courtyard instead by another Spanish word, *patio,* which is the term used in this book. The earliest documentary mention is by Fray Motolinía, around 1540: "The patios are very large and hand-

Fig. 2.16 *Last Judgment*, mural painted on the north end wall of the portería at Cuitzeo. Photograph by Jorge Pérez de Lara.

Fig. 2.17 Looking east toward the convento of San Francisco, Tlahuelilpa, Hidalgo. Photograph by Jorge Pérez de Lara.

Fig. 2.18 Looking north from inside the "basilica," convento of Santiago, Cuilapan, Oaxaca. Photograph by Jorge Pérez de Lara.

some, for the people are many and cannot fit in the churches. For this reason the chapel is outside in the patio because all hear Mass every Sunday and holidays, while the church serves for the week-days."[30]

Much argument has been raised about the origin of the Mexican convento patio and open-chapel arrangement. The friars arrived in the New World already with an apocalyptic image of New Jerusalem in their medieval mind's eye—a "shining temple" in an enclosure walled off to protect the faithful from the temptations of the venal world. There is also the question as to whether or not the patio plan had some derivation from the similar-appearing early Christian church courtyard that was always called *atrium,* such as once extended from the facade of old Saint Peter's Basilica and is still extant and adjacent to the church of San Clemente in Rome.[31] The purpose of the early Christian atrium was also to serve in the conversion of pagans during the first centuries after Christ and, again like the Mexican patio, was an enclosed courtyard where crowds of newly converted adult catechumens should await confirmation before being officially accepted into the church. Similarities in appearance and

Fig. 2.19 Convento of Nuestra Señora, Izamal, Yucatán, looking through the western entrance eastward into the patio (note carved stone in threshold). Photograph by Jorge Pérez de Lara.

Fig. 2.20 Stone carved with preconquest relief imbedded in the facade of the seventeenth-century Dominican church at Teotitlán del Valle, Oaxaca.

function notwithstanding, the friars in Mexico never mention this. It would seem, therefore, that the Mexican patio developed in response to needs that were special to the friars' mission in Mexico with no overt nostalgic link to the apostolic evangelization of ancient Rome.

Another precedent that might have lurked in the minds of the friars as they thought up the idea of the convento patio was the Moorish *muṣallá,* or walled open court before the Mohammedan mosque. Prominent examples of these were surely familiar to the friars in Spain, especially in the great mosque at Córdoba, converted to a Christian church in the thirteenth century, and in the Cathedral of Seville where the muṣallá was retained as a forecourt when the old mosque was rebuilt as a Gothic church. Indeed, the open court at Seville was at one time even used for preaching purposes, and an early pulpit still stands at one side.

There is plenty of evidence that, like the conquistadors, the friars regarded the conquest of Mexico as a providential sequel to the Reconquista of Spain, which had reached its culmination just a quarter century earlier in 1492 when the Christian forces under Ferdinand and Isabella captured Granada, the last Islamic stronghold on the Iberian peninsula. Even if only in subconscious association, the Christianized muṣallá would have been an appropriate archetype to the Mexican patio. Interestingly, the Moorish muṣallá was often planted with orange trees, as indeed is the

Fig. 2.21 Section of ruined arch in the patio of the convento of Los Santos Reyes, Metztitlán, Hidalgo, showing rejoneado masonry.

Fig. 2.22 Detail after fol. 22, Codex Vindobonensis, showing Mixtec rebus sign for "architects." Staatsbibliothek, Vienna. Drawing by Mark Van Stone.

surviving court adjacent to the Cathedral of Seville, now called the Patio de los Naranjos (fig. 2.24). Similarly, the friars in Mexico planted orange and other such cultivated trees in the patios connected to their conventos. We also know that the first open chapel in Mexico, San José de los Naturales, had a plan quite similar to a Moorish mosque. Like La Mezquita at Córdoba, San José was multiple aisled, with a long open arcade fronting on the patio with no fewer than fourteen arched bays (the Great Mosque originally had only eleven). While San José no longer exists, its vaulted space was copied in a few other conventos, most notably the Capilla Real in Cholula where one may still experience a mysterious mosquelike interior (fig. 2.25).[32]

Whatever the Moorish connection, John McAndrew is correct in asserting that the most immediate inspiration for the postconquest patio was to be found in preconquest Mexico itself, in the very heart of "demon" Tenochtitlan.[33] Indeed, it had always been the custom in pre-Columbian Mexico for the Indians to perform their rituals and dances outdoors in quadrangular precincts similarly surrounded by a wall just like that which enclosed the Templo Mayor.[34] There is, however, more conclusive proof that this "pagan" ritual space, right under the friars' noses, was from the beginning the prime source for the standard patio plan of their Christian conventos. It was a deliberate replication—expedient selection—on the part of the friars to remind the Indians of how similar the Christian worldview was to their own traditional notion of an ensouled cosmos.[35]

Shared among nearly all indigenous societies in preconquest Mesoamerica was the concept that the universe was formed at creation in the shape of a quincunx oriented to the four cardinal directions, with the Indian nation in the center. This divine master plan was then reflected in microcosm in each Indian society's own turf, as it were, made manifest in a landscape surrounded by a wall of mountains holding up the sky, and then, as Nahuatl speakers would express it, *in tlalxicco onoc* [spread out on the navel of the earth] its figurative *axis mundi* being a tree on a hill above a cave from which issued the waters of the primordial sea.[36] The raised-up tree, the

Fig. 2.23
Patio looking southwest, convento of San Gabriel, Cholula. Photograph by Jorge Pérez de Lara.

Fig. 2.24
Patio de los Naranjos, Cathedral of Seville, Spain.

Fig. 2.25 Interior of the convento church of San Gabriel, Cholula, looking northeast. Photograph by Jorge Pérez de Lara.

Indians believed, connected the sky to the cave portal and thus to the underworld where dwelled the spirits of their ancestors. Here was the place from which all life on earth originated and ended. It was the destiny of each Indian nation to find and settle in such a sacred landscape, for only in the bosom of the primal quincunx could one expect to survive the whims of the capricious supernatural forces of deiform nature.

Not only the natural but the built landscape should mirror the cosmic quincunx. Angel García Zambrano has discovered that even after the conquest many Indian communities continued to lay out their towns in the traditional quincunxial form, with a central plaza (now containing a church) surrounded by four adjunct residential *barrios* oriented to the cardinal directions.[37]

Perhaps the most obvious and relevant example of this native tradition was observed in Tenochtitlan, capital of the Aztec empire. The city was originally founded on an island in Lake Texcoco, the Aztecs' proverbial "primordial sea" surrounded by mountains (most prominently the twin peaks of smoking Popocatépetl and "white lady" Iztaccíhuatl to the east). In the very center of the island the Aztecs built their great pyramid now known in Spanish as the Templo Mayor, originally dedicated to the two chief deities in the Aztec pantheon, Tlaloc, god of rain, and Huizilopochtli, the founder of the Aztec race and the god of war and Aztec imperial destiny. The temple sat in the midst of a vast precinct surrounded by a low wall and squared to the cardinal directions. It also marked the *tlalxicco onoc* of the three conjoined cities of the original Aztec "triple alliance" consisting of Tenochtitlan, Texcoco, and Tlacopan. This juncture was the mythical place from whence grew the nopal cactus tree with eagle perched upon it, the prophesied sign that signaled where the Aztecs were destined to build their city and launch their empire.[38]

In the Nahuatl language the concept of community represented by this cosmogram, including all the political, ideological, and ancestral creation rites that mystically bound the Aztec community together were summed up in the word *altepetl,* literally "water mountain," architecturally signified by the great pyramid of the Templo Mayor in the center of Lake Texcoco. The city proper, following the Mesoamerican norm, was divided into four cardinally oriented barrios. The Aztecs referred to these barrios as *calpolli,* literally "big houses." As subdivisions of the altepetl, each calpolli also symbolized a quadrant of the multicultural empire.[39] Furthermore, each calpolli had its own headquarters building in the city representing the places where the four legendary founding lineages had originated.[40] This ideogram of the founding of Tenochtitlan is illustrated in the Aztec Codex Mendoza, which shows the city in the shape of a rectangle surrounded and divided into equal sections by interlocking canals. Each section represents one of the four calpolli, and all are joined at the center under the eagle perched in a nopal cactus, the symbolic navel of the Aztec empire (fig. 2.26). It is revealing that Fray Motolinía used the word "patio" in describing this Nahua ceremonial center and its calpolli counterparts: "It seems as if the land was filled with patios of the demon . . . a very beautiful sight," he mused, and one can almost imagine him mulling over the thought that the Franciscans should co-opt and Christianize this native space.[41]

During each Aztec "month" of twenty days, a religious ritual, usually with a procession of priests and celebrants, took place in the precinct of the Templo Mayor. Fray Bernardino de Sahagún and Fray Diego Durán both recorded in detail these ceremonies, eighteen repeating every solar year. The most vivid was that of the fifteenth "month," called the Feast of Panquetzaliztli, occurring between November and early December in the Gregorian calendar.[42] For this ritual, the priests of the Templo Mayor made an amaranth-dough image of their principal deity, Huizilopochtli. On the last day of Panquetzaliztli, one priest, carrying the breaded god and followed by a procession, would race around a course that symbolically represented both the four corners of the Aztec realm and the directions of ancient Aztec "exodus" migration to Lake Texcoco. What is of special interest is that this route was traversed counterclockwise. Sahagún and Durán described it precisely. First the celebrants visited the separate "capulcos," as Sahagún called the calpolli, while the priest with the idol ran north from the Templo Mayor precinct to Tlatelolco, then west over the Lake Texcoco causeway to Popotlan, south along the western lake shore past Chapultepec to Tacubaya, eastward to Coyoacan and Churubusco, and finally northward across the southern Lake Texcoco viaduct and back to the Templo Mayor.[43] In the Codex Mendoza depiction of the founding of Tenochtitlan (fig. 2.26), the border of the image is made up of squares, each containing a tiny pictogram in a repeated sequence of four and surmounted by a sequence of dots counting from two in the square in the upper left corner, to thirteen halfway down the left side, repeating from one to thirteen squares three more times until the last square is reached in the upper center. This string of dotted pictograms represents a sacred fifty-two-year cycle in the Aztec calendar (a concept explored more fully in chap. 8). In fact, it connotes the first fifty-two years since the founding of the Aztec capital in 1325, which culminated in a celebration in 1377. For purposes of this discussion, however, what is important about this border design is that it also indicates a processional route around the perimeter of the city, in which sacred time is here transformed into sacred space, to be transversed in a counterclockwise direction.

The Aztecs were not the only ones who celebrated the founding and cosmic connection of their nation by parading in a counterclockwise direction. So did almost all preconquest Mesoamerican societies including the Maya and Mixteca. García Zambrano has documented the quincunx planning and counterclockwise sacralization rituals of dozens of Mesoamerican pueblos, original maps of which are still preserved in the national archives of Mexico and Spain.[44] Such a counterclockwise circuit indicated that the celebrants were actually paying homage to the nurturing sun by symbolically following its diurnal and solstitial path through a tropical year. As the procession goes north, it traces the morning sun's annual journey along the eastern horizon after December 22; then turning west the procession tracks the sun's passage across the sky during the day; then south along the western horizon following the evening sun after summer solstice on June 21; then east as the set sun moves beneath the earth at night; and finally the procession returns to the center from whence it began. By tracing the sides of this ritual quadrangle, celebrants should always have the sun at their right hand.

As the friars were aware, the Panquetzaliztli, and even more so the fifth-month Toxcatl ceremony commencing in May, bore intriguing likeness to the most spectacular of all public religious processions in Christian Europe and especially Spain, the festival of Corpus Christi.[45] Established by a papal bull in 1264 and decreed again by Pope John XXII in 1317, this movable feast on the first Thursday following Trinity Sunday was intended to emphasize that the transubstantiated bread of the Host is the true "flesh of God." It then became popular to carry the Host out from the church and into the community where the public could witness and share communally in

Fig. 2.26 *Founding of Tenochtitlan*, after frontispiece of Codex Mendoza. Bodleian Library, Oxford. Drawing by Mark Van Stone.

Christ's divine presence, celebrating with much rejoicing in the streets the redemptive power of the Host. By the fifteenth century, nearly every town in Europe boasted an elaborate processional ceremony to honor this mystery. As Miri Rubin has pointed out, Christ's body in the form of the Host thus signified and reinforced the people's sense of their own community body (like the Aztec altepetl), so the procession often symbolically demarcated the town's cardinal boundaries. In fact, Rubin noted, the Corpus Christi cortege in those communities with histories going back to ancient times would often visit the old pagan relics and resacralize them as Christian in the presence of the Host.[46]

Corpus Christi processions included religious theatrical performances (called *autos*), and portable palanquins (called *andas*) with live actors or posed mannequins representing the holy stories, all accompanied by music-playing and costumed dancers.[47] As the Corpus Christi procession moved through the streets of each community, sedge grass, boughs of poplar and pine, and flowers in abundance would be strewn in its path.[48] The celebrants often paused for benediction at four "stations" strategically located around the town, at which the Gospels were recited and *autos* presented. The Host itself was carried aloft in a hooded monstrance, often decorated with gilded rays, thus replicating the sun. Indeed, the image of the Corpus Christi in such a circular monstrance was derived from the ancient Roman notion of *Sol invictus,* which the early fathers of the church had Christianized as *Sol Justitiae,* Jesus as "Sun of Justice."[49]

It thus appears that the standard plan of the Mexican convento patio soon evolved into a "theater" for liturgical processions like that of Corpus Christi.[50] The friars openly encouraged Indian converts to perform their traditional processions and dances but now Christianized in symbol and content.[51] In each inner corner of the patio, a small square chapel was positioned known as a *posa,* or place for "pausing." Characteristic examples are extant at the Franciscan conventos of Atlatláuhcan, Morelos, and Huejotzingo (fig. 2.27). These squat buildings have no certain counterpart in European liturgical practice and were only subsequently adopted in South America by the Jesuits a century later. Their form, usually with a domical or pyramidal roof mounted on heavy stone piers, became more or less standardized in the conventos of all three mendicant orders in Mesoamerica.[52]

Unique to the patio's Mexican adaptation, however, was the layout of entrances, exits, and internal altars of the angled posas, which almost always compelled processional celebrants to move through them in a counterclockwise direction. (Note the placement of posa altars in fig. 2.5; the patios at Calpan and Atlatláuhcan once had the same arrangement.) At Huejotzingo, furthermore, each posa has a raised sculptural relief (skull and cross-bones) on but one face of its sloped roof, to be seen and contemplated only by marching celebrants as they turned left.[53] While counterclockwise movement was the norm in almost all indigenous Indian processional liturgies, I have found no evidence that this pattern was ever consistently followed or even mentioned as a ritual preference anywhere in Christian Europe at least until the seventeenth century.[54] Native-style counterclockwise processional routing was built not only into the fabric of the Mexican convento patio and posas but also frequently in the interior convento cloister as well.

San Miguel Huejotzingo, Puebla, begun before 1532, was one of the first four Franciscan conventos constructed in Mexico.[55] In figure 2.27, the posa in the northeast corner of the Huejotzingo patio is viewed just as if one had stepped out of the convento church and turned right, that is, facing north. Franciscan churches like Huejotzingo in fact frequently possessed a prominent north portal symbolically associated with the biblical Temple of Solomon (fig. 2.28).[56] Susan Webster has found documents describing how, during Holy Week (the week before Easter) in sixteenth-century Huejotzingo, Indian celebrants in procession would parade out from the church through the north portal and along the patio walkway toward our illustrated posa decorated with relief sculptures by a talented but unknown Indian artist depicting the instruments of Jesus' Passion. Here they would pause for a lesson and perhaps a scene from a miracle play. As the celebrants entered the narrow interior space of posa through the facing archway (and confronted an altar block that likewise faced in their approaching direction), the only way they could exit was through one other opening to the left, directing them to the west. When the procession then arrived at the next posa to the west, they again must turn left, and so on counterclockwise back to the church.[57] Not only would this circuit around the patio have mirrored in Indian eyes the microcosm of the ancient altepetl but also the posas vicariously imaged the old calpolli, each now representing the Indians' local barrio. During the eighteenth century when many old preconquest traditions had been forgotten and the patio in some conventos turned into a community cemetery, burials were clustered around the separate posas according to the home barrio of the deceased.[58] To this day the surviving posa chapels in the former conventos are used as meeting places for religious confraternities [*cofradías*] representing the various quarters of the local parish.

Fray Diego Valadés, a sixteenth-century Mexican-born artist and Franciscan friar charmingly if patronizingly captured the altepetl-like social and didactic functions of the convento patio in an engraving published in 1579 (fig. 2.29). At the top in a Latin caption, Valadés even observed the cosmic symbolism of his cardinally oriented diagram, depicted with a court of justice at the bottom eastern side and a funeral [*mortuus*] appropriately at the upper western entrance gate. In the upper corner to the left is a miniature of Valadés's mentor Fray Pedro de Gante conducting his school of music and "mechanical arts"; he is actually here demonstrating Testerian hieroglyphics painted on a large sheet of linen called in Spanish a *lienzo*. Note also the corner posas in the print, in each of which another friar gives lessons to a small group of catechumens: girls to the left and boys to the right at the top; women to the left and men to the right at the bottom.[59]

While not depicted here by Valadés, the center of nearly every convento patio in the Mexican altiplano during the sixteenth century was marked by a large stone cross raised on a pedestal. Whether by intention or again by extraordinary coincidence, the friars seem also to have realized that this conspicuous monument fulfilled the need for an appropriate *axis mundi* so that the patio might assume the sacred quincunx form revered by the Indians. Indeed in the patio before San José de los

Fig. 2.27 Posa in northeast corner of the patio, convento of San Miguel, Huejotzingo, Puebla. Photograph by Jorge Pérez de Lara.

Naturales once stood a huge wooden cross said to have been made from a mammoth cypress tree "taller than any tower in Mexico."[60] The patio cross, however, was rarely if ever a traditional European-style crucifix, that is, with a separate figure of Jesus affixed to it, but rather a plain cross with only Jesus' face, the instruments of the Passion, or both not on but imbedded in it, and the whole carved to simulate a living, branching tree, as at the Augustinian conventos at Atzacoalco and Acolman (fig. 2.30).[61] Indeed, many indigenous Mesoamerican societies believed that at the symbolic navel of their primeval territory stood a mystical World Tree out of which the human race was born. This ancient concept is quite graphically represented in the preconquest Mixtec Codex Vindobonensis where a stylized tree grows from a severed human head (sacrificial "seed" according to native tradition) while two deities carve on its trunk and branches (fig. 2.31). On the left, the deity is cutting out spindle whorls, symbolic of women's work as weavers. On the right, the other deity carves arrows, symbolizing the role of males. From the cleft between the arching branches of the tree spring the first human children, one a male, the other female.[62] By remarkable coincidence the patio cross at Acolman also rises symbolically over a human head, the skull of Adam (to the left of the small image of the seated Virgin Mary), whose "seed," according to the Judeo-Christian tradition, also begot the human race and was mystically buried at Calvary, the Hebrew "place of the skull." When the Spanish first saw such Indian images of the cross-shaped tree, as in the stone relief from the Classic Maya Temple of the Cross at Palenque, Chiapas, for example, they were convinced that Saint Thomas the Apostle had indeed introduced that holy sign to the "Indies" in biblical times, only to have his evangelizing work undone by the Devil.[63] In postconquest patio representations, in any case, Jesus is never represented hanging on the convento patio crosses. Indian artisans, obviously with the friars' blessing, conceived the Savior not on but *in* the cross. Indeed, Jesus *is* the World Tree, the symbolic center of the quincunx universe.[64]

Fig. 2.28 North portal to the church of the convento of San Miguel, Huejotzingo, Puebla. Photograph by Jorge Pérez de Lara.

Fig. 2.29 Fray Diego Valadés, engraving depicting the ideal convento patio, showing the activities of the friars and Indian catechumens, from his *Rhetorica Christiana*, Perugia, 1579, p. 107. Courtesy of the John Carter Brown Library at Brown University, Providence, Rhode Island.

Fig. 2.30 Patio cross, convento of San Agustín, Acolman, Mexico. Photograph by Jorge Pérez de Lara.

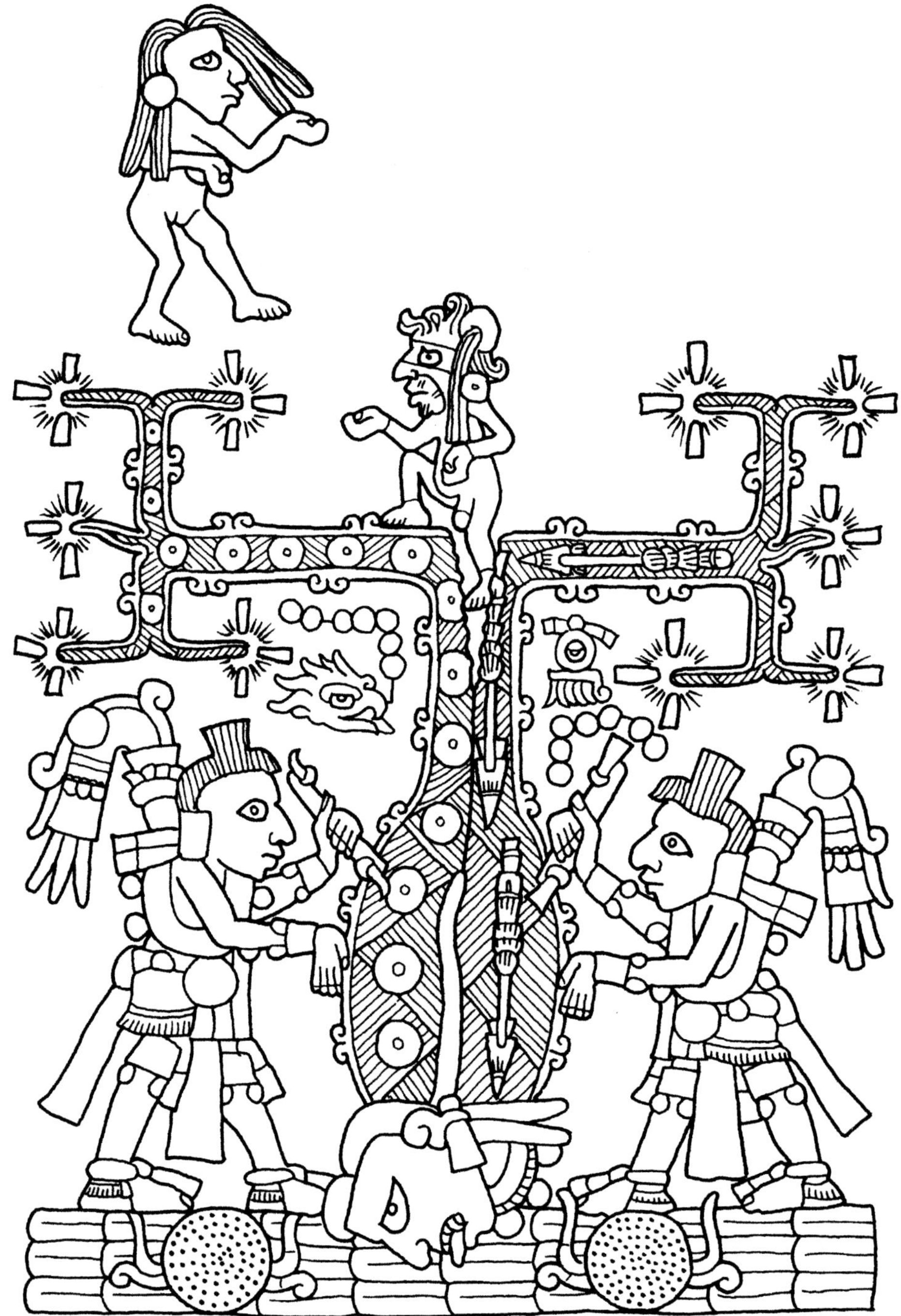

Fig. 2.31 Detail after fol. 37, Codex Vindobonensis, showing the Mixtec World Tree responsible for human creation. Staatsbibliothek, Vienna. Drawing by Mark Van Stone.

Fig. 2.32 Stone cross at the convento of San Salvador, Malinalco, Mexico, mounted at the northwest corner of the patio wall. Photograph by Jorge Pérez de Lara.

Often, a blossom-shaped disk made of obsidian or jade was inserted at the juncture of the arms of the cross, the cross's "heart," so to speak. This device was known in Nahuatl as *tezcatcuitlapilli* and in preconquest times represented the heart of the universe to which human blood is offered to the gods. At Malinalco, the stark five-foot-tall stone cross perhaps once in the convento patio (now mounted on the outer wall) has inset in its center an obsidian disk shaped as a flower, from which blood drips into a chalice (fig. 2.32). This is an overt reference to human sacrifice, yet it was tolerated by the friars because it so vividly prefigured the Christian mystery of Jesus' Sacred Heart. In sum, the uniquely Mexican patio, posa, and cross arrangement provides perhaps the paradigm example of the friar's special tactic of expedient selection—choosing from the vast store of ancient Christian symbols and Renaissance artistic motifs just those that would evoke in Indian eyes reassuring resemblances to preconquest concepts of their own. Curiously, even as evident as these concessions to native rituals are in the fabric of convento architecture, they are never mentioned in the numerous *Historias* and *Relaciones* written by the friars.

The Old World technology of the arch and vault, commonplace in Europe since the Roman republic, remained unknown in the New World until the sixteenth century. While the Indians of both North and South America were skilled builders—the intricate stonework of the Incas and the sturdy palaces of the Aztecs receive admiring notices in the writings of the conquistadors—native masons, even with their indigenous corbel compression vaults like the seventh-century Classic Maya Temple of the Cross, Palenque, were still unable to span the kind of broad, cavelike spaces Indians wanted to simulate in the sanctuaries of their own religious architecture. Fray Motolinía remarked that when the Indians for the first time saw a stone vault that a Spanish mason had constructed in the original church in Mexico City, San Francisco de México, in 1525–26, they were "much amazed, and were not able to believe that when the scaffolding was removed, it wouldn't fall down."[65] Motolinía continued that the Indians quickly learned the skill themselves. From the beginning, the friars intended that the Indians should master the keystone arch technique. The Nahuas even coined a new composite word for it in their language, *tenolli,* literally "curved thing in stone."[66]

In the grounds or patio . . . there is built a ramada of wood covered with . . . leaves of certain palm trees, very large, wide and long, holding many people, and very curious in that in all of it, there is neither nail nor rope, and withal it is most strong; it has no walls, by reason of which it is entirely open and the air enters from all sides . . . . In that ramada the people gather to hear the sermon and Mass which is said in a large [vaulted] chapel at the entrance of the same ramada. The Indians assist from the choir, which is at the side of the chapel, in which also there is usually the baptismal font, and on the other side is the sacristy.

Fray Antonio de Ciudad Real, Tratado curioso y docto

⊕

Chapter 3

THE ARCH AND THE CAVE

Open Chapels in the Yucatán

Arch and vault construction was one of the most important skills the friars wanted the Indians to learn. Both Motolinía and Mendieta recorded that the "first church in all the Indies," San Francisco de México built in 1525, had a masonry vault constructed by an unnamed Castilian mason supervising Indian laborers. Mendieta observed further that only the sanctuary of this church was vaulted, while the nave was roofed in wood.[1] Once trained in this new skill, as Motolinía continued in his *Memoriales,* "the Indians built as many things as they saw our masons

Fig. 3.1 Rosary Chapel, convento of Asunción de Nuestra Señora, Tlaxcala, Tlaxcala. Photograph by Jorge Pérez de Lara.

build; that is, circular, elliptical, and tripartite arches [*arcos redondos, escarzanos y terciados*], as in doorways and windows of much handiwork, and whatever Roman [classical/Renaissance] or bestial [Gothic/Mudéjar?] ornament they observed, they do it all, and very handsome churches and houses in the manner of the Spaniards."[2] In his *Historia,* Motolinía also described how, in preparation for the celebration of Easter 1538, the Indians by themselves built an arched chapel in the patio of the convento at Tlaxcala.[3] In the above quote from the *Memoriales* he added that the Indians also built two other small vaulted chapels in the same patio.[4] It remains a matter of scholars' contention whether any of these descriptions matches the beautiful Gothic-style Rosary Chapel, constructed before 1540 and still standing at the lower western entrance to the Tlaxcala convento (fig. 3.1).[5]

While all other vestiges of these earliest masonry vaults in the Americas have disappeared or been buried under later fabric, the form of their original structure, very similar to that of the first San Francisco chapel in Mexico City, may still be ascertained in the early churches of the Yucatán. However, one must detour from the superhighway now

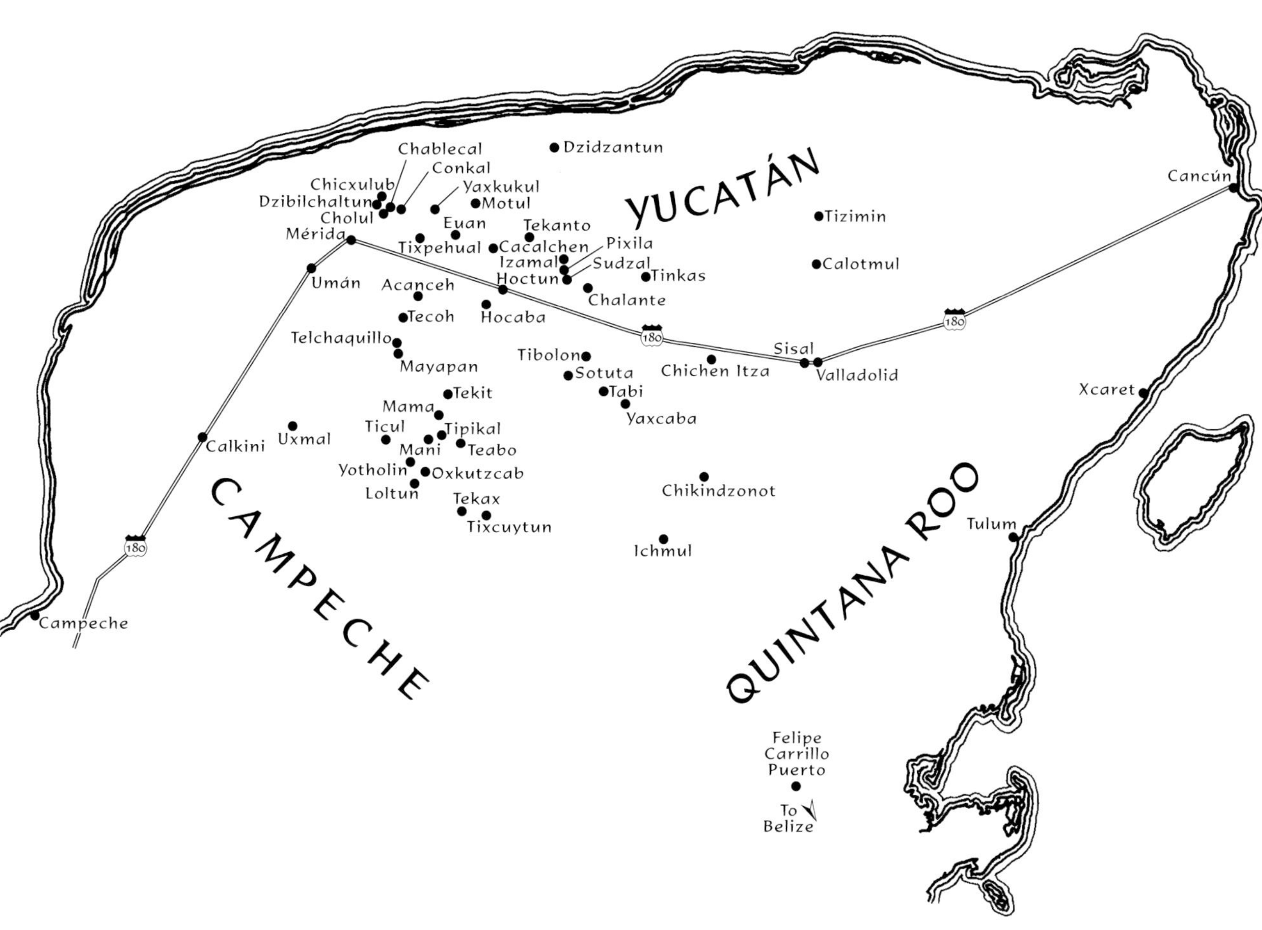

Fig. 3.2 Yucatán peninsula showing convento, visita, and other sites mentioned in chapter 3. Drawing by Mark Van Stone, typography by Melissa Tandysh.

transversing the peninsula (too easily tempting the tourist to race to the beaches of Cancún) and be willing to explore instead the lesser byways, especially those north and south of the highway between Mérida and Chichén Itzá (fig. 3.2). On the crisscrossing back roads of this rural region, one passes through dozens of indigenous Yucatec-speaking communities where local churches still have sanctuaries originally built in the sixteenth century. The singular feature of these primal buildings is a grottolike masonry-vaulted space surrounding the altar, of some six meters in depth and perhaps eight in height and width, and faced with an open *arco toral*, or prominently voussoir-outlined chancel arch.

The characteristic churches of this area (today consisting of three Mexican states in the Yucatán peninsula: Campeche, Quintana Roo, and Yucatán itself) functioned originally as visitas, frontier "missions of penetration" as Robert Ricard distinguished such buildings from the more sophisticated "occupation" missionary conventos in central Mexico.[6] The *visita* is a church that has no resident priest, being only "visited" periodically by an itinerant friar who would spend a day or two tending to all the baptisms, marriages, confessions, etc. that had been awaiting his call. He would then be off to the next neighboring visita and so forth around the circuit. In the meantime, there would be no Mass and no sacraments. Church upkeep and related lay affairs would remain in local Indian hands with an appointed native officer called the *maestro cantor*.[7]

Because of the Yucatán's geopolitical isolation and relative poverty, even less English-language scholarly attention has been paid to its sixteenth-century architecture. Kubler and McAndrew devoted only a few pages,[8] leaving Richard and Rosalind Perry's *Maya Missions* as the single indispensable guide. For further study, the reader limited to English must resort to articles. Albeit some are excellent they are in hard-to-come-by publications like the now-defunct Carnegie Institution's *Contributions to American Anthropology and History*, especially vol. 11 containing Ralph Roys's fundamental study of the topographical relationship between postconquest mission churches and preconquest Maya sites ("Conquest Sites and the Subsequent Destruction of Maya Architecture in the Interior of Northern Yucatán"). There are no pictures, and readers not already familiar with the towns and geography of the Yucatán will find Roys's essay hard going. Less formidable but in an equally obscure journal is Miguel Bretos's "Yucatan Franciscan Architecture and the Spiritual Conquest." Bretos's main concern, however, was less with the visitas and more with the principal Franciscan headquarter conventos in the Yucatán laid out in the manner of central Mexico.

An article by Craig Hanson, "The Hispanic Horizon in Yucatán," does deal specifically with the origins of the open chapel and thatch-covered nave church that became peculiar to the Yucatán mission, although his attempt at recreating a chain of developmental stages based solely on local archaeological evidence gives little consideration to the central Mexican convento tradition that the Franciscans certainly had in their mind's eye when they first arrived in the Yucatán. Two other relevant archaeological reports are William J. Folan's *Open Chapel of Dzibilchaltún, Yucatán*, and David M. Pendergast's "Worlds in Collision." Folan provides a detailed description of the archaeological remains, evidence for dating, and local legends about a monument of particular importance to this chapter. Pendergast similarly discusses the archaeological evidence of open chapels at Lamanai and Tipú in Belize, then the southeastern-most frontier of the Yucatán mission. He also provides revealing insights into how friars and Indians worked together in remote visitas like these. Finally, Eugene Logan Wagner of the University of Texas, Austin, presents for the first time in English a detailed study with plans drawn and measured on site of the great convento at Izamal, Yucatán, along with several of its neighboring dependency chapels in relation to its preconquest architectural antecedents.[9]

Evangelization of the Yucatán did not begin until some years after the friars had already converted most of central Mexico. Inhabitants of that forbiddingly hot and pancake-flat eastern Mexican peninsula were (and still are) Yucatec-speakers, the only Maya linguistic group at the time of the conquest still writing in the Classic hieroglyphic script and practicing an arithmetic based on numerical placement and the concept of zero. Architecturally too, their civilization was once as magnificent as that of the Classic Maya in the Petén region to the south, but it ended just as abruptly in the tenth century C.E., five hundred years before the Spanish arrived. Even the grandiose Terminal and Postclassic Yucatec cities of Chichén Itzá, Uxmal, Tiho, and Mayapán were only marginally inhabited and mostly lay in ruins as the Europeans moved in.[10]

Nonetheless, just before 1492, the population of the Yucatán countryside was again quite dense in the west and north, spread out in about two hundred *kahob* [communities; the Yucatec equivalent for the same concept as the Nahua *altepetl*] collected in sixteen provinces, or *kuchkabalob,* each dominated by a local lineage and usually at war with one or more of its neighbors.[11] No centralized authority had existed since the fifteenth century when the last great peninsular powers, Chichén Itzá and Mayapán, finally collapsed.[12] Many if not most of these Maya kahob centered around natural grottoes called *ts'onotob,* corrupted in Spanish and English as "cenotes," in which the natives believed their sustaining rain deities lived.

With no drainage valleys in the north, rain runoff from the southern sierras has since ages past seeped down through the porous limestone bedrock that forms the thumblike shape of the peninsula and eroded a network of subterranean channels leading to the sea.[13] There are no surface rivers; all fresh water flows through these underground caves, which occasionally become exposed when the shallow crust above collapses, creating eerie caverns and underground tunnels penetrating deep into the bowels of the earth (today providing special excitement to spelunkers, skin divers, and snorkelers). It was around these open cenotes that the Indians from ancient times gathered, attracted not only by the presence of fresh water but also by the deep caverns that seemed to connect the spirit realm of the underworld to the living earth above, much as the umbilical cord (in Yucatec, *kuxa'an suum*) sustains the fetus in its mother's womb (fig. 3.3).

Well before the conquistadors made their official entrada into eastern Mesoamerica, the diseases the Europeans inadvertently introduced in 1492, and to which the New World natives had as yet no natural immunity, had begun their

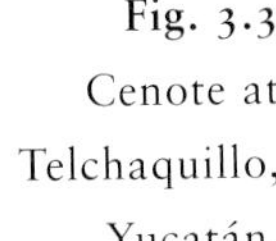

Fig. 3.3 Cenote at Telchaquillo, Yucatán.

deadly devastation. By 1540 the indigenous population of Yucatán had plummeted. While the Maya remained brave and determined against the Spanish, they were just too weakened to hold out against Francisco de Montejo, his namesake son, and his nephew who from the 1520s through the 1540s led assault after assault against them.[15] Yet even as the military conquest continued, the Friars Minor were preparing the task of conversion; in fact, they were granted exclusive right to proselytize in the Yucatán, now officially designated by the Holy See as the Franciscan Province of San José. In 1545 evangelization started in earnest when eight friars under brilliant linguist Fray Luis de Villalpando opened a mission in Campeche.[16]

The Franciscans, of course, had already established the basic architectural program and strategy for using visual aids to implement evangelization. In the Yucatán, they could now put into practice more than twenty years of field experience without interference from other competing orders. Furthermore, unlike in central Mexico where the great missions were rebuilt into their present monumental size well after the mass-conversion was over, the original form of frontline architecture can still be perceived in the small community churches of the Yucatán. Many of these humble structures preserve their original sixteenth-century components. Just east of Mérida, in small neighboring towns like Yaxkukul, Tixpéhual, and Euan, one can still observe the entire evolution of Yucatán architecture from preconquest platform foundation, to original sixteenth-century open visita chapel, to the extended nave and facade *espadaña* that finally complemented these buildings by the eighteenth century. The attractive church at Tixpéhual is illustrated in figure 3.4.

As the Franciscan friars were preparing for their Yucatán adventure, the preconquest Maya city of Tiho was chosen as the new Spanish capital, renamed Mérida after the ancient Roman city in Extremadura, Spain, which was itself built on pagan ruins. Upon the foundations of one of the former pyramids in Tiho, the Franciscans erected their first permanent convento and established, just as they had in Mexico City, a school for the training of native craftsmen. Two friars, Juan de Herrera and Juan de Mérida (another Extremeño who originally came to Mexico as a conquistador), had prior architectural experience and may have begun the training of Indian masons in the technique of keystone arch and vault construction. A similar training school was set up in Maní.[17]

While the Franciscans probably came to the Yucatán assuming they would simply apply the same architectural formula that had already worked in central Mexico, and in fact designed a number of major conventos with patios and posas as at Calkiní, Maní, Dzidzantún, Motul, Tekax, Tekantó, Tizimin, Izamal, and Valladolid (San Bernardino de Sisal),[18] their truly important contribution to the strategy of deploying architecture as a tool for conversion was the local community church, uniquely adapted to the environmental peculiarities of the peninsula. From their regional *guardianías*, or headquarters conventos, the friars fanned out into the rural hinterland. According to Fray Antonio de Ciudad Real who toured the Yucatán in 1588 (as companion of Fray Alonso Ponce, the just-appointed Franciscan commissary general to New Spain), only sixty-six friars were resident in the twenty-two guardianías then established.[19] This must have

Fig. 3.4
Church at Tixpéhual, Yucatán. Photograph by Jorge Pérez de Lara.

meant that only one or two friars at a time could be spared for proselytization in the 120 or so dependent visitas they were setting up in the interior kahob.[20] Moreover, once the local inhabitants were converted and a simple chapel constructed, the friars had to move on to the next community, leaving the nascent church in the hands of a native maestro cantor. With no spare friar to serve as resident *cura,* most of these new congregations could only hear Mass and receive the sacraments intermittently, that is, whenever the few itinerant priests were able to get around to them on the pastoral circuit.

While the guardianías maintained stricter control over the Indians in towns close by, forcing the natives to move into compacted communities [*congregaciones*] around the church and often prosecuting suspected apostasy with particular harshness, the friars further afield, isolated and alone among the Indians, had only their own individual authority to exert. Native communities were connected, if at all, by rude *sakbeob* [white roads] often little more than barely marked footpaths.[21] If assistance were ever needed in communities like Tipú or Lamanai in the far distant jungle south of Lake Bacalar, it could take days to make communication with and receive help from the nearest guardianía.

The first and most difficult task was to dismantle the old shrines of the Indians. It is not clear just how much military force, if any, the friars had to call upon in order to accomplish this in individual cases, but it is relieving to note that their efforts were quite selective. Roys has pointed out that at the time of the conquest, the Yucatán countryside was dotted with masonry temple structures, many already abandoned and so covered with overgrowth as to be indistinguishable from natural hills.[22] Whether recognized as such or not, many of these pyramids were left standing in communities where the friars had apparently converted the inhabitants and founded churches, as at Acanceh, Tibolon, and Dzibilchaltún.[23] At Izamal, once a preconquest center for Maya pilgrims seeking cures from disease, several mammoth pyramids served as temple platforms, but only the largest was partly razed to make the foundation for the Christian convento (and a special shrine to the Virgin Mary, to this day still attracting pilgrims seeking miraculous cures). Three other old pyramids remained, one of which had a giant sculpted stucco mask on its flank, visible as late as the nineteenth century when it was drawn by Frederick Catherwood.[24] Fray Diego de Landa, notorious *provincial* and later bishop of the Yucatán resident in Izamal during the 1560s, seemed to have tolerated this blatant pagan reminder even as he conducted inquisitions and burned native books as “works of the devil.”[25]

In northwestern Yucatán, the friars had their visita churches as well as guardianía conventos built right on top of former temple sites near the community cenotes, thus always at locations with special preconquest local religious significance. Even so, the old preconquest structures were not torn down completely, only truncated, leaving masonry foundations still visible aboveground to provide elevated stages as at Tecoh south of Mérida (fig. 3.5). As Roys observed, the awe-inspiring size and dramatic presentation of these new churches was an important factor in the Christianization of the Indians, an effective measure to “rival the impressive monuments of the earlier Maya with others commemorating the greatness of the new religion.”[26] Indeed, the newly established

Fig. 3.5 Church at Tecoh, Yucatán. Photograph by Jorge Pérez de Lara.

Christian parishes were not towns ex nihilo but only revamped former ceremonial centers to which the surrounding Indians would have been used to making religious pilgrimages even before the conquest. By the end of the century, churches had been built on nearly every former holy site in northwestern Yucatán, forming a network in which no guardianía or visita was more than a day's walk apart in any radial direction.[27]

During the early years of the mission, moreover, the friars in the remote communities had to negotiate with the inhabitants and could depend on little outside assistance. If the old temple was to be torn down and a Christian church erected in its stead, then the Indians should not be antagonized by being made to think they were desecrating their old site, but rather encouraged into believing they were preserving its sanctity, and that it should remain a place where supernatural forces continued to dwell. The friars in the field, while hardly advocating "superstitions," had to be tolerant. By urging that the new churches be built right on top of old temple remnants, they implicitly reassured the Indians that the Christian superstructure would osmotically assume the inherent primordial powers of the ancient location.[28] If the Indians were to be converted, they needed to be convinced that the succeeding shrine was going to bring them more benefits than whatever stood in the same place before. Interestingly, the Yucatec Maya continued to use the same term to denote a Christian church, *k'u* or *k'ul na,* literally "god" or "god house," as they had for their preconquest temples.[29]

Where the plaster veneer has fallen off the rough stone facade of the little church at Telchaquillo near Tecoh, one may still see fragments of stone carvings from earlier buildings, some with preconquest motifs and others with Christian. The former were clearly saved from the original preconquest temple; the latter probably retrieved from the first Christian masonry sanctuary built on the old temple's foundations (fig. 3.6). The present building is an eighteenth-century replacement, but the Indian masons even at this late date believed the original stones from both previous structures retained equal sacredness and so implanted them side by side in the new church to insure its divine continuity.

Archaeologist Craig Hanson has attempted to reconstruct a special "missionization model" worked out a priori by the Franciscan friars before embarking into the Yucatán hinterland. The first stage of his model required that the friars in the field put up simple pole-and-thatch structures to serve as provisional churches.[30] To this day Yucatec Maya people live in such thatched houses, called *palapas,* characteristically built with rounded ends as in figure 3.7. This form has remained unchanged in the Yucatán since preconquest times, adaptable also for corrals, storage barns, and as the Spanish invaders observed, for enshrining the pagan "idols" on top of masonry foundations.[31] In fact, the first friars probably took over some of these palapa tabernacles and consecrated them as temporary churches. A companion of Fray Bartolomé de Las Casas who traveled in the Yucatán in 1545, remembered: "We entered the church to hear Mass; it stands near the water [cenote] and is built of pole and thatch like the rest of the houses of the town."[32] One may still see the ruins of such a structure at Xcaret, built by the early

Franciscans at the edge of an important preconquest temple site beside an extraordinary cenote on the Caribbean coast in the state of Quintana Roo between Cancún and Tulum. The original palapa roof of the little church is long gone, but the stone walls with a rounded apsidal end that once supported the wooden thatch frame still stand.

Nevertheless, the humble palapa was an unsuitable Christian sanctuary and needed to be replaced as quickly as possible by a more permanent structure. Ciudad Real mentions several times that during his journey through the Yucatán with Fray Alonso Ponce in 1588, the commissary general wanted to make sure that the various churches he visited had a safe and secure place in which to store the Host. Hanson's "model" moves rather perfunctorily from provisional palapa shrine to second-stage masonry vault without considering either this sacred function of the sanctuary or how the Indians might have reacted as the friars reverently described to them the holy work they were performing as they built the new vaulted structures.

In all Christendom, whenever a church was to be put up where none had been before, the very first part constructed should be the altar sanctuary. Moreover, the form of this enclosure had to be visually dramatic in such a way as to inspire a feeling of spiritual uplift and thus concentrate the worshiper's attention on the sacrament within. Medieval scholastic exegeses on holy Scripture describe this sense of spiritual elation with a discrete Latin word, *anagogica* (sometimes *anagogia*). The English equivalent adjective, "anagogical," though little used in modern parlance is peculiarly suitable for revival in this context.[33] During the Middle Ages the word also described the same exhilaration one should feel when studying music and geometry among the Aristotelian liberal arts. Saint Augustine claimed that since architecture and music derived respectively from the Quadrivium sciences of geometry and arithmetic, they too were capable of producing heavenly harmonies, "leading the mind from the world of appearances to the contemplation of divine order," in Otto von Simson's paraphrase.[34] During the twelfth and thirteenth centuries, *anagogicus* was indeed the appropriate adjective to describe the soaring arches and vaults of Romanesque and Gothic cathedrals.

Fig. 3.6 Detail of western facade of the church at Telchaquillo, Yucatán. Photograph by Jorge Pérez de Lara.

Medieval ecclesiastics, citing Saint Paul's epistle to the Ephesians (2:20–22), often referred to the arched entrance of a church as the "gate of heaven," and the church itself as "built upon the foundations of the apostles and prophets, with Jesus Christ as the keystone."[35]

So moving were these metaphorical comparisons during the Middle Ages that parishioners often deposited gems and precious objects in the fresh masonry of each new church's foundations. One may well picture the Franciscans in Yucatán also resorting to such anagogical rhetoric as they exhorted their Indian catechumens. The friars may even have aroused the emotions of their congregations to such sublime heights that the Indians too wanted to deposit precious objects in the walls of the Christian church, just as was their ancient custom when pyramid temples were being built.

In fact, Indian artifacts have been frequently found buried in the fabric of the early Mesoamerican churches.[36] Allen Christenson reports that in Santiago Atitlán, Guatemala, local Tz'utujil Maya workmen making repairs on the sixteenth-century Franciscan-built church there, found that not only was it constructed over the pavement of a preconquest temple but also numerous dedicatory caches with artifacts of jade and even human bones were buried in the church foundations. The native workmen quickly reinterred the caches so as not to disturb these ancient pagan-Christian links.[37]

The missionary friars in the Yucatán seemed convinced that an arched space stimulated anagogical spirituality as no other architectural form could. In such a psychic setting with candles dimly flickering through the smoke of pungent incense, the sound of bells

Fig. 3.7
Palapa house near Sudzal, Yucatán.

and chanted prayers reverberating from the vaulted walls, the friars carefully orchestrated the most sublime moment in the Mass when the consecrated Host is raised. The Indians should then be so moved that they believed themselves in the very presence of the Christian God. While the friars were aware that the keystone principle per se was also a technical curiosity and probably added to the Indians' wonder, the real importance of its ubiquitous employment was for reasons of anagogical excitation and not simply to assert technological superiority, at least during the first century of Christian proselytization.

A contemporaneous engraving by Fray Diego Valadés, the Mexican-born (and possibly mestizo) Franciscan artist and author, shows a human sacrifice taking place in a pagan Aztec temple, which, amazingly, he depicted as a European-style vaulted open chapel atop a truncated pyramid base, not at all unlike an early Yucatán Christian church (fig. 3.8). By the late sixteenth century, some friars had apparently forgotten what an original pagan temple looked like, and others even believed the Indians had invented the arch by themselves.[38]

Figure 3.9 shows the archaeological reconstruction of the original open chapel at Dzibilchaltún, near Mérida.[39] While built late in the century (a stone fragment dated 1593 was found nearby), its simple plan and elevation follows a prototype that had already been standardized by the 1550s.[40] In its present stripped-down condition this structure represents the appearance of all early open chapels built of masonry during the frontier period of Mexican missionization. Dzibilchaltún was once a large preconquest population center with numerous temples that flourished from most ancient times until shortly after the Spanish arrival. The community slowly diminished and was entirely abandoned, including the Franciscan chapel, in the early seventeenth century. (The site is now being restored as a national archaeological park.) A plain stone vault about eight meters high from ground to keystone is open at one end and closed at the other. It is built of rough masonry and flanked at left by an equally simple connecting sacristy. A matching vestry on the opposite side was never completed. Note that the stones are laid according to the traditional Yucatec masonry technique with mud mortar known as *sahkab,* the same as in preconquest Maya pyramids.[41] At one time, the walls were plastered, and fragments of a painted mural were found on the altar wall.[42] Remains of curve-ended masonry foundation extend forward from the chapel's open face. This was to support a *ramada,* or open-sided pole-and-thatch sun shelter, in place of a nave. Other than the arches and vault, there is little European architectural influence. The whole structure was positioned in the center of the former sacred plaza of Dzibilchaltún almost on axis with the preconquest Temple of the Seven Dolls.

The friars had developed the open chapel architectural concept in central Mexico decades before as a convenient means of preaching to large numbers without crowding them into a confining church. The Indians were used to holding their own traditional religious rituals out of doors, so the friars adopted the same custom, thus inspiring the open chapel's popular Spanish name, capilla de Indios. The first such capilla built in the Yucatán was begun in 1549; it abutted the convento of San Miguel at Maní (fig. 3.10). It closely followed the central Mexican prototype by being separate from the church and opening onto an expansive patio originally with corner posas. The Maní open chapel is extremely large and was once divided into a lower and upper story. The seventeenth-century Franciscan historian Fray Diego López de Cogolludo described how Fray Juan de Mérida planned and finished the convento in seven months, employing, with permission of converted local Indian cacique Kukum Xiu, six thousand Indians of his powerful clan.[43] The chapel is thoroughly European in design and construction technique. No doubt Fray Juan used the occasion to train Indian workmen in the art of vaulting, native master masons who could then be made available to the friars in the hinterland for the building of visita chapels.

Fig. 3.8 Fray Diego Valadés, *Human Sacrifice upon an Aztec Temple*, engraving from his *Rhetorica Christiana*, Perugia, 1579, p. 176. Courtesy of the John Carter Brown Library at Brown University, Providence, Rhode Island.

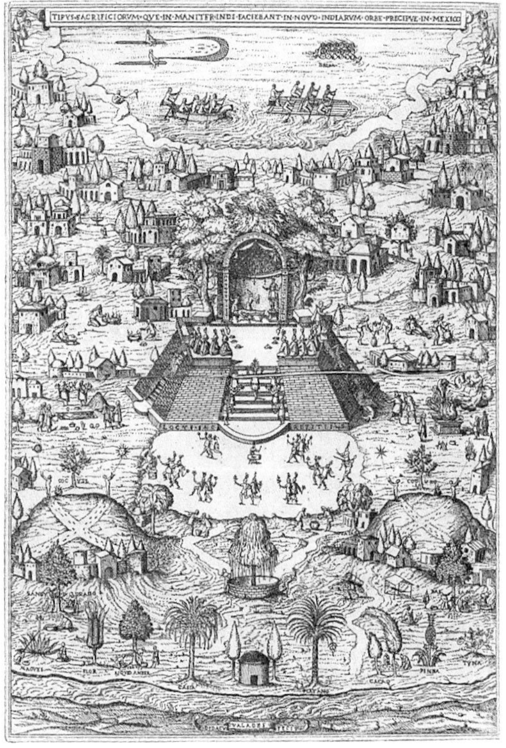

Traces of visita chapels like that at Dzibilchaltún can still be discerned in the fabric of dozens of Yucatán churches.[44] The general plan was to have an open-vaulted chapel flanked by a simple enclosed sacristy to the left side and "vestry" to the right usually serving as a place for the large stone baptismal font (fig. 3.11).[45] Arcuated space was usually de rigueur in these simple masonry structures. The facing chancel arch was emphasized still more. Today, one can observe the voussoirs of the arco toral looming like haloes above and around the later-added but lower nave roofs of many surviving examples, as at Sudzal near Izamal (fig. 3.12).

What did the Indians themselves think as they contemplated the novel vaulted Christian sanctuary pretentiously soaring above the sacred sites of their former temples? Just a hundred or so meters to the west of the Dzibilchaltún chapel is the cenote Xlacah [Old City], the largest of several cenotes in the site. In fact, the open altar side faces it directly. The Indian congregation that once heard Mass before the Dzibilchaltún sanctuary would have been standing exactly between it and the cenote. The same axial orientation of chapel to neighboring cenote is found at a number of Yucatán communities, for example, Cholul, Tabí, Tekit, Telchaquillo, and Chikindzonot (Yucatec for

Fig. 3.9
Open chapel
at Dzibilchaltún,
Yucatán.

"West Cenote"). In other cases the churches were built just as close but to the side of the cenote as at Yaxcaba, Mama, Maní, and Teabo. In one remarkable instance, the church was built right on top of the cenote as at San Bernardino de Sisal, Valladolid.

At Maní, local folklore has it that the adjacent cenote, and by implication the Christian convento, marks the "center of the world"; the cave underneath then supposedly makes umbilical connection with the cathedral in Mérida (preconquest Tiho) and even connects to Jerusalem![46] Surely, the friars were aware of the ancient Maya belief in the *kuxa'an suum*, the mystical "rope" that links the other world to this, through which divine "nourishment" passes from the gods to mankind. By deliberately placing their Maní convento with its conspicuous cavelike open chapel right at this location, the friars could manipulate the legend to their Christian advantage (fig. 3.10).

Several scholars in the 1990s indeed stressed the extreme importance of caves in the religious ideology of the ancient Maya.[47] That such a naturally vaulted space did evoke profound religious feeling is clear from the thousands of religious offerings placed in the depths of actual caves, as in the vaulted cavern at Balankanché near Chichén Itzá, not to mention the mass of offerings plus bones of sacrificed humans found in the celebrated cenote at Chichén Itzá itself. The Aztecs of central Mexico too believed their historical genesis occurred in a mythical womblike cave with seven branches called Chicomostoc. So important were caves as means of communication with the spirit world that some were actually man-made, like those under the Temple of the Sun at Teotihuacan, Mexico, and under the

Fig. 3.10 Convento of San Miguel, Maní, Yucatán, looking east. Photograph by Jorge Pérez de Lara.

Temple of Quetzalcoatl at Utatlán, Guatemala (the latter still venerated by K'iche Maya pilgrims). Indeed, for all human beings everywhere throughout history, the darkened expanse of a vaulted cave has inspired feelings of mystery and reverence. No doubt this primal emotion was mapped into the human gene as far back as the Pleistocene Age when our Paleolithic ancestors huddled in caves and pits, seeking refuge from wild beasts outside even as they were fearful of the supernatural forces inside. This same awe probably predisposed the medieval Christians' anagogical response to the vaults of the first Romanesque and Gothic cathedrals. Indeed, one of the original inspirations of the vaulted Christian church was the underground Roman catacomb. Caves and grottoes have from the very beginning fascinated Christians as mysterious places where miraculous events occur, just as much as they did pagan Indians.[48]

While the preconquest Yucatec Maya certainly considered the sanctuary atop the masonry pyramid as containing a sacred space (as at Mayapán, for example, [fig. 3.13]), the corbel arch, a simple compression rather than a tension system, is technically unable to span much more than a narrow gap. The awesome expanse of natural vaults as at Loltun, the most spectacular cave in the Yucatán peninsula, for instance, could never have been imitated by the corbel method. Yet Loltun does inspire any viewer familiar with semicircular vaults to reflect, "How like a cathedral!" In the same vein, would not a sixteenth-century Indian, upon entering a

Fig. 3.11 Prototypical sixteenth-century open chapel church in the Yucatán.

Fig. 3.12 Church at Sudzal, Yucatán. Photograph by Jorge Pérez de Lara.

European-style vaulted cathedral for the first time, have been inclined to imagine, "How like a cave"?

The newly introduced keystone vault with its ability to bridge so wide and high a space had metaphysical implications that surely encouraged the Indians' interest in the Christian religion. Even though artificial, the vaulted church provided the same darkened, mystical interior that had always intrigued the Indians as the proper place in which to commune with the supernatural.[49]

Thus it would seem that the Franciscans with some deliberateness planned their open chapels so near to the local cenotes in order to divert native attention away from pagan associations with natural caves. In fact, we have here yet another example of the missionaries' calculated selective expediency. By deploying the European masonry vault so ostentatiously in the Yucatán, they hoped to remind the Indians that the cavernous Christian church was not dissimilar in meaning as well as form from their natural sacred grottoes and thus ease their resistance to the new religion. After all, the visita church in the Yucatán was usually set upon a raised pyramidal rostrum, just as the former temples with their narrow corbel-arched entries also sat upon pyramid platforms. In preconquest times, the narrow darkened temple was believed to be the man-made surrogate of the cenote cave in the primordial mountain in the center of the world. Furthermore, inside many preconquest temples was a special inner sanctum called the *pib na* in Yucatec, or underground house, in which the most sacred objects were stored and rituals performed (in the Temple of the Cross at Palenque, for example).[50] It was this mystical symmetry between natural cenote and man-made pyramid that gave the temple with interior pib na its spiritual power. By no coincidence, these same ancient associations were allowed by the Franciscan friars to persist as Christianized symbols in nearly every community of the Yucatán peninsula.

As further evidence that the friars were attempting to co-opt the cenotes as places now of sacred Christian mysteries, small vaulted *hermitas* [shrines] were often built right at the cenote's edge, dedicated to Christian miracles associated with caves, as at Tabí and Yaxcaba. In Tabí the story is told of a horse and rider accidentally falling into the local cenote, then being miraculously levitated above the waters by the Virgin Mary. To this day the people who live in Tabí believe the Virgin resides in their cenote. Their lovely seventeenth-century church dedicated to this miracle faces the cenote a few meters to its left in figure 3.14.

William Folan has recorded similar legends about the cenote Xlacah at Dzibilchaltún where Saint Ursula is supposed to live and periodically visit the chapel. Saint Ursula is the patron of the nearby town of Chablekal;

Fig. 3.13 Maya pyramid at Mayapán, Yucatán.

the locals believe she is also the "sister" of the Virgen de la Concepción, patron saint of Izamal with which Chablekal and Dzibilchaltún were allied in preconquest times and perhaps joined by an ancient *sakbe* (and possibly even an umbilical underground cave extending from Xlacah).[51]

Once again the friars reveal little of these tactical accommodations in their official memoirs. On the other hand, and for the benefit of their Counter-Reformation audiences in Europe, some friars like Landa and Burgoa emphasized apprehension that the Indians were using the caves to secrete their pagan idols. In the main, however, it would appear that most of the friars in the field, especially in the more remote parishes, simply looked the other way when the Indians made covert pilgrimages to the caves. If the Indians did hopefully sense the adjacent vaulted church as exuding the same spiritual mystery as an indigenous natural cave, so much the better for expediting their conversion (and the less disclosed to the authorities in Rome, likewise the better).

In 1850, during the terrible Caste Wars when the native Yucatec Indians rose up against the white-creole and ladino ruling class, the event that most inspired the insurgents happened near the southeastern Yucatán town of Chan Santa Cruz (now Felipe Carrillo Puerto), where, beside a cenote that had once been a preconquest shrine, a wooden cross carved in a tree miraculously spoke. Beside this cenote, now resacralized by the "talking cross" (which "mysteriously" continued to preach revolution and overthrow of the whites), the Maya insurgents built a special temple known as *Balam Na,* or Jaguar House, deliberately recalling the preconquest shrine. Yet this revolutionary cult-temple and another that succeeded it were both vaulted in masonry and modeled exactly like the conventional Franciscan Yucatán church.[52] Still today, there are many similar and active cave-shrines with adjacent vaulted churches all over Mesoamerica, as at Esquipulas in Guatemala, Tila in Chiapas, Amecameca and Chalma in the state of Mexico. Each attracts Indian pilgrims who come by the thousands on special feast days to venerate sacred images associated with the caves, ostensibly Christian but the forms and devotions of which have clearly descended from the pagan past.[53]

The Yucatán climate is extremely hot, much more so than in the Mexican altiplano where the friars had first worked out the plans of their conversion architecture. To accommodate the Indians and expedite the conversion process, the Franciscans added another unique feature to their Yucatán open chapels, the palapa ramada. This thoroughly native-style pole-and-thatch construction simply abutted and extended from the open end of the masonry chapel (fig. 3.15).

Obviously this native form of sun-protection owed nothing to European architecture. Moreover, from the Indian standpoint, the Christian ramada chapel looked not unlike traditional preconquest temples that often had palapa shrines atop masonry terraces as in the reconstructed example from Classic Maya Piedras Negras (fig. 3.16). The manner of building the palapa ramada followed exactly the practice traditionally employed by the indigenous Maya in making their own private dwellings. While none of the palapa ramadas that once graced the sixteenth-century Yucatán open chapels has

Fig. 3.14 Church at Tabí, Yucatán. Photograph by Jorge Pérez de Lara.

Fig. 3.15 Prototypical sixteenth-century open chapel church in the Yucatán with palapa ramada.

Fig. 3.16 Reconstruction of a Classic Maya temple (Structure K5–3d), Piedras Negras, Guatemala. From Tatiana Proskouriakoff, *An Album of Maya Architecture* (Norman: University of Oklahoma Press, 1963).

survived, one may see vestiges of postholes and the characteristic curved-end form in the stone foundations still imbedded in some old church patios.[54]

Interestingly, near the outskirts of Maní on the road to Oxkutzcab stands a quaint example of a modern Franciscan revival, as it were, this time a Seventh-Day Adventist chapel (fig. 3.17). It seems that successes in spreading the Protestant faith to the Maya in the twentieth century inspired some resourceful minister to revive that old idea that had worked so advantageously for Catholic missionaries more than four hundred years ago.

The unique sixteenth-century Yucatán ramada chapel, even though laid out according to a preconceived Franciscan plan, was constructed according to traditional Maya building technology (approved of by the Franciscans who likewise preferred architectural abstinence). Only the European keystone arch was dramatically new. Nevertheless, the Maya appropriated even this foreign innovation into their enduring traditional symbol system. In truth, the sixteenth-century Yucatán chapel, a pastiche of ordinary Maya masonry and thatch, blended rather easily in the built landscape of the native community. From the Indian mason's point of view, the newly introduced keystone arch was a clear improvement on his prior technology, much as Roman arcuated forms offered expressive possibilities unrealized

Fig. 3.17 Seventh-Day Adventist chapel near Oxkutzcab, Yucatán.

Fig. 3.18 Convento of Nuestra Señora, Izamal, Yucatán, view of the western facade and patio. Photograph by Jorge Pérez de Lara.

in the trabeated architecture of ancient Greece. In this sense then, the vaulted Christian chapels built by natives in almost every one of their own kahob deserve to be admired as belonging to indigenous cultural history just as much as the Classic Maya pyramids themselves, no less an architectural accomplishment of ever-evolving Maya civilization.

Since the purpose of the ramada was to service the few hundred or so families in each local *kah* who could probably all fit under its protective thatch, there was less need for an enclosed patio and corner posas. Patios with posas in adapted form were included, however, in the planning of several of the larger guardianías like Izamal, but even those show no evidence of original crosses having been set up in the patio centers (fig. 3.18).[55] Perhaps the Franciscans simply left them out because they would get in the way of the extended ramada. In any case, the Yucatec Maya never relinquished the ancient custom of orienting their kahob to the cardinal directions. In fact, crosses, often in groups of three covered by small ramadas, are set up on each directional side of the town where the main roads enter, as at Tabí (fig. 3.19), still signifying the World Trees at the four sides of the universe. Every Yucatán kah thus continues to mirror the cosmic quincunx, except that now the vaulted Christian church has replaced the preconquest pyramid as guardian of the axis mundi.

By the seventeenth century, Italian Renaissance artistic motifs had begun to arrive in quantity in New Spain (as they were also in old Spain); Indian artisans themselves were becoming more Hispanicized and better trained in replicating the refinements of the latest European style. Meanwhile, under increasingly heavy-handed Spanish rule and

Fig. 3.19
Shrine with three crosses marking the entrance road to Tabí, Yucatán.

Fig. 3.20 Prototypical sixteenth-century open chapel church in the Yucatán, with rollizo masonry vault replacing palapa ramada.

with a population much reduced because of recurrent plagues, Maya society in the Yucatán was shifting to a new form of hierarchical control dominated by *criollos* and Hispanicized ladinos.[56] The community Christian church, just as the preconquest temple, became the power center of the new secular elite who sought to upgrade the church's appearance as a matter of bourgeois pride. The old and fragile palapas were removed and, whenever possible, replaced by a more permanent and stylish vaulted nave. Nevertheless, since this work was again carried out by indigenous artisans, traditional building techniques continued to be employed. Maya masons had always inserted wooden braces to reinforce their corbel vaulting, and they now devised a similar technique for reinforcing a European-style vault. They simply laid thin poles (trees in the Yucatán are characteristically short and thin because of the shallow topsoil) in parallel rows across the transverse masonry arches and then filled the interstices with plaster (fig. 3.20). This made for a cheap, lightweight vault, called locally a *rollizo*, that required minimum labor and scaffolding as at Calotmul south of Tizimin (fig. 3.21).[57] The vaulted nave, however, created a darkened tunnel in the church and raised the problem of lighting. It was not always easy to set windows into the massive walls supporting the vault, so that some smaller churches ended up illuminated only by one large window in the facade. Another interesting solution was to place a window at the juncture of the nave vault and the raised sanctuary, out of sight of worshipers in the nave but allowing light to fall directly on the altar. An example can be seen at Sudzal, where the vaulted ceiling is slightly lower than the great arch over the sanctuary, permitting a small window just under its soffit (see fig. 3.12).

On the other hand, wood-reinforced Yucatán rollizos were not fireproof, a weakness that was to be exploited during the Caste Wars of the nineteenth century, when rebelling Maya peasants set fire to many such churches, which had become symbols of creole oppression. This replicated the ancient Maya warfare tradition of burning the enemy's temples. Many roofless, gaping shells of these mutilated churches still scar the Yucatán landscape, rueful reminders of that terrible conflict. Note that the creole congregations were the objects of the Maya peasants' wrath and not the symbolic form of

Fig. 3.21 Nave of the church at Calotmul, Yucatán, showing rollizo vaulting.

Fig. 3.22 Detail of ruined church at Pixila (Cuauhtémoc), Yucatán, showing open chapel still in use.

Fig. 3.23 Western facade espadaña of church at Cacalchen, Yucatán. Photograph by Jorge Pérez de Lara.

Fig. 3.24 Western facade espadaña of church at Yotholin, Yucatán. Photograph by Jorge Pérez de Lara.

Fig. 3.25 Western facade espadaña of church at Tixcuytún, Yucatán. Photograph by Jorge Pérez de Lara.

Fig. 3.26 Ruins of late Classic Maya temple "Dovecote" at Uxmal, Yucatán. Engraving by Frederick Catherwood in John Lloyd Stephen's *Incidents of Travel in the Yucatán,* New York, 1843. Courtesy of the Chapin Library of Rare Books, Williams College, Williamstown, Massachusetts.

the Franciscan church. After all, the insurgent Indians built their own Balam Na temple in Chan Santa Cruz in exactly the same form. In any case, many of these damaged buildings have been partially restored by local Maya residents—always the grotto-like sanctuary first in order that Mass may immediately be celebrated, as at Pixila near Izamal (now renamed Cuauhtémoc) where the local parishioners still pay homage to their local "dressed cross" in a "cave" (fig. 3.22).

During the seventeenth century, considerable decor had been added to the Yucatán church, including painted *retablos* and sculptured santos.[58] The glory of the refurbished seventeenth- and eighteenth-century Yucatán chapel, however, is its signature facade with crenelated crowning belfry, or espadaña (moved from its original position above the original open chapel). While the sanctuaries and masonry-walled naves retained their standardized Maya-Franciscan simplicity, the towering espadaña, like the icing on a wedding cake, took on the special role of providing exciting individuality to each community church, as for instance at Cacalchen near Izamal and Yotholin near Oxkutzcab (figs. 3.23, 3.24). No two examples are ever alike; each town still prides itself on the special form of its confectionery espadaña, reshaping and adding to it to this day. By the nineteenth century, after the austere Franciscans had surrendered their churches to secular authority, traditional color returned to the Maya repertory. Many Yucatán espadañas are painted in the brightest hues; yellow and red are especially favored as at Tixpéhual and Cacalchen, not to mention the vivid yellow of the convento at Izamal.[59]

While the Yucatán espadaña officially owes its inspiration to the Spanish baroque variant known as churrigueresque, one could argue that once again an ancient Maya archetype lies concealed under the rococo frivolity. Look closely, for instance, at the espadaña in figure 3.25, then compare it to the engraving by Frederick Catherwood of the preconquest "Dovecote" at Uxmal (fig. 3.26).[60] "Dovecote" is but a modern nickname referring to the curious roof-comb atop the Terminal-Classic Maya temple in that famous Yucatán archaeological site south of Mérida that so captured the nineteenth-century romantic imagination. Catherwood's nostalgic scene dates from the 1830s, a time when many of the nearby Yucatecan churches were still being refurbished with new facades. There's no evidence that the clever Tixcuytún masons used nearby Uxmal as a model—although the comparison is beguiling—but it does seem that the characteristic Yucatán espadaña is a vestigial Maya architectural expression that unconsciously evokes the form and function of the ancient roof-comb frontispiece that once adorned preconquest temples, a rococo mutant that still animates the artistic resilience of the Yucatec people.

In the mechanical arts the Indians have made much progress, both in what they knew before and what has now come from Spain. After the Christians came, great painters have emerged. After the Spaniards brought models and images from Flanders and Italy, because where there is gold and silver, everything useful comes in search of gold; not a retable or image however excellent wasn't taken here and copied, especially by the painters of Mexico city, because here gathers everything good that comes from Castille. Before, [the Indians] knew only how to paint a flower or a bird or a naive but complex design [*labor como romano*], but if they were to paint a man or a horse they made it so ugly it looked like a monster. Now they make such good images, just like in Flanders.

Fray Toribio de Benavente Motolinía, Memoriales

⊕

Chapter 4

INDIANS AND RENAISSANCE ART

Fray Pedro de Gante's School of Art at San José de Los Naturales

If art history in the English-speaking world has paid little attention to the sixteenth-century missionary architecture of Mexico, it has shown even less interest in the mural painting and sculptural relief that once adorned these remarkable buildings, most of which were also created by Indian artisans.[1] To some degree this is understandable because the few convento paintings and sculptures that have survived the vicissitudes of church politics and secular revolution during the past four hundred years are largely in poor condition. Even perceptive connoisseurs find it difficult to reconstruct the faded imagery that originally transformed those grand old corridors into living theaters of Christian theology.[2]

Since the 1950s, however, the Mexican Instituto Nacional de Antropologia e Historia (INAH) has uncovered more and more wall paintings previously obscured under centuries of whitewash and grime. Many have now been reasonably restored, offering an expanding opportunity for art-historical evaluation. Indeed, a few scholars in the United States have at last taken notice of this unique but long-ignored genre. In 1987 Donna Pierce of the University of New Mexico completed a doctoral dissertation on the recently revealed sixteenth-century murals in the Augustinian convento church at Ixmiquilpan, Hidalgo, illustrating amazing native scenes of warfare in an allegorical Christian context. Another remarkable restoration in the convento at Malinalco near Mexico City prompted Jeanette Favrot Peterson to write her dissertation, which later became a prize-winning book, *The Paradise Garden Murals of Malinalco: Utopia and Empire in Sixteenth-Century Mexico*. As the title suggests, she attempts to relate the subject and style of these paintings to Augustinian visions of a Christian utopia under Hapsburg world empire. Yet another excellent doctoral dissertation, "Processions through Paradise: A Liturgical and Social Interpretation of the Ritual Function and Symbolic Signification of the Cloister in the Sixteenth-Century Mendicant Monasteries of Central Mexico" by Richard Phillips is currently being prepared for publication. It is probably the most comprehensive analysis in any language of the liturgical deployment and didactic purpose of the convento murals. In particular, Phillips has convincingly shown that even the convento cloister in the friars' residence, in Europe generally off-limits to lay persons, was opened by the friars to Indian processions and spectacles, at least during the second half of the sixteenth century, thus becoming another patio in both form and function.

In this chapter, I take issue with a disturbing trend in Latin American scholarship that, in its currently concentrated eagerness to reveal motifs and elements of style and iconography surviving from preconquest Indian art, tends to treat the imposed art of the European Renaissance as not only an imperialist intrusion but also an aesthetic antithesis to innate Indian sensitivities.[3] This is unfortunately manifest in the influential writings of French historian Serge Gruzinski, especially those books that have been translated into English such as his popular *Conquest of Mexico* and *Painting the Conquest*. While Gruzinski writes with eloquence concerning the twilight of the preconquest Indian style still visible in the images painted in colonial manuscripts (which he nostalgically if curiously terms the "Mexican Renaissance"), he takes the convento murals less seriously, even apologetically emphasizing the misunderstandings of the Indian painters who, in spite of their indigenous heritage, were still able to learn the style of the Flemish and Italian Renaissance. (The latter, interestingly enough, was arriving in Mexico almost at the same time it was spreading to Spain.)

Figure 4.1 is an outstanding example of the mastery that Gruzinski has chosen to ignore: a beautiful depiction of Saint Catherine of Siena, showing the fourteenth-century Italian saint dressed in a nun's habit with a crown of thorns and holding her attributes, a crucifix and the

Fig. 4.1 *Saint Catherine of Siena,* mural on cloister pier of the convento of San Juan Bautista, Tetela del Volcán, Morelos. Photograph by Jorge Pérez de Lara.

Sacred Heart of Jesus.[4] The image is rendered in black ink and red-earth wash, just as Renaissance artists in Europe frequently prepared their studio drawings, but here painted ca. 1560–70 in a mural cycle on the cloister piers of the Dominican convento at Tetela del Volcán, at the foot of smoking Mount Popocatépetl in Morelos.[5] Ironically, the very technical and stylistic sophistication of this European-mannered masterpiece has placed it in Mexican art-historical limbo. Not only Gruzinski but most scholars, Mexican included, have shied away from asserting that this mural could have been painted by an Indian. It is an unspoken assumption that the drawing is just too refined by European Renaissance standards. An Indian either could not, or should not, have become so competent in a foreign artistic mode imposed by conquerors.

Those who accept the above argument seem to be making a psychological distinction between the abstract forms of preconquest indigenous art, which they admire as attempting to communicate directly with the supernatural realm, and the European Renaissance style, which they tend to dismiss as merely descriptive of physical surface and thus lacking the same spiritual profundity that inspired the genius of native art.[6] I believe this is a rationale born from the triumph of "modern art" and its own corollary rejection of Renaissance "realism" that has prevailed in the West since the early twentieth century. Already by the mid-1800s many, mostly French, painters had become enamored with the arts of the exotic Orient, especially the quite un-Renaissance spatial arrangements created by the great masters of the Japanese wood-block print. By the 1900s avant-garde artists were more insistent than ever that Renaissance perspective be declared déjà vu, as they were further influenced by the fetish and often erotic "primitive" artifacts brought back from Africa and other non-European regions being colonized by the imperialist powers.[7] Such "unrealistic" but emotionally charged works offered a refreshing alternative to the jaded fin-de-siècle Western intelligentsia, for whom Renaissance aesthetics seemed tired signifiers of stuffy bourgeois conformity.

Slowly, aesthetic tastes everywhere in western Europe and North America began to shift in this direction as the expressionists, cubists, surrealists, and other revolutionary groups continued to eschew Renaissance three-dimensional illusion in favor of nonrepresentation. By the 1950s modern art had quite driven Renaissance perspective out of the academy and established flat abstraction as the new aesthetic dogma of Western civilization.

As a result, those non-Western art forms that had originally inspired modern art could no longer be regarded as primitive but rather as determinist vanguards in a progressive evolution in which abstraction was fated to become the ultimate achievement of the visual arts.[8] Proponents of this view would demote Renaissance linear perspective and chiaroscuro to simply a technical trick smacking more of mechanical science than art and that actually inhibits the artist from true self-expression.

Since this is only a recent assumption in the world of modern (and postmodern) Western art, it is inaccurate to assume it applied retroactively to the "period eye" of the premodern past, especially in regard to the interaction of still-medieval Spanish friars and naive Indians;

the latter in the beginning at least were more curious about, than resentful of, the new culture being thrust upon them. In fact, sixteenth-century Renaissance art, including Italian-style linear perspective, certainly as the missionary friars in New Spain understood it, was not conceived merely to replicate the illusion of three-dimensional physical reality for its own sake, but rather to reveal the metaphysical *Urform* of the world that was in the "eye of God" at genesis. And the Indians were able and even eager to learn all the conventions of the new Renaissance artistic style, including geometric perspective and light-and-shadow rendering, and did indeed become so expert that their mastery was indistinguishable from (and sometimes better than) professional artists emigrating from Spain and Flanders.

THE SCHOOL AT SAN JOSÉ DE LOS NATURALES

May 1523 was a month of twofold significance for Fray Pedro de Gante. It was the moment when he set sail for Mexico to spend the rest of his life teaching music and the visual arts to Indian converts and the same month that Pope Adrian VI proclaimed the official canonization of the Italian Antonino Pierozzi (1389–1459), late Dominican archbishop of Florence, hereafter to be known as Saint Antonine.[9] One of the early books that entered the Colegio de Santa Cruz Library, which Fray Pedro helped found after he arrived in Mexico, was a printed edition of Saint Antonine's *Summa theologica,* donated apparently in 1541 by Fray Francisco de Toral (Franciscan bishop of Yucatán and nemesis of Diego de Landa). Because Saint Antonine's canonization occurred so close to the time when the first contingent of Christian missionaries began their work in Mexico, his writings were decidedly au courant. Fray Geronimo de Mendieta mentions that Fray Andrés de Olmos, another early Franciscan historian and brilliant linguist, took advantage of Saint Antonine's imprimatur to verify certain writings of the Hebrews.[10] Fray Juan de Torquemada made frequent references to the *Summa theologica,* especially citing Antonine's ideas on moral government.[11] Assuming familiarity on the part of his readers, Torquemada called him *el Florentino.* The Dominicans, of course, were even more admiring, often displaying Antonine's portrait among the heroes of the order, as in the *sala de profundis* of their convento at Cuilapan, Oaxaca (fig. 4.2).[12]

The Colegio de Santa Cruz Library copy of Saint Antonine's *Summa,* still bearing an official stamp (of the Santiago de Tlatelolco convento where the original Colegio books were stored after 1600), is now preserved in the Sutro Library in San Francisco, California.[13] Saint Antonine had originally compiled the manuscript as an anthology of his public sermons in the Florentine Duomo. His persistent theme was the maintenance of Christian values in an increasingly secular mercantile society. Being a native and prestigious archbishop of that fecund city at the very moment when painting and sculpture were flourishing (he had previously served as prior of the Convent of San Marco when Fra Angelico was painting there), Saint Antonine, as one might expect, held a strong opinion about art—not of its

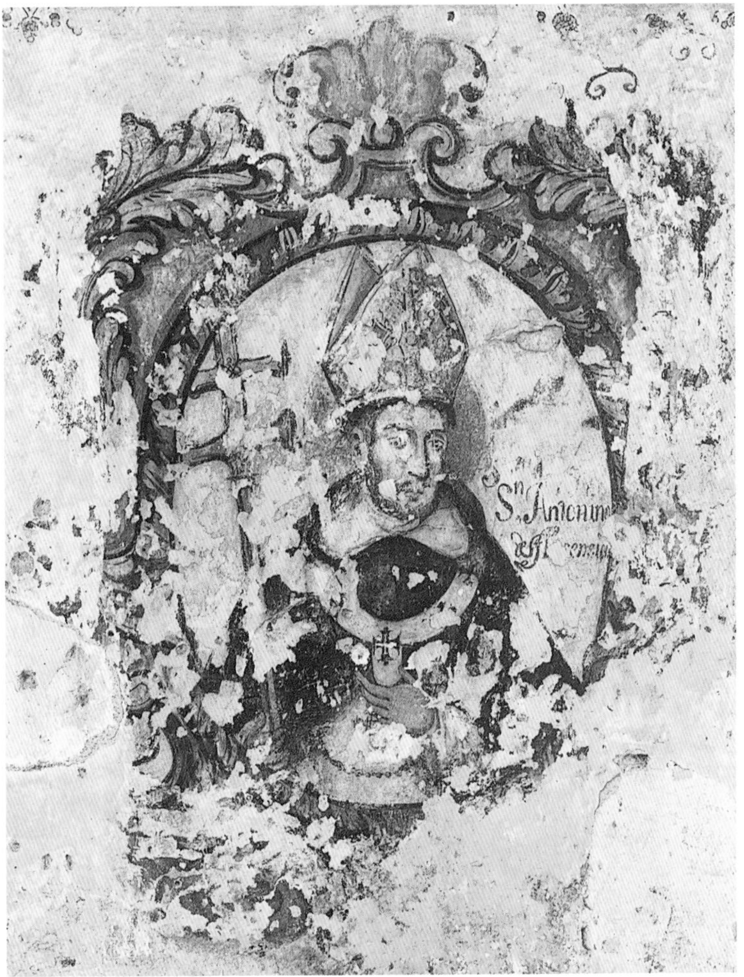

Fig. 4.2 *Saint Antonine of Florence,* mural in the sala de profundis, convento of Santiago, Cuilapan, Oaxaca. Photograph by Jorge Pérez de Lara.

aesthetic beauty but of its didactic function in the service of religious faith and morality.

Saint Antonine's views in the *Summa,* his vision of Christian values constantly threatened by the vanities of the secular world, were later carried to extremes by his Dominican and fellow-Florentine follower Girolamo Savonarola, and shared almost as adamantly by Dominican and Franciscan Observants in Spain and New Spain. All believed absolutely that the material world must never be quantified solely in "literal" (i.e., physical) terms, but equally comprehended as moral allegory and anagogical inspiration.[14] Here, for instance, is how Saint Antonine would uplift his fellow Florentine's obsession with Euclidean geometry: "Spiritual geometry works to measure temporal things. . . . It measures dimensions not as quantities but as virtues within God . . . as the length of eternity, the width of His charity, the height of His intense power, and the depth of His wisdom."[15]

While not being specific about a style of art he might have liked, Saint Antonine was quite clear about what he did not like, especially the ornate, frivolous character of fifteenth-century International Gothic-style painting that in his time was the rage of the European aristocracy. Such works often depicted elaborate courtly hunting parties promenading in affected poses and intermingling with exotic birds and animals, all thinly disguised with fig-leaf religious titles like *The Adoration of the Magi:* "Nor are those to be praised who paint curiosities in stories of the saints or in churches, which have no value in stimulating devotion, but laughter and vanity, such as monkeys and dogs chasing hares."[16] Saint Antonine's unmincing words were just as applicable to much of the stylish and increasingly mannered art in early sixteenth-century Flanders, the very painted artifice that a devout Flemish Observant like Pedro de Gante was convinced must be kept from the eyes of innocent but impressionable converts. Such a no-nonsense message, going right to the heart of the moral authority of art and written by a recently canonized saint of his own Observant persuasion, may well have prompted Fray Pedro to ponder just what sort of painting style Saint Antonine would have approved of, which would be appropriate for him to teach to his Indian novices.

Saint Antonine's austere artistic sensitivities were coincidentally shared by his Florentine contemporary the humanist Leon Battista Alberti (1404–72). In 1435–36, Alberti had written a short treatise on the art of painting in two slightly different manuscript editions, one in Italian *(Della Pittura)* and the other Latin *(De Pictura)*. Together, they introduced the first-ever discussion in Western art concerning the appreciation of artistic beauty as a means of moral ennoblement. Alberti also articulated for the first time in Western art a geometric explanation and method for constructing the illusion of optical perspective. It was based on the fact that a horizontal rectilinear floor plane (Alberti called it his *pavimentum*) divided into equal-sized geometric squares will look like a trapezoid when seen from a distance. The edges of the squares parallel to the viewer will seem to get closer together the farther they are away, and the edges at the sides of the squares will appear to converge toward the center (fig. 4.3). When a picture is painted with figures and other objects positioned on the various squares of the depicted gridded floor, viewers will believe they are looking through a window at a three-dimensional virtual space on the other side of the picture surface. This illusionistic optical phenomenon as drawn in pictures has come to be known as "Albertian perspective."[17]

Although only a few manuscript copies of Alberti's treatise were passed around, his ideas were spread widely by word of mouth and began more and more to affect the course of Renaissance painting in Italy and transalpine Europe. One reason for his appeal was that he seemed to address the uneasiness many laypersons (readers of his book tended more often to be patrons of the arts than artists) harbored on the eve of the half-millennial year 1500, the same anxiety that Savonarola was arousing to prepare the world for the Apocalypse and Second Coming. Mankind must immediately reject all superficial earthly conceits and return to the fundamental laws of nature set down by God at creation and reaffirmed by Christ on the cross. The black-and-white linear lattice of Albertian perspective seemed to replicate the primal skeleton of the universe projected from God's eye at genesis.[18]

Albertian ideas were especially evident in the latest artworks Fray Pedro would have seen in Rome if, as one may speculate, he went there in the entourage of fellow Netherlander Adrian VI, crowned Pope in August 1522.[19] It is not too far-fetched to presume that the Pope invited his friend to have a look at the Stanza della Segnatura, the papal library in the Vatican

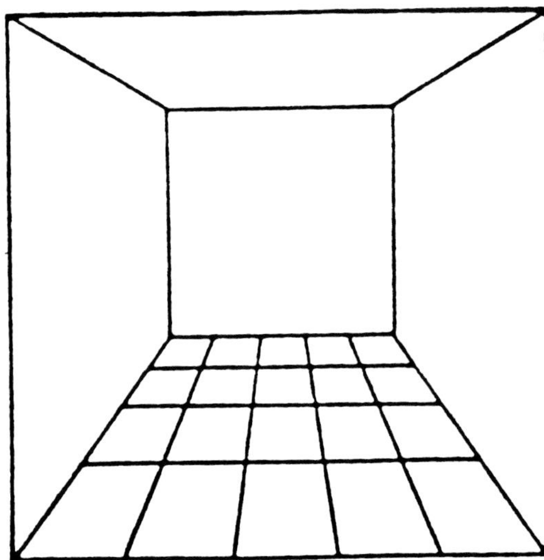

Fig. 4.3 Diagram of Alberti's linear perspective "window."

palace frescoed only a few years before by the great Raphael (who had just died in 1520). In his masterpiece in that room, the so-called School of Athens, Raphael expressed the very reticence and decorum that Alberti advocated (fig. 4.4). Both people and pictures, Alberti opined and Raphael painted, should contemplate God's primal vision according to Plato's *Timaeus* and exhibit the virtues of moderation and decorum (symbolized by the classical *contrapposto* pose eschewing gaudy colors and frenzied gestures) as expressed in Aristotle's *Ethics*.[20] Fray Pedro would also have observed that at the centric convergent point of Raphael's Albertian perspective, Plato and Aristotle are discussing the lessons of their two great books. As Plato points to the sky, one can almost hear him reaffirm the meaning of truth, just as Saint Antonine, Alberti, and Pedro de Gante would have understood it: "And knowledge is of two kinds, one turning its eyes towards transitory things, the other towards things which neither come into being nor pass away, but are the same and immutable forever. Considering them with a view to truth, we judge that the latter is truer than the former."[21]

In response to Alberti's widening influence, the Latin version of the treatise on painting was printed in 1540 (Basel) and in several more Latin and Italian editions shortly after.[22] There is no direct evidence that *De Pictura* was ever in the Colegio de Santa Cruz Library, but Alberti's equally influential "Treatise on Architecture," written in Latin as *De re aedificatoria*, in print since 1485, was definitely in Mexico, a copy of the 1512 (Paris) edition having been brought over by Antonio de Mendoza, the first Spanish viceroy of New Spain and cofounder with Pedro de Gante of the Colegio de Santa Cruz Library.[23] While no documents exist to prove that the Mexican missionaries consulted any of Alberti's writings, the latter's moral ideas expressed through architecture and painting were clearly in tune with the friars' own intentions for didactic use of visual images. Saint Antonine and Leon Battista Alberti supplied the spirit if not the letter of inspiration for Fray Pedro de Gante and the native students in his school for the arts at San José de los Naturales from the 1530s through the 1560s.

Perhaps Fray Pedro de Gante's most talented pupil and the only one we know for certain by name was a native-born Mexican named Diego Valadés (1533–82?), the son of a Spanish conquistador and possibly a native Tlaxcalan woman.[24] The Tlaxcalan Indians were Cortés's close allies during the conquest of the Aztec empire, and their reward was to

Fig. 4.4 Detail (Plato and Aristotle), Raphael, *School of Athens*. Stanza della Segnatura, Vatican Palace, Rome, 1510–11. Photograph from Alinari-Art Resource.

mestizo, he was allowed to join the Franciscan order. Fray Diego, as he was known in adulthood, was not only adept in the arts of drawing, painting, and engraving, but also an outstanding Latinist.

We know that Valadés, after many years of presumed activity as a friar-painter and missionary in Mexico, visited Europe for the first time in 1571. After sojourns in France and Spain, he went on to Italy and Rome, where his Mexican ethnicity and Latin fluency earned him such celebrity that he was elected procurator general of the whole Franciscan order. It was during this heady period of intense Renaissance exposure, yet tempered by church infighting and imperial politics, that Valadés wrote his Latin treatise *Rhetorica Christiana*. It was printed in Perugia (a short distance from Assisi, the world headquarters of the Franciscan order) in 1579, the first book ever published by an American-born author. It

be appointed the new native aristocracy in Mexico. In this tolerant Tlaxcalan atmosphere during the 1530s and 1540s, young Valadés grew up and was educated. Even if he were a

was even illustrated with some twenty-seven engravings by his own hand.[25]

Valadés wrote in elegant Latin and laced his book with numerous references to all the appropriate classical authorities—Virgil, Horace, Cicero, Pliny, Quintilian, plus the Patristic fathers. Indeed, his intent was to impress the intelligentsia of Europe, to explain to an international audience of educated and influential Catholics that not only was the conversion of the Indians in the Americas the most worthy of endeavors but that the Franciscans were carrying it out according to the latest and most esteemed methods of classical teaching. He wished to stress, moreover, that the Indians themselves were not savages but people of high culture and natural intelligence who, even though "without letters," were quite capable of learning the abstruse tenets of sacred doctrine and thus could become good Catholics and defenders of the faith. Valadés wrote this book at a time when the mendicant missionaries in the Americas, the Franciscans in particular, were being shunted aside by the bureaucratic Spanish king Philip II who wished to organize the Indians into parishes and dioceses under secular bishops and priests in direct chain of command from the Spanish crown. Fray Diego must also have felt a sting of resentment when he heard that the upstart Jesuits had been dispatched to the Americas in 1572, implying that the Franciscans were out of touch with the political ambitions of the Counter-Reformation church. The *Rhetorica Christiana* was thus a kind of Franciscan apologia, a *dernier resort* of traditional missionary autonomy in the New World.

Valadés paid special homage to his mentor, Pedro de Gante, under whose tutelage he had studied both literature and art at the Mexican Colegio de Santa Cruz and the school of San José de los Naturales. In fact, I argue, Fray Diego's engravings, in both style and subject, closely reflect Fray Pedro's own ideas. While Valadés's main subject was to explain in detail the art of literary rhetoric—how language can most effectively serve the teaching of Christian doctrine—he, like Pedro de Gante, believed that the same techniques and intention were equally applicable to the visual arts.

Figure 4.5 shows Valadés's well-known print, probably depicting Pedro de Gante (referred to by name just a few sentences earlier in the explanatory text) in the act of preaching to the Indians by means of pictures.[26] The Latin caption at the bottom translates, "The teacher makes perceptible to the senses the divine gifts of God; he moistens arid souls from the fountain of [his] eloquence." The letter *A* imprinted on the pulpit refers to the accompanying text, which states, "Here is the preacher of the word of God who makes perceptible to the Indians the celestial gifts, preaching about this in their proper language." With a touch of humor (Fray Pedro de Gante was no doubt a long-winded lecturer) Valadés drew in a little figure of a sleepy monk behind the pulpit pondering an hourglass. Underneath the pulpit cowers a humanoid monster wearing a half-moon headdress symbolizing paganism driven to despair by the brilliance of the teacher's audiovisual eloquence. Referring to the letter *B*, also on the pulpit, the text states, "Because the Indians lack letters, it was necessary to teach them by means of some illustrations; for this the preacher demonstrates the mysteries of our redemption with a pointer." A large audience of Indians is assembled before him on an Alberti-style gridded pavimentum, listening in rapt attention. Men and women are all dressed in *tilmahtli*, normally the native male garb but here worn by both sexes possibly to look like toga-clad

Fig. 4.5 Fray Diego Valadés, *Fray Pedro de Gante Preaching to the Indians*, engraving from his *Rhetorica Christiana*, Perugia, 1579, p. 111. Courtesy of the John Carter Brown Library at Brown University, Providence, Rhode Island.

ancients so that European readers would compare the Franciscan mission in Mexico to the original apostolic conversion of Rome. Some in the foreground of this audience hold batons; the letter C on the sleeve of one refers to the text explanation, "They who listen in this part and who hold batons in their hands are those who perform the duties of justice among our Indians, to whom is entrusted the government of the whole republic [*totius reipublicae gubernatio*]."[27]

Valadés goes on to express his fascination with the way the Indians were traditionally able to communicate with symbols, even to "confide secrets" by means of colored threads or arrangements of beans and stones. He further admired the Indians' picture-writing on bark paper [*amatl*], noting its similarity to Egyptian hieroglyphics. He mentions having often observed groups of Indians squatting on their haunches studying and discussing the meaning of a particular picture for an hour at a time. They even used pictures to indicate what sins they had committed when they came to confession.[28] In other words, Valadés concludes that since the Indians were a people with an instinctive predisposition for appreciating and understanding pictures, pictures should obviously be the principal tool of the missionaries for teaching Christian doctrine. In fact, Valadés went so far as to claim that his own Franciscan order first invented this "new method" of teaching with visual aids.[29]

Valadés was discussing this use of pictures as proselytizing tools in the section of his book devoted to *ars memoriae*, the popular sixteenth-century practice of the "art of memory," derived from the pseudo-Ciceronian *Ad Herennium* written in the first century B.C.E., on how orators should memorize their speeches by mnemonic association of the words with specific visual objects either in their own imagination or actually in the real world (see chap. 9). Fray Diego believed that this technique of disciplining the memory provided scientific basis for teaching the complexities of Christianity to the natives. Whenever they were presented with pictures of holy stories depicted in precise doctrinal detail, the images in those pictures should become implanted, point for point, in the Indians' minds, just as a piece of paper reproduces exactly the engraved image on an inked copperplate when pressed against it.

In Valadés's print the pictures to which the preacher is pointing are firmly in the European Renaissance style, displayed along the architectural entablature of an arcuated chapel that Fray Diego described as opening onto the same idealized patio he represented in figure 2.29. In actuality, didactic pictures strung along the wall like these would have been painted either on mounted strips of cloth called lienzos or as frescoes directly on the masonry surface. Although no lienzos have survived from the sixteenth century, framed spaces for such removable pictures are still visible on the splays of the magnificent vaulted open chapel abutting the Dominican convent of Teposcolula, Oaxaca (see fig. 7.12).

The seven pictures depicted in the background of Fray Diego's engraving illustrate in sequence the New Testament Passion of Jesus: *from left to right*, agony in the garden, flagellation, mocking of Christ, Christ carrying the cross, the crucifixion, harrowing of hell, and resurrection. These same scenes were among the most frequently represented on the walls of the Mexican conventos. An almost identical

Fig. 4.6 *Agony in the Garden,* mural in the northeastern corner of the upper cloister gallery, convento of San Salvador, Malinalco, Mexico. Photograph by Jorge Pérez de Lara.

but reversed image of agony in the garden, painted probably in the 1580s, is extant today (fig. 4.6). As the friars well knew, the story of Jesus' sacrifice had special resonance in Mesoamerican culture, all too familiar with the elaborate ceremony and immolation of human victims. Here is yet another example of the missionaries' clever tactic of expedient selection.[30] It is also interesting in light of the later and still continuing veneration of individual patron saints [*santos*] in native parishes everywhere in Hispanic America that almost all the mural imagery in the sixteenth-century conventos has to do with the life of Jesus. Except for Mary and the apostles, the only other saints depicted are those associated with the history of the orders. Indeed, it would seem that the friars quite avoided paying homage to the Cult of the Saints, even as it was becoming widely popular in Spain. The friars, in fact, were foremost among those Erasmian reformers who believed that such cults only masqueraded latent polytheistic paganism.[31]

Valadés recounted that Pedro de Gante conducted his art school in the patio (Valadés preferred the Latin term *atrium*) adjacent to the open chapel he depicted in the print, and it was there that Indian catechumens learned "to embellish, draw images of things with colors, and paint sharply" [*discunt etiam*

Fig. 4.7 *Flagellation of Christ*, mural in the upper cloister corridor, convento of San Agustín, Acolman, Mexico. Photograph by Jorge Pérez de Lara.

pingere, rerum imagines coloribus delineare, & acute pingere].[32] If Valadés's own art gives any clue, learning to "draw with colors" would surely have included rendering of light and shade with white and black (always included as true colors before the optical discoveries of Isaac Newton), a revived antique Greek and Roman technique called *chiaroscuro* [light-dark] in Italian. Although unknown in the arts of preconquest America, chiaroscuro had become an essential drawing convention throughout western Europe by the sixteenth century.[33] Figure 4.7 shows another mural scene from Jesus' Passion, this time the flagellation of Christ from the upper cloister of the convento at Acolman, painted probably in the 1570s. The seminude figure of Christ here reveals even in its present abraded condition the kind of training native artists were given in Renaissance-style figure drawing and how to model in light and shade.

As we see in the checkerboard-like floor depicted beneath Jesus' feet, Fray Pedro also had his pupils learn the rudiments of convergent linear perspective, although hardly following precise geometrical rules. This was another artistic technique unique to European tradition and unknown to any other culture in the world until introduced after the Renaissance. Even in still-medieval Spain, the representation of a gridded "pavement," the edges of which seem to recede behind the picture surface thus creating a mirror- or window-like illusion, had become a standardized convention as early as the mid-fifteenth century. Valadés himself makes it clear that the images he wants to implant in the Indians' memory should look like a perspective picture, with figures exactly positioned in space, and all in proper measure and proportion to one another just as God has arranged the four elements and the nine spheres of the heavens in their proper order in the universe.[34]

Figures 4.8 and 4.9 illustrate two more of Valadés's engravings, printed and textually identified in the opening pages of part 1 of his book.[35] They are usually called *Pagan Philosopher* and *Christian Philosopher,* and both accompany the author's chapter entitled "De proprietatibus Oratoris Christiani" [On the properties of the Christian orator]. (*Orator* was the common medieval Latin expression for "philosopher.") Looking first at *Pagan Philosopher,* we see a bearded figure also standing on a gridded pavement. He is viewing a suspended globe numbered *1* and with his right hand attempting to measure another globe on a table. According to Valadés, he thinks only of the material world, which he arrogantly tries to control with geometric (earthly) tools *3*. His "observation is not lacking in darkness" *[speculatio caligine non caret],* apparently because his vision depends on looking into mirrors perching atop the worldly sphere and on the vase of transient flowers at *4*, which, as Valadés continues, prohibits him from seeing the grace of God.[36]

Two more pictorial details hint especially at Valadés's and probably also Pedro de Gante's ideas about both the advantage and limitation of Renaissance-style art in the implementation of Christian teaching to Mexican Indians. I refer to the strange-looking oval-shaped grid marked *2*, which seems to entangle the pagan philosopher's feet, and the equally strange-looking spread-out manuscript on the shelf at the right of the print.

While the pagan philosopher is shown standing on a squared pavement in perspective, the oval grid entrapping his feet could just possibly signify the Franciscan artist's displeasure at something he unexpectedly encountered in Rome, namely, his Italian colleagues' obsession with the pure geometry of linear perspective for its own sake. Rather than merely being satisfied with the well-established Albertian convention, fellow artists in Italy, much more so than in Spain, were intent on producing endless geometric-perspective diagrams having no Christian purpose whatever, such as the many tour de force designs from book 2 of Sebastiano Serlio's Italian treatise on architecture (fig. 4.10). Incidentally, all sixteenth-century Spanish translations of the Italian architect omit book 2 on the rules of geometric linear perspective.[37] In any case, Valadés, offended by the secular atmosphere of Italian *scientia* (which at that moment was inspiring the young Galileo Galilei), was disappointed, interpreting such obsession as sinful pride. The pagan philosopher wallowing in geometry, Valadés captioned, "only thinks of the present

Fig. 4.8 Fray Diego Valadés, *The Pagan Philosopher,* engraving from his *Rhetorica Christiana,* Perugia, 1579, p. 5. Courtesy of the John Carter Brown Library at Brown University, Providence, Rhode Island.

Fig. 4.9 Fray Diego Valadés, *The Christian Philosopher,* engraving from his *Rhetorica Christiana,* Perugia, 1579, p. 10. Courtesy of the John Carter Brown Library at Brown University, Providence, Rhode Island.

life and does not foresee future things."[38] In other words, his literal mind is incapable of anagogical elevation.

Furthermore, the strange-looking manuscript laid out on a shelf at the upper right of the engraving represents something that equally offended Valadés in his native Mexico. Indeed, this object seems to be an indigenous Indian screenfold codex such as he was certainly familiar with in Tlaxcala. Figure 4.11 shows an actual unfolded example, the Codex Borgia, which may have been painted in Tlaxcala very close to the time of the Spanish arrival, demonstrating the characteristic way in which the native deer-skin sheets were joined accordion-style and filled with flat but colorful rebus pictographs painted without perspective or chiaroscuro modeling.[39] Such books were the repositories of native myths, calendrics, and divinatory recipes, and as we know from the infamous book burning carried on by Fray Diego de Landa in the Yucatán, anathema to

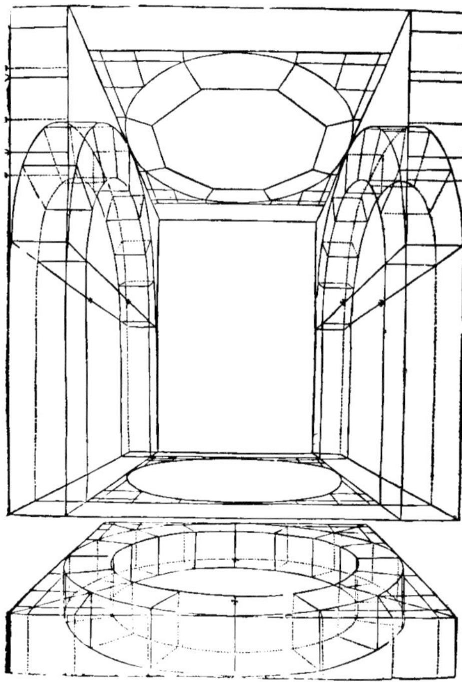

Fig. 4.10 Sebastiano Serlio, perspective rendering of an arched architectural bay, woodcut from his *Sette libri dell'architetura . . .* , Venice, 1540, Book 2, p. 16. Courtesy of the Chapin Library of Rare Books, Williams College, Williamstown, Massachusetts.

many of the first Christian missionaries.[40] In fact, it was the lack of illusionism in native Indian art in general, its dependence on garish colors and unnatural shapes, that prevented the pagan philosopher from perceiving Christian truth.

In figure 4.9 we see the Christian philosopher, *A*, seated at a desk like a New Testament evangelist. The desk likewise sits on a modestly foreshortened gridded floor, and under the desk is a sphere signifying the material geometric world properly subordinated beneath the Christian philosopher's feet. Bound European-style books are scattered about his desk and lie open on a shelf; in fact he's writing (or drawing) in such a book and being guided by his guardian angel, *B*, to contemplate memory images of his own self-mortifying chastisement (*left*, at *E*, another rigidly geometrical grid—that on which Saint Lawrence was martyred), reminding him of his mortality and the vicissitude of worldly fortune. The book has apparently induced the philosopher to conceptualize such "figures in the sense of the mind," as Valadés phrased how Indians should similarly be inspired to form mental images from the study of holy pictures because, as he remarked, even if the Indians "lack letters and are absent-minded," they are nonetheless "lovers of novelty and painting, this art [being] very fruitful and successful in explaining the divine word."[41] Interestingly, Saint Antonine addressed this same technique to his fellow art-loving Florentines, urging that they too study sacred Scripture and then mentally project the words *in figuram* [into a figure], as he called it, retaining the image in the memory for private anagogic devotion. In the far right corner at *D*, we see a framed crucifix atop a skull. Valadés emphasizes that this alone is the "mirror of nature" [*speculum talis est naturae*]. Its image reflects only truth and obscures nothing, thus exposing the hypocrisy of pagan occultism.[42]

In the confrontation of these two engravings, Valadés implies that the printed black-and-white illustrations in Latin-lettered books should be the prime source for learning and memorizing Christian doctrine, reaffirming what Motolinía had stated earlier, that before the Christians came to New Spain, the Indians drew the human figure "so ugly that it looked like a monster." Mendieta later recalled how the Indians "used to paint and sculpt their gods [to look] so fierce and horrible [*tan fieros y espantosos*]."[43] But now, under Pedro de Gante's supervision in the San José de los Naturales art school, they were learning at last to paint "beautiful images as in Flanders."[44]

In Fray Pedro's school, the glaringly colored figures that Indian artists had previously depicted in their native codices were especially offensive, like figure 4.12 of back-to-back deities Mictlantecuhtli and Quetzalcoatl depicted in the Codex Borgia, whose poses Alberti would have contemptuously dismissed as: "throwing their limbs about a great deal . . . casting aside all dignity in painting and copying the movements of actors."[45]

On the other hand, figures drawn in black-and-white chiaroscuro and posed in classical contrapposto, as in the Acolman mural *Flagellation of Christ* (fig. 4.7), accorded with the geometrical and sculptural way God envisioned the first human beings at creation, before Eve sinned and the world became corrupted with mankind's venalities (signified by emotion-stimulating bright colors).[46] This same rationale was in Alberti's own mind when he described in his treatise on painting how to model in dark and light before any superficial color was added: "Indeed, I agree that a wide range and variety of colors contribute to the beauty and attraction of painting. But I would prefer learned painters to believe that the greatest art and industry are concerned with the disposition of white and black, and that all skill and care should be used in correctly placing these two. Just as the incidence of light and shade makes it apparent where surfaces become convex or concave

Fig. 4.11 A typical Nahua screenfold manuscript unfolded.

Fig. 4.12 Nahua deities Mictlantecuhtli and Quetzalcoatl depicted in the Codex Borgia, fol. 56. Biblioteca Apostolica, Vaticana, Roma. Courtesy of Akademische Druck- und Verlagsanstalt, Graz, Austria.

. . . so the combination of white and black achieves . . . what the artist must above all desire: that the things he paints should appear in maximum relief."[47]

A great many if not the majority of all murals painted in the conventos of all three mendicant orders in Mexico were rendered in grisaille outline with dark chiaroscuro modeling before any color was overlaid. If, as I suggest, this "dark manner" was the trademark of Pedro de Gante's teaching, it apparently became accepted by other Indian training schools as well. Most extant murals in this style date between 1550 and the late 1570s, so that the Indian artists who painted them were of the second and even third postconquest generation, for whom preconquest artistic traditions were already passé.[48] During the years of the Counter-Reformation Council of Trent (1545–63), painting in Spain came strongly under the influence of Leonardo da Vinci's own "dark manner," no doubt as a gesture of moral self-control, and male fashion in both Spain and Italy eschewed the wearing of any color except black for the same reason.[49]

Donald Robertson attempted to define the various schools of Indian manuscript painters in the early colonial period. While few of the convento murals known today had been restored when Robertson was writing, he did observe a significant difference between native manuscript illumination and native painting of murals and retables in churches; whether qualitative or only stylistic he did not specify. However, he did search through all the written documents concerning Pedro de Gante's school in San José de los Naturales and found to his satisfaction that manuscript painting was not a subject taught there, which would seem to imply—although unmentioned by Robertson—that teaching the Indians to paint murals and lienzos in the current European Renaissance style was the primary preoccupation of Pedro de Gante's school of art.[50]

It is also worth mentioning that the mendicant art schools in postconquest Mexico did not emphasize the teaching of sculpture in the round. Since that art had already been practiced with great ingenuity and skill by Nahua sculptors in their creation of "idols," the friars no doubt wished to downplay sculpture lest the Indians be led to misunderstand the Third Commandment even in regard to Christian statues. For the friars, as for Alberti, the illusion of sculptural relief in two-dimensional images inspired a more profound anagogical contemplation of the divine, which they wished to impart to their Indian neophytes in order to discourage them from idol worship. The Franciscan mystic Fra Ugo Panzieri expressed it as early as the fourteenth century, using the same artistic metaphors to describe the five stages of Christian perfection: "The first time in which the mind begins to . . . think of Christ, he appears [only] written in the imagination. In the second, he appears drawn. In the third, he appears drawn with shades and shadows. In the fourth, he appears colored and in the flesh. In the fifth, he appears in the flesh and in relief. . . . This mental state of active moral will along with the virtuous corporeal life merits, through divine justice, the gift of meditation and contemplation."[51]

We should also consider it a very great gift to men that painting has represented the gods they worship, for painting has contributed considerably to the piety which binds us to the gods, and to filling our minds with sound religious beliefs.

Leon Battista Alberti, De Pictura, Book II, 1435/6

⊕

Chapter 5

CHRISTIAN MURALS BY INDIAN ARTISTS

Until the 1560s when a number of major Flemish and Spanish artists like Simon Pereyns (died ca. 1590) and Andrés de la Concha (fl. 1567–1612) came to live and work in Mexico, the few professionals who did drift to the Americas in the years immediately after the conquest and who helped teach the Indians the forms of European art in the newly established training schools were not stars from the great, sophisticated culture-centers of Renaissance Europe.[1] Like the conquistadors, most of these early migrating craftsmen probably came from the provinces where one may still see examples of their often awkward handiwork as they strove to ape the mannerist refinements of Seville, Madrid, or Antwerp, for example, the set of sixteenth-century murals conserved in the Palacio Carvajal in Cáceres, Extremadura, Spain, done for a provincial nobleman by a painter of obviously modest talent (fig. 5.1).[2] Furthermore, many early sixteenth-century artists in Spain and even Flanders continued to work in a flat, decorative Gothic manner barely influenced as yet by high Renaissance illusionism. One may get an instructive sense of this still *retardataire* aspect of Spanish art, no doubt exported to Mexico along with all the other stylistic variants, by visiting the recently restored Franciscan Convento of Santa Clara in Salamanca, Spain, where fifteenth-, sixteenth-, and even seventeenth-century murals overlap, any of which might easily be attributed to a novice Indian painter if the convento were in America instead of Europe.[3]

Such were the archetypes, often in the form of engravings or wood-block prints, that were taken to the New World in the 1500s and from which the Indians learned the rudiments of European art. With this in mind, it is unfair to judge Mexican examples as mere third-rate emulations of second-rate Renaissance models (as have Kubler and other critics). Rather they

Fig. 5.1 *Annunciation*, by an anonymous Extremeño artist, mid-sixteenth century. Palacio Carvajal, Cáceres, Spain. Photograph by Dorothy D. Edgerton.

Fig. 5.2 *Scenes of Augustinian Heroes*, mural in the stair hall of the convento of San Nicolás de Tolentino, Actopan, Hidalgo. Photograph by Jorge Pérez de Lara.

Fig. 5.3 Detail from the Actopan stair hall murals. Photograph by Jorge Pérez de Lara.

interior stair hall in the Augustinian friary at Actopan, near Pachuca in central Hidalgo, dedicated to Saint Nicholas of Tolentino. The adjacent wall surfaces running up two stories beside the open staircase are entirely covered by murals, all painted in crisp black and white with a few touches of color. They display the heroes of the Augustinian order in fictive cubicles arranged in five horizontal tiers. Except for the single figure of the patron saint at the top, each figure in the lower registers stands or is seated on a gridded pavimentum framed illusionistically behind a continuous arcade of plateresque pilasters. Several of the painted figures hold pens aloft, looking out of the picture space as if addressing the viewer (fig. 5.3). This is an ancient pictorial formula for the depiction of expostulatory saints, but note how Alberti humanized the old convention in his treatise on

should be seen as often first-rate, even original, adaptations.[4] When Indians achieved artistic quality in the Renaissance style, it was because they were talented creators not just servile imitators.[5]

Figure 5.2 is a view of the magnificent

painting. It is almost as if he were describing the popular "aside" artifice of actors during theatrical presentations: "I like there to be someone in the [painting] who tells the spectator what is going on, and beckons with his hand to look."[6]

This is not to say, of course, that the painter of these murals necessarily read Alberti's treatise or had even seen an Italian painted prototype. What we have here instead is the appropriation of certain currently stylish ideas that the artist vaguely heard about by word of mouth (and without even knowing they were Albertian) and then applied them because they were useful to the didactic purpose of his art. This is the same way, after all, that Alberti's ideas were first promulgated in Italy and everywhere else in Europe, by upper-class intellectuals or patrons who may have read the treatise and then stopped by an artist's *bottega* to talk shop with the leather-aproned artisans. At Actopan, similar new theories seem also to have been circulating even as the general forms of the murals followed in the style of the Spanish or Flemish lay teachers in Pedro de Gante's and other convento schools.[7]

At the bottom of the stairwell opposite the mural cycle is a single scene depicting three individuals, each with his name inscribed on an illusionistic scroll. The first is a friar identified as Fray Martín de Acevedo, prior of the convento after 1574. He may also have been a painter or at least the author of the mural program (fig. 5.4). Behind him stand two russet-colored Indians named Don Juan Atocpa and Don Pedro Izcuicuitlapico, local caciques (village chiefs) and loyal converts—and possibly also Fray Martín's assistants as painters of the murals.[8]

Fray Martín's predecessor and original planner of the Actopan convento was Fray Andrés de Mata, said to have studied architecture in Italy.[9] There is some evidence in fact that the Italian technique of *buonfresco* may have been utilized in the stair hall murals since sutures that divide the areas of fresh plaster laid up each day for painting have been discovered between the horizontal registers.[10] Usually, however, sixteenth-century Mexican muralists painted directly on the dry or perhaps slightly dampened wall.[11] This simple technique, referred to in Italian as *fresco a secco,* is, of course, less permanent, another reason why so many of the Mexican murals have become badly abraded. At Tetela del Volcán the artists modeled some of their mural images in *sinopia,* a pigment made from red earth (iron oxide) commonly used by Renaissance fresco painters. Interestingly, black (carbonate) and red silicates bond to dry plaster more readily than do organic pigments; another reason why these colors tend to survive while others are likely to flake off.

In Fray Pedro's Indian school, again just as in the painters' ateliers of Europe, apprentices were taught to copy from prints and drawings by master artists. Renaissance masters themselves copied from other masters. Young Michelangelo, for example, made drawings of Masaccio's frescoes in Florence. By the early sixteenth century, albums filled with illustrations of iconographic and other useful symbols exclusively for artists to copy were published in Europe. One of the most fashionable was Andrea Alciati's *Emblemata,* with dozens of allegorical images listed for easy reference. So in demand was it in New Spain that a plagiarized version was published in Mexico in 1577, one of the first books printed on America's earliest press.[12] An especially popular source for the fictive architectural frames in Mexican murals were the printed title pages decorated with swag borders and zoomorphic pilasters so stylish in Spanish typography, which showed up in America as early as 1535 (fig. 5.5).[13]

Nevertheless, before Indian apprentices could competently copy the European style, they had first to understand the basic geometry of shade and shadow rendering and know the standard drawing conventions for signifying Renaissance perspective.[14] This apparently was what Indian artists were taught at San José de los Naturales, and I believe it one of the main reasons why so many of the convento murals were painted in monochrome. Not just because European print sources were black and white; Indian artists were quite capable of enhancing copies with color, which, after all, had been the delight of their previous tradition. Rather, the newly trained Indian artists were now creating something never experienced in their painting before, the unprecedented illusion of sculptural relief, the three-dimensional, tactile effect of chiaroscuro modeling, which black-and-white enhances but color flattens.

An evocative example of this exciting

Fig. 5.4 Detail from the Actopan stair hall murals. Photograph by Jorge Pérez de Lara.

novelty may still be witnessed at another Augustinian convento, San Andrés Epazoyucán. Here in the friars' refectory is a chiaroscuro mural of the Last Supper (fig. 5.6), a subject that often decorates monastery dining halls. But notice that the artist has painted little shadows to the right of all the dishware on the table. The whole mural is just to the right of an actual window in the adjoining wall, and the artist has imagined that all his painted figures are being illuminated illusionistically by real sunlight streaming in from this direction and dutifully shaded his figures and had them cast shadows on their opposite sides.

San Andrés Epazoyucán indeed houses some of the finest examples of sixteenth-century mural painting in all Mexico. Miraculously, most are still in good condition. In the 1540s the Augustinians moved north from the capital to evangelize the Otomí Indians and erected this convento on a former temple platform in the bleak and chilly desert of southern Hidalgo. We are told by Fray Juan de Grijalva that it was built in seven months and seven days.[15] Unfortunately the seventeenth-century Augustinian chronicler makes no mention of the elegant murals, especially the scenes of Jesus' Passion and story of Mary in the lower cloister. Four are set in *testeras,* or shallow architectural niches in the walls at the corridor corners, a feature common in the monastery cloisters of Mexico intended to serve religious processions.[16] Figures 5.7 and 5.8 illustrate two of these cloister paintings, *Ecce Homo* in the southeast testera and *Death and Coronation of the Virgin* actually not in a testera but above an adjacent doorway in the same corner. All these murals date probably from the 1550s. Originally they were painted only in black and white, with colors added later.[17] In spite of the overt Flemish mannerist style (and dependence on German engravings), the rendering technique of these murals is peculiarly "Albertian" in the way the artist first outlined his figures on the wall, then heightened them with chiaroscuro.[18] Manuel del Castillo Negrete, the Mexican restorer of the

Fig. 5.5 Title page from Fernandez de Oviedo y Valdes's *La historia general de las Indias,* Seville, 1535. Courtesy of the Chapin Library of Rare Books, Williams College, Williamstown, Massachusetts.

Fig. 5.6 *Last Supper,* mural in the refectory, convento of San Andrés, Epazoyucán, Hidalgo. Photograph by Jorge Pérez de Lara.

Epazoyucán murals during the 1960s, has stated that "nothing like them has been encountered in any other Augustinian convent."[19] Both these paintings take advantage of sharply defined gridded pavements to give the illusion (enhanced in *Ecce Homo* by the inset testera) of looking through the wall at the holy figures standing in a virtual three-dimensional space.

Figure 5.9 shows a detail of another cloister testera from the Dominican convento at Cuilapan, Oaxaca, ca. 1570. It is empty of a picture but framed again by a quite emphatic fictive architectural embrasure painted to look like an illusionistic three-dimensional portal. Here again the black-and-white perspective was intended to increase the viewer's sense that the painted lienzo or sculptured image placed in the testera was within a recessed stage. While it is easy to dismiss this obviously more rudimentary perspective as evidence that native artists had difficulty comprehending Renaissance illusionism, the example is better understood by comparison

Fig. 5.7 *Ecce Homo*, mural in the southeast cloister testera, convento of San Andrés, Epazoyucán, Hidalgo. Photograph by Jorge Pérez de Lara.

Fig. 5.8 *Death and Coronation of the Virgin,* mural above the doorway in the southeast corner of the cloister, convento of San Andrés, Epazoyucán, Hidalgo. Photograph by Jorge Pérez de Lara.

with European pictures of the fourteenth century, that is, before any European had seen the "Albertian window."[20] From that point of view (the other end of the historical telescope as it were), we can appreciate how even this unrefined Cuilapan painting astonished its naive Indian audience, just as the novel but equally rudimentary frescoes of the life of Saint Francis at Assisi astonished naive European observers in the early fourteenth century (see chap. 7).[21]

Medieval Europeans all shared a classical Greco-Roman heritage, which the Indians did not, and had, historically at least, some familiarity with pictorial illusionism, if only vaguely remembered from the remnants of classical art still clinging to the ubiquitous leftovers of the fallen Roman Empire. Indigenous American Indians, on the other hand, had no such precedent to prepare them for the astounding psychological effects of Renaissance optical-geometric perspective and chiaroscuro. The relief and window illusion that these unique pictorial devices stimulate had never been independently realized in any other style of art before.

While various purely empirical means of depicting some sense of illusionistic volume by employing convergent lines to indicate distance and contrasting light and dark to make figures look three-dimensional had been achieved by artists in a number of pre-Renaissance cultures throughout the world (including even the ancient cave painters of the late Pleistocene age), none of these "perspective" techniques was based on the laws of optics, the geometric science of vision first studied in ancient Greece, modified by Mohammedan Arabs, rediscovered by Christian monks during the twelfth century, and translated into Latin as *perspectiva communis*.[22] This scientia had originally only to do with the way human vision works according to Euclidean principles of plane geometry. For example, it explains how we perceive the visual field as if it were a pyramid or cone, the apex being the eye and the base, the object seen. By Euclid's law of similar triangles, one can demonstrate how an image of a large object converges toward the eye and passes through the tiny pupil, forming a small-scale image of itself upon the lens, which—it was then believed—focuses that image upon the optic nerve at the back of the eye where it is transmitted to the brain.

Around the beginning of the thirteenth century, especially after the failure of the Crusades to capture the Holy Lands, Christians in the Latin West felt a desperate need to have their images of God and his saints appear in palpable, three-dimensional form as if actually standing as full-bodied human beings before their very eyes. European artists searched more and more for effective means of making their images appear "according to nature," often inspired by increasingly popular theatrical representations of the holy stories.

Inevitably, this peculiar urge to have two-dimensional pictures ape the illusion of three-dimensional, tactile reality, especially prompted as it was by the increased vividness of staged miracle plays, led artists in Christian Europe to explore various other technical and mechanical skills from whatever "scientific" sources were then available, which they might adapt to their art. One such was surely the geometry of optics, of much interest at the time to Franciscan monks who claimed that this Greek- and Arab-derived Euclidean offshoot seemed to explain not only how the human eye sees but also how God first conceived the essential structure of the universe in his mind's eye at genesis. By applying Euclid's law of similar triangles, the ancient puzzle of how very large images in the objective world are able to penetrate the tiny pupil of the eye and thus be "seen," could now for the first time be rationally comprehended. And so, likewise, it would seem that God at creation formed a priori in his divine mind's eye a similar miniature image and then projected it into the void in the form of an expanding cone, the base of which reproduced his vision in full-scale cosmic proportion, just as does a mechanical slide or movie projector when it sends a picture from film to giant screen by the same geometric principle.

Finally, about the year 1425, in the city of Florence, Italy, Filippo Brunelleschi, sculptor and architect, adapted these same optical principles, which heretofore had only been concerned with explaining the geometry of actual

Fig. 5.9 Testera framed by an illusionistic doorway, northeast corner of the cloister, convento of Santiago, Cuilapan, Oaxaca. Photograph by Jorge Pérez de Lara.

opposite. Brunelleschi's geometric method was exactly the same as employed today in the technology of computerized graphics imagery and special virtual effects for the motion picture industry.[23]

What Brunelleschi devised, and Leon Battista Alberti then modified in his "window" formula ten years later, was a simple adaptation of the optical law whereby the picture intersects the visual triangle in the same way as the lens does in the eye and upon which an object can be reproduced in precise scale to the real object seen in the visual field. This is the singular, unique quality of Renaissance linear perspective for artists, *perspectiva artificialis* as it is sometimes called in Latin. No other civilization in the world had as yet come up with such a mathematical means for the creation of an illusionistic picture before the Italian Renaissance—but then no other civilization in the world had the same peculiar cultural necessity for such optically based illusionism in its art.

vision, to the reproduction of a virtual reflection, that is, a painting, unfortunately now lost, of the Florentine baptistery as if viewed by one standing in the portal of the cathedral

While no documents have so far turned up revealing how indigenous American Indians first reacted to the new geometric illusionism in Renaissance pictures, we do have recorded responses from naive Chinese viewers of the early seventeenth century, as they were being similarly proselytized by Jesuit missionaries. The leader of the Jesuit mission in Beijing, the Italian padre Matteo Ricci, whose well-known dependence on the art of memory and the visual arts as conversion tools may have derived from the experience of the friars in Mexico, wrote an account of how the Ming Dynasty Wan-Li emperor supposedly responded when presented in 1602 with a Western-style chiaroscuro-enhanced painting of Jesus as Salvator Mundi.[24] Padre Ricci claimed that the emperor was so astonished he suddenly blurted out, "This is a living god!" Another Chinese who was also present recalled in his own words that "when seen from afar, [the image] was as if alive."[25] Some twenty years before, as Gauvin Bailey has vividly described, the Jesuits presented a similar perspective-enhanced engraving of a fourteenth-century-style painting of the Virgin said to have been originally created by the apostle Saint Luke (and still hanging in the Basilica of Santa Maria Maggiore in Rome) to the Mughal emperor Akbar in his capital at Agra in India. When the local Hindus were admitted to see it, so struck were they by its sculpture-like realism that a mass riot nearly ensued.[26]

Christian missionaries, of course, were little interested in Renaissance perspective science for its own sake and rarely bothered to teach their Indian artists much more than the standardized conventions. The friars were, however, convinced that perspective and chiaroscuro were powerful tools for Christian proselytization and must have been struck by the manifest amazement of non-Europeans experiencing for the first time the novelty of Renaissance illusionism. The Indians' favorable reception of Renaissance art could only have reinforced the friars' conviction that indigenous "idols" were rejected in heaven by the divine power of spiritual geometry and the "demon" among the Indians on earth was being simultaneously overwhelmed.

More research still needs to be done concerning just how the native artists were taught whatever rudiments of Renaissance perspective and chiaroscuro we have so far witnessed.[27] It would seem from casual examination of the Actopan murals, for instance, that the methods, like those in many contemporaneous paintings in Spain, were essentially still empirical, derived somewhat from variant perspective conventions devised by certain northern Europeans like the early sixteenth-century theorist Jean Pèlerin Viator.[28] In fact, some Spanish painters conceived their images more as illusionary relief sculpture than as "windows" in the strict Albertian sense, since their chiaroscuro-defined figures, rather than seeming to recede behind the picture surface, often had the illusionistic effect of projecting forward from it. A Mexican example of this peculiar effect can be seen in the Augustinian convento of San Agustín at Acolman. Giant black-and-white figures of Old Testament prophets and classical sibyls seated on looming yellow thrones are painted on the presbytery walls and seem to advance perceptually right into the viewer's space (fig. 5.10).[29] The native artist who painted these gigantic images must have seen a print of Michelangelo's Sistine Chapel frescoes created in

Rome only half a century before. He even added *ignudi*—Michelangelo's famous nude boys—sprawling on the fictive architectural frame painted between the thrones (fig. 5.11).

There can be no doubt that Indian artists were fascinated by the powerful tactile and optical illusionism of the imported Renaissance style and relished the opportunity to show off their own newly acquired skills in creating for themselves its astounding effects. Moreover, the native sculptors working in tandem with the painters were likewise fascinated. Still retaining the raised, "cookie-cutter" relief manner characteristic of central Mexican stone carving in pre-Columbian times, postconquest native sculptors achieved unique effects of Renaissance-style illusion by cutting deep outlines around anatomical details and drapery folds in order to take advantage of the natural modeling power of the tropical sun. An outstanding example is the beautifully carved relief, ca. 1550, of the Last Judgment on one of the corner posas in the patio of the convento at Calpan, Puebla, by an anonymous but ingenious native artist (fig. 5.12). The sculpture was inspired by a popular European woodcut circulating in the Spanish dominions in various versions in numerous religious treatises at the time. Figure 5.13 illustrates one such, printed in Venice in repeated sixteenth-century editions. In comparing the latter to the former, however, we observe right away how the sculptor improvised three-dimensional, modeled forms from his two-dimensional prototype by exploiting the natural chiaroscuro created in bright morning sunlight.[30] For instance, he allowed the cloud-like garment supporting the figure of Mary at the side of Christ to project several inches forward from the back plane. The shadow cast by this overhanging cut adds a wonderful effect of supernatural levitation. In the woodcut print, the graves of the emerging dead are drawn only in crude perspective, but the sculptor transformed them into hollow boxes projecting forward at a slant from the posa wall. The protruding front sides of each of these little tombs again cast real shadows, giving the convincing illusion of extending upward from an imaginary horizontal ground.

While frequently acclaiming the competence of the native artists trained in the new style, the sixteenth-century friar-historians rarely mention names.[31] Curiously, one of the few contemporaneous chroniclers who did was the old conquistador Bernal Díaz del Castillo in his *Historia verdadura de la nueva españa* written in the 1560s about his experiences in Mexico during and after the conquest: "There are three Indians today in Mexico City so excellent in their office of carvers [sculptors and engravers] and painters; they are called Marcos de Aquino and Juan de la Cruz and El Crespillo, and if they lived in the time of that ancient and famed Apelles, or of Michelangelo or Berruguete who are of our times, they would again be placed in their number."[32] Further in his text, Bernal Díaz praised the same three again but makes no reference to specific works. Another contemporaneous document in the Nahuatl language mentions "Marcos Cipak, Pedro Chachalaca, Francisco Xinmámal, and Pedro de San Nicolás" as the native painters of a now-lost altarpiece for the San José de los Naturales chapel around 1555.[33] Perhaps the "Marcos Cipak" here is the same person as Bernal's "Marcos," and, if so, one would like to know if he was trained

Fig. 5.10 *Prophets and Sibyls,* murals in the presbytery of the convento church of San Agustín, Acolman, Mexico. Photograph by Jorge Pérez de Lara.

Fig. 5.11 Detail of *Prophets and Sibyls* in the presbytery of the convento church of San Agustín, Acolman, Mexico. Photograph by Jorge Pérez de Lara.

in Pedro de Gante's school. And one is tempted to ask if this is also the same "Marcos, indio pintor" claimed by the Franciscans as the painter of the image of the Virgin in the *hermita* at Tepeyac/Guadalupe. The latter reference from 1556 is the earliest we have of a painting in what has come to be Mexico's most sacred national shrine.[34] Whether or not one believes a supernatural power created this image in 1531 (as has been proclaimed since the seventeenth century), it does bear stylistic qualities, especially the dark outlining and chiaroscuro rendering of the Virgin's face and hands, that I attribute to the teaching in Fray Pedro's school at San José de los Naturales (fig. 5.14).[35]

Perhaps the most original Indian painter known by both name and extant works in a sixteenth-century Mexican church is Juan Gerson, so called after the fifteenth-century French religious reformer whose writings were popular among the Franciscans. (At least four of Jean Gerson's books were in Mexican libraries.[36]) Only recently revealed as an Indian, this native painter who took Gerson's name and apparently tried to pass himself as a criollo developed his own colorfully medieval and decidedly un-Albertian variant of the European style (more similar to the manuscript styles than to contemporaneous mural painting). His sources seem to have been Flemish and Spanish woodcut prints after Albrecht Dürer, and his surviving masterpieces, ca. 1562, are twenty-eight scenes of the Apocalypse and Last Judgment painted not in fresco but on *amatl* (a native paper made from the inner bark of the fig tree) and pasted to the interstices between the vaulting ribs above the entrance hall in the Franciscan convento church at Tecamachalco, Puebla (fig. 5.15).[37]

In the sixteenth century the Nahuatl word for "artist" was *tlahcuiloh,* literally scribe-painter, indicating that in preconquest times one of the profession's most important occupations was as record keeper by means of rebus picture-painting. In the Latin-lettered languages of the West, there is no exact synonym; the English and Spanish words "scribe" and *escribaño* tend to connote a profession of bureaucratic anonymity and don't insinuate the artistic talents of the Mexican *tlahcuiloh.*[38] *Tlahcuiloqueh* were also called upon by the friars to paint and sculpt illusionistic frieze and dado moldings around the convento hallways in the crowded *horror vacui* manner of Spanish-style *grotescos* [grotesques], another modish Renaissance idea imported from Italy. Both Spanish and English words derive from *grotteschi,* as the Italians called the same decorative motifs, a technique they invented after discovering its antecedents in the grottolike ruins of ancient Roman palaces. Figure 5.16 illustrates a typical Mexican convento adaptation running along the upper friary corridor in the Franciscan monastery at Huaquechula, Puebla. Such motifs no doubt were adapted by Indian painters from the decorative woodcut borders around the title pages of printed books that were popular in Spanish typography and even published in Mexico during the sixteenth century (fig. 5.17).

Figure 5.18 shows a similar contemporaneous example of grotesco painting in Spain, in the chapel of the Franciscan convento at La Rábida, Andalusia. These mural designs were done generally for decorative and not didactic intent, and the Mexican version of the style, including the illusionistic rendering of classical acanthus leaves and festoonery often promiscuously mixed with native American flora and fauna, has come to be known by the demeaning Nahuatl word *tequitqui* [the tribute of laborers].[39] This is an unfortunate modern designation. We still do not know whether the painting of this decor was a lesser specialty or simply an added skill of the highly trained tlahcuiloqueh. It has sometimes been argued that the style of condensed surface decoration known as horror vacui [fear of emptiness] was unique to preconquest Indian art, but this is not so.[40] European medieval tapestry decoration and even Renaissance Italian classically derived grotesques show the same inclination to "scattered attributes" (Robertson's term) as the native preconquest tradition, which made it all the easier for tlahcuiloqueh to copy and adapt. Yet another favorite dado motif painted by the tlahcuiloqueh in all the Franciscan conventos was the distinctive knotted rope that the Friars Minor used to belt their habits thus signifying the order's penitential vows (fig. 5.19). Note the escutcheon below painted illusionistically to look as if hanging by a hook.

While pre-Columbian art, like most all other styles of art before the European Renaissance, had primarily been conceived in semiabstract images of natural and supernatural phenomena, such a tradition was again hardly peculiar to Mesoamerican culture. The same conceptual predisposition was and still is inherent in all human beings during early childhood. On the other hand, the desire to replicate in pictures what the

Fig. 5.12 *Last Judgment,* relief carving on east face of the southwest corner posa, convento of San Andrés, Calpan, Puebla. Photograph by Jorge Pérez de Lara.

human eye optically perceives in the physical world from a fixed viewpoint and illuminated from a single light source is not innate in anyone.[41] Geometric perspective and modeling with light and shade are a priori unnatural to artistic conception as any five-year-old creating a picture will tell you. They require a mature skill that must be learned through empirical observation, intellectual rationalization, manual practice, and most important of all, a distinct cultural necessity that pictures should replicate the physical characteristics of the visible world.

Until the Indians were converted to Christianity, there was no motive for them to create images of deiforms that looked like geometric volumes in illusionistic space. Had the Indians' original religion ever demanded such a representation, I am sure some ingenious native would have stepped forth to invent a method just as Brunelleschi did in Renaissance Florence. The same must be said

Fig. 5.13 *Last Judgment*, woodcut from *Nova contemplativa*, Venice, 1510–20. Courtesy of Chapin Library of Rare Books, Williams College, Williamstown, Massachusetts.

regarding any instance in non-Western art where some technique of illusionistic rendering has been discerned. There had to have been a cultural need a priori, and then a response by some particularly clever artist within the culture who would invent an appropriate technique and teach it to fellow artists.

Unlike loud music, which always startles the ears, trompe l'oeil images in perspective tend to become less shocking to the eyes after frequent exposure. Some modern critics, themselves overly satiated with ever more dramatic holographic effects since the Renaissance, seem no longer able (or willing) to appreciate how exciting even simple empirical perspective originally was (and occasionally still is) for indigenous peoples of America, Asia, and Africa upon first exposure. They conclude that Renaissance illusionism was just a Western cultural construct, no more and no less "resembling nature" than any of the myriad other world artistic styles.[42]

Fig. 5.14 Detail, *Virgin of Guadalupe,* painting in the Basílica de Guadalupe, Mexico City.

Another theory persistent among some today holds that non-Western peoples including indigenous American Indians do not comprehend optical perspective in the same perceptual way as Westerners, the implication once again being that even adult non-Western artists retain their innocent "conceptual" vision of phenomenal reality and are inherently averse to Renaissance-style "artificial" perspective and chiaroscuro. According to this view, the presence of any such alien forms in the art of indigenous peoples has to be negative, either coerced or an ethnic sellout, signifying the undermining perversity of Western cultural imperialism.

Ironically, the hypothesis that non-Western peoples visually perceive the world differently than "we" in the post-Renaissance "civilized" West goes back to the late nineteenth-century generation of anthropologists and psychologists who claimed it explained not the cultural integrity but rather the cognitive inferiority of so-called primitive societies. "Scientific studies," such as the infamous Hudson Depth Perception Test, were conducted among certain non-Western cultures supposedly having no familiarity with photographs or perspective pictures. "Subjects" from these groups were shown cartoonlike images of people and animals in differing scale and distance relationships. When the native viewers failed at first glance to "read" correctly the graphic conven-

Fig. 5.15 Juan Gerson, scenes from the Old Testament and the Apocalypse in the ceiling under the choir loft, convento church of the Asunción de la Nuestra Señora, Tecamachalco, Puebla.

tions of these pictures and misidentified which objects were near and which far in the fictive pictorial depth, they were summarily judged developmentally inferior to Westerners. The arrogance and falsity of the Hudson tests were finally exposed in the 1970s when perceptual psychologists proved that Western and non-Western peoples respond identically to all perspective images in whatever black-and-white or color medium as long as the pictorial conventions such as convergent lines signifying distance and dark smudges representing shade and shadow are mutually understood.[43]

In other words, there can be no doubt that all human beings of whatever race, creed, gender, economic condition, geographical location, or historical time were and still are genetically predisposed to perceive perspective convergence in the phenomenal visual world in the same physiological and optical way. Not an iota of verifiable scientific evidence indicates otherwise.[44] The fact that almost everyone sooner or later needs to wear glasses in order to read his or her native newspaper in whatever language should be proof enough that all human beings see, or don't see, according to the same fundamental optical laws.

On the other hand, the ability to replicate in pictures what we see optically and physiologically in nature is *not* inherent. Perspective drawing is a geometric skill that must first be invented for some particular cultural reason and then *taught* to everyone else thereafter. Notwithstanding, it can be learned easily and quickly by anyone, no matter what his or her ethnicity or artistic talent. Every academic year in my college course in Italian Renaissance

Fig. 5.16 Painted tequitqui molding around the wall in the convento of San Martin, Huaquechula, Puebla.

history of art, I teach the geometry and optics of linear perspective to a class of mixed-gender and ethnically varied students, most of whom have had no prior studio art experience. In one hour's class time I demonstrate how to draw a picture as if it were an imaginary window opening into a three-dimensional room with gridded floor filled with furniture and peopled with figures in different corners and proportionally sized, all in proper one-point Albertian perspective. Students must then draw their own examples. Most complete the assignment in another hour's time; a few may take two hours but never more to grasp the rules fully and apply them recognizably in a completed picture. This student exercise quite contradicts the assertion of some art critics that in the fifteenth and sixteenth centuries even experienced and talented artists took "years" to master the principles.[45]

In fact, so proficient did some Indian artists become at mastering the Renaissance style (just as Indian scholars became superb speakers and writers of Latin) the few, mostly second-rate European painters and sculptors who came to seek their fortunes in the New World during the early sixteenth century discovered that native expertise was often as good as if not better than theirs. To protect themselves, the controlling Europeans set up guilds aimed at limiting if not specifically excluding the Indians and did eventually drive them from the profession.[46]

While admitting that we do not know for sure who painted the beautiful Italianate mural of Saint Catherine of Siena at Tetela del Volcán, we must remain open to the distinct possibility that an Indian certainly could have.[47] The current fad for discerning the difference between indigenous and European participation in the painting of sixteenth-century convento murals based on degree of

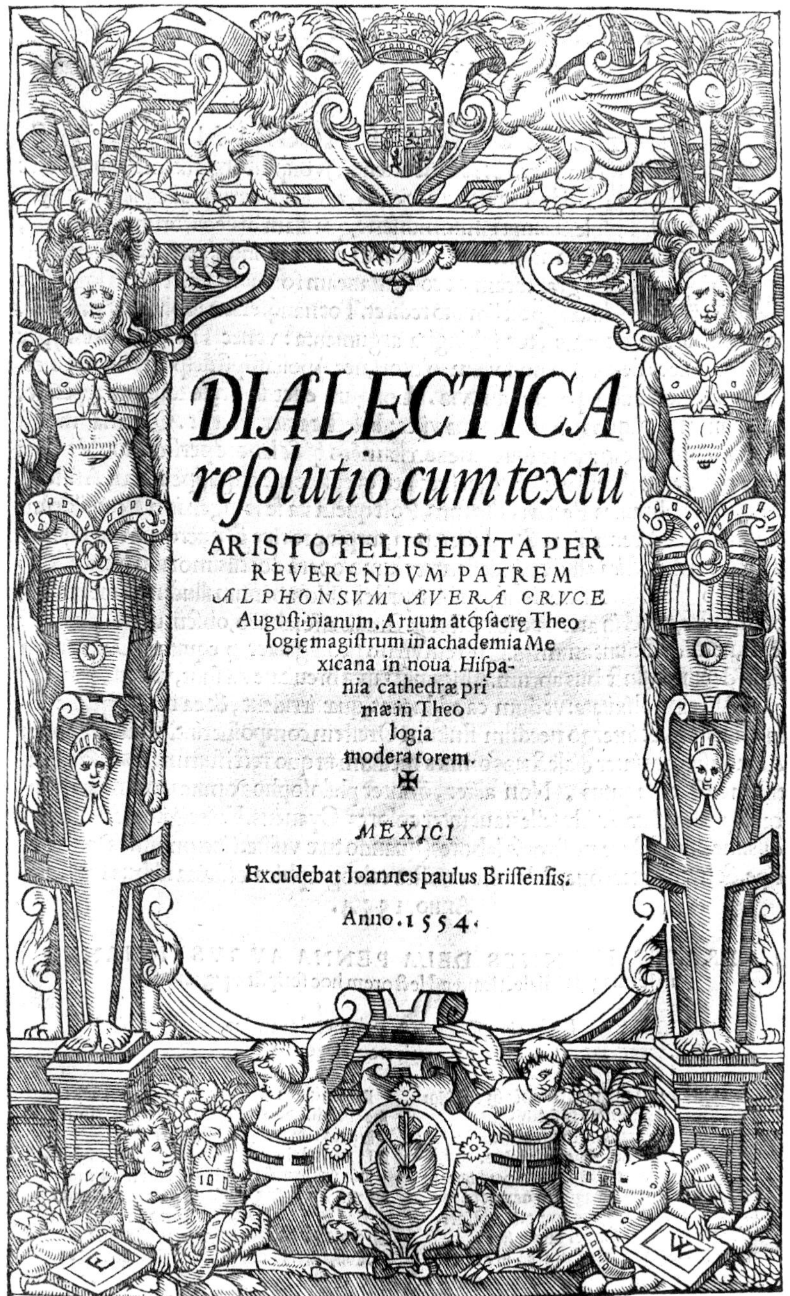

DIALECTICA
reſolutio cum textu
ARISTOTELIS EDITA PER
REVERENDVM PATREM
ALPHONSVM AVERA CRVCE
Auguſtinianum, Artium atq; ſacrę Theo
logię magiſtrum in achademia Me
xicana in noua Hiſpa-
nia cathedræ pri
mæ in Theo
logia
modera torem.

MEXICI
Excudebat Ioannes paulus Briſſenſis.
Anno. 1554.

Fig. 5.17 Title page of Fray Alfonso de Veracruz's *Dialectica . . . Aristotelis . . .*, Mexico City, 1554. Courtesy of Chapin Library of Rare Books, Williams College, Williamstown, Massachusetts.

Fig. 5.18 Interior of the chapel, convento of San Francisco, La Rábida, Spain.

Fig. 5.19 Painted illusionistic tequitqui molding around the cloister corridor wall, convento of San Martin, Huaquechula, Puebla.

competence in rendering Renaissance-style illusionism is simply wrong. During the early sixteenth century, Italianate ideas were not yet so imbedded in the art of all Spanish or Flemish practitioners that one should assume that just because some Mexican convento pictures seem lacking in either convincing perspective or relieflike modeling that they must then be by Indian artists. Conversely, there was (and is) absolutely nothing in the genetic or cultural predisposition of American Indians to prevent individuals, especially by the time of the second and third postconquest generations, from learning the most sophisticated optical principles and standardized Renaissance conventions for representing high Renaissance perspective and chiaroscuro with just as much cognitive understanding and manual dexterity as any European artist. To be sure, individual native abilities varied, as natural artistic talent does in every world culture, but in the main what is so remarkable is not how difficult it was for the Indians to adjust to the foreign style but how much of it and in so short a time they were able to learn and assimilate.

Moreover, the Indians had yet another incentive to master Western art. Their ancient statues and painted images, which they believed their former deiforms actually inhabited, had totally failed to thwart the Spanish invasion. From the native standpoint, the quality of any artifact used in religious ritual was not measured by its abstract "aesthetic" beauty (a purely Western Enlightenment assumption) but by its efficacy as a talisman. When an object's talismanic powers no longer worked, it was discarded. In this sense, the Indians observed that the talismans of the Spaniards (i.e., Christian images in the Renaissance illusionistic style) had worked only too well. I believe that this particularly explains why the Indians still today, even after having syncretized if not replaced Christian saints outright with aspects of preconquest divine forces in their current worship, rarely revert to preconquest forms in representation but rather continue to depict their hybrid santos in the sixteenth-century Renaissance style.

In any case, as far as Indian viewers apart from Indian artists were concerned, it was not so much the style or even the meaning of mural paintings per se that mattered, but where, when, and in what context they were shown. This is what touched the deepest chord in the native cultural and emotional psyche.

In order that the skill of these people may be seen I will relate here what they produced and represented . . . on the feast of St. John the Baptist on Monday [following Corpus Christi], June 24, 1538. I refer to the four autos. To produce these in prose—for history in prose is no less edifying than in verse—it was necessary to work all day Friday; wherefore it was only on the two days that remained, which were Saturday and Sunday, that the Indians learned the plays. On Monday they represented very devoutly the Annunciation of the Birth of John the Baptist, as made to his father, Zachary. The work lasted about an hour, ending with an excellent motet with organ accompaniment. Immediately after, on another stage [*tablado*], they represented the Annunciation of Our Lady. . . . Thereupon they marched in procession to the Church of St. John [Tlaxcala]. Immediately on arriving in the patio . . . the Visitation of Our Lady with St. Elizabeth was represented on another platform [*cadalso*]. It was a pleasure to see how gracefully the cadalsos were adorned and embellished. After Holy Mass, the Birth of St. John was represented. In place of the Circumcision [they represented] the Baptism. . . . The auto ended with the [canticle] *Benedictus Dominus Deus Israel.*

Motolinía, Historia

Chapter 6

THE CONVENTO AS THEATER

Medieval *Autos* and Nahua *Neixcuitilli*

If one tradition was shared in common by all indigenous peoples in preconquest Mesoamerica, it was obsession with pageant and spectacle. If one tradition characterized the Spanish Catholic Church in the sixteenth century, it was likewise obsession with pageant and spectacle (to the increasing disgust of northern European Protestants).[1] If no other reason explains the remarkable persistence of Catholicism in the Indian communities of North and South America, especially after five centuries of oppression, revolution, and secularization, it is this shared cultural need to demonstrate before heaven and earth that mortal humans march and sing to the music of the spheres. I argue that the Mexican conventos more and more evolved into *theaters*—literally—of pageants and spectacles celebrating the Christian religion. Their architectural layout not only accommodated the sacred direction of Indian processions but also allotted stage space for native plays with live actors, pictorial backdrops, movable scenery, locations for singers, dancers, musicians with instruments, and props for special dramatic effects. The convento also became a convenient "theater of memory" in which various elements of its architecture could be used as mnemonic cues to reciting the catechism according to the popular Renaissance revival of Ciceronian *ars memorativa*.

MEDIEVAL *AUTOS* AND NAHUA *NEIXCUITILLI*

In the languages of all Western Christendom during the sixteenth century, words derived from the Latin *theatrum* did not just refer to places of entertainment. Rather, the term was a common expression denoting a location, be it a stage or building or even a book, wherein images of any kind are presented for didactic purposes.[2] Within this context, the friars, from their proprietary point of view, took advantage of the traditional Indian fascination with spectacle in order to further consolidate their Christian proselytization, and the Indians, from their subservient position, were able to take advantage of the friars' tolerance of native spectacle in order both to preserve their preconquest traditions and to rehearse certain political grievances through impersonation and parody, much the way pre-Lenten carnival served to release the repressed tensions of the lower classes in medieval Europe.[3]

From the very beginning of their mission in America, the friars of all three orders approved of Indian spectacle, especially as accompanied by music, singing, and dancing, with little reservation as long as the form and content was overtly Christian.[4] Besides the celebration for the Feast of Saint John the Baptist described in the epigraph, Fray Motolinía wrote enthusiastically about four others, all personally witnessed by him during the years 1538 and 1539 when he was resident in the convento at Tlaxcala. Here is his description of an amazing three-dimensional mock-up of the Garden of Eden that the Indians prepared within the convento patio for a play about the fall of man on Wednesday of Easter week 1538.[5] The following long quotation, here translated (by Francis Borgia Steck) and only slightly abbreviated (by me), is worth reading in full because it inadvertently reveals how the Indians were mixing elements of their own traditional creation myth with biblical Genesis. Note the Indians' construction of terrestrial paradise as surrounded by a "sierra" with the "tree of life" in the center from which "four rivers or springs" flowed—and its similarity to the Indians' primordial altepetl in quincunx form.[6] Notice also the plethora of chattering birds. Surely the newly converted Indians who arranged this spectacle, even though being taught by the friars about the zoological abundance in Christian paradise,[7] would not yet have forgotten their ancient lore that birds were reincarnated *yolia* [souls] of dead and unborn human beings nesting in the World Tree.[8] Finally, note the detail of the Indian boy dressed as a "lion"—more likely a puma or jaguar since lions were hardly indigenous to the Americas—and devouring a real deer on a crag between three stones. Could this have been a covert reference to the preconquest myth of the violent dismemberment of Tlateotl, the act that begot the earth? In traditional Nahua imagery a jaguar killing a deer often symbolized human sacrifice and the jaguar's open jaws, like those of a serpent, the entrance to the primordial underworld.[9] Just as intriguing is whether or not Motolinía was aware of these pagan implications. I am sure that he was quite aware, but since he was writing this history for an orthodox Spanish audience, he must have thought it wiser to brush over these details as naive acts of Christian piety.

> The abode of Adam and Eve was adorned in such a way as closely to resemble Terrestrial Paradise. In it there were various fruit and flowering trees. Some of the latter were natural, others were artificial with flowers made of feathers and gold. In the trees there was a great variety of birds, from the owl and birds of prey to the little birds. Most conspicuous were the many parrots, whose chattering and screeching was so loud that sometimes they disturbed the play. I counted on a single tree forty parrots. . . . There were also artificial birds made of gold and feathers which were beautiful to look at. The rabbits and hares were so numerous that the whole place seemed full of them together with many other little animals, some of which I had never seen before. There were also two ocelots. These were tied because they are very fierce. . . . Once, during the play, Eve was careless and went near one of them and, as if well trained, the beast went away. This was before the sin; had it occurred after the sin, she would not have been so lucky. There were other artificial animals, all well simulated, with some boys inside them. These acted as if they were domesticated and Adam and Eve teased and laughed at them. Four rivers or springs flowed from the paradise, each bearing its label which read: Phiron, Gheon, Tigris and Euphrates. The tree of life was in the center of paradise and near it stood the tree of knowledge of good and evil with many beautiful artificial fruits in gold and feathers. Around the paradise were three large rocks and a high sierra. On these was a rich abundance of whatever can be found . . . on a refreshing mountain, together with everything that is characteristic of April and May. For making a thing look natural these Indians have a singular talent. . . .
>
> On the rocks there were animals, some of them were real, others were artificial. One of the artificial animals was a boy dressed like a lion [*leon*]. He was tearing to pieces and devouring a deer that he had killed. The deer was real and lay on a crag which was made between the two rocks. It was a thing worth noting.
>
> As soon as the procession arrived, the

auto began. It lasted a long time because, before Eve ate and Adam consented, Eve went from the serpent to her husband and from her husband to the serpent three or four times, Adam always resisting and, as if indignant, pushing Eve away; she on the other hand besought and molested him, saying that the love he had for her seemed small and that she loved him more than he loved her; then, taking him in her lap, she so importuned him that he finally went with her to the forbidden tree. Here, in the presence of Adam she ate of its fruit and gave him to eat. . . . Although they hid themselves as well as they could, they were not able to prevent God from seeing them. And God entered with great majesty accompanied by many angels. When God called Adam, the latter blamed his wife; whereupon she put the blame on the serpent. God condemned them all and imposed a penance on each one. . . . What made the greatest impression was to see the two depart, banished and in tears. Three angels carried Adam and three others carried Eve; they all left the place, singing to the accompaniment of the organ, *Circumdederunt me*. This was so well presented that all who witnessed it wept freely. A cherub remained, guarding the portal of paradise with a sword in his hand. Thereupon the world was represented, another land quite different from the one from which Adam and Eve had been banished. It was full of thistles and thorns and many snakes together with rabbits and hares. When the new inhabitants of this world arrived there, the angel showed Adam how he would have to work and cultivate the land, while to Eve were given spindles to spin and make clothes for her husband and children. After consoling, the two who remained there . . . showed great sorrow. . . . This auto was presented by the Indians in their native language, so that many of them were deeply moved and shed tears, especially when Adam was banished from paradise and placed in the world.[10]

In even more detail, Motolinía described a "siege of Jerusalem" performed on Corpus Christi Day the following year 1539. For this most elaborate spectacle, a blockbuster worthy of Cecil B. DeMille, the Indians built in the Tlaxcala town plaza a five-story artificial fortress complete with battlemented towers representing Jerusalem and defended by dozens of Indians dressed up in full warrior-regalia as Moors and Jews. Opposite, they built a replica of Santa Fe, the Spanish stronghold surrounded by walls covered with paintings that "very realistically simulated mason-work with embrasures, loopholes and many merlons."[11] This too was filled with dozens of Indians arrayed in feathers but representing Christian knights (including Tlaxcalan, Aztec, Mixtec, Huastec, and even Inca Indians) led by an Indian impersonating Don Antonio de Mendoza, viceroy of New Spain. Then, to the sound of trumpets and drums, the heroes immediately engaged the Moorish armies commanded by the sultan costumed as no less than Hernán Cortés! Motolinía again skips over this anomalous eyebrow raiser without another word. We are left to speculate only that the Indians were allowed considerable latitude in the production of such spectacles, even to making sport

Fig. 6.1 Crèche with artificial pool with live animals and plants. Erected January 2000 by the Indian parishioners of San Juanito church, Malinalco, Mexico, in celebration of the Feast of the Three Kings. Photograph by Jorge Pérez de Lara.

of their Spanish overlords. As it happened, Cortés and his conquistadors were at this moment suspected by the Tlaxcalans of reneging on certain political guarantees to their former allies.[12]

Back and forth raged the sham battle, complete with fake cannonballs filled with wet red mud, exploding prickly pears, and arrows tipped in red paint to give the semblance of blood and gore. The Christians were losing the battle until Saint James the Apostle (Santiago Matamoros) suddenly arrived on his white horse, charging everywhere and reinspiring the troops to renewed vigor. As the Christian army surged forward again, the figure of Saint Michael miraculously arose from the central tower of the enemy fortress to proclaim that God commanded the Moors to lay down their arms. Stunned by this divine apparition, the sultan's army fell back.

The Christians entered the Holy City in triumph amid a climactic crescendo of fireworks and skyrockets.[13]

Such splendid re-creations of miracles, holy stories, lives of the saints, and battles between Christians and infidels were of course common public entertainment in late medieval Europe. In the Latin of the church, they were called *exempla;* in vernacular Italian, *laude;* and in Spanish, *autos*. During holy days they were presented in public plazas with live actors before the portals of adjunct buildings that served as ad hoc proscenia and acoustic backdrops. Corpus Christi celebrations both in Europe and the New World were renowned for their pomp and ceremony.[14]

Along with the live *auto* as popular religious spectacle was the sculptured Spanish *paso,* a float carrying lifelike polychrome mannequins, often with hinged limbs, wigs of human hair, and real clothing, set up on wheeled carts or portable palanquins (andas), the latter carried in procession especially during Holy Week (the week before Easter) through the streets on the shoulders of members of religious confraternities.[15] For the January Feast of the Three Kings, elaborate scenery with real animals and live actors performing as the Magi are still set up with great fanfare in many indigenous Mexican communities. Figure 6.1 depicts a full-size mock-up with grass huts and even a painted lienzo backdrop constructed for the second millennial celebration of the holiday in the patio before the parish church of San Juanito, Malinalco.[16]

Before the Spanish conquest, native religious spectacles were commonplace, just as in Europe taking advantage of the natural human impulse for mimicry and artifice. Wherever the 365-day solar year and 260-day sacred calendar were reckoned, religious celebrations occurred at least every twenty days. Fray Diego Durán and Fray Bernardino de Sahagún described many of these in detail.[17] The great Aztec feast of Panquetzaliztli honored their principle deity, Huizilopochtli, whose effigy in amaranth dough they carried in procession on a palanquin similar to that which bore the Christian Host on Corpus Christi day.[18]

"Theater" in the ancient classical and modern Western sense of a fixed audience before an impervious proscenium is not the proper word to describe the organized spectacle in preconquest America, since Indian performers usually presented their spectacles in the round on raised platforms called in Nahuatl *momoztli,* without backdrops so that spectators could watch from all sides. These platforms, usually of masonry, were often in the form of low truncated pyramids with steps on one or more sides. Many are to be seen today in the great archaeological sites of Mexico and Guatemala, positioned in sunken courts surrounded by other buildings in such a way as to enhance the acoustics, as at Teotihuacan, Monte Albán, and Chichén Itzá.[19]

Not only groups of dancers performed on these raised stages but also individual actors dressed in colorful costumes in which they would impersonate deiforms, animals, and various human heroes and villains. In fact, they numinously *became* these other beings whose identity would be communicated through clever pantomime but without resorting to the degree of optical trompe l'oeil that the Western theater sought to achieve in the later Middle Ages. After the conquest Indian converts quickly and enthusiastically adapted to Renaissance-style illusionism in the visual arts. They would similarly infuse aspects of Western "realism" in their traditional spectacles, creating a remarkable and indivisible Native-European symbiosis that has persisted ever since.

One of the few extant descriptions of a preconquest Indian play in the precinct of the Temple of Quetzalcoatl was written by Fray Diego Durán. While not actually witnessing this spectacle, called by him a *farsia,* he had heard much about it from Indian elders.[20] Durán came to Mexico as a child in the 1540s, growing up among Indians and becoming fluent in Nahuatl and familiar with their customs before joining the Dominican order. It is worth comparing the form and presentation of this Indian spectacle to Motolinía's description of the fall of man above. The actors in both plays seem to have improvised much of their dialogue and actions as they went along, appealing to their audience with touches of bawdy humor mixed with Chaplinesque pathos, yet both plays were serious moral allegories with didactic messages about paying homage to divine authority (translated below by Doris Heyden and Fernando Horcasitas):

> This temple contained a fair-sized courtyard, where, on the day of the feast, were performed splendid dances, merry celebrations, and amusing farces. For these things a small stage or platform stood in the middle of the courtyard. It was about thirty feet square, and was adorned with branches and beautifully decorated for the feast. It was hemmed in by arches made of all kinds of flowers and rich featherwork which were hung at certain intervals. There were different birds, rabbits, and other festive things highly pleasing to the eye. After dining, the merchants and lords danced around that theater with all their finery and splendid dress. The dance then ceased and the players appeared. The first who came out played a farce of a man swollen with tumors, feigning to be sorely afflicted . . . mixing with these complaints many joking words . . . which caused much laughter among the people. When this farce ended, another . . . man appeared, representing a person with a cold, coughing constantly. Then the actors were a large fly and beetle; they came out imitating these creatures in lifelike fashion. One of them buzzed like a fly when it comes near meat. . . . Then this other, disguised as a beetle, poked about the rubbish. All these farces were highly amusing and pleasant, but were not acted without pagan meaning, for they stemmed from the fact that the god Quetzalcoatl was held to be the advocate for tumors, eye disease, colds, and coughing. Thus in these same farces they included words of pleading directed to this deity. They begged for his help, and so it was that all those suffering from these ills . . . came with their offerings and prayers to this idol and his temple.[21]

In preconquest Indian theater, as Durán's observation implies, the entire community participated. After the dancers and impersonators were finished with their special

Fig. 6.2 Detail, mural, south wall of the convento church of San Miguel, Ixmiquilpan, Hidalgo. Photograph by Jorge Pérez de Lara.

performances, they stepped back into the procession, and others might take their place in the next performance, everyone celebrating with equal feeling of catharsis and belief that by so participating they would transcend to the world of the spirits.[22] Actually, the same could be said of medieval Christian processions and spectacles.[23] In any case, the friars were pleased to incorporate this Indian theatrical style in the production of their own *autos*.

It is not certain just what the Nahuatl-speaking Indians of Central Mexico originally called these performances, but shortly after the conquest, the Spanish heard the word *tlamahuizolli,* meaning "miracle" or "something astonishing." Both Indians and friars, nevertheless, soon turned to another Nahuatl word, *neixcuitilli,* which can be translated as both "miracle" and "example." Since "example" seems to be a straight translation of the Latin *exemplum,* which is also a synonym for *auto*, it would appear that the Indians were already adapting to the imported Spanish mode of didactic religious theater.[24] One of the earliest Christian plays recorded as having been performed in the New World by Indians, a Last Judgment presented in Tlatelolco in the year 1531, was apparently called neixcuitilli.[25]

The most comprehensive historical study written so far on the Indian theater in Mexico is Fernando Horcasitas's *El Teatro Nahuatl,* unfortunately not yet translated into English.[26] As the title states, his coverage is almost exclusively Nahuatl, although he did include a brief chapter on pre- and postconquest spectacles in other indigenous linguistic communities like the Mixtec and Maya. In English, some excellent if more theoretical analyses of the Nahuatl theater have been published by Max Harris and Louise Burkhart. Harris's *Dialogical Theatre* argues that the medium served with special effectiveness as a disguised outlet for Indian frustration and resentment of the Spanish conquest, with the friars' (certainly Motolinía's) approval. Louise Burkhart's *Holy Wednesday* presents a translation and philological study of what may be the earliest known indigenous Christian play, originally presented only a few decades after the conquest. It celebrates Holy Week and is written in the vernacular for a Nahuatl-speaking audience.[27] Burkhart shows how the author, as he translated Christian concepts into Nahuatl (i.e., removed the terms from their European linguistic framework and reworded them in syntax more compatible to native speech), thereby gave these concepts a certain "pagan" nuance, thus transmuting the play into a peculiarly native version of Jesus' Passion.[28]

It is noteworthy that none of the existing texts of these Nahuatl *autos* gives much hint as to the type of scenery or what sort of building the plays were performed in. Horcasitas devotes much attention to the matter but acknowledges the lack of firm documentation. What little is known derives largely from Franciscan sources, especially from sixteenth-century eyewitnesses like Motolinía and Antonio Ciudad Real. Dominicans Bartolomé de Las Casas and Diego Durán left a few terse but useful clues, while the Augustinian friars left the least.[29]

Notwithstanding, the sixteenth-century Dominican evangelizers in Zapotec-Mixtec Oaxaca certainly sponsored native spectacles just as assiduously and enthusiastically as the Franciscans. Eleanor Friend Sleight has

Fig. 6.3 Detail, mural, south wall of the convento church of San Miguel, Ixmiquilpan, Hidalgo. Photograph by Jorge Pérez de Lara.

recounted how the Mixtec Indians performed a ritualized dance celebrating with weapons and mock violence their victory over the neighboring Zapotecs, which they reenacted every year in the patio of the Dominican convento at Cuilapan.[30] It was still being performed in the seventeenth century when witnessed by Fray Francisco de Burgoa. The Dominican chronicler described the dance admiringly, observing that even though it had now a more Christianized message, overtly paying homage to Santiago Matamoros the conqueror of paganism, the Indians had not foresworn its original intention, "having rehearsed for nearly two hundred years without forgetting the triumphant victories of their ancestors."[31]

In spite of Augustinian documentary reticence, a spectacle similar to what Burgoa described in Cuilapan may also have been performed in Ixmiquilpan, Hidalgo, in the late 1560s. In 1538 the Augustinian friars arrived in this northern buffer community consisting of friendly Otomí Indians who had traditionally served the Aztecs by protecting the empire from the savage nomadic Chichimeca tribes in the as yet uncolonized north. As Donna Pierce has demonstrated with much circumstantial evidence, confrontation with the Chichimecs, a matter reaching crisis after 1549 when the discovery of silver in the region began to attract more and more Spanish settlers to this isolated frontier, provided the subject matter for perhaps the most unusual and dazzling set of murals in all colonial Mexico. Moreover, these murals were painted not upon patio or cloister walls but uniquely within the convento church itself. They were later covered with whitewash and forgotten for four hundred years, only to be accidentally revealed during church repairs in 1960.[32]

The Ixmiquilpan convento church was first constructed between 1550 and the early 1560s, planned by the same Fray Andrés de Mata who designed the Augustinian convento at Actopan.[33] Along both sides of the nave from entrance portal to chancel arch spreads this series of brightly colored scenes of human warriors fighting with each other and also with mythical centaurlike semihumans. The figures on the south nave wall are drawn lifesize and even larger, and are engaged in such violent interaction that Pierce has labeled it the "battle wall." Those on the north side are depicted much smaller and seem mostly to be taking captives. She calls this the "triumph" wall (figs. 6.2–6.6).

The human figures are all drawn in an awkward European Renaissance contrapposto style. The artist was clearly fascinated by his newly learned but still unmastered ability to depict his warriors twisted in tour de force back view with foreshortened feet (fig. 6.2). On the other hand, he seems not to have applied the chiaroscuro modeling manner I have adduced to the school of Pedro de Gante. Instead, the artist resorted to perhaps a more native display of vibrant colors, predominantly light blue, yellow ochre, and russet red. While the scenes are separated by the piers of each nave bay, they are nonetheless unified by a giant leafy tendril, colored blue, that seems to wind through and connect all the images together in a continuous frieze. In the by-now standardized manner of tequitqui art, this tendril is composed of mixed swag and acanthus-like forms derived from

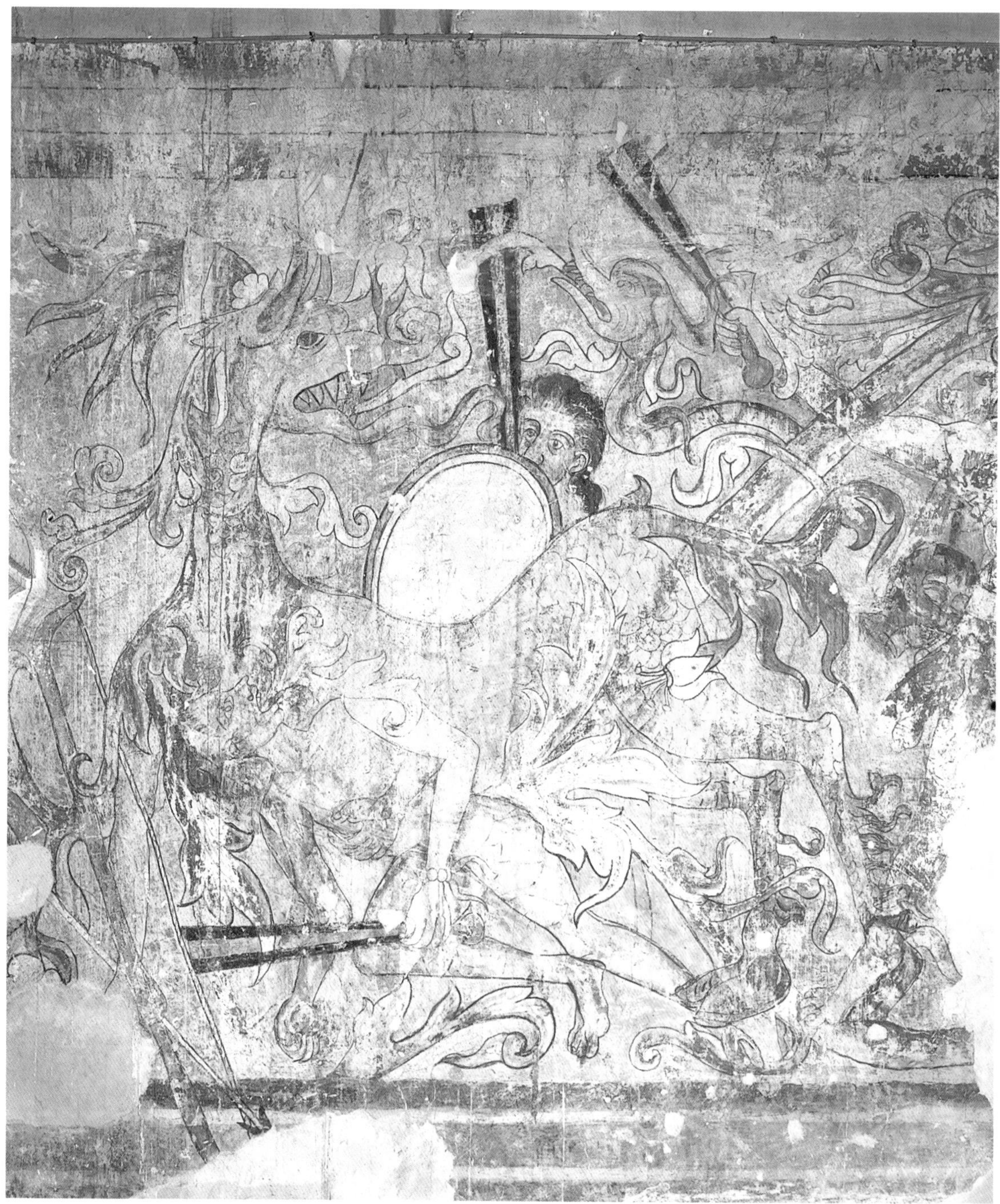

Fig. 6.4 Detail, mural, south wall of the convento church of San Miguel, Ixmiquilpan, Hidalgo. Photograph by Jorge Pérez de Lara.

European classical conventions as in the decoration of borders in printed books.

The most striking aspect of these murals, however, is the depicted dress of the battling figures. Without a trace of European trappings, each wears the garb and bears the weapon of a preconquest Indian warrior. One group appears to be uniformly attired in costumes made from jaguar and coyote skins, just like the elite guard of the Aztec empire. Others are nude except for loin cloths. The costumed warriors are also armed with typical Aztec obsidian-edged slashing swords called *macanas,* while their half-naked opponents all carry bows and arrows, a weapon that Pierce has argued with much evidence was a special favorite of the Chichimecs.[34]

On the "battle wall" of the Ixmiquilpan nave, severed heads fly through the air as the costumed warriors successfully slash away at their archer adversaries. Curling scrolls, Indian symbols for speech, pour from the gladiators' lips, no doubt signifying screams and curses. In one scene a sandaled centaur with bow and arrow and a trophy head hanging from his belt has lost his own head, which spouts blue-colored gore (fig. 6.3). Another horselike man-beast with a fire-breathing dragon head engages two naked macana-bearing warriors, one of whom he grasps around the waist and attempts to carry off (fig. 6.4).

Curiously, the binding blue acanthus tendril that meanders through all the scenes on both sides of the nave seems often to be reinfused by blue-colored material leaking from open wounds, severed heads, mouths, and even an anus. One is reminded here of another bloody Indian battle mural found at Cacaxtla near Tlaxcala, painted probably seven centuries earlier in the preconquest Terminal-Classic period but illustrating similarly dressed warriors some of whom are likewise dripping blue-colored gore. Perhaps in both instances, this anomaly refers to the indigenous tradition of reciprocal sacrifice where human blood is offered to the divine in return for crop-sustaining rain.[35] Indeed, the color blue employed so extensively here seems to have as much symbolic as decorative intent, perhaps even signifying *tonalli,* the vital force of Nahua natural science, contained not only in blood and water but also in seeds, semen, human breath, and all other body fluids and excrescences, which the Indians believed to animate the cosmos.[36] Furthermore, this same blue tendril also sprouts flowers from which more victorious warriors likewise dressed in animal costumes emerge to subdue the common enemy (fig. 6.5).

Why, Donna Pierce has asked, are these murals apparently so devoid of any overt Christian symbols? How could the Augustinian friars have permitted such blatant expression of indigenous "pagan" subject matter, especially within the sacred confines of their most holy church? Along with Mexican scholars Abelardo Carrillo y Gariel and Elena Estrada de Gerlero, she concludes that the Ixmiquilpan murals do in fact conceal a Christian lesson, a *psychomachia,* or cosmic struggle between the allegorical forces of good and evil disguised as a battle between the Christianized Otomí and the uncivilized pagan Chichimecs.[37] This would have been a timely and appropriate rationale

Fig. 6.5 Detail, mural, north wall of the convento church of San Miguel, Ixmiquilpan, Hidalgo. Photograph by Jorge Pérez de Lara.

Fig. 6.6 Detail, mural, south wall of the convento church of San Miguel, Ixmiquilpan, Hidalgo. Photograph by Jorge Pérez de Lara.

on the part of the Augustinian friars who in 1569 were being called upon to sanction an all-out "war of fire and blood" [*guerra de fuego y a sangre*] against the savage Chichimecs.[38]

The roots of such a Manichean allegory can be traced to the earliest wellsprings of Christianity in Middle Eastern Zoroastrianism, which as Pierce meticulously documents, became a popular propaganda subject in the woodcut prints circulated by both Catholics and Protestants in Europe during the sixteenth century. One is also reminded of a parallel example in classical antiquity, the sculpted *Battle of Lapiths and Centaurs* in the pediment of the fifth-century B.C.E. Parthenon where the mythical Lapiths exemplify the "good" Athenians, and the half horse–half man centaurs are the "evil" Persians whom the Athenians had recently defeated at the Battle of Marathon.

While the Parthenon sculptures could hardly have been known to the Augustinian friars, they did have this in common with the Ixmiquilpan murals: neither probably represented actual battles but rather mythicized theatrical spectacles performed in reminiscence of such battles in the temple precincts. I submit that the Otomí Indians of Ixmiquilpan at one or more times during the late 1560s and early 1570s also put on a mock-battle pageant, perhaps coincident with those aforementioned conferences being currently convened to deal with the Chichimec threat. For the same reason, Pierce speculated that the murals were painted between 1569 and 1572.[39] I add only that the friars, in apparent gratitude for Otomí military support, allowed native painters the unique and special privilege of recording their own native celebration dance in full regalia, comprehended however as a dualistic Christian allegory. And what better place to insure and reinforce such an association than within the Christian church itself?[40]

Figure 6.6 shows the first mural on the south wall of the church just inside the main portal under the choir balcony. In the upper or lunette portion, a rampant jaguar faces an eagle with wings spread wide while a second jaguar sits beside an organ cactus at far right. The first two figures flank an abraded escutcheon and also a topographical hieroglyph that seems to exemplify a local landmark. Pierce has argued that these images refer to contemporaneous Otomí military captains who were rewarded by being granted special Spanish titles and coats-of-arms. She does not venture an explanation, however, for the two curious volute symbols sharply outlined just above the cactus at the peak of the lunette arch. These emblems, looking like slips of coiled paper with decorative flourishes on the curls, bear remarkable resemblance to what Jeanette Favrot Peterson has identified as the "bee and song-scroll" motif, possibly representing the signatures of artists—and, as I argue, the presence of dancers, singers, and actors.

In other words, these innocuous-looking signs at the top of what was probably the first mural intended to be viewed in the series, were the Indian artists' way of proclaiming that the following scenes were representations of a spectacular native procession, perhaps even serving as backdrop to a unique theatrical neixcuitilli.

While circumstances have certainly changed since the sixteenth century, it might still be relevant to point out that murals showing the traditional Zuni Indian corn dance (having this time little to do with Christian ritual) are being painted by native artist Alex Seowtewa and son on the interior walls of Our Lady of Guadalupe. Built originally as a Franciscan mission in 1629, this Roman Catholic church is on the Zuni Indian reservation in southwestern New Mexico.

For another fiesta the same Indian residents of the city of Tlaxcala represented the day of Our Lady's Assumption [August 15], in the year fifteen hundred thirty-eight in my presence, and I sang the principal Mass because the fathers of Saint Francis asked me, and with me celebrated three choirs of Indian singers accompanied by an organ . . . and twelve expert flute players. . . . There were the apostles, or as the Indians represented them . . . (and it is to be supposed that no Spaniard understood nor mixed in the acts which they performed), and he who represented the Virgin Mary was an Indian, and all those who did understand were Indians. They spoke only in their own language, and all the actions and movements they made were with utmost prudence and devotion, and in that manner they aroused the audience who would see what was represented, along with the playing of the organ and much singing and music of the flutes when it was time for the elevation of she who was represented, Our Lady in a church-like setting [nave], from stage [*tablado*] until another height that they have fashioned into heaven, all of which was observed in a grand patio, according to our opinion by more than eighty thousand persons.

Fray Bartolomé de Las Casas, Apologética Historia de las Indias, ca. 1562

Chapter 7

STAGE AND SCENERY

After thirty years of thinking and writing about the origins of perspective illusionism so peculiar to the arts of Western civilization, I have come to the conclusion that popular street theater in medieval Europe was a primary, perhaps the prime, incentive pushing painters and sculptors to find ever more exacting ways to make their images look and feel as if "alive."

Indeed, both public theater and the visual arts during the late Middle Ages were called upon to alleviate the profound pessimism and depression European Christians sensed after the failure of

Fig. 7.1 Church of Santa Maria Sopra Minerva (formerly a temple dedicated to the Roman goddess Minerva), Assisi, Italy.

the Crusades and the bitter schism within the holy church (not to mention the trauma of the Black Death and recurrent plagues after 1348). More than ever, Christians felt the need for tactile evidence that God was immanent in their desperately uncertain lives. This same pessimism was shared by the Observant friars especially as the apocalyptic sixteenth century approached. What the missionaries in America in fact wanted to achieve by their evangelization of the Indians was nothing less than the redemption of the whole human race. God, they hoped, might be impressed and allay his final judgment if the last of the infidels in this world could be converted. Not only should illusionistic images help convince them of Christian truth but also the Indians themselves must invest their natural talent for spectacle and imitate these images through live impersonation. God would surely be pleased to see the Indians rehearse his moral admonitions in terpsichorean tableaux vivants.

What might have been in the mind's eye of the early missionaries as they watched Indian spectacles and thought of co-opting them for didactic purposes? To reconstruct such a mental picture, it will be useful to visit vicariously the small Italian hill town of Assisi, the birthplace of Saint Francis and the mother convent of the Franciscan order and major Mecca for Christians ever hoping to discover God's divine presence in late medieval Europe.

The great basilica honoring Saint Francis in Assisi was begun and completed in the thirteenth century as sepulcher for the town's favorite son who had been canonized in 1228, only two years after his death. Within months after confirmation of Saint Francis's miraculous stigmata had spread through Europe, thousands of pilgrims flocked to the new shrine in order to touch his tomb, witness his relics, and perhaps just as importantly, to re-create the events of his life for themselves as street performers in public laude.

To stimulate further these popular responses, the interiors of the upper and lower churches of the two-tiered basilica were painted from top to bottom with fresco cycles narrating Christian stories and theological themes by various Italian artists. The most popular cycle was and still is that of the life of Saint Francis himself, painted at the very end of the thirteenth century. Twenty-eight scenes follow in left-to-right sequence around both sides of the lower nave in the upper church, to be read like a modern comic strip. They are arranged in groups of three on each side of the first three bay walls and in groups of five on the two sides of the entrance bay. Each event of the saint's life is depicted as if it were an individual stage set of a miracle play, and all are framed together under a fictive modillion cornice that runs around both sides of the church, very much reminiscent of a real cornice that covers the colonnaded portal of an ancient Roman temple just down the street, still standing as a converted Christian church called Santa Maria Sopra Minerva (fig. 7.1).

In the very first painted scene of Saint Francis's atavistic life (the left-most in fig. 7.2), we see a citizen of Assisi laying down his cloak before the young charismatic, right in front of that very Santa Maria Sopra Minerva Church. What we have in this fresco, I believe, is not so much an imagined recapitulation of what

Fig. 7.2
Scenes from the Life of Saint Francis, by an anonymous Tuscan painter (possibly Giotto but more likely the so-called Master of the Saint Cecilia Legend), late thirteenth century. Upper church, Basilica of Saint Francis, Assisi.

happened to Saint Francis in true life, but what the artist and contemporaneous viewers would have witnessed in a theatrical representation of the event performed in the public square before this familiar local landmark.[1]

What the Assisi painter ingeniously did was to stretch the architectural motif of Santa Maria Sopra Minerva's classical cornice around all the painted scenes as a reminder that each was really a tableau vivant taking place in the Assisi piazza.[2] The painter of this fictive architecture (with solomonic columns alluding to Saint Peter's Basilica in Rome) may have been Giotto di Bondone of Florence (ca. 1270–1337). In any case he would seem to have been familiar with ancient Greek and Roman theories of stage design based on the science of optics and called *scenographia* in antiquity.[3] Here is what the first-century B.C.E. Roman architect Vitruvius had to say about scenographic illusion:

> Scenography is also the shading of the front and the retreating sides, and the correspondence of all lines to the center of a circle. . . . For to begin with: Agatharcus at Athens, when Aeschylus was presenting a tragedy, was in control of the stage, and wrote a commentary about it . . . in order to show how, if a fixed center is taken for the outward glance of the eyes and the projection of the radii, we must follow these lines in accordance with a natural law, such that from an uncertain object, uncertain images may give the appearance of buildings in the scenery of the stage, and how what is figured on vertical and plane surfaces can seem to recede in one part and project in another.[4]

Looking closely now at the fictive projecting modillions of his painted cornice, we notice that the artist has angled them so that they

Fig. 7.3 Perspective overlay, *Scenes from the Life of Saint Francis,* late thirteenth century. Upper church, Basilica of Saint Francis, Assisi.

Fig. 7.4 Giotto, *Scenes from the Life of the Virgin Mary [Expulsion of Joachim from the Temple; Presentation of the Virgin]*, ca 1305. Arena Chapel, Padua.

appear illusionistically to converge over the center of each group of three scenes (fig. 7.3). The perspective convergence at this point compels the viewer to stand fixed in the middle of the bay and observe the scenes as if they were being performed sequentially on separate stages behind a single colonnaded proscenium.

Art historian Charles Parkhurst has further shown that the painted background architecture in the early fourteenth-century frescoes surely by Giotto in the Arena Chapel, Padua, and pictorially narrating the lives of the Virgin and Christ, actually represents convertible stage props that could be reassembled into different settings from one narrative scene to the next (fig. 7.4).[5] In other words, the mural paintings of both Assisi and the Arena Chapel, long considered as the formative models of all subsequent narrative representation in Western Renaissance art, seem to have been motivated not so much by attempts to imagine the past but rather to represent the illusion of a stage setting for a contemporaneous miracle play. Even southern Spain was touched by this influence as early as the fourteenth century. In a fresco showing the coronation of the Virgin by an anonymous Andalusian artist in the Basilica of Santa Maria de la Asunción in Arcos de la Frontiera, for example, we see a fictive row of converging modillions below, implying that the viewer is observing the scene as if it were raised up on a classical architectural stage centered before him (fig. 7.5).

Italian laude and Spanish *autos* were frequently performed in front of or within church portals. So popular was the portal-proscenium in making spectators believe they were eyewitnessing the holy stories that painters and

Fig. 7.5 *Coronation of the Virgin,* by an anonymous Andalusian painter, early fourteenth century. Basilica of Santa Maria de la Asunción, Arcos de la Frontiera, Spain.

sculptors quickly borrowed and conventionalized the association in their own religious painting. Illusionary Gothic doorways replete with trompe l'oeil grisaille statue niches were often depicted as framing proscenia around the sacred events, such as figure 7.6, a late fifteenth-century panel from the so-called Cambrai Altarpiece showing scenes of Jesus' Passion by a follower of Rogier van der Weyden now in the Prado Museum, Madrid. The fictive framing format of this painting, apparently invented by Rogier in Flanders, soon became quite popular in Spain. Queen Isabella herself commissioned similar examples for the Capilla Real in Granada.[6] In Italy, the more classical rounded arch was favored over the Gothic proscenium, but still for the same purpose as painted by Pintoricchio for example, ca. 1480, in the Piccolomini Library, Siena, depicting scenes in the life of Pope Pius II (fig. 7.7). Note how the painter rendered a fictive archway as a *frons scenae* standing before the panoramic narrative sequence with the perspective deliberately exaggerated and differentiated from the scene behind so the viewer might imagine it taking place in a Roman-style amphitheater.

Spain too had its own rich classical theatrical heritage, perhaps the best-preserved Roman theater in all the ancient empire, in Mérida, Extremadura (fig. 7.8). While probably not looking so restored as it does today, the remembered image of the old theater with its trabeated frons scenae may well have been in the mind's eye of those Extremeño missionary friars from the Franciscan province of San Gabriel as they contemplated appropriate backdrops for the sacred *autos* they planned to have performed in the New World. After all, the friars maintained that their enterprise was but a divinely mandated extension of the apostolic conversion of Rome.

One of the first artistic conventions apparently taught to Indian painters in Pedro de Gante's school of the arts at San José de los Naturales was the framing of convento murals in fictive classical entablatures. This convention quickly became commonplace in the mural paintings of all the mendicant orders, as on the cloister corridor walls of the Augustinian convento at Acolman, where painted classical columns and tequitqui frame scenes of Jesus' Passion, or in another example at Charo, where fictive pilasters similarly frame scenes of Augustinian martyrdoms (figs. 7.9, 7.10). While surely copied from printed bookplates (which themselves recall theatrical prosceniums), the original iconographical inspiration for these mural framings was in scenographic association with Christian *autos*. I submit that the friars of all the orders were aware of this and intended the murals to serve as backdrops to the religious processions of their Indian converts as they passed through the various ritual spaces of their conventos. In fact, even the tequitqui borders of these murals are an artistic offspring of the fictive hanging fabrics painted below the Assisi Saint Francis fresco cycle, which in turn signified actual tapestries and carpets hung out of windows and over balustrades and balconies during festivals when processions and *autos* were taking place in the public street—a custom still observed in Spain and other Catholic countries of Europe and Latin America.[7] Fray Diego Valadés admired the same custom among the converted Indians. In his *Rhetorica Christiana* he observed how the natives "weave quite ample carpets [*tapetes*] with . . . flowers glued to reed mats, and they also draw all sorts of forms, figures and histories, in the same manner that one sees in the tapestries of Flanders [*belluatis Flandricis*]. Then, they cover the steps and walls of the sacred buildings and chapels with these carpets and adorn them with various figures made from weavings of flowers that appear very alive."[8]

Motolinía tells us that the four *autos* celebrating Saint John's Day in Tlaxcala in 1538 were performed in the vicinity of the Franciscan convento at Tlaxcala, and all were similarly staged on "gracefully adorned and embellished platforms," which he called by either of two Spanish words, *tablados* or *cadalsos*. According to Horcasitas, both these terms might refer to a raised wooden scaffold with a vertical frame supporting a curtain.[9] This superstructure might even be divided laterally into separate spaces for sequential scenes or vertically with another second-story platform or balcony onto which actors could climb from a ladder as if ascending to "heaven."[10] There might even be a trap door in the floor of the main platform below, opening to a lower space for dramatic descent into "hell."[11] If Horcasitas's reconstruction of the Tlaxcala cadalso is correct, it would seem that it was similar in form to the stages used for miracle plays everywhere in Europe at the time, in Italy called *edifizi,* and perhaps with interchangeable sets like the background "architecture" in Giotto's Arena Chapel paintings.[12] In any case, the cadalsos to which Motolinía referred were temporary and movable, and could be set up ad hoc in any number of convenient places in the streets of the neighboring town as well as on the convento premises.[13]

Fig. 7.6 *Crucifixion,* by a follower of Rogier van der Weyden. Prado Museum, Madrid, late fifteenth century. Photograph from Alinari-Art Resource.

Perhaps most importantly, Horcasitas has observed that a number of convento murals, for example *Death and Coronation of the Virgin* from the lower cloister corridor in Epazoyucán (see fig. 5.8), are actually representations of theatrical scenes, with figural poses, costumes, and props derived directly from those of the actors and actions in contemporaneous Indian neixcuitilli, just as in all likelihood were the frescoes of the life of Saint Francis in the Basilica at Assisi and in *Life of the Virgin* by Giotto in the Arena Chapel, Padua.[14]

Certain architectural spaces where Indians could assemble outdoors were standard features in the conventos of all three orders since the early days of the sixteenth century: a portería with a narthex-like arcade as vestibule to the friary; a patio before the church surrounded by a wall with open-arched posas at the angles; and an open chapel of various sizes and shapes fronting on the patio and adjacent to the church.[15]

The initial reason for all these structured spaces, of course, was to accommodate the thousands of Indians who could not immediately fit into the enclosed church, hence it was necessary to service the multitudes out-of-doors. By the second half of the sixteenth century, however, the great conversion had pretty much run its course. Most of the urban Indians were by now enrolled in the parishes and professed at least superficial allegiance to the Catholic faith. "Paganism" for all intents and purposes was relegated to covert cave-shrines in the remote back-water. Furthermore, the native population as a whole had dramatically and tragically declined due to epidemic diseases, while at the same time the mendicant missionaries themselves were under increasing pressure from the new Spanish King Philip II (crowned in 1556) and the new Archbishop of Mexico Alonso de Montúfar (appointed in 1554) to cede their control of native religious affairs to the secular, that is, parish churches under diocesan episcopal authority in the towns.[16]

Paradoxically, even as half of the original native population had died during the plagues of the 1540s and 1570s, and the autonomy of the mendicants was more and more curtailed after 1556, the friars chose just this time to aggrandize their old conventos and to have their cloisters and

Fig. 7.7 Pintoricchio, *Scene from the Life of Pope Pius II,* ca. 1480. Piccolomini Library, Duomo, Siena. Photograph from Alinari-Art Resource.

patios covered with permanent mural paintings. How is this to be explained? What was the continuing function of these ostentatious convento embellishments once the diminishing Indian population was converted and already in its second and third generation as practicing Christians? As John McAndrew remarked as he puzzled over the grandiose size of many of the Mexican open chapels, "Why build [such structures] for the few survivors who did not need them?"[17]

Meanwhile in contemporaneous Europe, the Catholic Church in response to the Lutheran Reformation was ever more suspicious of unsupervised religious expression on the part of the laity. In 1545 Pope Paul III called together the famous synod of Counter-Reformation known as the Council of Trent. Meeting off and on for the next eighteen years, the council, made up of a large contingent of Spanish delegates including the brother of the first viceroy of New Spain, issued a bevy of decrees demanding greater than ever Catholic conformity. Among the council's expressed concerns was that the conventional forms of religious art and public spectacle be brought more strictly under the church's ideological guidance. In the Americas at this time, no doubt the friars began to worry that Christian spectacles performed by Indians in the secular towns were becoming a bit too disorderly and out of the convento's control.[18]

In any event, after the 1560s, as the mendicant orders were increasingly challenged by lay settlers demanding more access to Indian labor and the secular episcopate as it extended its control over Indian education, the friars sought to gather their still-loyal converts more closely to the bosom of the convento. To do

Fig. 7.8 Ancient Roman theater, Mérida, Spain.

this, it was important that the architecture and decor of the conventos be made conducive to the Indians' obsession with religious spectacle. The friars hoped to entice the natives to hold more of their rituals and processions on convento premises rather than in the licentious byways of the worldly towns.

I now examine how the open chapel in the convento patio metamorphosed into a unique indigenous Indian theater. Fernando Horcasitas has already suggested that the open chapel offered both acoustical and visual advantages for the staging of *autos*. Many open chapels did indeed have space enough for setting up elaborate cadalsos, like that which also served as the portería to the Franciscan convento at Cuernavaca (fig. 7.11).[19] The great open chapel at Maní in the Yucatán might have been another example (see fig. 3.10). Originally the vast vaulted opening was divided into two stories by a wooden balcony, an ideal stage setting for miracle plays. Ciudad Real recorded a number of organized Indian spectacles performed for him and the commissary general of the Franciscan order, Fray Alonso Ponce, when they visited the Yucatán during 1588. At Tinum, the local Maya presented a "dance of the Moors" inside the ramada before their church. At Maní, the friars were greeted by Indians not only singing and dancing but also putting on a puppet show.[20] That the friars were so taken by such theatrical spectacles in the late sixteenth century should not be surprising. Everywhere in Western Europe at that time there was increased interest in public theater. The popularity of the commedia dell'arte in Italy, for example, had inspired the planning of more and more permanent theater buildings with elaborate stages and stage machinery. This was especially true in Spain where the *corral*, similar in form to the famous Shakespearean Globe Theater in England, was developing as a distinctive feature of civic architecture for the popular public performance of farsias. Indeed, in the last quarter of the sixteenth century, Spain was about to enter its golden age of theatrical production, introduced by the great dramatist Lope de Vega (1562–1635), author of nearly two thousand plays. Not to be outdone by such secular attention, the Roman Catholic Church, especially after the Council of Trent, began to stress the need for more theatricality in the presentation of the Mass, the inclusion of instrumental music, live reenactments of holy stories, and dramatic lighting and stage effects designed in the very architecture of the churches themselves.[21]

Motolinía's account of the fiesta of Saint John the Baptist on Monday, June 24, 1538, states that the first of the four sequential *autos* took place at the starting point of the Indians' procession, presumably in the patio proper of the Tlaxcala convento and perhaps before one of the small vaulted chapels mentioned earlier by the Franciscan as having been built there by the Indians. But exactly where in the compound, and whether any vestiges of these structures survive, has troubled scholars and archaeologists ever since.[22] A few pages later in the same chapter, Motolinía described one of these chapels thus:

> For Easter the Indians had completed the chapel in the patio, which, when finished, was a magnificent structure, which they

Fig. 7.9 *Crucifixion*, mural in the upper cloister corridor, convento of San Agustín, Acolman, Mexico. Photograph by Jorge Pérez de Lara.

called Bethlehem. On the outside of the chapel, they painted pictures in fresco in four days, because then the rains would never efface them. In one space of [the] chapel's exterior they painted the works of the first three days of creation of the world and in another space the works of [the] other three days. In one of the remaining two spaces is the "Tree of Jesse" with the lineage of the Mother of God very beautifully placed over it. In the other space is Our Father St. Francis. Elsewhere in the chapel is a picture of the Church, His Holiness, the Pope, cardinals, bishops and so on; and next to it a picture of the Emperor, kings and knights. The Spaniards who have seen this chapel say that it ranks with the most graceful piece of its manner in Spain. The chapel has well-shaped arches and two choirs, one for the singers and one for the musicians with wind instruments. All this was produced in six months and thus, like all the churches, the chapel is very ornate and well arranged.[23]

What Motolinía tells us above is that on the outer facade *(parte de fuera)* there was enough solid wall space *(octavos)* for four large paintings, two framing the central opening of the chapel and the other two flanking the arches on the left and right sides, plus other unidentified solid spaces elsewhere for at least six or seven more images.

The still-standing Rosary Chapel, with its three beautiful Isabelline arches at the western entrance to the Tlaxcala patio (see fig. 3.1), does not quite match this description nor has any trace of the murals described by Motolinía ever been found here or anywhere else in the Tlaxcala convento. Nevertheless, precise identification is not so important as what Motolinía further hints about how the Indians venerated their Tlaxcala capilla de Indios, surrounding its entrance with holy images just as traditionally demarcated sacred precincts in preconquest days. As Mesoamerican Indians were also

Fig. 7.10 *Martyrdoms of Augustinian Friars,* cloister corridor of the convento of San Miguel, Charo, Michoacán.

wont to do with sacred places and fetishes (like rubber game balls), they gave the chapel a pious name, Bethlehem [*Belén*]. Interestingly, the word in Hebrew means "house of bread," while "Tlaxcala" in Nahuatl means "the place where tortillas are made." This bilingual pun on "bread" is significant because tortillas bore the same sacramental significance for preconquest Indians, even having the same round shape and symbolic association with human flesh and sacrifice, as the Christian Host. We have here yet another instance of the missionary tactic of expedient selection where the friars would choose from the vast store of Christian typological lessons a particular story that would resonate with the Indians' own local history and traditions. Motolinía's vivid recall of how the Tlaxcala chapel was used as a backdrop for sacred images, however, would almost seem to fit the form and one of the apparent functions of the vast, imperial Roman-scale open-chapel at Dominican Teposcolula, Oaxaca (fig. 7.12). The diagonally extended splays of the Teposcolula chapel even have ruled panels for convenient attachment of painted lienzos, indicating that this chapel too was used for the presentation of didactic pictures (fig. 7.13).

Fray Augustín Dávila Padilla, a late sixteenth-century Dominican historian chronicling the evangelization of the Mixtec and Zapotec Indians in Oaxaca, provides a further graphic example of how the friars intended the chapels from the beginning to serve as theaters for the dramatic presentation of images.[24] Although he did not mention Teposcolula, Dávila Padilla recounted how Fray Gonzalo Luzero, one of the original Dominican apostles and founder of the Dominican mission in Oaxaca in 1530, carried detachable lienzos "to whatever city" he visited.[25] According to the chronicler, Fray Gonzalo, fluent in the Mixtec language, would begin his presentation by holding up a three-dimensional model of the earth (probably an armillary sphere) large enough for all his Indian audience to see, and then, imitating God the prime mover of the universe, the Dominican would illustrate with sweeping hand how the cosmos worked like a machine, with sun, moon, and stars all revolving uniformly around the earth.

Next, Fray Gonzalo would turn to one of two large painted lienzos he had set up at each side of the chapel. This was a depiction of the Last Judgment with God the Father enthroned in glory at the top and adoring angels and saints at his feet. To God's lower right were more adoring Indians. Images of their souls were also shown being wafted to eternal paradise to the accompaniment of angelic music. At God's left hand, sinful Indians who refused conversion were represented burning in hell and being horribly tormented by demons.

After explaining the eschatological implications of this image, Fray Gonzalo would turn and point his stick at the other lienzo. As described by Dávila Padilla, this must have been an extraordinary painting indeed. It is now unfortunately lost, although some traces of its fire-and-brimstone subject matter may be discerned in a faded later sixteenth-century mural depicting the miracle of the Virgin of the Rosary still partially visible in the Dominican convento at Tetela de Volcán (see chap. 8).[26] Dávila Padilla surely had seen Fray Gonzalo's lienzo firsthand, for he recalled admiringly every detail. Here follows my loose translation, necessarily edited since the chronicler's quaint medieval Spanish would otherwise be incomprehensible in English:

> [The lienzo depicted] . . . a great body of water signifying the movement [inconstancy] and lack of solidity in the present life. In these waters were two large boats that the Indians know by the name of canoes, carrying different kinds of people and [following different] directions. In one boat which was traveling toward the top [of the picture], were Indian men and women with rosaries in their hands, some mortifying themselves, others with hands together praying, and all accompanied by angels with paddles; [the angels] gave the paddles to the Indians in order to row in search of Glory which would be discovered at the top of the lienzo, the message of which [Fray Gonzalo had already explained] in the other complementary painting. There were many demons beside the boat, trying to restrain it and fighting against the angels and those Indians armed with the holy rosary. Some [demons] with fierce faces struggled on, others turned away dazed and exhausted to make it to the other boat where they [felt themselves] contented and happy just as if they were

Fig. 7.11 Open chapel–portería at the convento of the Anunciación de Nuestra Señora, Cuernavaca, Morelos, looking south.

Fig. 7.12 Open chapel at the convento of Saints Pedro y Pablo, Teposcolula, Oaxaca, looking east from the patio.

home [in hell]. Some of the Indian men and women [in this second boat] were getting drunk on large glasses of wine; others were fighting and killing each other, and others were doing dishonorable acts with men or women. . . . Angels flying above this infernal boat offered rosaries to its unfortunate [occupants] whose heads were bent over and focused on their pleasures, turning their backs to the angels' entreaties on behalf of God. The wretched [Indians] fixed their eyes and hands [only] on the wine glasses or on the women that the demons offered. The demons then paddled this other boat with much contentment and intensity, indicating their eagerness to arrive at the terrible entrance to hell which was [depicted] beginning at the bottom corner of the painting and extended to the other side. With much sentiment and vivacity this servant of God [Fray Gonzalo] showed the sympathy he held and should give to the damned, [explaining how] they were envious of the fortunate [in heaven] who were secure in eternal happiness. After the Indians had listened to the significance of these paintings, they conferred amongst themselves, the brighter ones repeating [the message] to the less so. The blessed father invited all to his sermon, and with the sentiment and spirit of an apostle, gave the most marvelous and lively [interpretation] to the picture.[27]

The open chapel at Teposcolula, with its magnificent and diaphanous Gothic rib-vaulted ceiling just recently restored, may be the most sophisticated example of sixteenth-century European-style architecture in all Mexico and Mesoamerica (fig. 7.14). Robert Mullen has attributed its elegant design to Dominican Fray Francisco Marin, ca. 1548–55.[28] Interestingly, an earlier, smaller open chapel on the same site had first to be torn down, and the materials from it, including carved column capitals evincing a more humble style (and conventional use), were reset into the decor of the contemporaneously reconstructed and much-overwhelmed facade of the convento church.[29] The sheer size of the Teposcolula open chapel and the fact that it was built at the very time when the local population was decreasing suggest that it was planned for events even more theatrically ambitious than Fray Gonzalo's animated lectures.[30]

While the arched openings on either side of the central sanctuary at Teposcolula were no doubt spaces for musicians and singers just as at Tlaxcala, mezzanine floors on wooden joists were also inserted behind the back wall of each of these side openings facing only into the central sanctuary, thus out of sight from any viewers in front (the author is pointing to that on the left side in fig. 7.14). These probably had some offstage special effects function from which ropes and pulleys could be manipulated to raise or lower objects and even actors "miraculously" onto the central stage.[31] Fray Agustín de Vetancurt, for example, recorded a neixcuitilli performed in the chapel at San José de los Naturales in Mexico city where, during the Feast of the Ascension, the Indians "raise the *Señor* by means of ropes [*con cordeles*] and a cloud receives him."[32]

Franciscan Fray Antonio de Ciudad Real described in even more detail a special effect that he witnessed during a neixcuitilli celebrating the fiesta of Epiphany by Indians in the patio of the Franciscan convento at Tlajomulco de Zúñiga, Jalisco, during December 1587.[33] The Indians had built a *Belén,* with images of Joseph, Mary, and the Christ child (*Niño;* unclear whether impersonated by actors or only by effigies) near the portal of the patio and then stretched a rope from the church to a nearby hill outside. To the rope was fixed an imitation star made of tinsel *(oropel),* which Indians hid behind "small wooden towers" *(torrecillas de madera)* manipulated by pulling two more ropes, slowly guiding the star on a trolley in the direction of the manger while actors impersonating the three kings followed it into the patio. Finally, another actor dressed as an angel was revealed *(se descubrió)* rising from one of the "towers" to announce to the audience that the fiesta was concluded.

We even have a crude picture of such a "wooden tower" and perhaps even the native word for it in the late sixteenth-century Aztec Codex Aubin (fig. 7.15). Three times on separate folios of the codex the death of Fray Pedro de Gante in 1572 is mentioned in the Latin-scripted Nahuatl text with Aztec glyph for the year Two Flint, giving a description of an Indian spectacle in commemoration that took place in the patio before San José de los Naturales, the first open chapel in all the Americas (where Fray Pedro had operated

Fig. 7.13 Open chapel at the convento of Saints Pedro y Pablo, Teposcolula, Oaxaca, looking west toward the patio. Photograph by Jorge Pérez de Lara.

his school of music and the visual arts since the 1530s). The spectacle featured a sham battle between Moors and Christians, including perhaps a representation of the great naval victory at Lepanto the year before when a Christian fleet under Spanish command defeated the Turks in the eastern Mediterranean thus buoying up the flagging spirits of Reformation-riven Catholic Europe.[34] The climax of the drama came when the Christians attacked the Moors ensconced in a structure described in the Nahuatl text both by the loan-word *castillo* and the combined-word *cuauhteohcalli*, which means literally "wooden temple."[35] In the same text, the latter term also referred to the open chapel of San José de los Naturales itself, which decades before had provisionally been made of wood in the manner of a Moorish mosque. One can only surmise that the fictive Moorish castillo erected for this Indian neixcuitilli was either a separate cadalso made to look in some ways like the original wooden open chapel or, more likely, was the open chapel itself, decorated with a wooden superstructure to look like a Moorish castle.

Although the accompanying illustration on folio 58r is crudely drawn (Donald Robertson has characterized the Codex Aubin as representing the "disintegration of native tradition") it does reveal a flattened plan-view of the square convento patio with circular posas at the corners and a two-story boxlike structure in frontal elevation at the center.[36] At ground level of this structure is an arched doorway. The upper tier seems to be a mansard-shaped open framework with two faces peering out, and the whole is crested by a vertical element looking like a tower with feathers or fictive smoke rising from the top.

Not far from Teposcolula and still in Oaxaca state, another grand Dominican open chapel that was once also covered by a Gothic rib-vault can be seen at Coixtlahuaca; it was completed just a year or two before Teposcolula and designed, according to Mullen, by the same Fray Francisco de Marin (fig. 7.16).[37] The entire convento at Coixtlahuaca is built on what was once a native ceremonial platform. However, while the church and friary are in good condition, only the ten-meter high central arch and sanctuary of the open chapel still stands today. Originally, two splayed arches flanked the central arch just as at Teposcolula. The entire chapel adjoined the church at its north side but with no passageway between. Inside the open chapel on its south wall, however, are two arched doorways, a smaller one at ground level and another overhead with threshold some four meters above the ground (within the arched chapel to the right in figure 7.16). Both lead into enclosed rooms linked internally by a stairway. Mullen does not mention them, and McAndrew admitted his perplexity as to their purpose, hypothesizing only that the larger upstairs vaulted chamber might have served as a space for musicians or perhaps a sacristy, but then he dismissed both ideas as illogical. Music would certainly carry poorly from such an enclosed chamber, and whatever could be the usefulness of an external doorway a dozen feet above the ground without an outside staircase?[38] I suggest that these rooms were installed for theatrical reasons only, as places where actors could enter from below and emerge above for special "miraculous" effect. The upper opening, for instance, framed as it is by a fancy arch supported on carved plateresque pilasters, would have made an excellent tabernacle for fictive apparitions, with actors impersonating apotheosized holy personages just like the similarly framed saints depicted in the painted murals in the Actopan stair hall.

Coixtlahuaca and Teposcolula (as well as Yanhuitlán), were Dominican houses near one another in the bleak but beautiful mountains of northern Oaxaca known as the Mixteca Alta. Traveling through this dramatic region (easily traversed today by way of the new superhighway between Puebla and Oaxaca City) one passes through some of the most stunning desert landscape in all Mexico, especially so during late afternoon as the colors of the hills and dry arroyos change from tan to pink to misty purple. This is of course ancient Mixtec country, although the Indians who currently live in Coixtlahuaca speak a language called Chocho; the town was once called Yodzo Coo in Mixtec. Indeed, until the Aztecs renamed it in their own language after brutally subjecting the region in the fifteenth century, Yodzo Coo was a center sacred to all the various Mixtec communities and lineages, regarded as one of the many *Tollans* [places of cattail reeds] where the Indians believed their race was created in primordial times.[39] Moreover, Yodzo Coo may have been one of those special sites to which Mixtec princes, like the renowned twelfth-century warrior hero Eight-Deer-Jaguar-Claw of Tilantongo, were required to visit in order to be legitimized as *teuctli,* or full-fledged lords, and have their noses pierced with a special pendant *yacaxiwi* as a badge of high office.[40]

Interestingly, Yodzo Coo in the Mixtec language means "plain of the snake." Among the various place-name hieroglyphs of the town identified by Mary Elizabeth Smith, one has intertwined serpents with feathers at the ends of their tails.[41] Figure 7.17 is a detail from a 1590 map of the region with a sketch of that very symbol beneath a church positioned on a truncated pyramid identified in Latin letters as "couayxllabaca." The relationship of this entwined serpent symbol to the present convento is further confirmed in situ as a prominent sculptural-relief decoration on the central arch of the open chapel (fig. 7.18). Here we see the same motif of two intertwined serpents with tail-feathers repeated all along the soffit and extrados.

Curiously, this figure has always been identified as a cryptic reference to the pagan god Quetzalcoatl, which is odd because Quetzalcoatl was not a named deity in the Mixtec pantheon, and his nearest Mixtec clone, God Nine-Wind, was never associated with a feathered serpent.[42] In fact, the choice of the feathered-serpent motif as place-sign stems directly from a Mixtec pun also discussed by Smith.[43] In Mixtec, *yodzo* can mean both "plain" and "large feather." Since the Mixteca often employed homonymic punning in their place-names, Yodzo Coo means both "plain of the snake" and "feathered snake." The Dominican friars at Coixtlahuaca had their Indian artists Christianize the symbol by inserting a pelican piercing its side (symbolizing Jesus' similar wound as he suffered on the cross) and inscribing in distinct Latin letters along the body of the top serpent in each of the pairs the acronym INRI [*Iesus Nazarenus, Rex Iudaeorum*].[44]

Like the Yucatán and so much of the Mexican terrain, the Mixteca Alta has many

Fig. 7.14 Open chapel at the convento of Saints Pedro y Pablo, Teposcolula, Oaxaca, view of the interior looking northeast (author is pointing toward the left-side wooden mezzanine). Photograph by Jorge Pérez de Lara.

natural geological caves. As everywhere in preconquest Mesoamerica, these caves played a crucial role in the preconquest religious ideology of the indigenous Oaxaceños. Mixtec rulers, for example, were traditionally buried in a great cave at Chalcatongo. Fray Francisco de Burgoa, seventeenth-century chronicler of the Dominican mission in Oaxaca, actually visited this cave as well as several others in the region. He was much impressed and described in detail how the Indians worshipped their idols inside, filling the caverns with statues and paintings. Concerning the cave at Chalcatongo, he mused that the Mixtecs believed it a mystic gateway to their own pagan counterpart to the classical Elysian fields where the spirits of the dead lords would be revivified in eternal paradise.[45] Indeed, the friars were both in awe and in fear of the anagogical power of these mysterious grottoes, worrying that they continued to tempt the Indians to relapse into idol worship.[46] I propose that one of the reasons the friars had the vaulted open chapels at Coixtlahuaca and Teposcolula built so large was to reinforce these structures in Indian eyes as magnificent alternatives to the pagan cave, wherein the Indians could set up Christian images and perform Christian dances and spectacles in the same anagogical space as in a natural grotto. At Coixtlahuaca, the arched opening to its cave-like chapel was even lined with a "sky-band" of images of open-mouthed serpents, a traditional zoomorphic symbol everywhere in Mesoamerica of the primordial cave.

Fig. 7.15 Detail after fol. 58r, Codex Aubin. Bibliothèque Nationale, Paris. Drawing by Mark Van Stone.

In Hidalgo state far to the northwest of Oaxaca is yet another cavelike open chapel, one painted inside to look like the very bowels of hell itself, adjacent to the Augustinian Convento of San Nicolás de Tolentino, Actopan (fig. 7.19). This huge barrel-vaulted structure is still intact, with its interior covered with images of every sort of infernal punishment, arranged in horizontal registers reminiscent of Mixtec and Aztec codices. A blank space remains in the center of the back wall where a real-life interlocutor, an Augustinian Fray Gonzalo, might have stood to explain the meaning of these grim scenes, which present the same themes as the Dominican's portable lienzos. Just below the soffit of the vault, images of the dead arise from their graves to present themselves before Jesus seated on a rainbow. On either side of the back wall are narrative scenes of Genesis and the Apocalypse. Flanking these on each side wall is a giant leviathan head with open jaws,

Fig. 7.16 Open chapel at the convento of San Juan Bautista, Coixtlahuaca, Oaxaca, looking southeast. Photograph by Jorge Pérez de Lara.

Fig. 7.17 Detail after map of Coixtlahuaca diocese showing the convento raised on a truncated pyramid platform with the entwined-serpent place-sign of the community below, 1590. Drawing by Mark Van Stone.

which again would remind the Indians of a cave, in the process of devouring the souls of the damned, no doubt a deliberate allusion to the bicephalic serpent once sacred to the Indians but now transformed into a two-headed monster-demon (fig. 7.20). Other scenes include torture by humanoid demons wielding iron pincers, here colored bright blue so as to be seen distinctly (and felt kinesthetically) by an audience of Indians identifying with the brown-colored victims (fig. 7.21). The message of how to avoid these grisly torments is summed up in a quaint scene depicting a light-skinned Spaniard having convinced a dark-skinned Indian clothed in a white surplice with hands folded in prayer to turn his back on his former pagan pyramid (fig. 7.22).

In contrast to the decorous black-and-white murals of the Actopan stair hall, the figures in this open chapel are crudely drawn and painted in gaudy colors. According to the logic adduced to the Pedro de Gante school of art, this duality may have been intentional. Just as chiaroscuro signified Christian humility, bright colors and wild gestures should then be appropriate to visions of hell and human degradation. Surely these striking murals were intended for an Indian audience, but why in such a large and cavernous space? Is it possible that the pictures served as scenery for live neixcuitilli? Was the special intention of the Actopan open chapel to provide a proper stage for native spectacles?[47]

The Last Judgment was indeed a popular subject, perhaps the earliest *auto* performed by Christianized Indians in sixteenth-century Mexico. Another example of a stage having been similarly set for Last Judgment neixcuitilli may be the great open chapel at Franciscan Tlalmanalco, Mexico state, an important early pilgrimage site where Fray Martín de Valencia was originally interred after his death in 1534. The imagery in this chapel, however, is not painted but carved in high-relief sculpture, taking advantage of the handsome cinnamon-colored limestone of the region (fig. 7.23). Tlalmanalco, in fact, had been a major preconquest production center of Aztec sculpture, and the Franciscan convento itself probably rests on the remains of an ancient Aztec temple. It was here that one of the most striking of all preconquest Aztec monuments was carved, the famed in-the-round statue in the same reddish stone of the flower deity Xochipilli, now in the Museo

Nacional de Antropología of Mexico City (fig. 7.24). Compare the ecstatic grimace on Xochipilli's face to the expressions on the carved heads of the Tlalmanalco arches in figures 7.25 and 7.26.

As architecture, the Tlalmanalco chapel consists of a never-completed trapezoidal exedra fronted by a proscenium of five arched openings reminiscent of the facade of San José de los Naturales.[48] An interior arch opens onto a central altar space with no roof, although a wooden trabeated cover of some sort may have been originally intended. All the arches and supporting capitals and pilasters are carved with horror vacui ornaments consisting of unusually volumetric tequitqui motifs and intermingled with even more naturalistic, high-relief human faces, many with mouths agape like Xochipilli. There are also skulls, cross-bones, apes, and other monsters all apparently witnessing either the glories of heaven or the horrors of hell. Over the central internal arch looms the bust of a stern-looking Jesus as *Salvator Mundi* holding the orb of the universe in one hand and raising his right two fingers in a gesture of absolute judgment

Fig. 7.18 Place-sign of Coixtlahuaca as repeated relief motif carved along the arch of the open chapel, convento of San Juan Bautista, Coixtlahuaca, Oaxaca. Photograph by Jorge Pérez de Lara.

Fig. 7.19 Open chapel at the convento of San Nicolás de Tolentino, Actopan, Hidalgo, looking east. Photograph by Jorge Pérez de Lara.

(fig. 7.27). On either side of him a pair of apocalyptic angels flies and below are shields emblazoned with his five wounds. What was the purpose of this remarkable sculptural display? Was it too intended as backdrop to a neixcuitilli presentation?

Kubler has suggested that the unique open chapel at Tlalmanalco was constructed by the Franciscans to entice the local Indians away from the neighboring Dominican convento at Amecameca where a rival pilgrimage cult was paying homage to Fray Martín de Valencia's relics after they had been removed from Tlalmanalco and sequestered in the sacred cave site of Sacromonte in 1565.[49]

In any case, Tlalmanalco presents another stylistic conundrum like that of the murals at Tetela de Volcán. In 1948 Kubler opined that the sophistication and quality of the sculpture at Tlalmanalco seemed much too European to be the work of Indians.[50] Most Spanish and Mexican scholars, on the other hand, have detected at least some indigenous influence, although Constantino Reyes-Valerio has insisted that a Spanish friar armed with European prints as models must have been the leading instigator.[51] Moved by this sentiment no doubt, Kubler himself changed his mind by 1959, stating now that the Tlalmanalco sculptures were altogether done by Indians. While still claiming the motifs as overtly Christian, Kubler likewise detected "Aztec echoes" including skulls, monkeys, masks, and "Xipe Totec heads," as he wrote: "Here is a living synthesis of European and Indigenous art . . . extraordinarily rich and ingenious, but medieval in flavor. In contrast to the frequent flatness of tequitqui carving, the Aztec feeling for volume is preserved." John McAndrew agreed, adding enthusiastically: "The decoration manages to reconcile passages of Renaissance Plateresque, late Gothic, Mudéjar, and what may be indigenous ornament in an exuberant and original synthesis, more plastic than planar, too bulgingly carved to be typically tequitqui, yet with such unmistakable indigenous flavor that it could never be mistaken for Spanish work. The varied motifs . . . are all fitted into a repetitive, sparkling, coloristic light-and-shade pattern—half-Indian, half-European, all-Mexican."[52]

Fig. 7.20 Detail, murals painted inside the open chapel at the convento of San Nicolás de Tolentino, Actopan, Hidalgo, looking east. Photograph by Jorge Pérez de Lara.

Curiously, none of the sixteenth-century friar chroniclers ever allude to these striking works of art. Fray Antonio de Ciudad Real during his journey with the commissary general was in and out of Tlalmanalco several times in 1587, yet says nary a word. Were he and his contemporaneous colleagues ignoring these sculptures for the very reasons that inspire our twenty-first-century admiration? Had they so succumbed to Italian high Renaissance tastes by 1587 that the Gothic (and native?) intensity of the Tlalmanalco images was no longer pleasing?

Mexican scholar Gustavo Curiel in perhaps the most exhaustive study to date of the style

Fig. 7.21 Detail, murals painted inside the open chapel at the convento of San Nicolás de Tolentino, Actopan, Hidalgo, looking east. Photograph by Jorge Pérez de Lara.

Fig. 7.22 Detail, murals painted inside the open chapel at the convento of San Nicolás de Tolentino, Actopan, Hidalgo, looking east. Photograph by Jorge Pérez de Lara.

Fig. 7.23 Open chapel at the convento of San Luis Obispo, Tlalmanalco, Mexico, looking southeast. Photograph by Jorge Pérez de Lara.

and iconography of the Tlalmanalco sculptures has challenged all prior theories, insisting in no uncertain terms that whoever the artists, the program itself is "Christian in its totality."[53] He claims that there is not a single image in the entire ensemble that can't be explained with a conventional European prototype. Moreover, his thesis holds that the general theme of the sculptures had not to do with the Last Judgment but rather a psychomachia, the ancient Manichean heavenly battle between the mystical forces of good and evil, just as has been claimed regarding the church murals at Ixmiquilpan. Tlalmanalco, however, asserts a strictly Franciscan view of the apocalyptic end of the world, according to Curiel.

I think his argument goes a bit too far in this direction, especially his denial of any indigenous iconographic input, but Curiel is

Fig. 7.24 Statue of the Aztec deity Xochipilli, ca. 1495. Museo Nacional de Antropología, Mexico City. Photograph by Jorge Pérez de Lara.

right in implying that even if the artists were Indian, they were perfectly capable of adapting to European prototypes (whatever the form of their models). Such models indeed had many precedents in Spain, as for instance, the similarly expressive sculptures in the capitals of the sixteenth-century cloister of the Convento de las Dueñas in Salamanca. Romanesque and Gothic examples depicting the horrified expressions of sinners in hell abounded everywhere in Europe, and no doubt many prints of such images found their way to Mexico.

On the other hand, I suggest that the Indians had before them a more immediate and exciting source, the actual faces of live actors mugging contorted expressions as they played their parts in *autos* of the Last Judgment. Mendieta tells us that Fray Andrés de Olmos wrote a version of the Last Judgment in the Nahuatl language that was performed by Indians in Mexico City around 1535.[54] This play may or may not be the same as that reported in Tlatelolco in 1531, regarded by some as the first

Fig. 7.25 Detail from the open chapel at the convento of San Luis Obispo, Tlalmanalco, Mexico. Photograph by Jorge Pérez de Lara.

Fig. 7.26 Detail from the open chapel at the convento of San Luis Obispo, Tlalmanalco, Mexico.

Christian neixcuitilli in the New World, but does indicate how appealing the subject was to the Indians.[55] Fray Andrés himself served in the Tlalmanalco convento in 1530.[56] Ciudad Real describes further how Indian boys in the Yucatán put on a similar show in which they "dressed as little black people representing devils. . . . Hearing the name of Jesus, all fell to the ground and trembled, making a thousand grimaces and writhing as a sign of fear and consternation."[57] In other words, Indians seemed to revel in this kind of theatrical mimicking. Whatever the source of the Tlalmanalco images, the native artists who carved them would have had no dearth of quick and willing models.

Fig. 7.27 Central arch of the open chapel at the convento of San Luis Obispo, Tlalmanalco, Mexico. Photograph by Jorge Pérez de Lara.

And then the year changed to the companion to follow, Thirteen Rabbit. But the year Thirteen Rabbit was about to come to an end, was at that time of closing, when the Spaniards came to land. . . . And then the stewards came to inform Motecuhzoma. . . . Thus he thought—thus it was thought—that this was Topiltzin Quetzalcoatl who had come to land. For it was in their hearts that he would come, that he would come to land just to find his mat, his seat. For he had traveled there eastward when he departed.

Fray Bernardino de Sahagún, The Florentine Codex, ca, 1570

⊕

Chapter 8

THE CLOISTER AS THEATER

Adam and Eve Lost in Aztec Paradise

Not only the outdoor chapel and portería but also another open space inside the convento complex was apparently taken advantage of for public theatrical purposes during the latter half of the sixteenth century, to wit, the cloister enclosed within the residential friary itself (fig. 8.1). Architecturally, the cloister consists of a corridor surrounding a central garden, separated from it only by a low wall supporting an arcade. Usually, a second arcaded gallery rises over the lower corridor, to which the cells of the friars have access. The garden in the center is open to the sky, often planted with neatly tended flowers and manicured trees around a sculptured fountain. In Europe this pleasant space traditionally was reserved for friars' use only, especially for solitary meditation and education of younger neophytes.

Ideologically, the cloister was the soul-center of the whole convento complex, the *hortus conclusus* [enclosed garden] symbolizing the purity of the Virgin's womb. European Renaissance paintings of the annunciation frequently show such a garden adjacent to the Virgin's bedroom emphasizing her chastity, as in the detail of a late fifteenth-century Flemish painting from the workshop of Rogier van der Weyden now in the Metropolitan Museum of Art, New York (fig. 8.2; note that the Virgin is shown not only inside her private room but also standing in her adjoining walled garden tending the tonsured trees).[1] Just off the cloister corridor at Huejotzingo is a large mural showing the Virgin of the Immaculate Conception based on contem-

Fig. 8.1 View into the cloister of the convento of San Andrés, Epazoyucán, Hidalgo. Photograph by Jorge Pérez de Lara.

poraneous paintings of this subject so cherished by the Franciscans during the sixteenth century (fig. 8.3).[2] She is surrounded by symbols of all her attributes including the hortus conclusus at her lower left, practically pointing to the Huejotzingo cloister just to the right of the mural.

Fig. 8.2 Workshop of Rogier van der Weyden, detail of *The Annunciation*, late fifteenth century, Metropolitan Museum of Art, New York, Gift of J. Pierpont Morgan, 1917 (17.190.7).

The origin of this popular Marian association derives from the Old Testament vulgate version of Song of Solomon 4:12–15, wherein Solomon, prefiguring God of the annunciation, sings to his beloved, in turn prefiguring the Annunciate Virgin, and referring to her as "a garden inclosed is my sister, my spouse; a spring shut up, a fountain sealed. . . . A fountain of gardens, a well of living waters." Significantly, hortus in Latin was also a vulgar metaphor for female pudenda.[3] Notwithstanding the prurient insinuation, medieval iconographers took advantage of the double meaning of hortus conclusus as denoting Mary's absolute virginity. In this sense, the real enclosed garden of the monastery symbolized both Mary's immaculateness and the friars' own rule of celibacy. Positioned in the very center of the monastic complex, the enclosed garden epitomized the collective sanctity of the entire convento.

The fact that murals were commonly painted on the cloister corridor walls in sixteenth-century Mexico has long begged the question as to their purpose and intended audience. Since cloister paintings were more or less protected from the elements, many have survived, but patio, posa, portería, and outdoor chapel walls were likewise once covered with

Fig. 8.3 *Virgin Immaculate,* mural in the convento of San Miguel, Huejotzingo, Puebla. Photograph by Jorge Pérez de Lara.

very similar murals, now mostly disappeared, and all were intended for the same didactic purpose: the edification of Indian catechumens. In other words, the very presence of such murals suggests that Indians had access to them and that the cloister corridor and garden served as one of the places where Indians performed their processions and spectacles just as in the patio, posas, portería, and open chapel.[4]

Furthermore, at each corner of most convento cloister corridors was a shallow testera intended for an image, usually painted directly on its recessed back wall or sometimes only as a framed lienzo or statue temporarily placed on its retracted shelf, in any case, conspicuously positioned as focal points for persons circulating around the four corners of the cloister garden. Moreover, the testeras in many if not most of the Mexican conventos were so set at the ends of corridors that persons desiring to confront each in order could do so only by proceeding in a counterclockwise direction—just as with the posas in the convento patios—again reflecting the traditional ritual direction of indigenous religious processions.[5]

Richard Phillips has characterized the convento cloister as an "interiorized" version of the patio and posas in both form and function. He has argued with strong evidence that by the second half of the sixteenth century the cloisters in most of the Mexican conventos were actively used by Indian cofradías, religious confraternities dedicated to a particular saint or holy day for their special devotions and ritual processions.[6] The actual depth of the testera niche was sometimes taken advantage of to enhance the fictive perspective illusion of the painting. This is particularly the case in the convento cloister at Epazoyucán even though its testeras were set so that processions could confront them from both a clockwise and a counterclockwise direction. Nonetheless, the Epazoyucán testeras not only had their natural recession intensified by Albertian perspective but also around the outer borders of these niches, as in the scene of the Crucifixion in the southwest corner of the Epazoyucán cloister, arches of twisted vines and flowers were painted (fig. 8.4). While modern eyes may see these borders as nothing more than innocuous tequitqui embellishment, sixteenth-century Indian catechumens would have related such floreate arches to an important aspect of their own ceremonial tradition. In his famous account of the Indian spectacles in Tlaxcala in 1538–39, Motolinía observed: "Where a procession is to pass they [the Indians] erect numerous triumphal arches made of roses and adorned with trimmings and garlands of the same flowers. The wreaths of flowers they fashion are very attractive. This is the reason why in this land everybody is bent on having rose gardens."[7] In other words, the cloister at Epazoyucán was painted to replicate the decorated avenue along which an Indian procession would march during religious celebrations, pausing at each testera just as it would before the intermittent shrines along the ceremonial route through a city.

Among the most iconographically intriguing as well as aesthetically pleasing examples of convento painting in all Mesoamerica are the murals in the lower cloister corridor of the Augustinian house at Malinalco in the present State of Mexico. Only discovered in 1974–75 after centuries of oblivion under whitewash, these unprecedented paintings, finished around 1571, depict what appears to be a native American forest in chiaroscuro (fig. 8.5). Originally the murals ran uninterrupted around the north, east, and south corridor walls between a chest-high dado and overhead cornice decorated with a continuous Latin inscription in ornamented Roman capital letters quoting from the Psalms. Behind these the forest imagery continues onto the vaults, changing only to a greenish bluish grisaille with touches of russet. Gamboling in the tangled branches of the fictive jungle on the lower walls is a veritable zoo of indigenous fauna, including deer, monkeys, coyotes, rabbits, opossums, squirrels, snakes, lizards, and birds of all sorts likewise painted in chiaroscuro indicating European influence but interspersed with enough preconquest stylisms to convince most scholars that the artists here were native Indians.[8] While the overall appearance of the Malinalco murals superficially suggests conventional tequitqui, the individual details owe little to the standardized forms of Renaissance grotescos. Rather, we have here an extraordinary, almost Dioscourides-like encyclopedia of New World biology with dozens of actual species of native plants and animals drawn from life, yet so artfully arranged they give the effect of a woven tapestry.[9] No comparable painted murals exist anywhere else datable to the sixteenth century in postconquest colonial America.

Malinalco, a Nahuatl word that means "at the place of the grass," was originally an Aztec stronghold about seventy kilometers southwest of Mexico City, located in a fertile valley surrounded by heavily forested buttelike hills with steep rocky cliffs. On one of these cliffs, the Aztecs were in the process of building an elaborate temple complex at the time of the Spanish invasion. One may still visit the unfinished remains today, including an eerie man-made cavern carved from solid rock in the form of an open serpent's maw through which

Fig. 8.4 *Crucifixion,* mural in the southwest cloister testera, convento of San Andrés, Epazoyucán, Hidalgo. Photograph by Jorge Pérez de Lara.

celebrants could literally enter the underworld and pay homage to the jaguar and eagle, patrons of the Aztec military elite (fig. 8.6).

Following the Spanish conquest, Augustinians moved into Malinalco and began constructing their convento some time after 1540 in the valley town at the base of the hills. The earliest structure was built of pole and thatch with perhaps a crude masonry open chapel appended. In its final architectural form, achieved by the late 1570s and more or less as it is today, the open chapel was absorbed into a magnificent portería that stretches across the entire western front of the friary and lets directly into the cloister (fig. 8.7).[10] The portería itself is entered from the outside through seven arches, seven being a sacred Christian number signifying, among other associations, the first Augustinian apostles to arrive in New Spain (their individual portraits were once painted on the inside of the support piers). Above these arches are a series of twenty-four inset stone medallions with repeating sculpted insignia including the preconquest-style glyph of a bound bunch of grass, the Aztec place-sign of Malinalco (fig. 8.8).

Before the portería extends a medium-size patio with no corner posas. A stone cross about one meter tall that may once have stood in the middle of the patio now adorns the northwest corner wall. It too was surely created by an Indian who carved in its center a jarring vestige of his preconquest ideology, an inlaid obsidian tezcatcuitlapilli shaped as a blooming flower with a tiny crucifix sprouting from its "heart," below which a stream of blood drips down into a chalice (see fig. 2.32).[11]

The Malinalco cloister was built in two stories, the lower of which was apparently ready for mural painting sometime after the 1560s. The upper cloister gallery was not completed until the 1580s. While this gallery has no inset testeras, two abutting murals were painted at each upstairs corner, with chiaroscuro scenes of Jesus' Passion cycle in left-to-right clockwise series (see fig. 4.6). The lower cloister, however, has testeras only at the right corner of each side outer wall (fig. 8.9). They are now empty of images, but their presence indicates that counterclockwise processions were at one time planned through this passage. The mural images are carefully shaped around these testeras indicating that the testeras themselves were intended to play a role in whatever the intention of the painted program.

Several investigators have already identified the iconography of these lower cloister paintings as an Indian representation of the Christian terrestrial paradise.[12] In her wide-ranging examination of the Malinalco murals, Jeanette Peterson has assiduously examined not only the Augustinian religious iconography and Spanish political context but also how the native artists syncretized indigenous zoological and botanical lore with traditional Christian subject matter. She explains how garden imagery was regarded by both European Christians and preconquest Nahua Indians as signifying human rejuvenation and moral redemption, and how this imagery indeed provided ideal scenery for miracle plays serving as didactic tools of conversion.[13]

Nevertheless, according to Peterson, the purpose of the Malinalco murals, in spite of being executed by Indian painters, was not primarily to serve a native audience. Since the cloister was the friars' private space and generally off limits to all but a few trusted Indian

Fig. 8.5 Eastern cloister corridor, convento of San Salvador, Malinalco, Mexico. Photograph by Jorge Pérez de Lara.

Fig. 8.6 Temple of Eagle and Jaguar Knights, Malinalco, Mexico.

converts, she believes the principal intent of the murals must have been to edify the friars themselves. As she then postulates, the basic pictorial message was an "idealistic vision . . . a utopian scheme" of monastic life in the newly discovered Americas.[14]

Essentially, Peterson's argument has it that the Augustinians at Malinalco would have wanted to depict in their convento the same "Thebaid" theme that was traditional to their order since the early Middle Ages. Such scenes of celibate monks abandoning the contemplative privacy of their solitary abbeys in order to evangelize publicly in the temporal world were especially expressive of the intensifying missionary zeal during the great age of monastic reform and are frequently painted in Europe.[15] Similar images can be seen in Augustinian conventos in Mexico, as at Acolman and Actopan.[16] The subject matter of these paintings generally includes a forest with trees and exotic animals plus winding roads along which itinerant monks are shown wandering and conversing.

What is evident in the Malinalco murals is that there are no human inhabitants in this supposed Thebaid. Not a single monk is represented strolling in its fictive landscape. Instead, the painted scenes show only masses of unruly trees and vines inhabited by a plethora of untamed animals, resembling the stage set described by Motolinía for the scene showing paradise lost in the "fall of man" neixcuitilli performed by the Indians of Tlaxcala: "Thereupon the world was represented, another land quite different from the one from which Adam and Eve had been banished. It was full of thistles and thorns and many snakes together with rabbits and hares. When the new inhabitants of this world arrived there, the angel showed Adam how he would have to work and cultivate the land, while to Eve were given spindles to spin and make clothes for her husband and children."[17]

The Malinalco murals were painted around the outward sides of the cloister across the corridor opposite the inner garden and fictively behind a row of shieldlike medallions, three to each side of the cloister, painted as if illusionistically suspended along the south, east, north, and part of the west walls (fig. 8.10).

Each medallion bears one of three common Christian symbols. They are the same as those carved above the portería arches on the friary facade. There, they are to be "read" left-to-right as follows: the thrice-pierced heart, emblem of the Augustinian brotherhood; an A interlaced with an M, which stands for Ave Maria and thus an insignia of the Annunciate Virgin Mary; and third, IHS (applied by Saint Bernadine of Siena in 1424 to the phrase Iesus Hominum Salvator [Jesus, the savior of mankind] but originally the first three letters of the Greek name for Jesus, which resemble the English capital letters IHS). Each group of three (six groups in all along the portería) is separated on the portería facade by a Malinalco place-sign. Inside the cloister corridor the same groups of three are represented again in paint, one group to each wall but here separated by a corner testera instead of a Malinalco place-sign. However, on these cloister walls the three Christian emblems are so arranged as to be read in mirror-reverse, right-to-left sequence. While the individual insignia are all standard tequitqui decor in most Augustinian conventos, their repeated presence on the portería facade and then in reverse order in the cloister at Malinalco reveals a deliberate ritual purpose.

A celebrant exiting the convento church through the west portal and turning left to walk along the portería facade toward the entrance of the cloister would first see the sculpted medallions above the portería arches at the celebrant's left and would then pass, in this order, Augustinian insignia, Annunciate Virgin Mary insignia, IHS insignia, and Malinalco place-sign. The same sequence is then repeated until the celebrant turns left again and enters the cloister. Inside the cloister and along each of the cloister corridor walls, the celebrant once more observes the same arrangement of medallions but now at the right as he or she walks around the corridor in the counterclockwise direction compelled by the testeras. Inside the western entrance of the cloister and turning toward the southern corner where at least two IHS images can still be made out, the celebrant enters the south corridor facing in the direction of the testera on the eastern wall. The first medallion encountered on the south wall, now at the celebrant's right, is the Augustinian insignia, followed by the Annunciate Virgin Mary's insignia more or less in the middle section of the wall, and third the IHS medallion just before confronting the east wall testera. Next, turning left along the east wall, the same order is repeated again at the right, ending with the IHS preceding the empty testera at the east corner of the north wall. Finally, turning left along the north wall, the series is once more restated with the IHS symbol preceding the testera at the corner of the west wall.

What is the peculiar meaning of this arrangement in which the same repetitive order of carved medallions as perceived on the left as one walks along the portería facade is then continued in painted versions, but only as perceived from the right as one moves counterclockwise along the cloister corridor wall? Furthermore, why is the IHS emblem always third and just before the Malinalco place-sign in its left-hand order on the portería, and similarly just before each testera in its right-hand order inside the cloister?

Surely we have here a set of directional indicators mapping a processional route leading from the church along the portería facade, then into the cloister through its west portal, then around the south corridor facing the testera on the east wall, then left along the east corridor facing the testera on the north wall, left again along the north corridor facing the testera on the west wall, and finally out through the western portal once more, but not before pausing at one last IHS medallion and its adjacent testera at the southwest corner. This pattern demonstrates beyond any doubt that the Malinalco cloister entertained processional functions just like the convento patio, with the corner testeras serving exactly like patio posas (there are no true posas in the Malinalco patio). At each testera processions might momentarily stop to contemplate lienzos or other didactic effigies associated with the occasion.

We may further assume with some assurance that the consistent order of all the medallions had its own didactic message, reminding the passing celebrants first of the holy mission of the Augustinian order, then of Jesus' miraculous conception in the sacred womb of Mary (prompting a glance toward the symbolic hortus conclusus in the center of the cloister to the left of the moving procession), and finally of Jesus' sacrifice on the cross as savior of mankind just before pausing for a further inspirational message at each corner testera.

Interesting as all this is, however, what has it to do with the imagery of the terrestrial paradise behind the medallions? When observed from within the central cloister garden, the forest imagery appears to be occluded by this continuous row of large painted medallions. Indeed, the depicted jungle seems illusionistically beyond the very convento itself, thus figuratively outside the protective environs of Malinalco's "spiritual fortress." The medallions also have their own outer edges bound by what looks like twined or braided rope, perhaps in reference to the etymological meaning of "Malinalco." Bound grass was indeed a Nahua symbol for a topographical boundary. Angel García Zambrano has examined numerous manuscript land titles extant in the Mexican National Archives from both before and immediately after the conquest showing that whenever the Indians established a community, they marched counterclockwise in ceremonial procession around the perimeter, during which the elders would set the community's borders by "joining together boughs and pasture grass, one with the other, and in this manner they were capable of identifying their borderlands, tying the branches as it was mentioned, isolating the lands pertaining to this town."[18] Following this ritual, markers of stone or some other permanent material, known as *teteles,* were then set up along the borders. In the manuscript land titles, these are often depicted as circular in shape, similar in form to the Augustinian medallions.[19] They also resemble traditional Aztec warrior shields, reminding the friars of one of their own favorite metaphors, the Erasmian "shield of the

Fig. 8.7 Portería facade, convento of San Salvador, Malinalco, Mexico. Photograph by Jorge Pérez de Lara.

faith" figuratively wielded by them as "soldiers of Christ" against the Devil and all his pagan minions in the New World.

I submit that both Indian painters and Augustinian friars saw these medallions as framing an allegorical boundary analogous to the actual demarcated boundaries of native Indian communities, but here tropologically separating orderly Christian community life within the convento from paganism and the chaotic secular world without. In other words, the lower cloister corridor murals at Malinalco were not intended to depict a contiguous extension of the actual garden in the center of the cloister but rather its dualistic, symbolic opposite, the savage wilderness of terrestrial paradise lost as Adam and Eve fell from God's grace.[20]

Peterson tends to conflate the Old Testament terrestrial paradise with the Marian hortus conclusus as if together they were a single entity in Christian theology. To be sure, they are typologically related, but only in the sense that the former was the source of the moral dilemma that was to be redeemed in the latter. I propose instead that the planners of the Malinalco convento meant from the beginning that there be two gardens in their cloister, the outer primordial but fictive, the inner orderly and actual, each a separate exegetic cue to friars and their neophytes that the birth of Christ by Mary, the new Eve of the garden enclosed, finally granted divine salvation (IHS) from the original sin of old Eve in paradise lost.[21] Furthermore, the quadrangular cloister garden with fountain in center once again replicated the sacred quincunx form of the Indians' traditional cosmic landscape. As Angel García Zambrano goes on to explain, the Indians would then sacralize their particular microcosmic territory by not only marching counterclockwise around its four corners but also returning to the center to pay homage to their community's primordial umbilicus.[22] Processions through the Malinalco cloister would similarly define and consecrate the moral boundary between the depicted paradise lost of the murals on the outside, and paradise regained in the actual hortus conclusus in the Augustinian convento's inside. I suggest further that the Malinalco artists and friars chose to paint the murals in grisaille to reinforce this very opposition—to contrast the world before God's grace with the living color in the garden of Jesus' salvation.

Peterson's most important contribution is her identification of a number of flora and fauna motifs with preconquest occult associations, deliberately and perhaps "subversively" disguised among the otherwise European-style and Christianized painted details.[23] Of special importance to the endurance of Indian culture under Spanish dominance, Peterson argues, is the motif she identifies as a "bee and songscroll," looking like a segmented caterpillar winding its way among the horror vacui flora in the vault of each bay in the north, east, and south corridors (fig. 8.11). Convincingly, she

Fig. 8.8 Detail of portería facade, convento of San Salvador, Malinalco, Mexico. Photograph by Jorge Pérez de Lara.

Fig. 8.9 Testera at northeastern corner of the cloister corridor at the convento of San Salvador, Malinalco, Mexico. Photograph by Jorge Pérez de Lara.

has matched this figure to the glyphic form of the traditional Aztec speech-scroll with a flower above, in particular, one that emanates from the mouth of a drum-playing musician before the deity Huehuecoyotl, as painted on one of the calendar pages in the Aztec Codex Borbonicus (fig. 8.12).[24]

Huehuecoyotl was an Aztec god whose powers related to sportive pleasures, mischief, and eroticism just like the native coyote whose zoomorphic features as well as name he bears.[25] Huehuecoyotl was also worshipped as patron of fiestas, music, dancing, and singing. Finally, Huehuecoyotl was the lord of the Fourth Trecena, that is, the fourth of twenty thirteen-day cycles (trecenas) making up the 260-day ceremonial year in the Aztec *tonalapohualli* or calendric "count of days."

Twenty named days are included in the Aztec calendar, each of which occurs thirteen times in sequence (fig. 8.13). Imagine a gear-wheel with twenty teeth, rotating against another smaller wheel with thirteen teeth in this order: starting with the first gear-tooth at One Alligator (the first day of the First Trecena), the next day will be Two Wind, then

Three House, Four Lizard, Five Serpent, Six Death's-Head, Seven Deer, Eight Rabbit, Nine Water, Ten Dog, Eleven Monkey, Twelve Grass, and Thirteen Reed. Then the Second Trecena begins on One Jaguar, followed by Two Eagle, Three Vulture, Four Motion, Five Flint-knife, Six Rain, Seven Flower, Eight Alligator, Nine Wind, Ten House, Eleven Lizard, Twelve Serpent, and Thirteen Death's Head. The Third Trecena commences with One Deer and continues in the same sequence through Thirteen Rain, with the Fourth Trecena starting on One Flower, which is why its name-glyph appears atop the song-scroll on this particular calendar page of the Codex Borbonicus.[26] Each numbered day-name can occur only once every 260 days.

Peterson observed that the tiny "parallel-hook" motif, known as the *ilhuitl,* within each segment of Huehuecoyotl's song-scroll also

Fig. 8.10 East corridor of the cloister as viewed from the west corridor, convento of San Salvador, Malinalco, Mexico. Photograph by Jorge Pérez de Lara.

Fig. 8.11 Detail, central vault of the south cloister corridor, convento of San Salvador, Malinalco, Mexico. Photograph by Jorge Pérez de Lara.

have the first known instance of a tlahcuiloh-artisan leaving a sign of his profession—some fifty years after the conquest."[28]

As Peterson goes on to point out, a number of significant trees, flowers, and animals are depicted on the east corridor wall, namely two indigenous American trees, one a white sapote that bears a sweet applelike fruit (to the left of the medallion in fig. 8.14), and the other the singular cacao plant (fig. 8.15), so treasured by the Indians that its seeds were not only brewed as the "drink of the gods" but also circulated as money.[29] The animals represented climbing among these trees include, besides a number of bird species, two native spider monkeys picking cacao beans and a coyote eating grapes while what looks like another smaller coyote with head turned almost full-face to the viewer clings to its back (fig. 8.16). Nearby, rabbits nibble on grapes and pomegranates (fig. 8.17).[30] Roses, flowers not indigenous to the New World but introduced by the Spanish, are also depicted. The rose was not only especially prized in the Old World (having traditional Christian association with the Virgin Mary: "a rose without thorns") but also

appears in the fourth from last segment of the similar song-scroll in the center vault of the south corridor of the Malinalco cloister (see fig. 8.11). This motif, she argues, was an ancient Indian good-luck sign associated with artisans and painters, a fact confirmed in a number of other Aztec codex representations.[27] As she then stated, "In the Malinalco frescoes we may quickly gained esteem among the Indians. Indeed, it was by the sign of the rose that the Virgin of Guadalupe supposedly communicated her miracle to the Indian Juan Diego in 1531. In Nahuatl, the newly introduced rose was called *castilxochitl,* or Spanish flower.[31]

The east side of any convento cloister, of course, had special theological imprimatur.[32] Not only does the Bible specify that God planted terrestrial paradise "eastward in Eden" (Genesis 2:8), and that east is the source of the sunrise (important to all civilizations in the world), but it was from this sacred direction that the Angel Gabriel supposedly came to the Virgin Mary in her own cloistered domicile. Throughout the Middle Ages in Europe, the terrestrial paradise as Garden of Eden was always represented on cartographic maps as being in the Orient, indeed, even in the preferred "up" position on these charts.[33] Any image depicted on the east side of a convento cloister would have enhanced iconographical importance. At Malinalco, the depicted grapes and roses on this wall, as Peterson pointed out, certainly referred respectively to Christ's sacrifice and the Virgin Mary's purity.[34]

There is no doubt, as Peterson further averred, that the sapote tree was intended here to represent the biblical Tree of Knowledge and its fruit likened to Eve's apple. In fact, in the tree to the left of the cacao, the Indian artist indicated a serpent coiled around a branch and menacing a small bird, an overt reference to the Devil's temptation in the Garden of Eden (fig. 8.18).[35] Also related to Eve's temptation was the pair of monkeys, about which Peterson has much to say in respect to their differing European Christian and native Aztec iconographies.[36] The Christian meaning of monkey imagery in association with Eve and the Virgin Mary has been cogently summed up by Erwin Panofsky: "The monkey symbolized all the undesirable qualities thanks to which Eve brought about the Fall of Man and was thus used as a contrastive attribute of

Fig. 8.12 Detail after fol. 4, Codex Borbonicus. Bibliothèque de l'Assemblée Nationale, Paris. Drawing by Mark Van Stone.

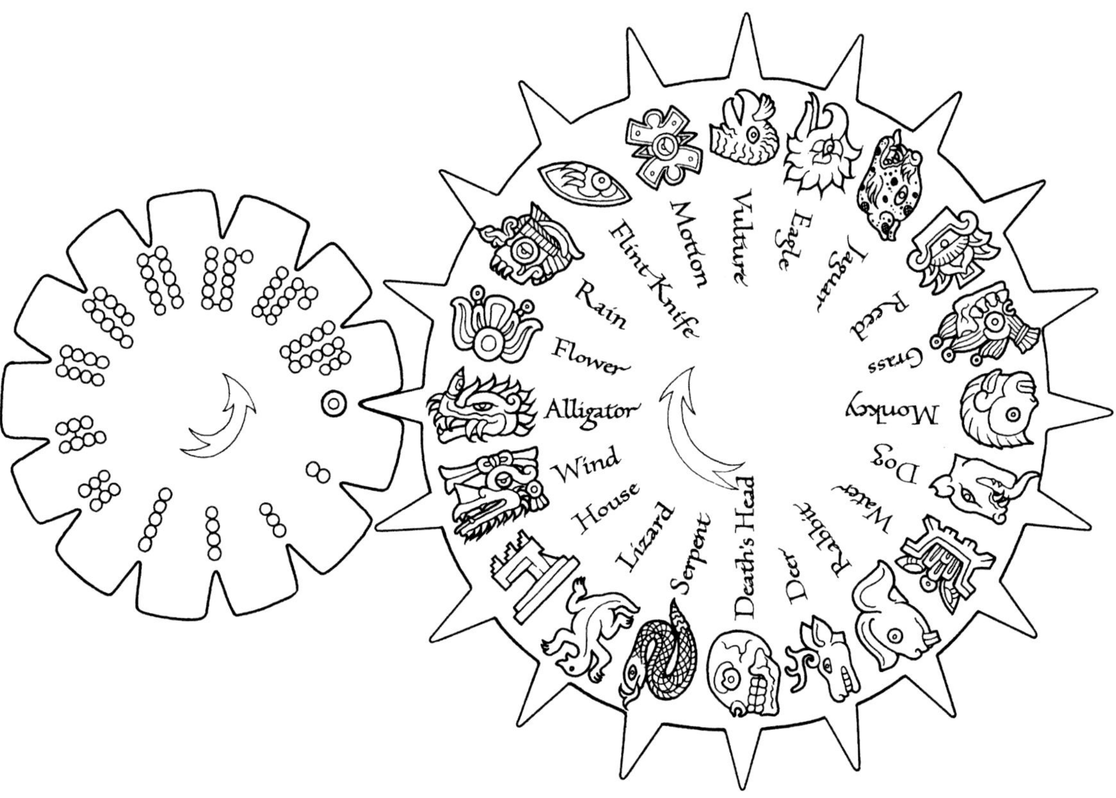

Fig. 8.13 Aztec 260-day ritual calendar. Drawing by Mark Van Stone.

Mary, the 'new Eve,' whose perfection blotted out the sin of the 'old': Eva occidendo obfuit, Maria vivicando profuit."[37]

I expand on Peterson's contribution by adding that the Huehuecoyotl–Fourth Trecena connection she has correctly related to the Malinalco murals has more aspects and further meaning for the sixteenth-century native artists and catechumens in the convento, not only reminding them of their preconquest past but also reinforcing their recently acquired Christian religion, and that the presence of such preconquest symbols in the Malinalco murals was hardly "subversive," in fact, they were surely included in full collusion with the Augustinian friars.

The Codex Telleriano-Remensis, painted by Indian tlahcuiloqueh sometime around 1563 at the very time the Malinalco cloister was under construction, is filled with Spanish commentary inscribed under the preconquest Indian-style pictures by several European hands including a Dominican friar named Fray Pedro de los Ríos, known to have been stationed and probably writing his comments in Puebla, some two hundred kilometers east of Malinalco.[38] He and the other Christian commentators attempted not only to interpret the pagan imagery for Christian readers but also to make comparisons between the old Indian iconography and similar Christian stories, characters, and rituals.[39] The commentators apparently belonged to that school of sixteenth-century missionaries like Mendieta, Durán, and Sahagún who thought that in ancient times the natives of the "Indies," perhaps descended from a lost tribe of Israelites, had originally been converted by Saint Thomas the Apostle. In the meantime, the Devil intervened and forced the Indians to revert to idol worship. Convinced of this prior evangelization of the Indies, many friars believed that vestiges of the old Christian rites could still be discerned in pagan Indian rituals even though blasphemed and obfuscated by the "demon."[40]

Like the Codex Borbonicus, the Codex Telleriano-Remensis contains a traditional *tonalamatl,* or book of the days, depicting the twenty thirteen-day trecenas that make up the Aztec 260-day ceremonial year. Turning to the Codex Telleriano-Remensis representation of the Fourth Trecena, we find the same association with the deity Huehuecoyotl, only here represented with human rather than coyote facial features and holding a disembodied human arm with blood spurting from the stump (perhaps referring to the same native symbol sculpted on the facade of the convento church at Acolman; see fig. I-3). On the facing

Fig. 8.14 Detail, east cloister corridor wall, convento of San Salvador, Malinalco, Mexico. Photograph by Jorge Pérez de Lara.

Fig. 8.15 Detail, *Cacao Tree with Monkeys*, east cloister corridor wall, convento of San Salvador, Malinalco, Mexico. Photograph by Jorge Pérez de Lara.

folio continuing the same trecena, a kneeling female figure labeled Ixnextli with tears streaming from her eyes turns her head toward Huehuecoyotl as she holds a pot of bulging brown substance (fig. 8.19). The Spanish commentator has drawn a short line from this pot to his one-word caption, *mierda*.[41]

Considerable textual commentary is inscribed in Spanish under both images, with crossings-out, corrections, and insertions by a number of different hands at different times including that of Fray Pedro de los Ríos. Eloise Quiñones Keber has published a facsimile edition with English transcriptions plus her own commentary.[42] Following is her translation of the long text under the picture of Huehuecoyotl (fol. 10v). I have abridged it slightly and also italicized certain words and phrases because they bear obvious relevance to my argument:

> Huehuecoyotl . . . mischief-maker, the deceived one, or he who lets himself be deceived; god of the Otomí; *the same as Adam,* survived the flood. . . . Here they celebrated the feast. . . . They said [there was] an omen in the *year One-Rabbit,* on the day one rose [*One-Flower*], that a rose blossomed on earth and then withered. . . . [Huehuecoyotl is] lord of these thirteen days . . . those born here would be singers and doctors and weavers and important persons, *here on this week of One Flower when a Rabbit year occurred they fasted to commemorate the fall of the first man.*[43]

The similarly abridged text under the figure of the female (fol. 11r) then follows:

Fig. 8.16 Detail, *Coyotes,* east cloister corridor wall, convento of San Salvador, Malinalco, Mexico. Photograph by Jorge Pérez de Lara.

Fig. 8.17 Detail, *Rabbit Eating Pomegranate,* east cloister corridor wall, convento of San Salvador, Malinalco, Mexico. Photograph by Jorge Pérez de Lara.

They paint Ixnextli as if she [were] always crying and looking at her *husband Adam. The same as Eve . . . this year of 1562 on the 27th of July was the feast of she who sinned* [this last sentence was inscribed then crossed out]. Her name is Ixnextli, which means eyes blinded with ashes, and she is like this since she sinned by picking the roses, and thus they say that now they cannot look at the sky. *And in memory of that idleness that they lost, they fasted . . . every eight years to commemorate this fall . . .* and they fasted eight days *before this one rose [day One Flower?] arrived and when it occurred they adorned themselves in order to celebrate it. They say that all the days with five in this calendar refer to this fall, for on such a day she sinned.*[44]

My analysis of the cryptic Nahua calendar references in the commentary above begins with 1562, the Christian year mentioned in the Codex, which indeed corresponds to Nahua year Five Rabbit. The Codex even repeats on folio 49r that "Eve's sin" was commemorated in "this year of Five Rabbit on the day One Flower."[45] While the Christian (Julian) month and day, July 27, 1562, inscribed and then crossed out by the commentator above, does not convert to a native date beginning with Trecena One Flower according to the generally accepted correlation system worked out by Mexican scholar Alfonso Caso, it may have conformed instead to a local calendar adjustment in the Puebla region.[46] In any case as late as 1562 and even later, decades after the conquest and the élan of the great Christian conversion, not only were many Indians still keeping track of their traditional calendar but also many of the missionary friars were co-opting the same "pagan" dating for their own Christian purposes.[47]

Like the Maya, the traditional Nahua calendar consisted of two day-counting systems running simultaneously. First there was the solar 365-day count, similar to the Western calendar but without intercalating the extra quadrennial leap-year day. Then there was the 260-day ritual year that one may again imagine as like a cogwheel of 260 teeth rotating against and intermeshing endlessly with a larger cogwheel of 365 teeth. Unlike the Maya, however, the Nahua did not name each sequential solar year after its initial interlocking day with the *Tonalpohualli,* but rather after its 360th, five days before the solar year's end. Because of the arithmetic relationship of these two intermeshing systems, the year-ending day could only fall on four day-name possibilities: Rabbit, Reed, Flint-knife, or House (numbered sequentially from one to thirteen and then repeating in the following order for fifty-two consecutive years: One Rabbit, Two Reed, Three Flint-knife, Four House, Five Rabbit, Six Reed, Seven Flint-knife, Eight House, Nine Rabbit, Ten Reed, Eleven Flint-knife, Twelve House, Thirteen Rabbit, One Reed, Three

Fig. 8.18 Detail, *Serpent Threatening Bird,* east cloister corridor wall, convento of San Salvador, Malinalco, Mexico. Photograph by Jorge Pérez de Lara.

Flint-knife, Four House, etc., etc., so that the same numbered year-ending day-name could not occur again for fifty-two years).

Thus, for example, according to the Caso correlation, the Nahua year-name for Christian 1561, Four House, would also be the Nahua day-name for January 8, 1562, the 360th day of that year. Before the next year Five Rabbit (the day-name likewise for its 360th day, or January 8, 1563, according to Caso) could only be celebrated, however, after five interim "nameless" days were counted off, which the Nahua considered a special time of atonement.

Fig. 8.19 Detail after fol. 11, Codex Telleriano-Remensis. Bibliothèque Nationale, Paris. Drawing by Mark Van Stone.

These were called the *nemontemi,* or bad-luck days, and must be endured with much penance and mortification before the new year was officially inaugurated. The first day of year Five Rabbit, again according to the Caso correlation, should then have commenced on the sixth day after Four House, or Ten Water, on January 14, 1562.

Since Rabbit years can only happen after four-year intervals, and thirteen Rabbit-year endings must pass before another year Five Rabbit returns, fifty-two solar years, known as a "calendar round," always separate the same year-ending day from repeating itself. The year One Rabbit was of particular significance in this respect because it was always followed by Two Reed, the crucial year in which the Aztecs celebrated their famous "new fire" ceremony. At that time the emperor would sacrifice a human victim and beg the gods to permit the sun to rise and the world to continue for yet another sacred fifty-two-year calendar round.[48]

The Codex Telleriano-Remensis commentator relates that according to native lore on the day One Flower in the year One Rabbit, "a rose bloomed and then withered." This legend provided a convenient parallel to the Christian allegory of Eve's temptation and fall. Coincidentally, day One Flower began exactly forty days after the beginning of the Aztec ritual calendar, reminding Christians of Noah's flood, Christ's fasting in the wilderness, the duration of Lent, and the number of days after Easter until Christ's ascent into heaven. The Fourth Trecena then ended on day fifty-two, which had equally traditional significance for the Indians. Moreover, the Nahua year One Rabbit could also be construed as metaphorically preceding the arrival of Christianity since the Aztec believed that the year One Rabbit was associated with a "place of thorns," while the following year, Two Reed, was associated with the direction east from which the first newborn sun of the succeeding age arises.[49]

It is not clear just who—friars or Indians—first made all these syncretic connections with Christian allegories of sin and redemption, but as Michael Graulich has argued, there may have existed a legend among the preconquest Nahua concerning the creation of the first humans in a garden called Tamoanchan, and these first humans transgressed against the gods and fell from grace when the original woman picked a forbidden flower from the sacred World Tree in the center of their primordial paradise.[50] In sixteenth-century Spanish, the word *rosa* was often a generic alternate for "flower," no doubt deliberately substituted here to relate the trecena day-name to the Christian concept of "two Eves," Adam's wife and the Virgin Mary.

During the sixteenth century, the only two possible One Rabbit years were 1506 and 1558. On folio 48v of the codex, in reference to the Rabbit year 1558, which just as in 1506 had undergone a disastrous harvest (and now suffered the added misery of the plague), the commentator remarked that all such Rabbit years were prone to "famine and death."[51] Thus as the commentary continues, a fiesta solemnizing "Eve who sinned" should be performed every eight years and only during a Rabbit year, and the celebrants should "adorn themselves" and begin fasting "eight days" before the Fourth Trecena. They should also regard any calendric day "five" as bearing reference to "this fall of man."[52]

According to the alleged Nahua legend, "first mother" (named Ixnextli in the Codex Telleriano-Remensis) picked the forbidden flower on the day One Flower, year One Rabbit, at the ominous moment of Venus rising as morning star; subsequent commemorations of this event should repeat whenever a One Flower day is in conjunction with the first morning appearance of Venus.[53]

The problem with this facet of the legend, however, is that the Nahua 260-day ritual calendar bears no relation to the seasonal cycles of the sun and Venus.[54] Perhaps for this reason, the Codex Telleriano-Remensis commentators do not mention an astronomical association regarding the Fourth Trecena. Nevertheless we are assured that the fiesta not only took place every eight years but that it actually transpired in 1562, Nahua year Five Rabbit. This occasion would have been just four years after 1558, the last possible One Rabbit year in the sixteenth century. The only other One Rabbit year was 1506, which as the codex commentary text on folio 41v relates, preceded the Two Reed year 1507 during which the last "new fire" ceremony of the Aztec empire was performed prior to the Spanish conquest.[55]

Since fateful 1506 fell exactly fifty-six years before 1562, that is, seven times eight years, we have reason for assuming that 1506 was the likely moment when the Christian friars construed the story so that Ixnextli-Eve should have picked the forbidden rose on that date, thus setting the schedule for calculating the commemorative fiesta every subsequent eight years apart thereafter. In the Nahua calendar, every fourth year has a Rabbit number, and so the same with every eighth year after 1506. Thus, 1514, 1522, 1530, 1538, 1546, 1554, 1562, and 1570 would all be suitable

Rabbit-year dates for celebrating the fiesta of "Eve who sinned." Obviously this Christianized ceremony could not have begun until after the conquest, and we may assume that accompanying it would have been a neixcuitilli performance of the fall of man.

The earliest recorded instance of this Indian *auto* in the New World was that witnessed in Tlaxcala by Fray Motolinía on the Wednesday following Easter, April 24, 1538, Nahua year Seven Rabbit.[56] Motolinía explained that the Indians at first had wished to produce their play during Lent, which he says was not permitted. They performed instead during Easter Week, a fortuitous coincidence since Easter Week—the octave after Easter Sunday—was traditionally called in Spanish, *Pascua Florida,* or floral Passover.[57]

I now consider the Malinalco murals' peculiar allegorical imagery in relation to the Codex Borbonicus and the Codex Telleriano-Remensis calendric iconography. The sapote tree, the serpents, and monkeys must allude to "Eve who sinned." The coyote was certainly intended, by way of covert reference to Huehuecoyotl, to signify Adam. The second coyote clinging to its back with uncharacteristic frontal face was probably meant to signify a demon and thus infernal punishment, often so represented in medieval Christian as well as preconquest Indian art.[58] Among several crude images of hell and damnation reminiscent of Fray Gonzalo Luzero's famous sermon, one may still make out in a faded black-and-white mural in the Chapel of the Miracle of the Rosary in the Dominican convento at Tetela del Volcán a figure of a nude Indian woman holding what appears to be an apple (thus representing Eve?) and with a Devil's frontal face where her genitalia should be. Two demonic claw-footed animals of the same shape and relative size as the smaller coyote in the Malinalco fresco cling to her arms while they gnaw upon both her shoulders (fig. 8.20).[59] Finally, the five painted rabbits on the east wall (plus two more, one each on the north and south walls) probably allude to the Aztec cyclic years when the sin of Eve should be commemorated. The intertwining grape vines and roses surrounding these animals are tropological references to Christ and the Virgin Mary.

Yet despite all this edenic activity on the east wall, no human figures are depicted, here or anywhere else in the lower cloister murals. The reason should now be apparent. People were not painted into this fictive Aztec garden of temptation and sin because they were intended to be impersonated by living actors performing neixcuitilli, perhaps brief scenes in the lives of Adam and Eve before each testera. Images set up in the testeras would then be integrated with the murals as scenic backdrops to a grand procession celebrating the "Eve who sinned" fiesta, occurring possibly in the Fourth Trecena of Thirteen Rabbit year, 1570, perhaps even on the day One Flower. According to Nahua tradition that special day favored not only artists but also dancers, singers, and actors participating in religious processions and neixcuitilli.[60]

There is yet another circumstantial reason why a postlapsarian exegesis was so appropriate to the Malinalco murals at just this time, particularly if their completion and accompanying celebration occurred near the end of the year 1570 or early 1571. One should keep in mind, as surely the friars and their native converts did, that while 1570 was Nahua year Thirteen Rabbit with its stressful "fall of man" message to the neophyte Indians, the following year, 1571, was One Reed, a uniquely opportune moment, especially in Aztec calendric terms, to remind the Indians of the providential event that led to their Christian redemption from Eve's sin. Exactly fifty-two years before, one sacred Aztec calendar-round ago in the same-name year One Reed, Hernán Cortés first arrived in Mexico, dropping anchor off Veracruz on Maundy Thursday, 1519. That day, April 21, either by amazing coincidence or perhaps prompting this whole Aztec-Christian fall of man scenario, was also Nahua day One Flower.[61]

Many of the mendicant friars from the beginning believed that Cortés was a divinely chosen "new Moses" whose "return" to Mexico had been foretold to the Indians by way of their own preconquest legend of the hero-deity Quetzalcoatl. Whether or not this legend was laundered for Christian purposes, Mendieta added the story of how Quetzalcoatl had supposedly tried to stamp out human sacrifice but was instead driven out of "Tula" (Tollan) by his sinister twin, Tezcatlipoca. Quetzalcoatl then vowed to come back as a "bearded white man" from the direction "east" in the year One Reed.[62] According to Sahagún, Motecuhzoma sent messengers to Cortés's landing at Veracruz to greet the Spaniard as no less than returned Quetzalcoatl.[63] After all, the biblical Moses was himself born appropriately among "reeds" (bulrushes). Cortés as Moses-Quetzalcoatl, likewise arriving from such an eastern Tollan [place of the reeds] was thus hailed by the Augustinians as well as the Franciscans as the proverbial messiah, divinely delegated to lead the Indians to an enlightened Christian utopia.[64]

Peterson, without considering any of the above calendric correspondences, interprets a contemporaneous Spanish document dated January 29, 1571, stating that "the [Malinalco] cloister is . . . almost finished and is also vaulted," as evidence that the murals were ready to be painted at that moment.[65] Furthermore, she points out that a famed Spanish naturalist and court physician named Francisco Hernández arrived in Mexico in February 1571 at the behest of King Philip II to gather information for a series of volumes on the medicinal properties of various flora, fauna, and minerals unique to the New World. Dr. Hernández apparently spent some time at Malinalco, and Peterson believes his prestige and repertoire of biological knowledge may have stimulated the project.[66] Be that as it may, the Indian painters themselves had as much to contribute to, as to learn from, Dr. Hernández, and the great naturalist's presence could only have enlivened their already enthusiastic cooperation with the friars in planning a spectacular procession and neixcuitilli to celebrate the providential succession of two such significant years.

Just what day, even what month in the Christian calendar, when these Aztec years conjoined, is still a matter of scholarly contention. According to Caso, "new year's day" for One Reed should have been January 12, 1571, but this is unconfirmed by any contemporaneous record keepers in or near Malinalco. Moreover, one of the Christian commentators in the Codex Telleriano-Remensis claimed that in his Puebla region the native new year began in late February.[67] In Mexico City, on the other hand, Sahagún was hearing from his Indian informants during the 1560s that early February was the proper season.[68] In any case, the Aztec year Thirteen Rabbit did overlap into Christian

1571 by nearly a month or more, so it would appear from the documents that the Malinalco cloister was being rushed to completion by the earlier Aztec year's end, perhaps so that the murals would be painted in time for a special event related to the calendar-round anniversary of Cortés's coming in the next year One Reed. It would have been another amazing coincidence indeed if the Caso correlation were operative in Malinalco in 1571, because in his system day One Flower would have fallen on April 8, Palm Sunday, the beginning of Holy Week and five days of penance and self-mortification before Easter, the Christian alternative to the Aztec nemontemi.

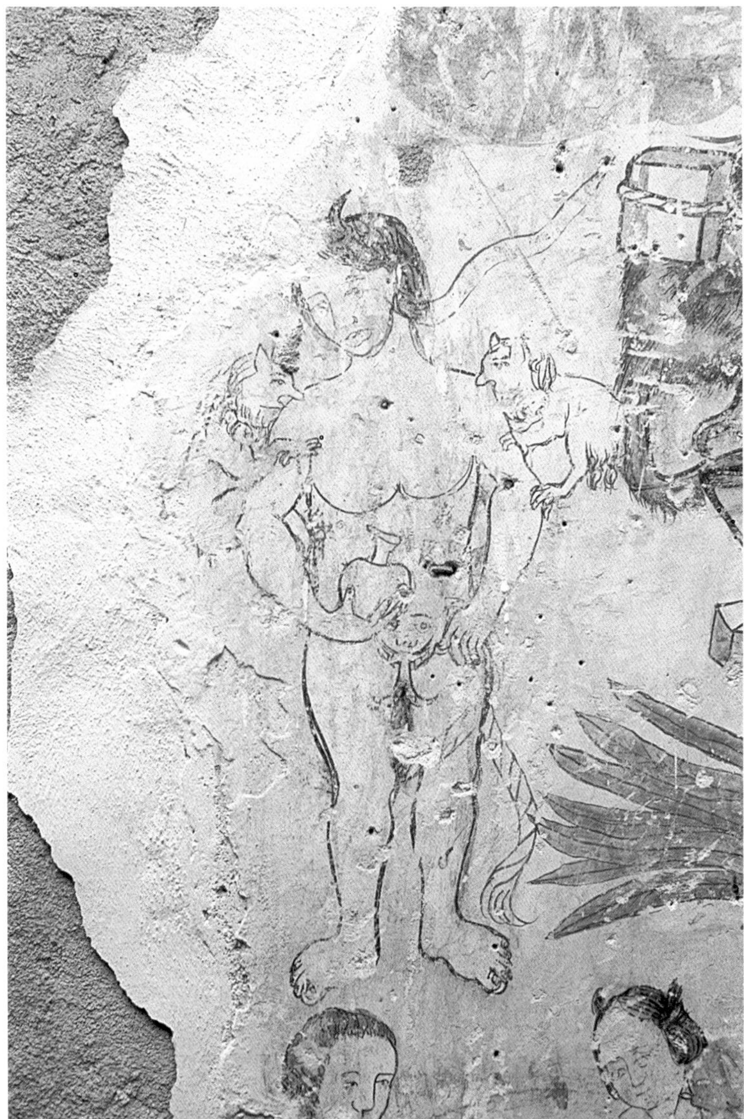

Fig. 8.20 Detail, mural in the Chapel of the Miracle of the Rosary, convento of San Juan Bautista, Tetela del Volcán, Morelos. Photograph by Jorge Pérez de Lara.

Certainly, if a neixcuitilli was to be performed in the Malinalco cloister, the number of persons admitted into this constricted area would have been small. Nevertheless, there is structural evidence that before the upper cloister story was built in the later 1570s and a massive connecting staircase inserted in the lower west wall (actually overlapping a section of the previously painted murals), a much broader opening to the portería existed on this side, meaning that not only could more of the interior of the cloister be observed from outside but also the original entrance was wide enough to allow a substantial procession to both enter and exit with impressive pomp. Whatever the number of participants, spectators, or both, they would all feel themselves on an "interiorized" momoztli as it were, in the same tropological paradise with Adam and Eve, together experiencing with the first parents the Devil's guile, Eve's sin, and Adam's punishment, and the new Eve's giving birth to Jesus the Savior.

If I am correct that these terrestrial paradise murals represented the scenery for just such a native procession and neixcuitilli, then reevaluation is in order regarding not only how cloisters were used by friars and Indians during the sixteenth century but also how Indian painters were still being allowed to preserve many of their old cultural traditions, now represented by the forms and conventions of the European Renaissance style.

In respect to the latter, the Malinalco murals are indeed a magnificent achievement. What the Indian painters did in effect was to create a two-dimensional illusion of a three-dimensional forest. As the sixteenth-century friars were wont to admire, the Indians had always a talent for "realistic" theatrical effects, even including live plants and animals in their spectacles. Where Malinalco diverges from this native tradition, of course, is that its murals were a deliberate counterfeit of live plants and animals. By coloring their murals only in Renaissance-style chiaroscuro, the Malinalco painters presented the illusion not only of raised tactile relief but also of the Christian God's own primordial, black-and-white vision of the world at genesis.

The Malinalco cycle, arguably the most original extant masterpiece of Indian mural art in the postconquest period, had, unfortunately, no painted successors. At least, none has been uncovered so far that exhibits the same ingenious attention to both native biology and pictorial composition. One reason surely has to do with the demise in general of the convento in the life of the indigenous Indians. More and more after the third quarter of the sixteenth century, administration of the rapidly diminishing native population was being taken away from the mendicant friars and given over to the secular church, the newly arrived Jesuits, and the tender mercies of Spanish lay colonists. In the visual arts, sophisticated Flemish mannerism and Spanish baroque, now practiced in Mexico by a larger number of professionally trained European masters, assumed the high style of the increasingly Hispanicized cities. The grand architectural retablo with its gilded sculpture and inset oil paintings replaced the mural fresco as the prominent art form in churches and friaries. By the seventeenth century, the old murals were already quite out of fashion, and most had been erased or whitewashed over, as indeed happened in Malinalco.[69] Indian mural painters, increasingly obsolete, had often to pass themselves off as Spanish criollos, or at least mestizos, if they would continue their craft, and to abandon their old convento stylisms in favor of the latest fads from Spain.

In this final moment of the mendicant friars' autonomy, the Malinalco murals sing the swan song of constructive cooperation between native artists and the European Renaissance—the light of convento art burning brightest just before it went out.

Memory is a strong perception of the soul, of things and of words and of [their] placement. It is of the greatest necessity to the orator, and not without reason is called the treasury of inventions and custodian of all parts of rhetoric. It is much reinforced and agumented by exercize, that is by art and preconception, making use, to be sure, of places and images.

Fray Diego Valadés, Rhetorica Christiana, 1579

⊕

Chapter 9

THE CONVENTO AS THEATER OF MEMORY

On page eighty-eight of his *Rhetorica Christiana,* Fray Diego Valadés published an engraving by his own hand showing a human head in profile, inset with a diagram indicating the so-called three ventricles of the brain into which, according to the Galenic medical theory of the time, the five classical senses directed their external stimuli. In the Middle Ages it was firmly believed that seeing, hearing, tasting, smelling, and touching each conveyed their sensations to a point just behind the eyes known as the *sensus communis,* or common sense (fig. 9.1). (This is where Leonardo believed the soul was located; see fig. 1.9.) From thence the sensory messages were distributed to the appropriate ventricles: the foremost part of the brain where "fantasy" and "imagination" were aroused; the center where "thought" and "judgment" [*cogitativa, estimativa*] formed; and the hindmost, where "memory" was stored (separated from the rest by the *vermis,* or "red worm," as the choroid plexus was then called).[1]

The source of Valadés's engraving, as René Taylor has shown, was the woodcut frontispiece of *Congestiorum artificiosae memoriae* ([Book of] compilations of artificial memory) by the Dominican Johannes Romberch, printed in Venice in 1520 (with a second edition in 1534).[2] This treatise was but one of many being published in Europe throughout the sixteenth century concerning a popular fad among intellectuals of that time known as *ars memoriae,* or art of memory. In fact, Romberch's woodcut was itself derived from

Fig. 9.1 Fray Diego Valadés, *The Five Senses and the Human Brain,* engraving in his Rhetorica Christiana, Perugia, 1579, p. 88. Courtesy of the John Carter Brown Library at Brown University, Providence, Rhode Island.

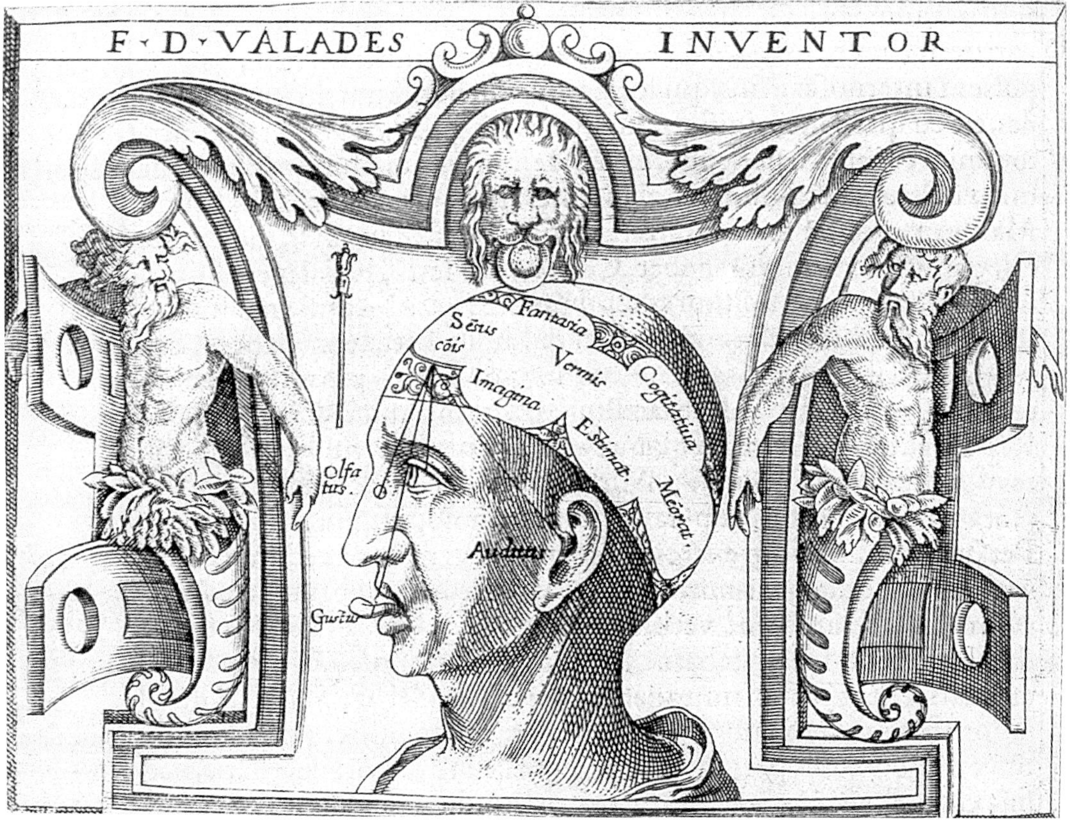

the standard medieval diagram of the human brain, appearing in anatomical manuscripts even before the invention of printing. The image then became, as in Valadés's own use, the logos introducing several subsequent treatises on the art of memory.

Ars memoriae was intended to train public orators to take note of various physical objects such as architectural details in the buildings wherein they were speaking and have these serve as mnemonic cues. The orator should first associate a particular object with a particular thought. In the course of his speech, he would spot that object either in his imagination or actual visual field, and thus his memory would be jogged and the thought recalled.

This sixteenth-century fad was actually a revival of an ancient practice that, according to the Roman orator Cicero, was invented by a Greek poet named Simonedes of Ceos. However, the earliest texts surviving on the subject are from first century B.C.E. Rome, especially a very popular treatise often erroneously attributed to Cicero entitled *Ad Herennium* [To Herennius] after the unknown Roman to whom it was dedicated. Cicero did write a similar treatise *On the Orator [De oratore]*, and both these, along with a very similar first century C.E. work by the Roman author Quintilian, were frequently printed during the sixteenth century. In fact a 1527 printed edition of Quintilian's *Institutio oratoria* [The institution of oratory] was one of the early books deposited in the first American library at the Colegio de Santa Cruz in Mexico City. This copy has been preserved, still bearing its original seal, in the Adolph Sutro Library in San Francisco, California.[3]

Well before its Renaissance printed-book revival, the art of memory had been employed by the early Christian clergy for the teaching of sacred doctrine to neophytes by placing images of the holy stories in strategic locations along the liturgical procession routes within the church.[4] In the thirteenth century the newly founded Dominican order, whose defining mandate was public preaching, especially emphasized the art of memory, advocated by no less a personage than Saint Thomas Aquinas.[5] The Florentine Dominican Saint Antonine also urged that readers of his *Summa theologica* learn the art of projecting sacred concepts into memory figures. Franciscans likewise practiced their own version of the art of memory based on the mystical writings of Ramon Lull. It was even generally believed at the time that if one tilted back the head, as in Raphael's portrait of the pensive Cardinal Inghirami, ca. 1512 (fig. 9.2), gravity would cause "vital spirit" to flow into the posterior ventricle of the brain, thus inciting memoria and anagogic contemplation of the holy images therein stored.

One is inclined to wonder just how the learned Pedro de Gante took advantage of ars memoriae in his own strategies for teaching Christianity to the Indians by means of visual aids. Had he seen, for example, Guglielmus Leporeus's popular *Ars memorativa* printed in Paris, 1520, in which the author demonstrated how mnemonic associations be made with the use of separately numbered parts of an imaginary edifice, the woodcut diagram of which very much looks like an open patio surrounded by four corner posas (fig. 9.3)?[6] Leporeus's diagram is labeled "House of Ten Places." Starting from the doorway and proceeding to

Fig. 9.2 Raphael, *Portrait of Cardinal Tomaso Inghirami,* ca. 1513, Isabella Stewart Gardner Museum, Boston, Massachusetts.

roof, is *Sextus,* and so on around the right side of the "house" and back to the entrance. Each *locus* should be related to an image *(imago)* retained for recall in the senses.

In his 1579 *Rhetorica Christiana* Fray Pedro's student Diego Valadés devoted five whole chapters to the art of memory—termed by him *scientiarum thesaurus* (treasure of all knowledge).[7] According to the classical tenets of ars memoriae there are two kinds of memory: natural and artificial. While natural memory is inherent, artificial memory, as Valadés paraphrased the ancient sources, is that which induction confirms and is the reason of perception. It consists of places and images and is amplified by the rationale of doctrine. . . . Images are certainly forms and signs and representations of those things we want to remember; which it is necessary for us to collect in certain places like the genus of horses, lions, books, and stones. For places are like wax tablets or writing paper. Images are like letters; the disposition and collocation of images like writing.[8]

For Valadés, what was so attractive about

the left, *Secundus* is the wall space before the circle marked *Tertius,* which is the base of a column marked *Quartus,* with its capital the circle marked *Quintus.* The entablature, or the art of memory was its obvious applicability to the teaching of Christianity to the Indians, already disposed to "reading" images in their own indigenous picture-writing. Like so many of his fellow Franciscans in Mexico, he saw connections between native Indian culture and that of the ancient Mediterranean world; Mexican picture-writing was like Egyptian hieroglyphics, he mused (based on his reading the popular Renaissance-revived text on the subject by fifth-century C.E. Horapollon).[9] Therefore, the Indians, even though unlettered in the European sense, were, like the ancients of the Old World, still capable of communicating complex and arcane concepts by means of pictures, especially exemplified in their calendar. Interestingly, Fray Diego made an engraving of the dual Mexican calendar in the form of concentric circles, an emblematic device he surely intended the more erudite among his European readers to connect with the arcane combinatory wheels for explaining the mysteries of the universe by Isadore of Seville and Ramon Lull.[10]

As René Taylor and Pauline Moffitt Watts have shown, Valadés rehearsed all the antique and contemporaneous Renaissance sources, but he was especially concerned with those that actually illustrated methods that would be relevant to teaching the Indians the letters of the Latin alphabet and Christian doctrine by association with the architecture of church and convento. From Lodovico Dolce's *Diologo nel quale si ragiona del modo di accrescere et conservar*

Fig. 9.3 Guglielmus Leporeus, woodcut diagram of his *House of Ten Places, Ars memorativa,* Paris, 1520.

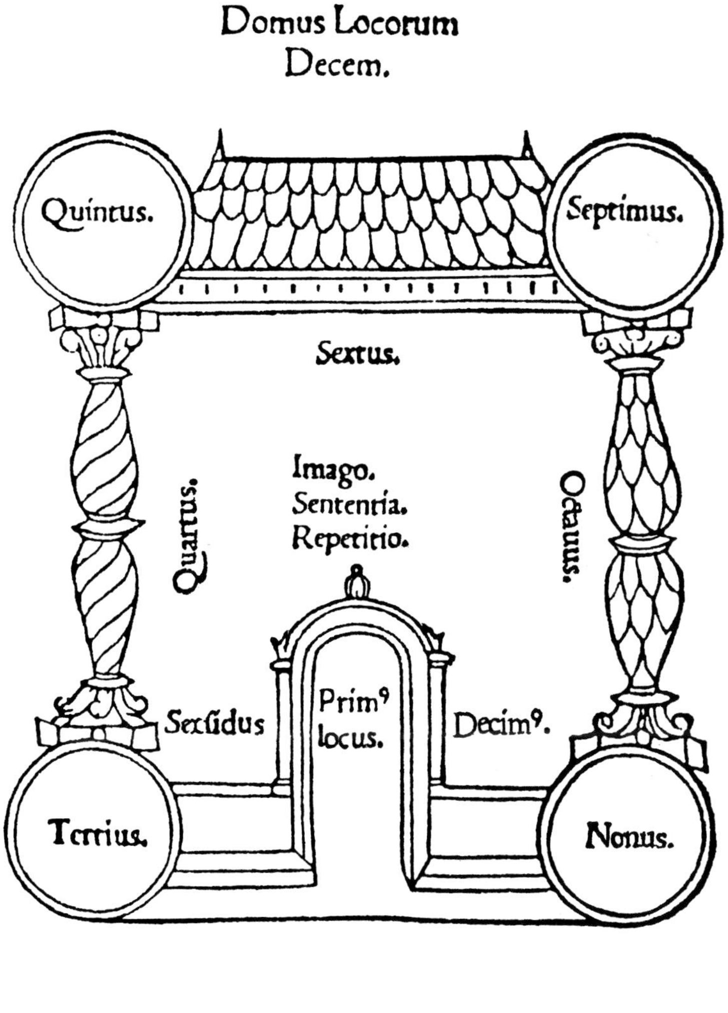

Fig. 9.4 Fray Diego Valadés, Latin letters converted to pictographs, engraving in his *Rhetorica Christiana*, Perugia, 1579, after p. 100. Courtesy of the John Carter Brown Library at Brown University, Providence, Rhode Island.

la memoria (Dialogue in which one reasons the means for increasing and saving the memory) (Venice, 1552), he copied line for line one of the Italian author's rebus diagrams identifying Latin letters with various physical objects having the same general shape.[11] He also included a mysterious diagram of his own invention in which the letters of the alphabet were related to hieroglyphic-style emblems (fig. 9.4). Some of these were deliberately drawn to look like Indian symbols, as for the letter *E*, which appears to have been derived from the native calendric glyph for the day-sign *calli*. Others are obviously European, like the image for the letter *D*, which shows the imprint of a Spanish "piece-of-eight."[12] Valadés's intention here remains unclear, since there is no recognizable visual or phonetic correlation between any of these emblems in Nahuatl or European languages. He seems to have invented these images simply to resemble exotic, perhaps even Testerian, characters and thus impress his European readership with the proselytizing ingenuity of the missionary friars in America. In fact, in the upper left-hand corner of his engraving of the ideal convento patio (see fig. 2.29), he represented Pedro de Gante actually demonstrating to the Indians (*discunt omnia;* "they discuss everything") certain similar figures that appear to be Testerian glyphs painted on a hanging lienzo (fig. 9.5).[13]

Many more pages were devoted by Valadés to his method for teaching holy doctrine by means of association with church architecture. While inspired no doubt by the woodcut images in Romberch's book that showed how even the various community buildings adjacent to a Christian abbey (including barbershop and beauty parlors, library, and animal barns) could be deployed as memory prompts, Fray Diego did not add any illustrations of his own. Instead, he set out in words only an elaborate plan based on similar descriptions in the Bible like the "ark of the tabernacle" envisioned by Ezekiel. He even applied scriptural measuring terms like "cubits" and described pillars and capitals of "silver and brass" just as in Solomon's temple. In this imaginary setting, Valadés envisioned a vast atrium framed on all sides with columns, each cluster of which should represent from east to west the names of both Old and New Testament authors in special orders of precedence, all in all furnishing six hundred general and specific architectural *loci* to serve as memory cues to the various passages and meanings of Scripture.[14]

Valadés's intention in this abstract example was once again to appeal to European intelligentsia who would, of course, be quite familiar with the biblical references and could thus more conveniently share in his memory method. However, there is no doubt that Fray Diego was implicitly alluding to the Mexican conventos in which he had been educated, and where I believe he first encountered the ars memoriae in practice. In his text he also referred to a more mundane route through "a city, monastery, church, theater, house, garden, or whatever of this sort," during which one should mentally assemble things like doors, windows, stairs, columns, etc. and the distance between these objects along a continuous wall. Each object and interval would then provide a prompt to be recalled in serial order. One is reminded here of the famed "memory palace" that the Jesuit missionary to China Padre Matteo Ricci (1552–1610) constructed in his own imagination, enabling him to memorize all forty-thousand characters of the Chinese alphabet and even to recite the Chinese writings of Confucius backward.[15]

Perhaps the tour de force example of the mnemonic art most talked about among intellectuals in Europe during the early sixteenth century was the Theater of Memory devised and actually built by the Venetian Giulio Camillo. Here is an excited description sent to Erasmus by a friend visiting Camillo in Venice in 1532:

> They say that this man has constructed a certain amphitheater, a work of wonderful skill, into which whoever is admitted as spectator will be able to discourse on any subject no less fluently than Cicero. . . . The work is of wood, marked with many images, and full of little boxes. . . . He gives a place to each individual figure and

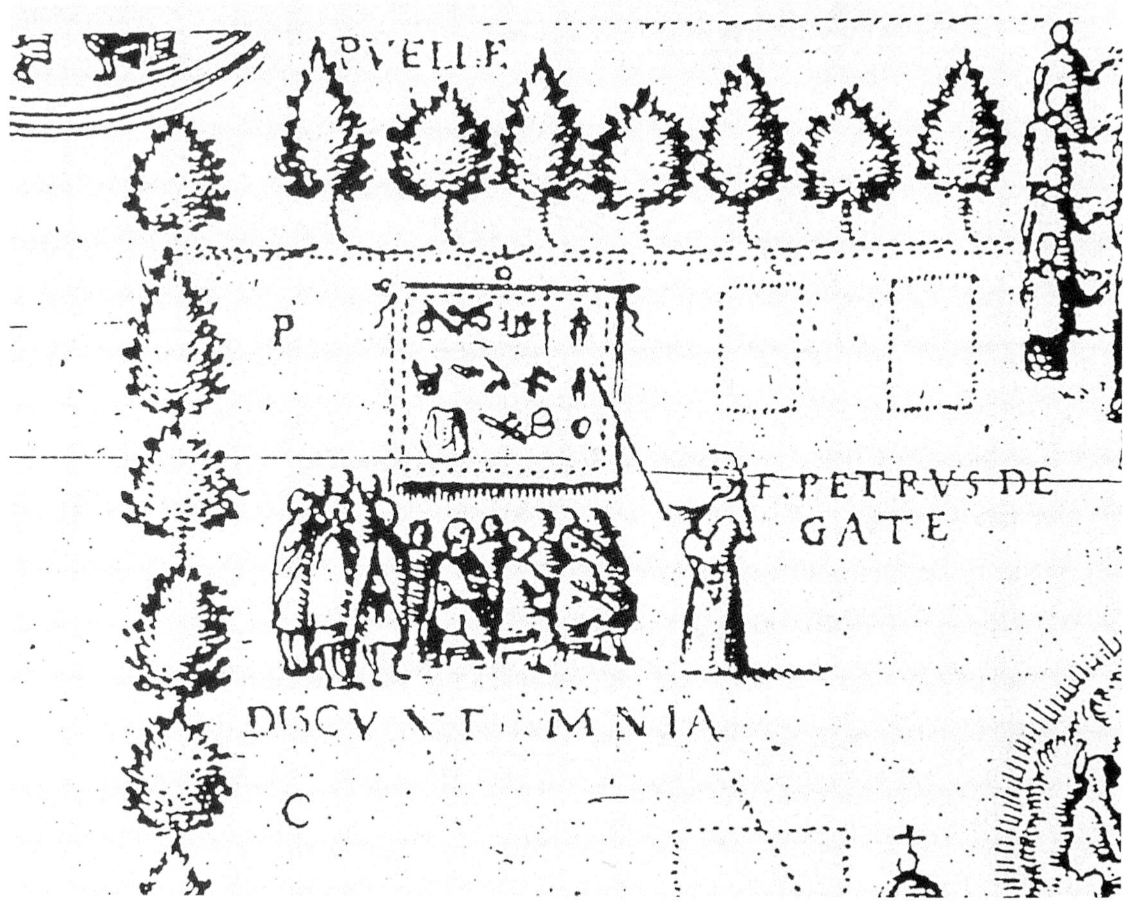

Fig. 9.5 Fray Diego Valadés, detail (from fig. 2.29), Fray Pedro de Gante teaching the Indians Testerian hieroglyphics, *Rhetorica Christiana,* Perugia, 1579, p. 107. Courtesy of the John Carter Brown Library at Brown University, Providence, Rhode Island.

ornament. . . . He calls this theater of his by many names, saying that it is a built or constructed mind and soul, and now that it is a windowed one. He pretends that all things that the human mind can conceive and which we cannot see with the corporeal eye, after being collected together by diligent meditation may be expressed by certain corporeal signs in such a way that the beholder may at once perceive with his eyes everything that is otherwise hidden in the depths of the human mind. And it is because of this corporeal looking that he calls it a theater.[16]

As Frances Yates has explained, Camillo belonged to an intellectual movement in Europe at the time increasingly fascinated by

Hermeticism and occult religion. He devised his memory theater as a means for collating and reconciling all these exotic references, many of which had been inspired by revelations coming from the newly discovered lands of Asia and America. Camillo's theater particularly appealed to contemporaneous philosophers like Giordano Bruno, Paracelsus, and J. J. Scaliger, forerunners of modern science.[17] Indeed, Camillo's curious concept was of no small importance to the eventual development of scientific taxonomy.

Although Valadés and the Franciscan missionaries in Mexico would hardly have admitted to such pagan dabbling, many were much intrigued by the thought that American Indians had ancient Hebrew and possibly cabalistic contacts. In this sense the *Rhetorica Christiana* sits within the same intellectual movement as inspired Camillo. Many of Valadés's other engravings in which he attempts to schematize Christian doctrine seem just as convoluted as the Venetian's elaborate construction. Nevertheless, beneath all the abstruse rhetoric of Valadés's long-winded discussions, can still be perceived a palimpsest of his original exposure to the art of memory, formed not after he arrived in Europe but from personal experience in the Franciscan conventos where he grew up and was educated. Whatever else were the architectural sources of these uniquely Mexican structures, they most practically if only coincidentally served as ideal theaters of memory.

[The Pueblo Indians] have notable affection for the things of the Church, as all the churches and monasteries they have made fully testify. All of which it will seem an enchantment to state that sumptuous and beautiful as they are, the [churches] were built solely by women and by the boys and girls of the curacy. For among these nations, it is the custom for women to build the walls, and for the men to spin and weave their mantas, and go to war and the chase; and if we [try to] oblige some man to build a wall, he runs away from it, and the women laugh. And with this [work of women] there have been built more than fifty churches, with roofs, very beautiful carvings and fretwork [*lacería*], and the walls very well painted. For there are marvelous highlands of every sort of timber; and with the care that we religious have put to teaching the Indians of the curacy, there are very good craftsmen in carpentry and in all the crafts.

Fray Alonso de Benavides, Memoriales

Chapter 10

"EL DORADO"

The Desolate Desert Conventos of New Mexico, 1598–1700

Out of respect for a utopian vision that never squared with geopolitical reality, the Spanish crown may have waited until the death of Fray Pedro de Gante before administering the coup de grâce to the mendicant friars' dream of an autonomous Indian Republic in New Spain. In a series of decrees between 1573 and 1583, King Philip II finally removed the friars from control of Indian education, a duty they had assumed since 1523, and reverted all authority to the secular priesthood, who should henceforth organize the natives of Mexico into official parishes under episcopal

Fig. 10.1 Ruins of the Nuestra Señora de los Angeles pueblo church with kiva in foreground, Pecos, New Mexico. Photograph by Jorge Pérez de Lara.

rule. Moreover, the upstart Counter-Reformist Jesuit order was posted to Mexico to further moderate mendicant activities, perhaps even to keep an eye on the Franciscans, whom the king often suspected of being crypto-Lutherans.[1]

In book 4 of his 1596 *Historia eclesiastica indiana,* Fray Gerónimo de Mendieta lashed out at this unhappy turn of events. He excoriated Philip's dependence on bureaucratic advisers ignorant of true conditions in the distant Americas and claimed the current reign compared poorly with the glorious golden age of predecessor Charles V. With biblical invective, he railed against the "Babylonian captivity" of the evangelized Indians now being placed under secular authority.[2] In fact, Mendieta's whole *Historia* is a *dernier resort* justification of the heroic, messianic Franciscan mission in Mexico. Unfortunately, it was neither read by the Spanish king (who died in 1598) nor published until modern times. In the face of such autocratic indifference, the regulars were left with but two choices: retire to their cloisters in secluded irrelevance or leave their comfortable quarters in Mexico and seek new souls in the harsh frontier of the still-uncolonized north.

Such was the booby prize the Spanish sovereign offered to the mendicants. In his wide-ranging Laws of the Indies, the king decreed that conversion of the northern Indians "was the principal objective for which we mandate that these discoveries and settlements be made."[3] Philip was all too aware that Francisco Vásquez de Coronado's vain search for El Dorado three decades before had yielded no gold, not even a promise of prosperous agriculture, only rambunctious natives scattered in squalid villages in a vast and lonely desert. If the mendicants still insisted on having their "primitive church," let them found it among the pesky savages in the uncivilized wilderness.

After the discovery of silver in the Zacatecas region of old Mexico in the 1540s, Augustinians and Franciscans as well as Jesuits sought to help in "pacifying" the wild Chichimec Indians who were continually attacking the isolated mining communities and the tenuous trails linking them to the settled south. Because of the violence that characterized this frontier, few of the early churches and conventos constructed by the missionaries in what are now the Mexican states of Sonora, Chihuahua, and Coahuila

Fig. 10.2 Church of San Francisco de Asís, Taos, New Mexico, as viewed at its altar end.

have survived in their original form.[4] Even less remains across the Gulf of Mexico in what is now the southeastern United States where the Franciscans made another determined effort to proselytize as early as 1565. Unfortunately, not one of the more than a hundred missions originally set up from Florida to the Chesapeake Bay is any longer extant. Disease, Indian uprisings, and English expansion after 1763 put an end to any art and architectural heritage the Spanish Catholic missionaries may have bequeathed to the North American eastern seaboard.[5]

In New Mexico, on the other hand, enough of the picturesque architecture built during the early seventeenth century is still to be seen, permitting comparison with immediate precedents in central Mexico, Counter-Reformation Europe, and even South America. Most remarkably, the pueblo style that the friars and their Indian converts devised for these Christian monuments perfectly complements the awesome geology of the desert, as, for example, the massive adobe church at Pecos, New Mexico. Even in russet ruin it looks like a wind-sculpted desert butte (fig. 10.1). So environmentally compatible was this form that it has remained the regional trademark distinguishing both native and non-Indian architecture ever since. Long after the 1680 Pueblo Revolt, even as Christian missions in neighboring Arizona, Texas, and California were being constructed in updated, arcuated Hispanic style, churches in New Mexico still adhered to their original post-and-beam model.[6] The eighteenth-century adobe church of San Francisco de Asís at Rancho de Taos is a striking instance (fig. 10.2). Its simple geometric masses have especially appealed to twentieth-century cubist-inspired painters like Georgia O'Keeffe who reclaimed the primal structure as an icon of modern art.

In any event, the seventeenth-century New Mexican pueblo church is the culminating example of my theory of expedient selection, the friars' tactic of choosing from the stock of Christian forms just those that blended comfortably with the traditional visual symbols of whatever native society they were at the moment proselytizing.

Not since George Kubler's classic *Religious Architecture of New Mexico,* published in 1940, has there been a comprehensive attempt to set this unique regional adaptation into the larger context of post-Tridentine reform, nor has there followed a comprehensive study of how this style related to the mendicants' prior sixteenth-century experience in building missionary conventos elsewhere in the Americas. I hope to validate Kubler's original observation that the New Mexican style was a provincial extension of that great creative expression in the seventeenth-century Christian world known as the baroque, in which theater, once only the inspiration for religious art, became its essential purpose.

I also examine the peculiar natural and social environment under which the churches were constructed, and pass judgment on the breezy enthusiasm of Fray Alonso de Benavides who wrote the encomium cited in this chapter's epigraph. Fray Alonso was custodian of the Franciscan mission to New Mexico from 1626 to 1629, and the quotation is from his official report when he returned to Mexico City in 1630.

Conquest Northwest

While settlement and evangelization of what was then regarded as even more remote than the barbarous Chichimec frontier of New Spain did not begin in earnest until the early seventeenth century, the desire to find and reap its imagined riches goes back to an event that occurred in the very first decade of Cortés's conquest. In 1527 an expedition led by Cortés's rival, Pánfilo de Narváez, set out to explore the northern coastal regions of the Gulf of Mexico from Florida westward. Near what is now Galveston, Texas, some sixty of his followers lost contact with the main force and found themselves suddenly stranded, alone and abandoned in an uncharted savage wilderness.

Fortunately, among these lost adventurers was another of those exceptional Extremeños like Cortés, blessed with what Renaissance Italians admiringly called *virtù,* the ability to persevere and triumph under the most adverse circumstances. His name was Alvar Núñez Cabeza de Vaca (ca. 1490–ca. 1560), and for the next eight long years he and his ever-diminishing band of survivors toiled through steamy forests and arid desert, suffering capture and enslavement by hostile Indians. Somehow they managed to escape (often by posing as "medicine men") and make their way across what are now the states of Texas, New Mexico, and Arizona before reaching Mexico and home.

All save four eventually perished along the way. In March 1536, Cabeza de Vaca and his last three companions, including a remarkable Moroccan slave of equal virtù named Estéban, staggered into Culiacan, then the most northern settlement of New Spain (now capital city of the Mexican state of Sinaloa).[7]

What a tale they had to tell! Summoned to Mexico City, Cabeza de Vaca was the celebrity guest of Viceroy Antonio de Mendoza. There he met and was eagerly questioned by Bishop Juan de Zumárraga. Although Cabeza de Vaca accurately described the modest conditions of the northern natives living in crude but multistoried stone houses compacted together in pueblos (which simply means "villages" in Spanish), his hearers were certain that what he had witnessed gave truth to a congeries of Old World legends that now seemed relevant to the western side of the New World, all having to do with a mythic gilded king—El Dorado—who reigned in "seven cities" somewhere in terra incognita. One variant of the legend had it that this elusive "Eldorado," as the words were condensed into an imagined name for the "land of gold," was an island supposedly defended by Amazons situated near the terrestrial paradise "to the right hand of the Indies." That would place it, according to the Ptolemaic cartographic theory of the time, just to the west of New Spain. Cortés himself had led an expedition in search, discovering nothing but the eastern shore of lower California which he did not realize was only a peninsula.

The most enticing version of the story, however, held that long before Columbus, seven Portuguese bishops pursued by Muslims had managed to cross the "ocean sea" and found "seven cities of Antilia," presumably in the Azores, but later thought to be much farther west somewhere in the "Indies." The Spanish even named the Caribbean islands Antiles.[8] Now with the stunning report of Cabeza de Vaca, rumors transmogrified into certainty;

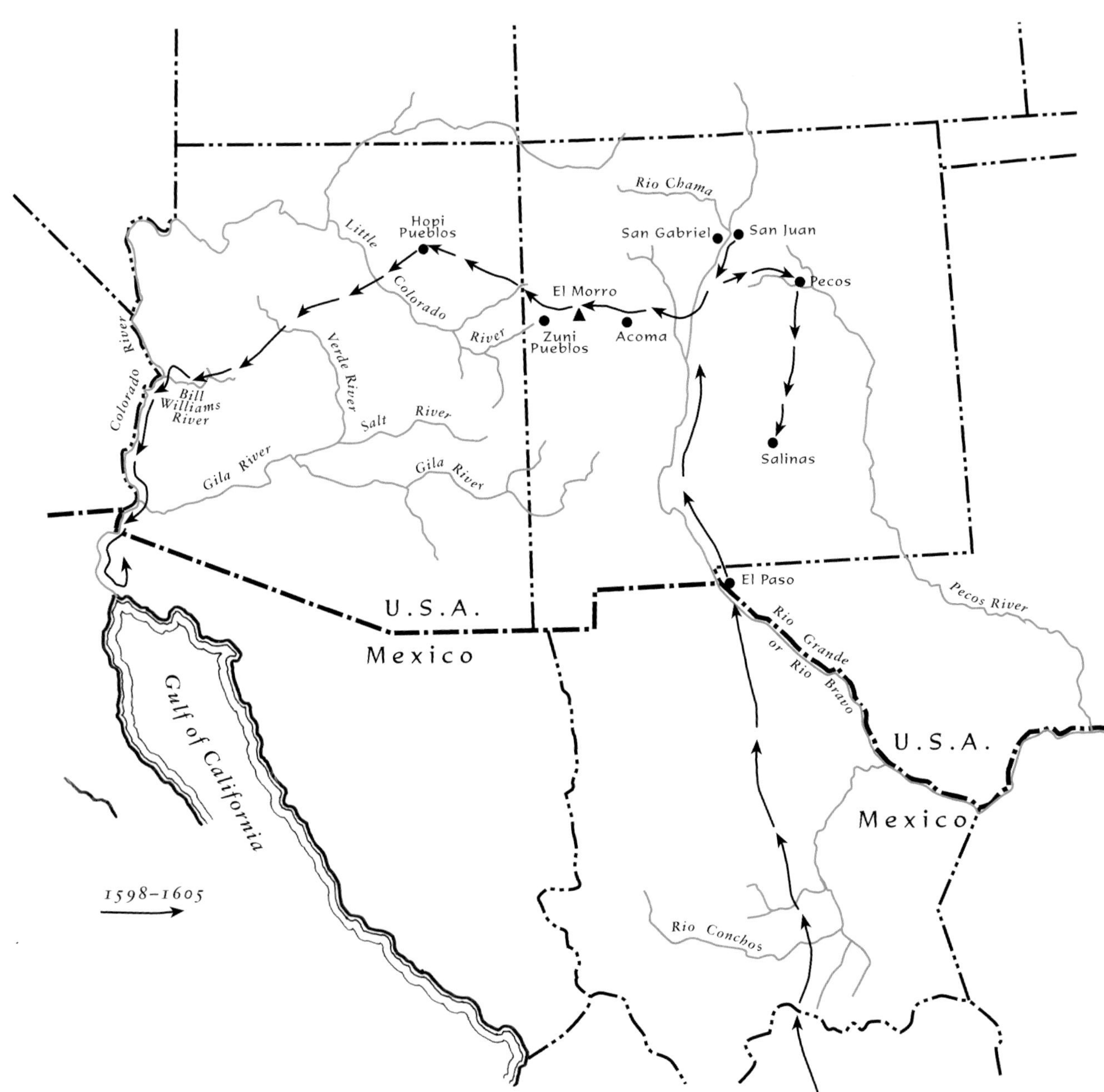

Fig. 10.3 Routes of Juan de Oñate's entradas into the present-day U.S. Southwest 1598–1605. Drawing by Mark Van Stone, typography by Melissa Tandysh.

Eldorado and the seven cities must be just a few leagues beyond the outpost pueblos described by Cabeza de Vaca. Here was surely a paradise more lush even than the kingdoms of the Aztecs and Incas, just waiting to be conquered by whoever could get there first.

Eager to beat the competition, Viceroy Mendoza decided to organize his own expedition under command of a swashbuckling young captain recently arrived from Spain named Francisco Vásquez de Coronado (1510–54). At the insistence of Bishop Zumárraga, Coronado was to be accompanied by an equally youthful and adventurous Franciscan friar named Marcos de Niza. Once again, the sword and the cross were to cooperate in this hoped-for new harvest of gold and souls.[9]

The idea was to send Fray Marcos in advance. He, along with a small caravan including Estéban, the veteran companion of Cabeza de Vaca, left Culiacan in March 1539. Traveling north along the western slope of the Sierra Madre, turning eastward following the Sonora River valley, they headed for what is now the U.S.-Mexico border. Estéban the scout ran ahead. It was he who first heard the word "Cíbola" in reference to the so-called seven cities, which local Indians informed him also included pueblos known as "Marata," "Acus," and "Totonteac." "Cíbola" apparently was the name the neighboring Ópata Indians gave to the Zuni nation of present-day southwest New Mexico.[10] Estéban and Fray Marcos were also told that these cities were ruled by a single king, and that their inhabitants dressed sumptuously and lived in houses of stone and mortar, sometimes four stories high with the doors of the "principal houses covered with many decorations of turquoise stones, of which there is great abundance in this land."[11] Again Estéban ran ahead, reaching one of the Zuni pueblos (Kiakima or Háwikuh?[12]) southwest of Halona, the present and only occupied Zuni city in New Mexico, in May 1539. There, in dramatic circumstances that are still recounted among the legends of the Zuni, he was killed.

Frightening as was this news, Fray Marcos was determined to see Cíbola for himself. He pressed on, but discretely did not try to enter the Zuni town. Instead, he climbed a neighboring hill, from whence he was able to see what he later described:

> [Cíbola] has the appearance of a pretty pueblo, the best I have seen in these parts. The houses, the Indians told me, are all built of stone, with their stories and flat roofs, as it appeared to me from the eminence which I climbed to see it. The settlement is larger than the city of Mexico. At times I was tempted to go to it, because I knew that I risked only my life, and this I had offered only to God the day I began this expedition. But the fact is I was afraid, realizing my peril, and that if I should die it would not be possible to have an account of this land, which in my opinion, is the largest and best of all those discovered.[13]

As much as Fray Marcos praised Cíbola, his native guides kept telling him that this was but the least of the seven cities, that Totonteac yet farther to the north was even larger and richer than all the others put together. (Totonteac has since been identified as the Hopi nation of eastern Arizona; Acus, with Ácoma, the famous Sky City of central New Mexico.)

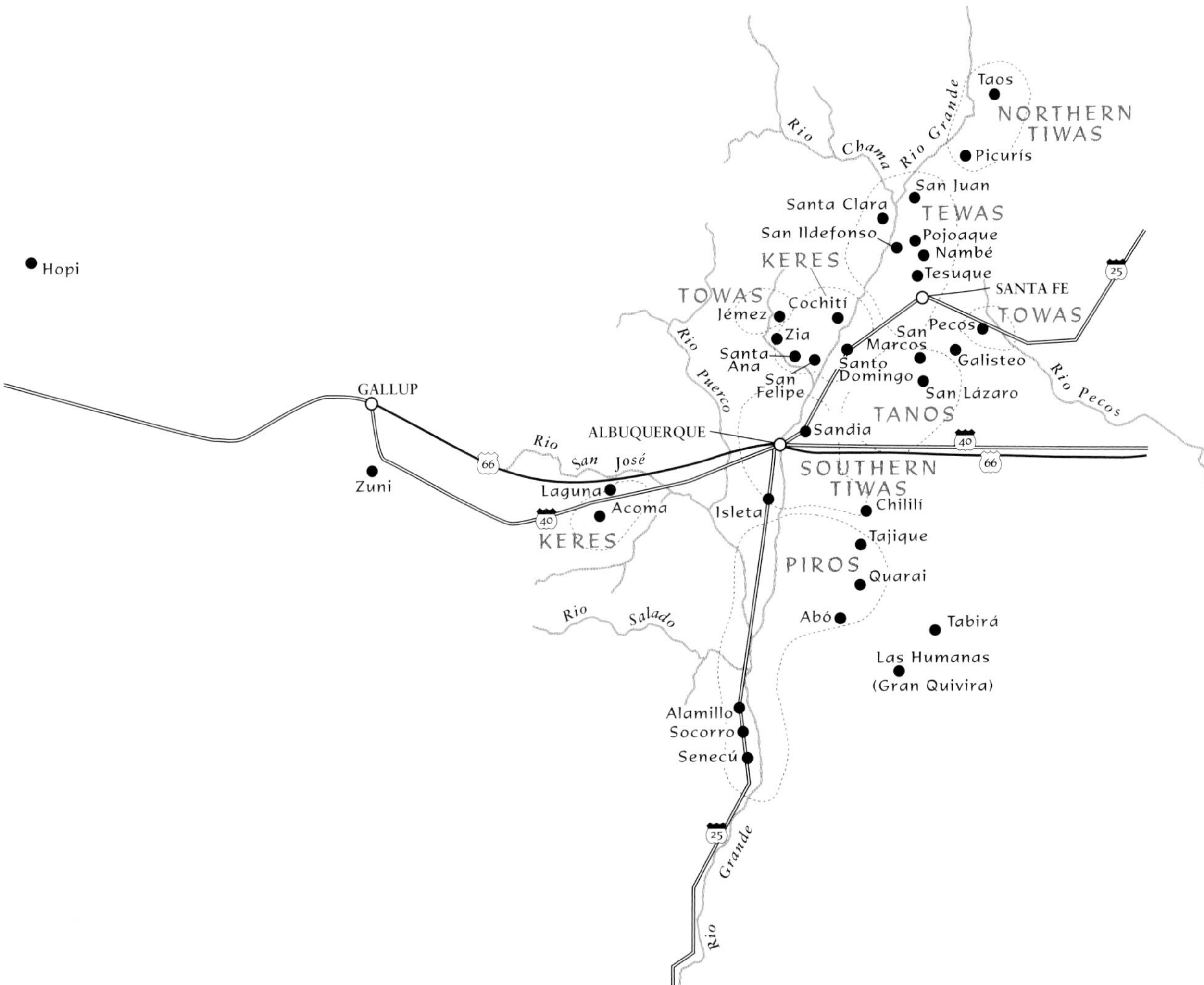

Fig. 10.4 Pueblo Indian settlements and language groups along the Rio Grande and vicinity in eastern New Mexico during the seventeenth century. Drawing by Mark Van Stone, typography by Melissa Tandysh.

This was enough for Fray Marcos who immediately decided to go back to Mexico with his news. As a marker for Coronado's imminent return to Cíbola, he set up a cross and vicariously "took possession" of all seven cities, proclaiming this as-yet unvisited territory, "the new kingdom of San Francisco" now under the authority of Viceroy Mendoza, the Pope, and the Holy Roman Emperor.

Fray Marcos, it turned out, was a man of vivid imagination. His stories to Coronado grew taller with each retelling. The stone houses he had seen were now described as made of timber; their multilevels heightened to palace proportions; their turquoise ornaments transmuted to gold. Also inhabiting the rich lands of Cíbola, moreover, were "unicorns and cows . . . and camels and dromedaries."[14]

Bishop Zumárraga and Viceroy Mendoza insisted that not only Fray Marcos but an entire contingent of Franciscans should accompany the return expedition "so that the conquest may be Christian and apostolic and not a butchery." By early 1540 Coronado's great adventure was launched. It was to last more than two years and cover thousands of miles of territory heretofore unseen by Europeans. To the north and east, Coronado apparently got as far as Kansas in search of another ephemeral land of gold called "Quivira."[15] To the west, his lieutenant García López de Cárdenas discovered the Grand Canyon, which halted his advance but failed to impress him aesthetically. Indeed, all Coronado's expectations of finding gold faded into nothing more than unappreciated natural wonders and desert mirages. Suffice only to mention that he was the first European to make face-to-face contact with Zunis, Hopis, and the many Pueblo Indians to the east and north along the Rio Grande valley from Ácoma to Tiguex (Bernalillo, New Mexico). Coronado was certain that the Zunis dwelled in seven cities—archaeology so far has found the remains of only six—but the Hopis he discovered really did inhabit seven original pueblos. Unfortunately, Coronado and his men did not always reciprocate the hospitality shown them by the Indians, thus sowing seeds of mistrust and bitterness that would plague Pueblo-Spanish relations in the north ever after. Coronado also dropped off five of his Franciscan friars, the first Catholic missionaries to dedicate their lives to converting North American Indians west of the Mississippi.[16]

In spite of Coronado's disappointing reports, numbers of Spanish fortune-seekers continued to adventure north during the third quarter of the century, still hoping to find Eldorado. It was to curtail these often irresponsible entradas leading to frequent abuse of the Indians that the bureaucratic Spanish ruler issued his ordinances, the so-called Laws of the Indies in 1573.[17] Henceforth, under penalty of death, no one was to "make a new discovery by sea or land, or enter a new settlement or hamlet in areas already discovered" without an official license from the king or his viceroy.[18]

Despite the king's decree, unauthorized incursions continued. Several missionizing attempts were however authorized, with often tragic results.[19] In 1582 a search party seeking to learn the fate of certain missing missionaries returned with news that two Franciscan friars had been martyred by Tewa Indians. At the same time the searchers had seen an abundance of rich-looking land just begging for the taking. So much clamor followed this announcement that the authorities in Mexico City decided to organize an expedition of "pacification" to what was now being hailed as the "province of Nuevo México." This land should now be officially subjected to the full measure of the ordinances of 1573, meaning that a colonial administration with a governor be duly appointed, a capital city with a permanent military garrison established, the surrounding land divided into encomiendas with access to Indian labor *(repartimiento)*, and above all, churches and conventos constructed for converting the Indians.

More years of delay elapsed before this last great Spanish enterprise of exploration and colonization could safely get under way (the Chichimec threat was only resolved in 1595). The leader was to be Don Juan de Oñate (1550?–1630), a criollo already wealthy from the silver mines discovered by his father in Zacatecas and newly hidalgo by virtue of his marriage to Hernán Cortés's granddaughter (who was also great-granddaughter of Aztec emperor Motecuhzoma). Finally, in January 1598, with a party of some five hundred prospective settlers including 129 men-at-arms and ten Franciscan friars, and driving a huge herd of livestock including 1,600 horses, Oñate, the "last conquistador" as he has been called, thrust north. After four months on the trail, the expedition made its first rendezvous with the Rio Grande, crossing the river where now is the city of El Paso, Texas (figs. 10.3, 10.4). Here, on April 30, 1598, they paused for Mass and to witness an *auto* performed by the pioneers acting in costume as if they were Indians begging the friars on bended knee that they be baptized and received into the church as Christians. Afterward, the friendly local natives treated the Spaniards to a sumptuous banquet of fish and waterfowl.[20] This event, as the citizens of present-day El Paso proudly and loudly proclaim, was North America's original Thanksgiving, a full twenty-two years before Plymouth, Massachusetts.

The colonists continued northward along the Rio Grande. By June 24, 1598, the feast of Oñate's personal patron Saint John the Baptist, the advance party reached a Tewa-speaking pueblo not far from present-day Albuquerque and there the Franciscans may have built their first crude church. In the weeks following, however, the strung-out units of the long wagon train converged a few miles distant at the juncture of the Rio Chama and the Rio Grande about halfway between modern Santa Fe and Taos. Here, beside another Tewa pueblo called Okeh, they decided at last to settle, naming their community San Juan de los Caballeros (just off Route 68, north of modern-day Española), honoring both Oñate's patron and the famous Crusader Knights of Jerusalem. Again a church was established. When the church was completed on September 8, Oñate's men-at-arms dressed as Moors and Christians and performed a mock-battle *auto* in the patio, no doubt to impress the local Indians with Spanish equestrian and military prowess.[21]

After settling in at San Juan, Oñate sent out expeditions east and west to explore his new domain. It was during the first western sortie in 1598–99 that Oñate ordered the atrocity that would stain his name ever since. In an attempt to collect provisions from the Indians of the high mesa Sky City pueblo at Ácoma, several Spanish, including Oñate's nephew, were killed. In retaliation, the governor ordered a scorched-earth attack on the pueblo resulting in the slaughter of hundreds of Indians including women and children. All captured males over the age of twenty-five were then sentenced to twenty years of servitude and to have a foot or hand amputated in a series of deliberately humiliating public autos-da-fé. Captured women were likewise sentenced to serve as slaves for twenty years. Indian children who survived were taken from their families and turned over to the Franciscans to be reared and educated as Christians.[22]

For some reason, perhaps out of fear of more native uprisings, the colony decided two years later to move across the river to another site called Yunque Oweenge. The native inhabitants were persuaded to move away and cede their pueblo houses to the colonists. Most of the Spanish settlers, increasingly restless and angry at not finding any gold or silver, were unwilling to become farmers, so the new town, rechristened San Gabriel, depended almost entirely on tribute extracted from the local Indians, themselves barely surviving on the meager produce of this land.

To explore further his vast domain, Oñate continued to dispatch sorties (and now angered his settlers at home by appropriating provisions from the sparse community reserve). In the east, he demanded allegiance from the inhabitants of the so-called Salinas region and the populous pueblo at Pecos. To the west, the Spaniards again confronted the Zunis and Hopis, and then followed the Colorado River south to the Gulf of California. On his return in 1605, Oñate chiseled his name, date, and erroneous claim that he had "discovered the South Sea" on a sandstone promontory beside a desert spring now called Inscription Rock in the El Morro National Monument, New Mexico.

In the meantime, conditions at San Gabriel were deteriorating. Not only were the colonists disappointed by the lack of mineral treasure but also the agricultural potential of the land itself was utterly inadequate. So bad indeed were living conditions that open rebellion broke out from all sides against Oñate's rule. Many settlers, including a number of friars, decided to abandon the colony and head back to the south. In the face of these difficulties and imminent censure by the viceroy, Oñate resigned as governor in 1607. In 1610 his former fiefdom was officially assumed by the Spanish crown and its capital moved to Santa Fe.

Oñate's earlier decree that the missionizing prerogative in New Mexico belonged exclusively to the Franciscan friars, to whom he granted "full faculty and license to build in each of [the Indian pueblos] the churches and conventos they deem necessary for their residence and the better administration of Christian doctrine," not only prevailed but was reinforced under the succeeding colonial administration.[23]

The vast land area originally claimed by Oñate and now to be evangelized by the Franciscans consisted of some 125,000 square miles of sagebrush desert and forested mountains covering what is now New Mexico, northeastern Arizona, and a corner of western Texas, all sparsely inhabited by some twenty-five thousand Indians gathered in threescore or so widely separated pueblo villages of populations varying from a hundred to a few thousand souls and belonging to at least six different mutually unintelligible language groups. Among the largest was the Towa-speaking Pecos Pueblo east of the Rio Grande with two thousand inhabitants. Farther south and east of the Manzano Mountains along

Fig. 10.5 Ruins of the San Isidro pueblo church, Las Humanas, New Mexico, looking toward the original forecourt patio.

several salt lagoons called by the Spanish *salinas* were a string of fourteen smaller pueblos including Chilili, Tajique, Abó, Quarai, and Las Humanas (later called Gran Quivira), speaking either Piro or Tiwa. Extending from south to north along the Rio Grande between Socorro and Taos was another string of pueblos including Isleta, Sandia, Santa Ana, Zia, Giusewa (Jémez), San Felipe, Santo Domingo, Cochití, and Picuris, speaking either Tiwa, Tewa, Keres, Tano, or Towa. Some distance west of the river (sixty-five miles from Albuquerque off U.S. Highway 40) the Keres-speaking survivors of Ácoma struggled to rebuild their pueblo atop its 350-foot-high *peñon,* and farther west still, lived the Zuni (to the south of present-day Gallup) and the Hopi (in the northeastern corner of Arizona) again with their own separate languages and customs.[24] To an indoctrinated Christian eye, the geographical distribution of all these far-flung pueblos might appear on the map to resemble a cross, and so it seemed to the Franciscan friars who took this to be a providential sign that God commanded their holy mission.

The obstacles to be faced by the Franciscan missionaries in New Mexico were more difficult than any their predecessors had ever encountered in New Spain. Perhaps they initially expected to repeat the experience of the Yucatán, a land of similar size and scrubby terrain where climate and natural topography likewise demanded a special solution for the founding of churches. Yet the indigenous Maya of the Yucatán all spoke the same language, followed a common native religion, and answered to the rule of only a few principal lineage heads through whom the general population could be reached. In New Mexico, the various Indian communities were quite independent of one another, speaking many languages, with different rituals, and socially more guarded and suspicious than the outgoing Yucatecans. There was also the problem of Indian raids, as the migrating *Navaju,* later called Apaches, now mounted on horses, were

Fig. 10.6 Reconstruction of the first church of San Gregorio, Abó, New Mexico. Drawing courtesy of James E. Ivey.

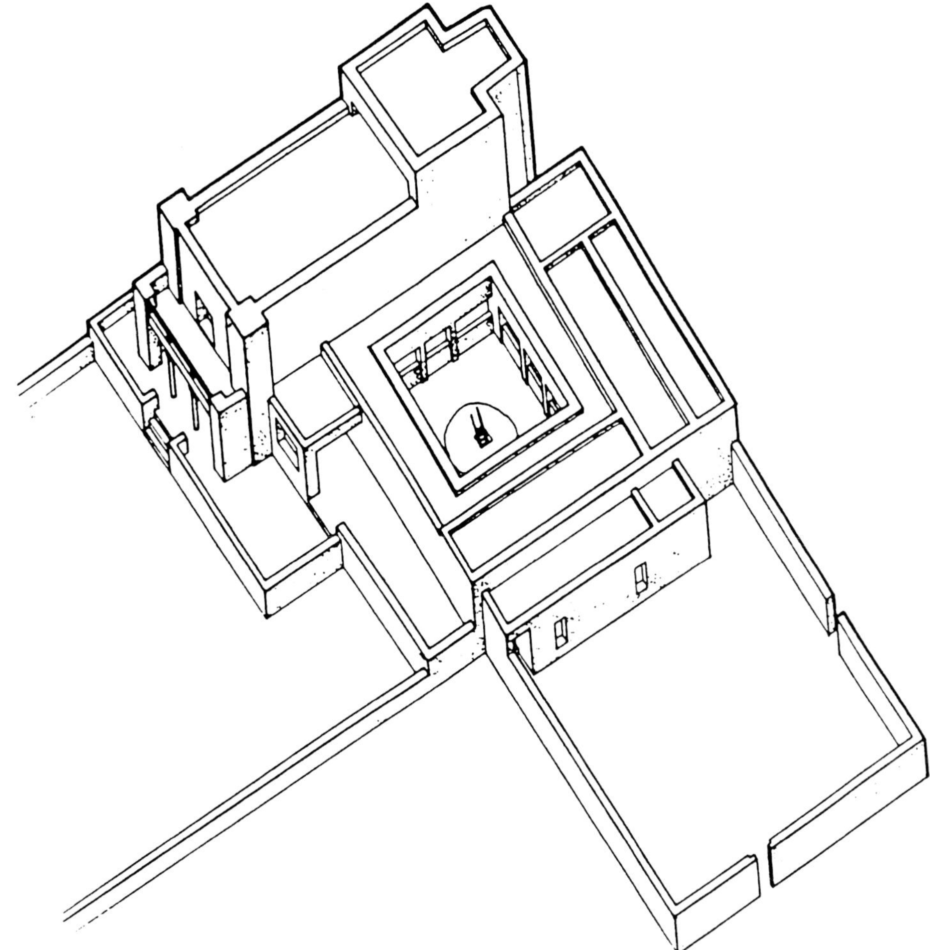

able to pillage the sedentary pueblos with impunity. These attacks became increasingly frequent during the period of severe famine in the 1660s and 1670s. In fact, they were so ferocious in the already drought-ridden Salinas region that the missionaries, along with the entire native population, were forced to abandon the pueblos and flee north, leaving their once-noble churches to disintegrate like sand castles in the wind.[25] For the most part, it was the utter loneliness and isolation of the desert that truly tested Franciscan endurance and dedication. To get a sense of the solitude—and indeed it pervades the region to this day—one needs but to contemplate the ruins at Las Humanas (fig. 10.5) in a setting that eerily recalls Shelley's "Ozymandias":

> Round the decay
> Of that colossal wreck, boundless and bare
> The lone and level sands stretch far away.

It is a terrain often so arid (especially during the extended drought that afflicted the region in the mid-seventeenth century) that its aboriginal inhabitants had to save their urine for watering their meager gardens and for mixing adobe mortar.[26] Making life even more precarious were the formidable winters in the desert, as bitterly cold as the summers are blistering hot, with bone-chilling winds and sometimes heavy snow.

From 1610 to 1680 the fledgling New Mexican colony—*aquellas provincias remotisimas* (those most remote provinces) as Fray Juan de Torquemada put it in 1615—maintained umbilical contact with central New Spain only by way of a single wagon train that arrived in Santa Fe from Mexico City every three years.[27] After a tortuous six-month trek through fifteen hundred miles of dangerous Chichimec territory, each triennial caravan brought just enough supplies, news and the latest fashions, and sufficient additional or replacement personnel to supplement whatever the colony and its mission could not produce for themselves, barely enough communion with "civilization" to keep body and soul together for another thirty-six months of Siberian isolation.

In 1629 only forty-six Franciscan friars are known to have been in all New Mexico.[28] In his *Memoriales* of 1630, Benavides stated that fifty churches had already been erected in as many pueblos before his departure from Santa Fe the year before.[29] Whether or not Benavides's figure is exaggerated—archaeologists have so far only traced some twenty sites where mission churches were built before the 1680 revolt[30]—hardly more than two friars could ever have been available together at any one time to supervise each construction, all of which must have been going on more or less simultaneously.[31] Nevertheless this was the crucial period in which the New Mexican adobe style achieved its archetypal and most attractive form (fig. 10.6).

In the remote Indian villages, the resident friar lived under the same conditions as the indigenous inhabitants on whom he depended for his daily subsistence. He had to learn the local language as best he could with no prior preparation and no pocket phrase book or dictionary. With whatever words or signs he was able to communicate to his often suspicious hosts, he had to convince them (1) of his own goodwill and peaceful intentions, (2) that they should reject their traditional religion and

Fig. 10.7 East-facing entrance facade of the San Estévan church, Ácoma Pueblo, New Mexico. Photograph by Dorothy D. Edgerton.

adopt his, and (3) that they should stop their own occupations and volunteer to help him build a church in their own pueblo style and technique, yet larger and more labor-intensive than any structure they had ever taken part in building before.

That so many large and handsome churches were erected before 1680 would seem to indicate that the early friars had succeeded on all three counts above. Certainly there were many instances of resistance on the part of the Indians; indeed, the first church at Giusewa (Jémez) was burned by its native builders in midconstruction in 1624, and elsewhere a number of Franciscans were murdered.[32] Nevertheless, the archaeological evidence in the surviving architecture itself makes clear that the greater number of inhabitants in each Indian community did cooperate in the construction of their new Christian churches. Once again the question arises as to how much the Indians were "forced" against their will to work on these massive structures. I reject the explanation suggested by some authors that the Indians only begrudgingly participated, in servile submission out of fear of physical punishment.[33] Everything about the pueblo churches reveals pride of craft and joy of creation. The artisanship and engineering of these remarkable buildings, setting an architectural style that has continued to be followed in the region right through to the present century, are just too inspired to have been the work of halfhearted or sullen laborers. Furthermore, the original mission churches that have survived in still-active Indian communities as at Zuni, Isleta, and Ácoma, despite the horror stories about the human cost of their construction which modern-day native guides relish rehearsing to arouse guilt in Caucasian tourists, are nonetheless proudly shown off as monuments to the enduring Indian spirit (fig. 10.7).

By 1660, however, the airy optimism expressed by Benavides in his 1630 report was truly no longer warranted. Relations between the lay government and the friars over rights to repartimiento labor, always a thorny issue, grew even more strained on the short-tempered and increasingly hair-trigger frontier. Conditions deteriorated further as the pueblos were more and more subjected to Apache raids, which contributed to the abandonment of the Salinas missions by the 1670s.

Furthermore, the Franciscans themselves made matters worse by tightening the screws on their Indian neophytes. The friars had always employed a relatively lenient strategy of conversion in New Spain, but this policy began to be called into question after the Council of Trent. While the Franciscans seem to have continued their original policy in New Mexico for at least the first four decades of the seventeenth century, they too succumbed to the paranoia of the Counter-Reformation.[34] As suspicions mounted that the Indians were reverting to idol worship, the friars turned intolerant. Kivas, originally permitted even inside the conventos, were suddenly forbidden to the Indians and often wantonly desecrated.[35] Suspected Indian backsliders were publicly whipped and humiliated, and some even were hanged for alleged sorcery and sedition. To the disillusioned Indians, the new religion, which originally had inspired them to such church-building zeal, brought little benefit, only drought, famine, disease, Apache violence, and more reactionary Spanish oppression.[36] The Christian god the Indians so ardently accepted during the 1620s and 1630s was, hardly three decades later, perceived to have failed.

As tensions on all sides heightened, the Spanish crown seemed unable and even uninterested in tending to the crises of its far distant, expensive, and not very productive colony. Explosion was inevitable, and it happened on Saint Lawrence's Day, August 10, 1680, when a preplanned massive revolution suddenly broke out involving seventeen thousand Pueblo Indians from two dozen varied communities uncommonly united by a charismatic Tewa Indian from San Juan pueblo named Popé (?–1692). Sweeping down the Rio Grande valley from Taos, the rebels fell on the Spanish settlements, burning haciendas and killing some four hundred colonists in a matter of a few days. Pueblo churches were also torched and twenty-one Franciscan missionaries murdered. Those Spanish settlers who got away fled to Santa Fe, which the Indians immediately surrounded and besieged. After three weeks of bitter fighting, Santa Fe too was abandoned on September 21.[37] As the city went up in flames, the last of the settlers retreated to El Paso, three hundred miles distant. For all intents and purposes, Pueblo New Mexico was now cleansed of any living Spanish and Franciscan presence.

For twelve years thereafter the Indians maintained their independence. Then, in 1692, after several failed attempts to wrest back the territory, a more spirited Spanish army under determined General Diego de Vargas, hearing perhaps that Popé had died, reentered New Mexico, and after a relentless four-months' campaign retook Santa Fe. In remembrance of his victory, Vargas engraved his name, date, and exploits alongside those of Oñate on Inscription Rock.

Several more years were needed to take

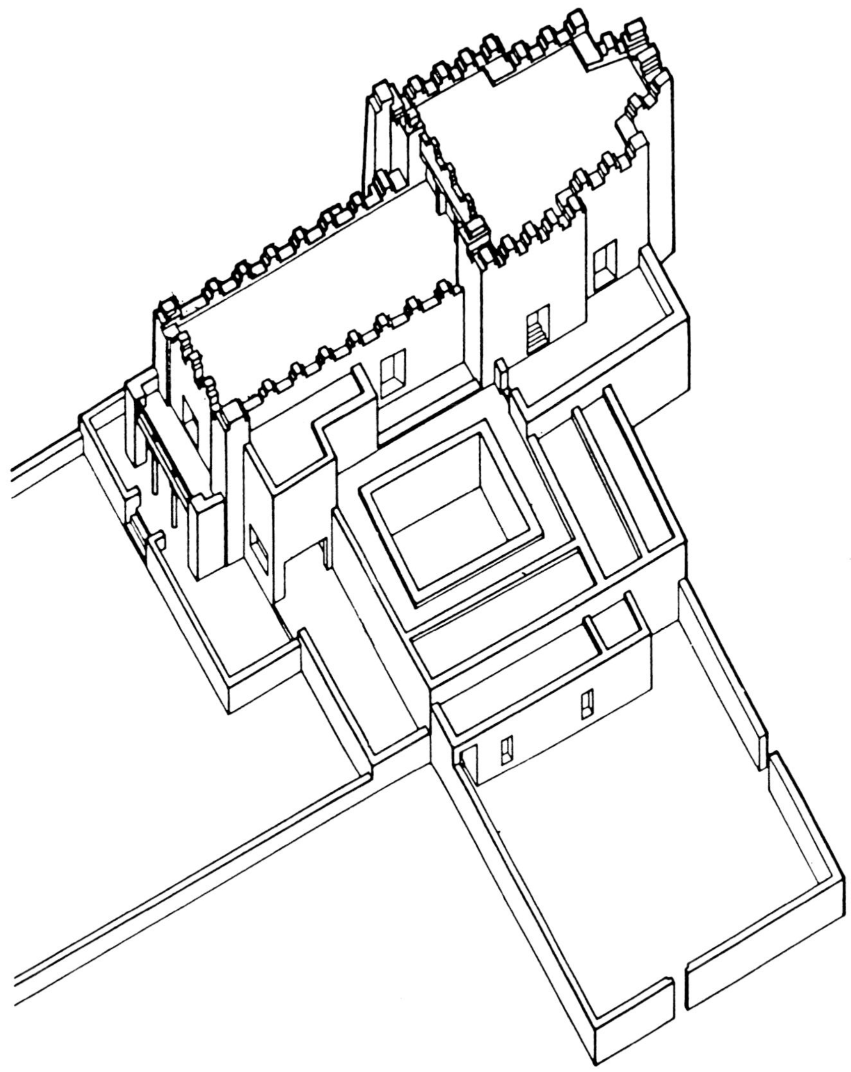

Fig. 10.8 Reconstruction of the second church of San Gregorio, Abó, New Mexico. Drawing courtesy of James E. Ivey.

Fig. 10.9 Ruins of La Purísima Concepción church, Quarai, New Mexico, looking toward its south-facing entrance. Photograph by Jorge Pérez de Lara.

control of all the now disunited and much-reduced Indian pueblo communities. By 1700 Hispanic and Franciscan dominion along the Rio Grande had been restored more or less to its antebellum condition. Native pueblos at Ácoma, Zuni, and Hopi continued to hold out for awhile, with the Hopi successfully resisting almost to the present day. Meanwhile, war and disease had taken a desperate toll on the indigenous population, now for the first time being outnumbered by the settlers. The Franciscan friars nonetheless returned warily to rebuild their churches in native villages, although no longer daring to live alone without military protection. The static lifestyle of the missionaries on this still uncertain and ever lonely frontier even until the nineteenth century has been sensitively described by Willa Cather in her beautifully written novel *Death Comes for the Archbishop*.

Of the twenty or so still-detectable mission sites established before the 1680 revolt, five are now under federal protection.[38] At Pecos National Historical Park, New Mexico, stand the ruins of two churches, the first and largest edifice dating from 1617 (and destroyed in 1680) and the smaller Nuestra Señora de los Angeles de Porciúncula, built after the 1692 restoration and finished in 1717 (see fig. 10.1). At Salinas Pueblo Missions National Monument (with headquarters at Mountainair, New Mexico) are four churches: San Gregorio, Abó, built first in 1623 and enlarged after 1629 (fig. 10.8); La Purísima Concepción at Quarai built after 1627 (fig. 10.9); and two churches at Las Humanas, San Isidro and San Buenaventura, the former begun in 1635 and the latter left uncompleted in the 1670s (figs. 10.10 and 10.11). The ruins of one more large church, San José de Giusewa, dating from 1626, are now conserved by the State of New Mexico in the Jémez Springs State Park (fig. 10.12).

Several other seventeenth-century churches remain the property of the Indians, are in good repair, and are still in use on their reservations today. Of special interest in this book are the churches of San Agustín, Isleta, claimed to have been first built in 1613 (fig. 10.13), with much reconstruction since;[39] San

Fig. 10.10 Plan of the Church of San Isidro, Las Humanas, New Mexico, ca. 1635. Drawing courtesy of James E. Ivey.

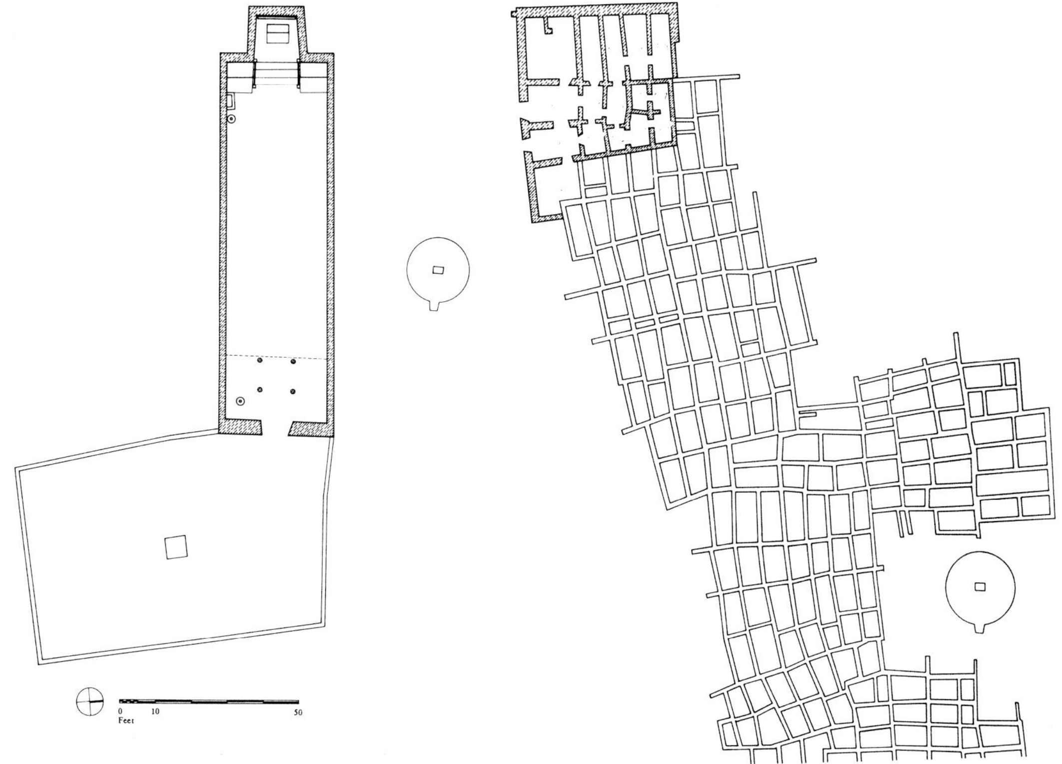

Fig. 10.11 Ruins of the church of San Buenaventura, Las Humanas, New Mexico, looking toward its east-facing entrance. Photograph by Jorge Pérez de Lara.

Estévan, Ácoma, originally constructed between 1629 and 1664 with restorations after 1680 (see fig. 10.7); and San José, Laguna, begun in 1699 (fig. 10.14).

While Kubler's classic *Religious Architecture of New Mexico* is still the most comprehensive study of the subject in its broader Hispanic context, his archaeological observations are quite outdated. Considerably more excavations have been carried out since, with new conclusions drawn. These have been meticulously analyzed by James E. Ivey in his provocatively titled *In the Midst of a Loneliness: The Architectural History of the Salinas Missions.* Despite the local limitation suggested by his title, Ivey offers far more than just a description of Salinas. His chapters on construction techniques and daily life and times of the various friars apply to the entire period and region. Although published in special U.S. National Park Service "historic structures report" format and therefore not intended for the general reader (in fact, now out of print and difficult if not impossible to obtain), this book is the definitive work on the whole subject. More accessible as well as being lavishly illustrated is Marc Treib's *Sanctuaries of*

Fig. 10.12 Ruins of the church of San José de Giusewa, Jémez, New Mexico, looking toward the altar through its south-facing entrance. Photograph by Jorge Pérez de Lara.

Fig. 10.13 Church of San Agustín, Isleta Pueblo, New Mexico, looking toward its south-facing entrance facade. Photograph by Jorge Pérez de Lara.

Spanish New Mexico. It also deals with all religious architecture of New Mexico from the seventeenth through the nineteenth centuries. Nonetheless Treib's archaeological information derives in the main from Ivey. For a general survey of indigenous building practices in North America before Europeans arrived, with useful information on how the Pueblo Indians of the Southwest adapted to Spanish customs and vice versa, see Peter Nabokov and Robert Easton, *Native American Architecture*.

Fig. 10.14 Church of San José, Pueblo of Laguna, New Mexico, looking toward its east-facing entrance facade. Photograph by Jorge Pérez de Lara.

[At Pecos] there was a magnificent temple, Nuestra Señora de los Angeles de Porciúncula, with six towers three adorning each side, with walls so thick that in its concavities were built workshops. . . . There were more than two thousand [Indian] Christians in the neighborhood. . . . and on a plateau about a league away the Apaches brought hides of buffalo [*sibolas*], tanned deer skins [*gamuzas*], and other things to trade for maize, stones of various colors which they call *chalchiguites* [turquoises], and tobacco, and more than fifty of these merchants came with their dog-teams laden every year. This is the pass to the realm of Quivira. Here it developed that they killed Padre Fray Fernando de Velasco, born in Cadiz, son of this [New Mexican] Province, former missionary, and then they burned the temple.

Fray Augustin de Vetancurt, Teatro Mexicano, 1698

⊕

Chapter II

RELIGIOUS ARCHITECTURE IN "THOSE MOST REMOTE PROVINCES"

Indigenous Pueblo peoples hardly suffered the same self-mortifying loneliness that the friars did. For the Indians, the desert teemed with invisible yet animate supernaturals including the spirits of their ancestors inhabiting every purple mountain, salmon-tinted butte, and sun-baked mesa wafted by the pungent aroma of the summer cliff rose. Each community had its natural canyon and arroyo tabernacles wherein dwelled not only the ancestors but the souls of descendants yet unborn. In one ritual form or another, all Pueblo peoples paid homage to the sun, which coaxed

Fig. 11.1 Kiva at Chetro Ketl, Chaco Canyon, New Mexico. Photograph by Jorge Pérez de Lara.

both the life-sustaining corn and human life itself from the arid sand and rock.[1] Contrary to recent archaeological evidence, the friars reported no instances of human sacrifice or ritual cannibalism.[2] Rather, they observed the Pueblo world energized through the medium of kachinas, supernatural spirits who emerge periodically from the earth to visit the living community by way of underground shrines in which masked human impersonators act as intermediaries.

Unlike their Uto-Aztecan brethren to the south, the Indians of the desert pueblos did not erect tall pyramids with temples on top. Instead, many communities worshipped in masonry-lined rooms usually submerged some six or more feet below ground, which allowed for a comfortable year-round temperature. These are the kivas, whose origins go back to the cavelike pit-houses of the earliest Paleolithic inhabitants of the American continent.[3] In plan, the kiva can be either circular or rectilinear, and some are even formed like a D. The remains of dozens of kivas are found in many ancient pre-Columbian Anasazi sites of the U.S. Southwest such as Chaco Canyon (fig. 11.1) and Mesa Verde. Some are large enough that an entire community could gather there; others are only large enough for a few people. Some are altogether belowground; others extend above, enclosed under squat structures shaped like pillboxes (fig. 11.2).

While most kivas were entered by means of a wooden ladder through a hatchway in the timber-and-earth-covered roof, some had side doorways with steps to the lower level. The roof opening also served as an oculus. In the reconstructed circular kiva at Aztec Ruins National Monument, Aztec, New Mexico, one may still observe how the rays of the sun stream through this overhead opening, shifting its focus like a spotlight around the perimeter of the room, which must have added mystery and drama to the ancient ceremonies once performed there (fig. 11.3).

The roof in such large communal kivas was often supported by four heavy wooden posts set in stone sockets on the earthen floor. The inside walls were usually coated with adobe and often painted with kachina images. Around the lower sides were sometimes benches and on the floor a number of raised masonry boxes (perhaps covered with stretched skins on which the Indians danced) and sunken fire pits, plus a shaft to the outside for ventilation. The most important floor opening was the *sipapu,* a small hole that serves as conduit for direct communication between the kachinas in the deeper underworld and the living celebrants in the kiva above. From the original sipapu, the "navel of navels," human beings are said to have originally emerged into the present world. The kiva itself symbolizes the primordial underworld cave where human beings were first created and then arose to inhabit the earth.[4]

When the Spanish first encountered kivas in the Pueblo communities, they did not perceive them as temples, at least not in the same sense

Fig. 11.2 Exterior of reconstructed kiva at Aztec Ruins National Monument, Aztec, New Mexico.

as the monumental "kues" with which they were familiar in southern Mexico. In fact they called them *estufas,* or warming rooms, perhaps in confusion with the steam baths they had seen among the Aztecs and Mixtecs, which likewise served a purifying religious function.[5] In any case, the kiva was, and still is, more of a meeting hall and council house than a symmetrical temple formally focusing on a central altar. While the different Pueblo peoples are notoriously reticent about divulging the meaning and symbolism of their individual ceremonies, one may speculate with some assurance that the elements of every kiva bear analogy to the almost universal notion among American Indians that the cosmos is in the form of a quincunx with the sky supported on four corner mountains or trees, and that human creation occurred in a cave in the center of the world.[6]

Just as in central Mexico and the Yucatán, the Franciscans in New Mexico sought to give their new churches a size and form more imposing and anagogically inspiring than the traditional religious architecture of the natives. In one famous instance, at Awatovi in the Hopi Reservation in northeastern Arizona, the Franciscans seem to have built their church right on top of a former kiva, reminiscent of the southern Mexican churches similarly erected on old temple foundations. Since this discovery at Awatovi, there has been much discussion about its significance.

In spite of rising resistance to Spanish authority by many neighboring Hopi pueblos, the village of Awatovi in the high mesa country of

Fig. 11.3 Interior of reconstructed kiva at Aztec Ruins National Monument, Aztec, New Mexico.

northern Arizona was successfully converted by Franciscan missionaries during the 1630s. At the outbreak of the revolt that suddenly swept the area in 1680, Awatovi refused to join with fellow Hopis in overthrowing the Spanish and driving out the Christian friars. When Awatovi tried to recall the Franciscans after the revolt, the town was attacked by its own neighbors who destroyed its church, murdered the priest, and slaughtered all Awatovi's male inhabitants. The pueblo was leveled and Awatovi women and children carried off for rehabilitation in other Hopi communities. No Christian church has ever since been allowed inside the boundaries of any Hopi community.[7]

In the 1930s the still-abandoned ruins of the Awatovi pueblo were excavated by a team of archaeologists from the Harvard Peabody Museum. Subsequently, the investigators published several reports analyzing their most intriguing find, namely, that beneath the remains of the old Franciscan church, a small rectangular kiva was discovered, fully intact including most of the original timber roof.[8] Moreover, the structure, which still contained handsome original wall paintings, had been filled with clean sand, and its sipapu had been sealed by means of a specially shaped plug. In other words, the kiva had been carefully "embalmed" for ritual burial. The archaeologists also determined that the sanctuary of the superseding Franciscan church was set directly above the buried kiva.

In explanation of this discovery, which they also assumed would lead to others like it, the authors proposed what they called the "theory of superposition," based on the practice in early Christian Europe of building new churches right on top of Roman temples as icons of triumph, much as victorious warriors might be depicted as ceremonially standing with feet implanted upon the backs of prostrate and defeated victims. "The Christians wished to obliterate the pagan shrine and in its stead to erect their own. It was reasonable to accomplish both purposes by superimposing the Christian fane upon the pagan counterpart, thus demonstrating the dominance of the new Faith over the old, and at the same time perhaps translating the established sanctity of the particular locale into the substitutional structure."[9] In the main, this interpretation has held sway ever since, in spite of the fact that the condition of the Awatovi kiva, so carefully preserved beneath the church, might suggest something other than "obliteration."

U.S. National Park historian and archaeologist James E. Ivey reexamined the Awatovi data and observed that there was not just one but several kivas partially under the Franciscan church, and that the famous kiva in question was not at all directly on axis with the Christian sanctuary above. Moreover, after many more years of archaeological digging in New Mexico since the original Awatovi excavations, no other example of churches built on top of kivas has ever been found. The best revised explanation, according to Ivey, is that the Awatovi Indians granted the Franciscans the right to build a church in an area containing some no longer active kivas. So long as the Franciscans covered and filled the old shrines in a respectful manner, the Indians were happy to cede the space to the church. In other words, "superposition" as a general theory of kiva "obliteration" and thus intentional desecration by being buried under Christian churches

Fig. 11.4 Ruins of the second church of San Gregorio, Abó, New Mexico, with round kiva in its cloister patio/garth. Photograph by Jorge Pérez de Lara.

remains unsustained by any other examples in Arizona and New Mexico.[10]

Furthermore, the kiva is essentially a masonry-reinforced hole and thus the architectural negative of the aboveground temple of old Mexico. By its very lack of imposing profile, the kiva would hardly have intrigued the Franciscans to use it the way they did the truncated pyramid in the Yucatán, that is, to enhance the visual drama by elevating the new church on the old temple platform as if on a theatrical stage.

On the other hand, Ivey points out that in nearly all the pre-1640 convento sites so far excavated in New Mexico and Arizona, kiva remains are indeed found right in the middle of convento cloisters, including that at Awatovi. The most conspicuous examples have been restored at Abó and Quarai in the Salinas National Park.[11] The kiva at Abó is round (figs. 11.4 and 10.6), that at Quarai is square (fig. 11.5), and both are in the middle of their respective convento cloisters. Oddly, in all the current literature on New Mexico architecture, the word "cloister" refers only to the corridor around the central open space. What is usually a garden in European and old Mexican conventos is in New Mexico called instead the patio or garth. The latter is an old English term for a small courtyard beside a house or inn with no particular religious connotation.[12] The use of this word implies that the convento cloister "garden" in New Mexico served the same role of public gathering place as the convento patio/atrios to the south.

While some have argued that the kivas at Salinas were inserted after 1680 by apostate Indians as a kind of "reverse superposition" to show their rejection of Christianity in the abandoned conventos, archaeologists have noted that the material used to construct them is identical to that in the fabric of the original conventos proper, thus indicating that the kivas were built not separately but simultaneously with the conventos. At Abó, for instance, the kiva is so aligned in the foundations of the cloister/garth that it must have been built at the same time as the earlier church (see fig. 10.6) that was later razed in 1630 to make way for the second much larger structure (figs. 11.6 and 10.8).[13] At Pecos, a kiva has been discovered adjacent to the cloister/garth again related to the first church and is not only composed of the same black adobe brick but the red mortar between the bricks is also identical to that used in the church.[14] (This kiva, which has been reconstructed, is shown in the foreground of fig. 10.1.) What then is the reason for this anomalous architectural *convivencia*? Why would the friars tolerate such an obvious token of heathenism in the Virgin Mary's symbolic hortus conclusus?

Fig. 11.5 Plan of the convento and church of La Purísima Concepción, Quarai, New Mexico, showing square kiva in its cloister patio/garth. Drawing courtesy of James E. Ivey.

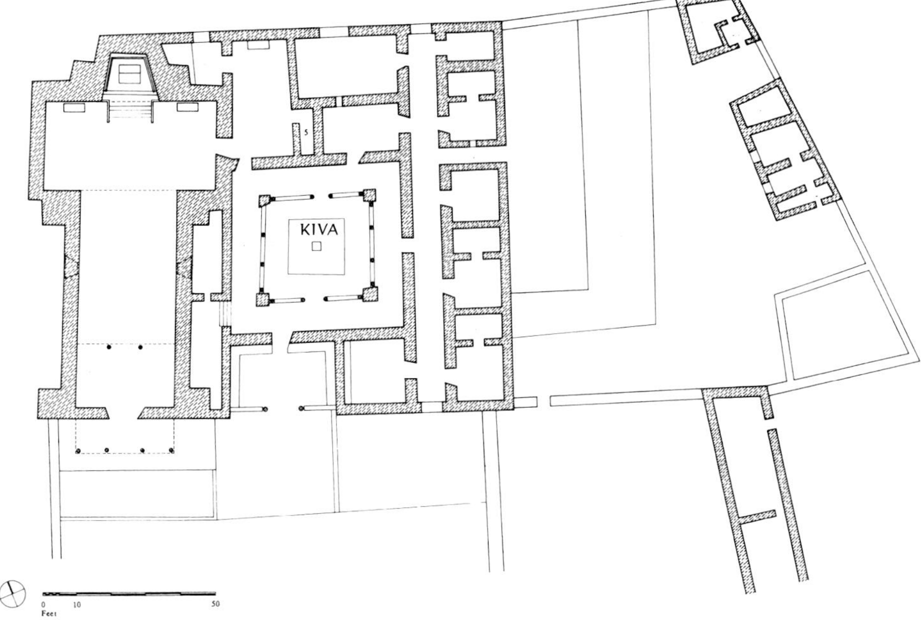

Ivey believes that the friars so located these kivas in keeping with their original policy of toleration, deliberately co-opting this native religious form for their own proselytizing purposes. I suggest further that this curious practice had its precedent in the Franciscan Yucatán experience. When the few friars in the Yucatán were similarly plying the backwoods villages alone and with little military protection, they too appreciated the necessity of compromising with local Indians, especially in the delicate matter of imposing a new set of sacred symbols without being overly insulting to those they were replacing. Just as the friars wanted their new churches built close to sacred cenotes and on top of former temple platforms so the Indians might perceive an osmotic link between the church and the still-visible foundations of the former sacred shrine, so the New Mexico Franciscans sought a means to take advantage of the sunken kiva to enhance the symbolism of their own Christian architecture. By setting—literally lowering—it into the center of the cloister/garth, the friars could draw an exegetic

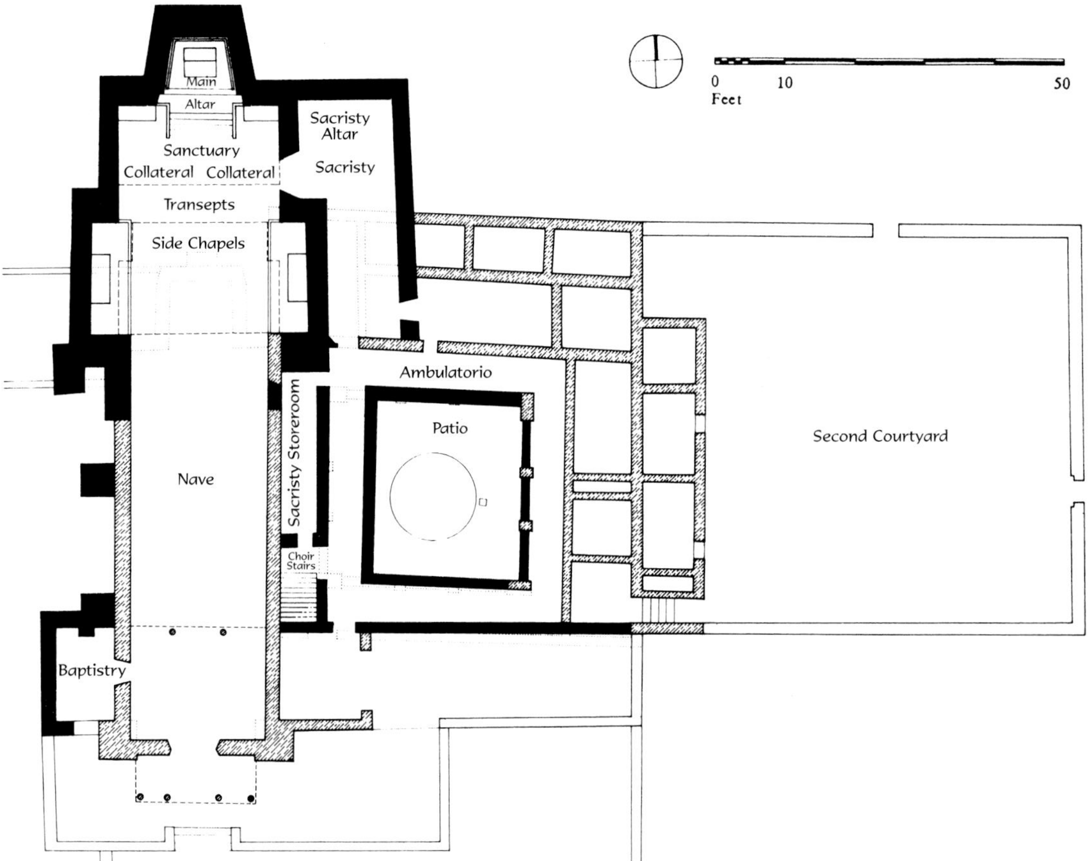

Fig. 11.6 Plan of the second church and convento of San Gregorio, Abó, New Mexico, ca. 1652. Drawing courtesy of James E. Ivey.

correlation between the pagan space of the kiva and the Christian space of the surrounding cloister looming above it.[15]

To the Indians, the mystic *Urform* of their universe was signified by the kiva. It represented the primeval underworld from which human beings, finally fashioned to the satisfaction of the gods, at last emerged and were permitted to live and prosper in the present world. To the friars, the convento cloister symbolized the enclosed garden where the new Eve, the Virgin Mary, received her divine fecundation thus ensuring mankind's salvation. By placing an open kiva in the very center of the convento cloister, the friars could argue that the native structure really signified the Indians' own *ante legem* world of arrival, not yet to full acceptance by the true God, but only to the level of Eve's primal sin. The cloister above represented yet a higher level of moral achievement leading to their ultimate redemption through acceptance of Jesus' birth, just as in the convento at Malinalco where the murals depicting the terrestrial paradise at the moment of the fall of man were juxtaposed to the convento's actual hortus conclusus. Vertical ascendance was as much a Pueblo Indian metaphor of moral virtue as it was a Christian one.

Indeed, this teleological relationship of kiva to cloister fit well as a visual aid for teaching the Indians the threefold method of Christian contemplation, as paraphrased from Fray Diego Valadés's 1579 *Rhetorica Christiana*: In the literal sense one considers the order of things on earth; in the tropological, we arise from the literal to consider its moral meaning; in the anagogical, we pass to things yet more superior, leaving behind earthly matters altogether, we approach the city of the living God, the heavenly Jerusalem.[16] Perhaps too, the friars even used the kiva as a stage set for scene one of an *auto* in which the Indians begin their worldly existence in an innocent but limbolike kiva, to be followed by scenes two and three respectively representing their Christian conversion and, finally, heavenly redemption.

By 1610, when New Mexico was declared a royal colony, the Franciscans had renewed their zeal for evangelizing the Pueblo Indians and seemed to have finally devised a building type suitable to the peculiar environmental and social conditions of the region. As Ivey points out, a distinct difference occurred between the humble structures first erected by the friars during the uncertain years of the mission before 1610, and afterward. The earliest church at San Gabriel, for example, was little more than a crude room or two appended to the pueblo complexes taken over by the friars for their conventos.[17] By the 1620s, however, construction of such great churches as the first edifice at Pecos and the rebuilding of Giusewa (Jémez) truly took on monumental and sophisticated proportions.[18]

As was ever the case, the friars in the field had little prior architectural expertise. At best, they were only amateur carpenters and few could do little more in planning a church than staking out its general proportions full-size directly on the ground by means of "rod and cord." Ivey has described in detail this basic method as it was applied to the New Mexico churches and conventos.[19] While sophisticated architectural drawings to scale were gradually becoming an accepted building procedure in Europe by the seventeenth century, they were not yet a standard prerequisite, and there is no evidence that the friars took predrawn designs with them into the field. Ivey avers, however, that Fray Francisco Acevedo made elevation drawings on paper for his reconstruction of the church at Abó in 1629, based on measurements he must have taken from the old building before the new work began.[20] Fray Francisco was indeed one of the very few friars with obvious engineering experience. His knowledge of reinforcing high walls against the dangers of wind thrust is evident in the still-standing massive buttresses, yet just as in medieval Europe (the Gothic cathedrals of France; the great cupola over the cathedral of Florence), similarly reinforced walls were also built without architectural drawings. Still, if Fray Francisco did make use of sketches, it would be intriguing to know how they were then perceived by the Indian workers, and whether they could make sense of unfamiliar Western architectural units of measurement and drawing conventions, and especially understand the novel concept of geometric scale.

In any event, the friars on their way to New Mexico doubtlessly shared a common mind's eye image of what an ideal missionary complex should consist. Most of the friars in New Mexico, as Fray Agustín de Vetancurt stated in his 1697–98 *Menologio Franciscano,* had been resident in the Convento of San Francisco in Mexico City where Pedro de Gante had established his famous school of the arts at San José de los Naturales and where the original and unique Mexican convento plan was first conceived a century before.[21] In fact, all the friars on their way to New Mexico had first to stop off in Mexico City where they received their instructions and picked up their supplies. Presumably they spent some time looking around the San Francisco convento (under reconstruction during the last decade of the sixteenth century[22]) and possibly visited the nearby library at the Colegio de Santa Cruz, now being removed to the convento of Santiago de Tlatelolco where illustrated architectural books might still have been available. (Pedro de Gante no doubt collected some of these to aid the friars in the planning of their missions.)[23]

They would also want to inquire about the experiences of other friars elsewhere.[24] A number of Franciscans on their way north apparently knew fellow Fray Juan de Torquemada, resident at the convento of Santiago de Tlatelolco during the first two decades of the seventeenth century.[25] Torquemada was there writing his *Monarquía indiana,* the history of Mexico and its evangelization by the Franciscans in twenty-one books (mostly derived and sometimes copied verbatim from Mendieta's manuscript).[26] Several chapters in his book 5 are original, however, and reveal familiarity with the geography, agriculture, and habits of the native peoples of New Mexico, which he must have learned in conversation with returning missionaries. He expressed particular concern for the vexed conditions in the new colony and was dismayed that so many friars had decided to abandon their proselytization of the Pueblo Indians. He even reprinted letters filled with complaints about Oñate from two friars trying to secure the troubled mission.[27]

Torquemada was especially interested in religious architecture. He was brought to Mexico City in the first place to supervise the rebuilding of Santiago de Tlatelolco, originally constructed on the ruins of the great pyramid where the Aztecs had made their last stand against Cortés. He was also overseeing the painting of a retable by Indian artists. In his *Monarquía,* Torquemada devoted the entire eighth book, consisting of twenty-three somewhat pedantic chapters (much dependent on the usual classical and Patristic literary sources), to discussing the similarity of pagan "temples" from classical antiquity to the present Aztec and Inca in the New World. It is significant that he was little interested in practical construction problems but only in the liturgical layout of such buildings, the disposition of altars, patios, and entrances for ritual purposes. Torquemada observed that both ancient Egyptians and Indians in America built towering temples, inadvertently acknowledging the true God in heaven even though the "demon" kept them ignorant. Both similarly adopted other symbolic forms such as quadrangular patios and altars oriented to the cardinal directions that, Torquemada further implied, were likewise in recognition of the true God and proper to be recycled in Christian churches even if previously profaned.[28]

Surely some of the Franciscans headed for New Mexico were aware of the revolutionary architectural ideas currently being promulgated in Italy in the wake of the Council of Trent. Of immediate interest would have been news of the new Jesuit mother church of Il Gesù in Rome, consecrated in 1584, engravings of which, such as the well-known Francesco Villamena print (fig. 11.7), were quickly disseminated to all the proselytizing orders and had extraordinary influence on the building of mission churches all over the world. Il Gesù had only a single broad nave with no continuous side aisles, only independent lateral chapels. It also had only a narrow transept that concentrated light (incoming from a fenestrated dome unseen by viewers in the nave) and directed it upon the altar with remarkable theatrical effect. The intent of this hall-like arrangement was to encourage both good acoustical and unimpeded visual communication between worshipers in the nave and the clergy in the shallow sanctuary. Preaching was to be especially stressed, so a raised pulpit was carefully situated where the priest could most advantageously be seen and heard. No choir or choir screen should block the public's view of the splendid main altar from the body of the church.[29] In the first decade of the seventeenth century, Il Gesù hosted one of the most spectacular religious theatricals in all Europe, the "forty hours devotion" before Easter and again at Advent when all the windows in the nave would be covered with black cloth. The audience in the darkened hall then beheld the Host on the altar illuminated by mysterious "divine light" from the out-of-sight dome thus seeming to emanate illusionistically from heaven (further enhanced by candles and lamps concealed behind an elaborate false proscenium).[30]

No doubt the friars also talked of how they should adjust these novel Counter-Reformation concepts to the environmental peculiarities of the northern desert and the social and ideological idiosyncrasies of the native inhabitants. They seem to have reached an early consensus that their New Mexico churches consist of a single enclosed nave opening directly onto a recessed, often splayed and stagelike altar sanctuary with only a short crossing transept (or none at all) that did seem to reflect the Il Gesù precedent.

It was also an early decision that there be only a single entrance portal to their churches for which each friar carried into the field "a large [iron] latch."[31] The eventual church facade should then be flanked by one or two adjunct espadaña bell towers. The friars at Jémez, however, taking advantage of a bedrock hill at the altar end, had the tower built in an odd position (fig. 11.8) and inside the entrance a balconied choir overlooking the nave according to the Spanish custom. Outside, a small portería could be built beside the entrance, and at the altar end a separate but connecting sacristy. Before 1640 baptisms were held inside the churches, but afterward in separate buildings adjoining the church near the entrance. The adjacent friary should contain living quarters and kitchen and also a cloister with surrounding ambulatory. Because the conventos in New

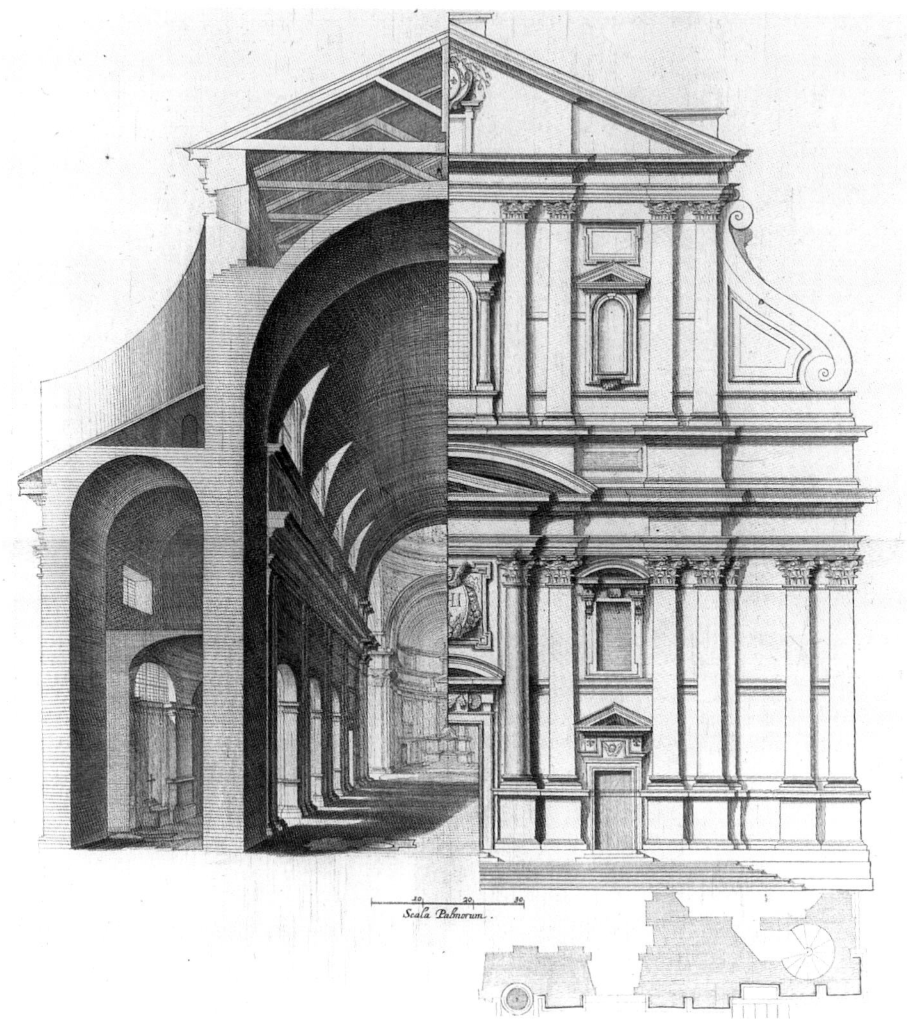

Fig. 11.7 Francesco Villamena, engraving of the Jesuit church of Il Gesù, Rome, after 1586. Courtesy of E. J. Johnson, Williamstown, Massachusetts.

Mexico were intended to be completely self-sufficient, there had also to be farming facilities including workshops, corrals, and ample space for storing foodstuffs as insurance against the frequent droughts.

Since the Indians to be evangelized in New Mexico lived in widely scattered communities of generally low but condensed population, there was no need, nor much room, for an extended atrio-patio with posas. The Franciscans entered New Mexico realizing there would not be the same conditions as earlier in the south when thousands upon thousands of Indians once crowded the grand patios before the open chapels.[32] Even though Torquemada parlayed the post-Oñate Franciscan propaganda that "more than eight thousand souls" had been baptized in New Mexico by 1608, those missionaries actually in the field felt no pressure to build large patios adjacent to their New Mexico conventos.[33] Instead, they were content with only small low-walled courtyards before the church (sometimes with a pedestal for a wooden cross, as in the partially restored ruin at San Isidro, Las Humanas [figs. 10.5 and 10.10]). While suitable in the early days perhaps for Oñate's *autos*, these small churchyards served the community better in the long run as *camposantos* (cemeteries), as at Ácoma.

The dispensing of religious instruction and other ministerial functions, on the other hand, seems to have taken place in the cloister, hence its designation as patio or garth. Open chapels seem likewise to have been eschewed in the standard New Mexico convento plan, although Kubler claims vestigial possibilities at Zia and Santa Ana.[34] More likely in terms of utility, the nearest New Mexico parallel to the old Mexico open chapel was the raised porch above the entrance portal that once graced many seventeenth-century pueblo mission churches like Quarai (fig. 11.9) and can still be seen at Zuni and the beautiful eighteenth-century parish church of San José de Gracia at Las Trampas (fig. 11.10). Such facade porches were also common to many European churches during the seventeenth century.[35]

Especially eye-catching is the buttelike silhouette of the New Mexico church. While bearing some resemblance to the "fortress" form of the convento church of New Spain, in no other region of native America did this squat archetype achieve such harmonious blend with the geology of the natural surroundings. For once, the friars did not insist on the arch and vault, a form curiously discordant in that most straight-edged of landscapes. Instead, the friars took advantage of what the Indians already well knew, that is, how to build masonry-bearing walls with roofs supported on horizontal wooden joists, or vigas, laid across the parapets. Having only stone hatchets, the Indians could not fell large trees, hence their vigas were usually too slender to support heavy roofs, and so the basic units of pueblo architecture tend to be rather small. To amend this, insofar as they wanted to make their new churches awe-inspiring, each friar assigned to New Mexico brought with him an assortment of hardware including ten metal axes for distribution to the Indian laborers.[36] This is a good indication that the Franciscans planned from the beginning to build trabeated churches with roofs on wooden beams rather than attempt to teach the Indians the technology of arch and vault. Interestingly, another architectural theory current in Counter-Reformation Rome at the time had it that flat-roofed naves provided better acoustics for preaching than vaulted ceilings with their propensity to reflect disturbing echoes and overtones.[37]

Whatever may have been the friars' original thought, another very good reason why they chose not to introduce the keystone arch had to do with the peculiar tradition of division of labor among the Pueblo Indians. Curiously, among Pueblo peoples of the Rio Grande valley, masonry houses were only built by women and children, while the men did the weaving and hunting. To the amusement of Fray Alonso de Benavides and the Indian ladies mixing adobe, men would run away when asked to help lift stones to the walls. In these circumstances, it would have been difficult indeed to introduce vaulting, which depends on the strength of men to dress and set the heavy voussoirs necessary to support a vaulting system.

Not only were the Pueblo Indians unskilled in the practice of shaping large building stones but also the crude masonry materials that were available, consisting mostly of soft sandstone ledge and adobe mud, lacked sufficient tensile strength for vaulting the broad naves the friars anticipated.[38] In a few instances, as in the later church at Pecos where small arched doorways open from the sanctuary

Fig. 11.8 Reconstruction of lateral section through the Church of San José de Giusewa, Jémez, New Mexico, looking toward the altar. Drawing courtesy of James E. Ivey.

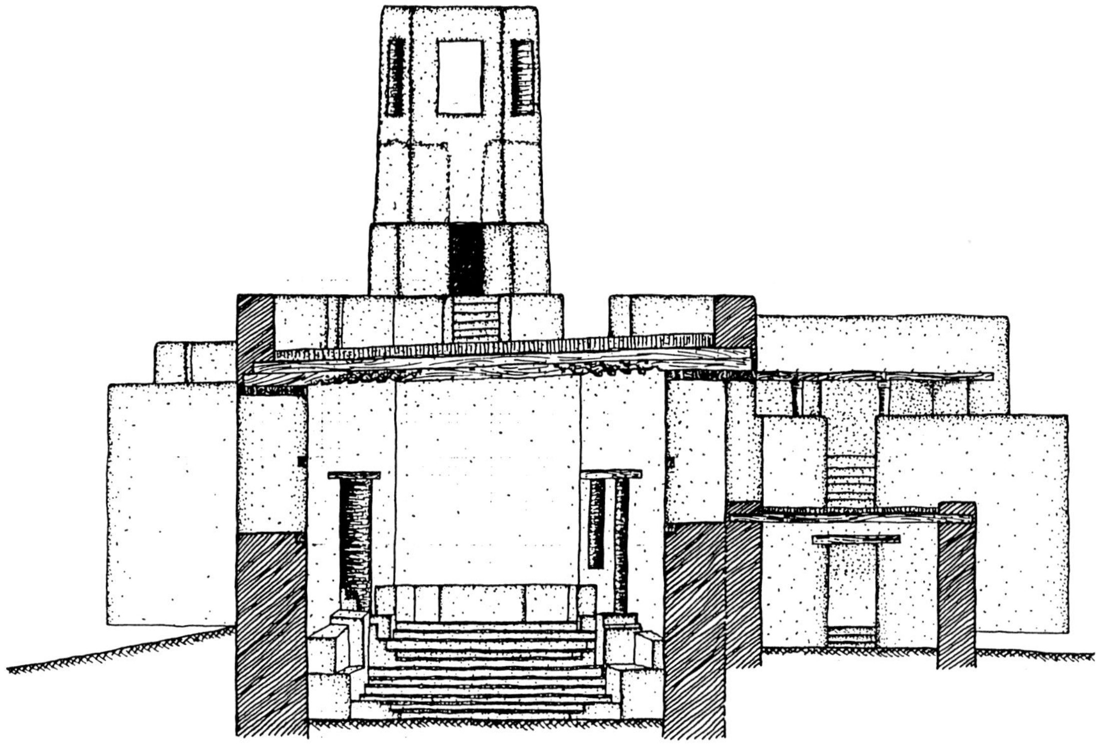

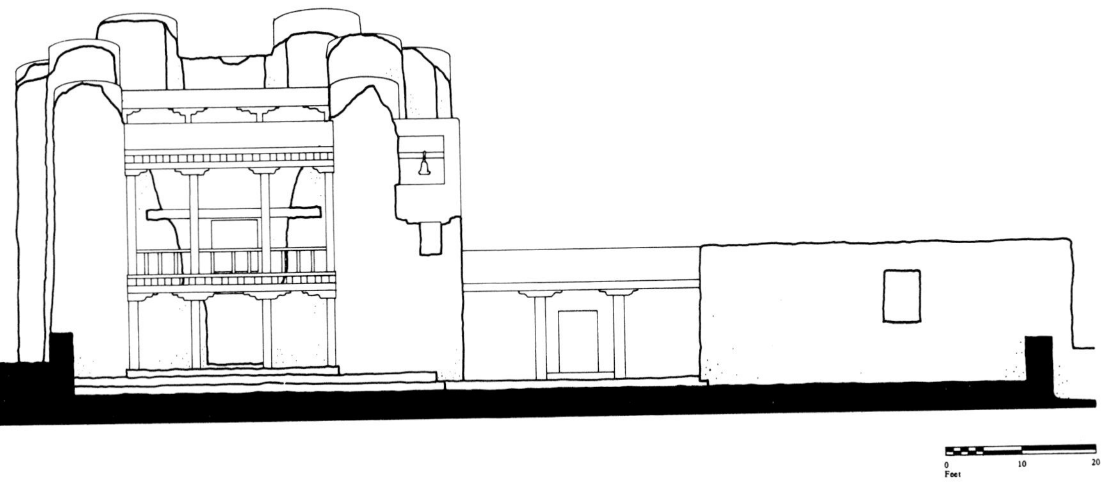

Fig. 11.9 Reconstruction of south elevation of the church and convento of La Purísima Concepción, Quarai, New Mexico, ca. 1632. Drawing courtesy of James E. Ivey.

into the side sacristy and vestry,[39] arches were built of dried adobe bricks, which the friars taught the Indians to make in molds, but these never spanned more than a few feet and do not appear before the eighteenth century. Anyway, it is unlikely the friars would have entrusted the construction of something so technically demanding as wide-spanning arches and vaults to women, although female masons managed to erect, as Benavides attested, amazingly sturdy walls for the New Mexico churches, the massiveness of which no Pueblo man had ever seen before.

The friars brought with them from Mexico City a variety of metal tools, including adzes, saws, and drills, for the purpose of cutting and shaping extra-large vigas to support the wide roofs of their monumental churches. Woodcutting and carpentry were the accepted work of Pueblo men, and the construction of San Estévan at Ácoma provides an epic example of how such projects were carried out. This great building, erected some time after 1629 with many repairs since, still preserves its original dimensions. The roof of the nave is covered by nearly forty vigas, each over thirty feet long and resting on massive walls of adobe brick nine feet thick at the base.[40] The work was directed by Oaxaca-born Fray Juan Ramírez (?–1664), still well remembered in Ácoma for his leadership in restoring the pueblo after its destruction by Oñate.[41] He was apparently able to inspire the men of the pueblo to cut the timber from a mountain forest twenty miles to the north and, according to the local story, carry on foot the heavy logs, each of which weighed about as much as a modern automobile, on their shoulders all the way to Ácoma without ever letting them touch the ground. The giant beams were then hoisted up the steep and narrow path to

Fig. 11.10 Parish church of San José de Gracia, Las Trampas, New Mexico. Photograph by Jorge Pérez de Lara.

the top of the 350-foot high mesa, and finally set in place atop the 35-foot high walls of the church.[42] Since one is not allowed to photograph inside the church at Ácoma, I illustrate here the much less monumental but similar and still visually pleasing interior ceiling set on vigas in the nearby eighteenth-century pueblo church of San José de Gracia, Laguna (fig. 11.11). Here are the same fine decorative carvings of the supporting corbels and patterned woodwork as at Ácoma, all carried out by skillful native artisans who built the church in order that a friar be sent to them in 1699.

The most distinctive characteristic of many surviving New Mexico pueblo churches (although not at Ácoma) is the so-called transverse clerestory window, noticeable on the exterior profile of the flank of the church by the kick in the roof at the juncture of the nave and transept or sanctuary as in this longitudinal section drawing of the second church at Abó (figs. 11.12 and 10.8). Technically, it is merely a long, low slit between two stacked vigas separated by stilt-blocks, the upper one supporting the stepped-up roof over the crossing. The opening at this separation of the two roof heights permits sunlight to fall directly on the altar beyond the nave without viewers in the nave seeing the window source. In effect, it functions somewhat like a fenestrated dome, but open on only one side. It is a device that had no precise precedent in Europe, although various means for illuminating churches in such controlled ways were being experimented with by many architects in late sixteenth-century Italy.

Irving Lavin has pointed out that the very notion of controlled illumination can be traced back to the Pantheon in ancient Rome where some of the original pagan altars were lit by hidden windows.[43] Marc Treib has suggested that a similar clerestory method was devised in Moorish Spain for lighting the multiple vaults of mosques, as in the great Mezquita at Córdoba.[44] In the ceiling vault of the important Franciscan convento church of San Luis Obispo at Tlalmanalco, not far from Mexico City and rebuilt in 1591 (Fray Martín de Valencia had originally served there), one may observe a small hidden opening just behind the chancel arch, allowing afternoon light to stream in upon the altar without viewers in the nave spotting its source. It has also been argued that certain late sixteenth-century structures in northern Mexico possessed hints of clerestory-like windows that might have inspired the friars on their way to Santa Fe.[45]

Whatever the possible precedents, the friars

Fig. 11.11 Interior of the church of San José, Pueblo of Laguna, New Mexico, looking east. Photograph by Jorge Pérez de Lara.

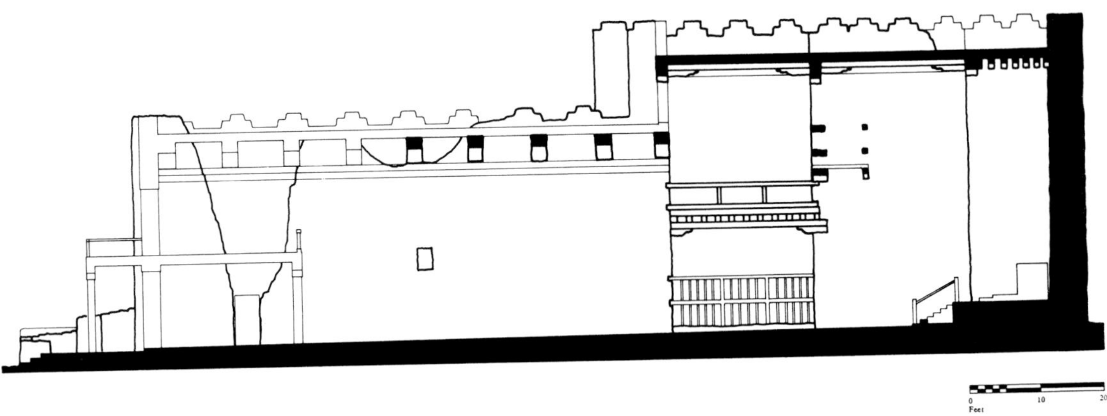

Fig. 11.12 Reconstruction of longitudinal section through the nave of the second church of San Gregorio, Abó, New Mexico, ca. 1652. Drawing courtesy of James E. Ivey.

hardly needed to be motivated by a particular prototype. They were already primed by the Counter-Reformation charge that the clergy infuse more excitement into the presentation of the Mass.[46] In fact, just as in post-Tridentine Italy, the friars in New Mexico during their first forty years were experimenting with varying ways to illuminate and thus dramatize their church interiors, particularly the altar sanctuaries. James Ivey and his team of archaeologists have found at Jémez, for example, that in the rebuilding of the south-facing church after its 1624 destruction, very large windows were inserted high up along the side walls in order to allow the morning and evening sun to angle in upon the altar alternately from east and west (fig. 11.13).[47]

The Jémez flank-windows experiment, however, seems not to have been repeated. Instead, the unique transverse clerestory emerged as the most satisfying solution to the New Mexico lighting problem. No one as yet knows exactly when, where, or by whom the transverse clerestory was first realized, but after 1620 it was quickly adopted by most of the churches put up in that flurry of activity described by Fray Alonso de Benavides. Moreover, the transverse clerestory was wholly feasible within the traditional building technology of the Pueblo Indians, since its timber framing was not so dissimilar from that of the traditional flat entrance openings in the roofs of both kivas and secular Pueblo dwellings. It is quite possible that the Indian workers themselves, perhaps even one of the women, first came up with the structural solution.[48]

It has also been proposed that these very high roof openings were so placed for a more practical reason, to let in light but keep out flaming arrows shot by Apache warriors. If Torquemada's quite liturgical attitude toward church architecture is any indication of how the friars in New Mexico reasoned, then such a consideration would have been but a fortuitous afterthought. More revealing is the fact that in nearly all the New Mexico structures, the ground plan—the very first act of construction—was aligned not with the altar at the east end as had been canonical in both Europe and old Mexico as late as the sixteenth century, but rather with it at the west or north, for reasons that seem to have had much relevance to where to place the eventual windows. To be sure, the old rule of east-end altar alignment had been eased during the Counter-Reformation when the many new order churches had to be adjusted to crowded, often directionally restricted sites. While no such crowded conditions existed in New Mexico, the wide-open, big sky natural environment of the region does suggest that the friars had another excuse for the unorthodox alignments of their churches; namely, to take advantage of the native Indians' traditional veneration of the sun. The spectacular desert light should be emphasized as a tool for Christian inspiration. In Christian Europe, interestingly enough, two remarkable exceptions to the standard orientation were no less than the ancient Basilica of Saint Peter in Rome and the thirteenth-century Basilica of Saint Francis in Assisi, which, because of original site restrictions, had to have their facades facing east. The symbolic rationale, however, was that these two great churches should greet Sol Justitiae, Jesus the "Sun of Justice, each breaking dawn."[49]

In any case, assembling the Indians to morning Mass seems to have been the friars' daily practice in most of the New Mexico communities where churches were newly present. At Ácoma and Laguna (and originally at the first church at Pecos), for example, morning sunlight brilliantly illuminates the beautifully textured east-facing adobe facades, still impressive sights today just as they must have been to the first hesitant converts on their way to Christian service. The splendid effect of morning light streaming in through transverse clerestory windows upon the altar sanctuaries would have been even more awe-inspiring. More than half the known total of pre-1680 church sites, according to both Ivey and Kubler, indicate that the original alignment was with facade and altar both facing toward

Fig. 11.13 Reconstruction of longitudinal section through the Church of San José de Giusewa, Jémez, New Mexico. Drawing courtesy of James E. Ivey.

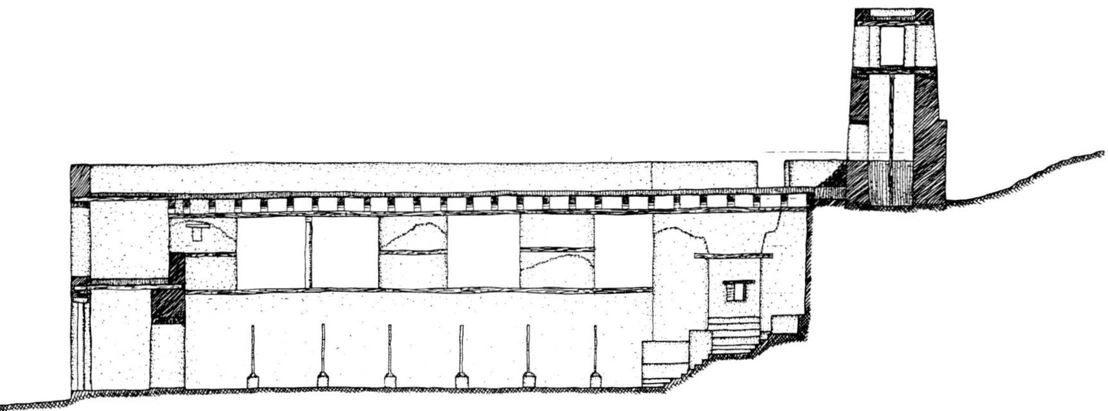

the rising sun—appropriate (and quite spectacular) between the feast of the Annunciation (March 25) and Easter (the first Sunday after the first full moon following vernal equinox).[50]

A lesser but still significant number of New Mexico churches have their facades facing south or southerly, as at Jémez, Isleta, Quarai, and Abó. A reasonable explanation for this choice is that the sun in all regions of the world north of the Tropic of Cancer (twenty-three and a half degrees north latitude) never rises to zenith, but remains instead slightly in the south, even in summer. In New Mexico (between thirty-one and thirty-seven degrees north latitude), if one desires a church facade, interior, or both to be illuminated uniformly in the morning and afternoon, both summer and winter (and especially in winter between Christmas and Easter), a south-facing facade and altar would be ideal.

Ivey has actually discovered a striking fact about the south-facing altars at Abó and Quarai. At noon on December 22, the day of winter solstice, sunlight entering through their respective transverse clerestory windows would have concentrated dead center upon the sanctuary altars in both churches.[51] The friars knew, of course, that winter solstice was among the most important calendric rituals celebrated by all the Pueblo Indians of New Mexico and that each community had its own signposts fixed on the horizon marking exactly where the sun would reach its most southerly point during its annual journey through the sky. At that moment the Indians would dance, imploring the sun to turn back north, restoring warmth and fertility to the land once again.[52] The fact that the solar alignment of these churches allowed the incoming light to dramatize both the winter solstice and the advent of Christmas, indicates once more how the Franciscans applied their tactic of expedient selection. Better to co-opt than ignore the old pagan belief; let the astronomical significance of the latter be associated henceforth with Jesus whose miraculous nativity was likewise timed to signal the return of light and warmth—justice and charity—to the world.

What the transverse clerestory window also permitted was the same theatrical lighting effect that became so popular in the Counter-Reformation churches built in seventeenth-century Rome. It is intriguing to realize that around the year 1630, as the Indian congregation assembled in the darkened nave of the Church of San Agustín, Isleta, New Mexico, and admired its altar brightly lit from a hidden transverse clerestory window (fig. 11.14; the present altar arrangement is of course modern, but the natural lighting effect in this photograph is probably as it was in the seventeenth century), they were receiving a baroque theatrical experience worthy of the great Italian sculptor-architect Gian Lorenzo Bernini (1598–1680). However crude, the transverse clerestory windows of the New Mexico churches worked by the same mechanical principles Bernini was at that very moment applying to heighten the visual drama of his sculpted *Miracle of Santa Bibiana* in the church of that name in Rome. Eighteen years later, Bernini would astound the sophisticated citizens of the Holy City with his *Ecstacy of Santa Theresa* in the Cornaro Chapel, Santa Maria della Vittoria, again exploiting this same basic technology (fig. 11.15).[53] In order to give spectacular illumination to his fictive ensemble, Bernini installed a shaft behind the chapel outside the

Fig. 11.14 Interior of the church of San Agustín, Isleta Pueblo, looking north toward the altar as illuminated by the transverse clerestory window. Photograph by Jorge Pérez de Lara.

church, with a window hidden above the chapel's framing entablature, unseen by viewers in front who must then wonder from what mysterious source comes the brilliant glow that irradiates the imagery. How coincidental that this quintessential effect of baroque theatrical illumination was already being anticipated in many "heart of darkness" desert outposts thousands of miles away in "savage" America.

Kubler was so struck by these baroque-style improvisations that he devoted a whole chapter of his 1940 book to optical effects and treatment of light, including a section on perspective illusion of architectural space.[54] In fact, he discerned certain "irregularities" in the alignment of the lateral walls of the churches at Quarai, Las Humanas, and Jémez among others that he attributed to a deliberate attempt on the part of the planners to have them converge slightly toward the sacristy, thus enhancing the illusion of depth to the nave and theatrical focus upon the altar. The creation of such architectural perspective effects was also a tour de force in Italy during the late sixteenth and early seventeenth centuries, inspired by theater designs illustrated in popular architectural treatises such as those by Sebastiano Serlio and Andrea Palladio.

Intriguing as was Kubler's interpretation, Ivey and the national park archaeologists believe that most of these irregularities (particularly observable at San Buenaventura, Las Humanas [fig. 11.16]) had more to do with simple misalignment due to site problems or faulty measuring.[55] Nevertheless it is still quite evident that the friars wanted to dramatize the altar ends of their mission churches by having them set back in often sharply splayed niches framed between lateral "shoulder walls," again as in San Buenaventura, Las Humanas, and the rebuilt church at Abó, or raised up on steps like a theatrical rostrum as at Jémez (see figs. 10.12 and 11.8).

By intent or intuition, the friars also took subtle advantage of certain visual similarities between standard Christian symbols and what the natives would also consider as signifying sacredness. Just as in the Yucatán where the vaulted Christian chapel seemed to replicate the mysterious form of a cenote cavern or pib na [underground house], so the pueblo church must have reminded the Indians of a natural desert formation wherein their own spirit forces dwelled. Some might even have noticed how the overhead clerestory window is similar to the roof opening in the native kiva as well as pueblo dwelling, which also sought to take advantage of the mystical effects of focused light in a dark interior.[56]

One aspect of the New Mexico churches about which we know little is how they were originally decorated with painting or sculpture. Fray Alonso de Benavides indicated that they were covered with "very beautiful carvings and fretwork [lacería], and the walls very well painted." Nonetheless, surviving evidence is scanty. It is also true that even in old Mexico, mural painting had gone out of style by 1600. Pedro de Gante's school for Indian artists at San José de los Naturales was no longer active; in fact, the visual arts in Mexico City were being taken over more and more by newly arrived European professionals. Old murals in the Mexican churches by the earlier Indian artists were now being whitewashed and replaced by lavish architectural retablos with painting and sculptured elements framed in

Fig. 11.15 Gian Lorenzo Bernini, *Miracle of Saint Theresa,* Cornaro Chapel, church of Santa Maria della Vittoria, Rome.

gilded wood in the form of baroque solomonic (spiral) columns and classical entablatures. Documentary records exist that indicate that the New Mexico friars were eager to have these stylish retablos exported north from Mexico City via the triennial wagon train. Archaeological remains of wooden beams for mounting a large retablo have been found in the sanctuary at Quarai, for example.[57]

At Jémez, fragments of a painted Mexican-style tequitqui ornament with fleur-de-lis-like figures have been uncovered on the eastern nave wall, but again this manner of decoration seems only to have been a temporary ornament tolerated until the commissioned retablos arrived.[58] Benavides does mention that Indians were being taught in "trade schools," and Donna Pierce has found records that during the 1630s there was a workshop for native painters in Santa Fe. At some point, the friars permitted the Indians to paint abstract geometric designs in the native tradition, acceptable even on the nave walls of churches as long as they were not overtly pagan, as for example in the restored interior of the eighteenth-century church of San José de Gracia at Laguna where hieroglyph-like symbols for hills, caves, and rainbows presumably signify Christian afterlife, and birds with cornstalks growing at their feet represent departed human souls (see fig. 11.11). Such mural designs are not dissimilar, at least in the manner of their stylized forms, from kachina figures on the walls of preconquest kivas, as in the restored Kuaua kiva at Coronado State Park, Bernalillo, New Mexico (fig. 11.17).

At Laguna can be found a style now recognized as the ultimate achievement of Indo-Christian art in New Mexico: the splendid retablo on the main altar by the so-called Laguna *santero,* an anonymous artist who flourished from 1796 to about 1808 (fig. 11.18).[59] At one time the side walls of the sanctuary were covered with similarly brightly colored designs presumably by the same painter, but these were unfortunately whitewashed in 1968.

The Spanish word *santero* refers to a genre of folk painters and sculptors with little formal

Fig. 11.16 Plan of the convento and church of San Buenaventura, Las Humanas, New Mexico, ca. 1670. Drawing courtesy of James E. Ivey.

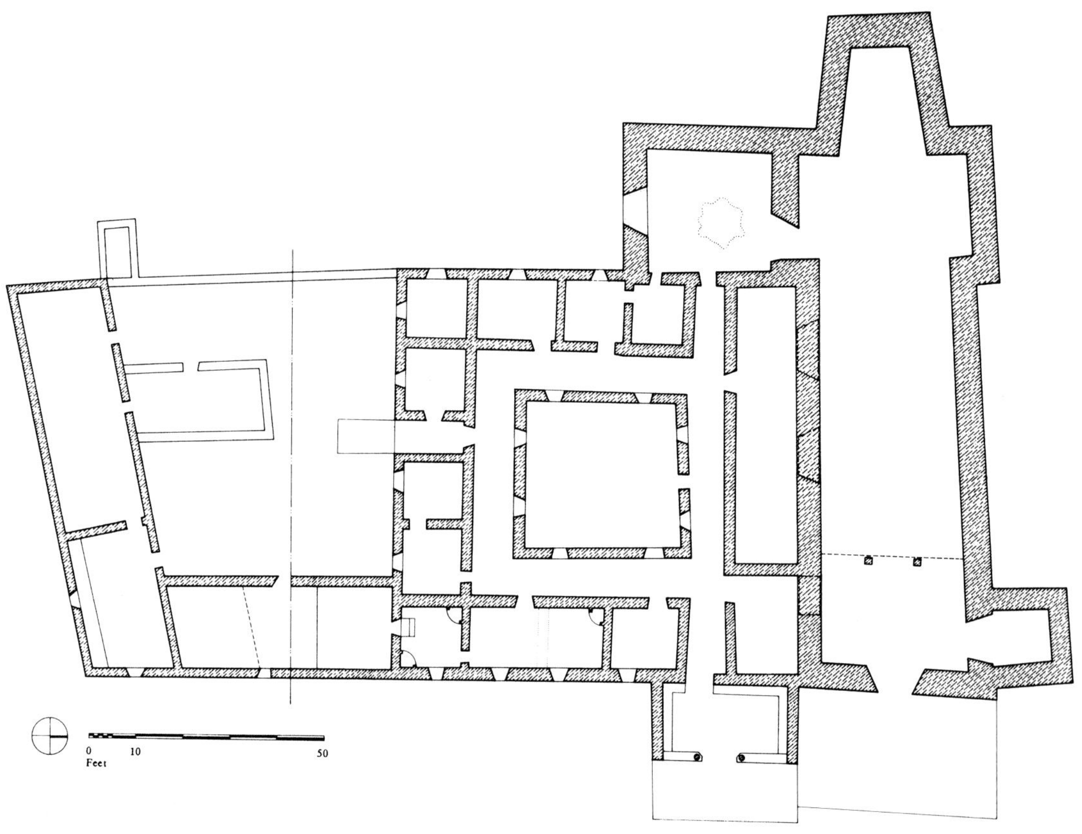

Fig. 11.17 Interior of kiva at Coronado State Park, Bernalillo, New Mexico. Photograph by Jorge Pérez de Lara.

training and only apocryphal knowledge of Christian iconography. While their ethnicity, whether native Indian, mestizo, Spanish, or whatever, is still a question, they apparently all began their careers after the suppression of the Pueblo Revolt when many damaged or decayed retablos and sculptured santos needed to be replaced in the rebuilt churches. While adopting the popular Spanish baroque retablo form and aping its general ornamental vocabulary (solomonic columns, elaborate volutes, and floral arabesques around the borders), these santero painters infused their revisions with regional native motifs, all in unrestrained color. Curiously, their figural representation seems almost to have returned to preconquest stylized flatness. However upon close inspection, the details still appear to be European-Renaissance in derivation and rather akin to the *retardataire* Byzantine-like folk art one would also have seen practiced by naive artists in provincial Europe during the same centuries. A considerable body of santero work is attributable to the Laguna master, including an almost identical

Fig. 11.18 *Retablo with Saints and Synthronous Trinity,* by the anonymous Laguna santero, church of San José, Pueblo of Laguna, New Mexico. Photograph by Jorge Pérez de Lara.

retablo at Ácoma. The iconography of both these altarpieces contains a peculiar reference to the Christian Trinity, represented as three identical figures of synthronous Jesus each with a triangular halo. This was a widely popular iconographic theme in the Christianized native art in both North and South America during the seventeenth century and later, although several times proscribed as heretical by the Holy See.[60]

As fascinating as is the subject of santero painting, it is a phenomenon primarily of the eighteenth and nineteenth centuries and thus beyond the scope of the present book. Indeed, santero painting in New Mexico has attracted its own specialized scholarship in recent years, which has already revealed new insights into a remarkable regional and multicultural art form heretofore little appreciated by art historians.[61] Suffice to say only that the unknown Laguna santero's masterpiece is the ideal illustration with which to conclude this book, perhaps the paradigm masterpiece descended from the sixteenth-century friars' strategy of expedient selection. This ad hoc policy was in the long run amazingly successful in setting the groundwork for a unique and truly syncretized (I may now safely use that word) native American religious art, openly flourishing (accepted and even encouraged by the post-Vatican II Catholic Church) from Maya Guatemala to Pueblo New Mexico, whether or not Saint Antonine, Leon Battista Alberti, or Fray Pedro de Gante would have approved.

NOTES

Citations for sixteenth-, seventeenth-, and early eighteenth-century chronicles of missionary activity in New Spain include not only relevant page numbers from publications in the bibliography but also, following the modern citation, book and chapter number from the authors' original editions. This information is provided to help readers use *Theaters of Conversion* for further research. Scholars with modern reprints different from those cited may find that page numbers vary, but all retain the book and chapter divisions of the originals. This information is provided for the following authors: Burgoa, Cervantes de Salazar, Ciudad Real, Cogolludo, Dávila Padilla, Duran, Escobar, Grijalva, Las Casas, Mendieta, Motolinía, Sahagún, Torquemada, Valadés, and Vetancurt.

INTRODUCTION

For the full text and discussion of the first epigraph, see Klor de Alva, "Aztec-Spanish Dialogues."

1. Neumeyer, "The Indian Contribution"; Reyes-Valerio, *Arte Indocristiano;* Gruzinski, *Painting the Conquest.*
2. Unfortunately, the earthquake of 1650 so damaged most of the sixteenth-century Christian structures in Cuzco, Peru, that they had to be rebuilt, and little evidence of their earlier forms can be discerned today.
3. A good start has been made by Gauvin Bailey; see Bailey, *Art on the Jesuit Missions.*
4. George Kubler in an insightful essay, "On the Colonial Extinction of the Motifs of Pre-Columbian Art," likewise avoided the singly defining word "syncretism"; instead, he saw the matter as multivalenced, divisible into at least five categories coexisting simultaneously, their differences depending on power relationships between colonizer and colonized in *local* circumstances:

   Juxtaposition: among the same people, coexistence of forms, drawn from two different cultures, without interaction. Only here has native culture any chance of intact survival.

   Convergence: unconnected cultural traditions produce similar behavioral patterns, which are interchangeable in the colony for aims approved by the ruling group.

   Explants: connected portions of native behavior continue to evolve for a period under colonial rule.

   Transplants: isolated but meaningful parts of native tradition are taken into colonial behavior, without major changes or development.

   Fragments: isolated pieces of the native tradition are repeated without comprehension, as meaningless but pleasurable acts or forms.
5. I distinguish this process from the "guided syncretism" characterized by Nutini and Bell, 291, insofar as the phenomenon they describe implies a conscious toleration by the friars of certain pagan motifs implanted in the fabric of Christian art. What I discern, on the other hand, is not so much the friars' attempting to Christianize Indian idolatrous forms as the Indians' attempting to rationalize standard Christian visual symbols in terms of sympathetic similarity to their own traditions. As a rule, with some remarkable exceptions, the friars were careful not to permit Indian artists to include pagan motifs in their newly learned Christian representations. Instead, the friars chose to teach just those forms of Christian iconography that would comfortably remind the Indians of the former motifs.
6. Thomas Dacosta Kaufmann, "Italian Sculptors and Sculpture Outside of Italy (Chiefly in Central Europe): Problems of Approach, Possibilities of Reception," in Farago, *Reframing the Renaissance,* 47–67.
7. Lockhart, *Nahuas after the Conquest.*
8. In the same vein, see also Freedberg.
9. Gombrich, 181–291.
10. Sylvest, 100.
11. The Spanish word *encomendero* refers to a lay settler granted an *encomienda,* a large plot of land in the Spanish colonies from which the grantee had the privilege of enriching himself. He also had the right of *repartimiento,* to claim a certain amount of free labor from the Indian inhabitants of his lands. The encomenderos' only obligation to the Indians was to contribute to their Christianization and support a local church. Because this latter requirement was often ignored and the friars' need for Indian labor in the building of their conventos conflicted with the encomenderos' demands for labor on the estates, considerable friction quickly developed between the friars, the Indians working in the autonomous Christian conventos, and the colonial civil authorities trying to adjudicate the encomenderos' claims. For a brief but helpful review of the complications of the encomienda system, and the Spanish government's difficulties in trying to control it, see Gerhard, *Guide to the Historical Geography of New Spain,* 8–10.
12. Concerning whatever architectural training and building skills the friars as well as lay-colonists possessed before coming to the Americas in the early sixteenth century, see Kubler, *Mexican Architecture,* 1:109–33; see also McAndrew, 125–28. Mendieta, *Historia eclesiástica indiana* (1945), 4:14–15 (bk. 5, chap. 1), notes that Fray

Martin de Valencia may have had some prior Spanish experience in planning church structures. Kubler, *Mexican Architecture,* 1:115, further makes the point that the friars, the Franciscans in particular, actually resisted having European craftspersons work on the construction and decoration of their conventos and churches, preferring always to employ Indians or members of their own order.

13. Lockhart, *Nahuas after the Conquest,* 203–61.
14. McAndrew, 586–90.
15. The story is told in Mendieta, *Historia eclesiástica indiana* (1945), 1:87–88 (bk. 1, chap. 4). Also repeated in Torquemada, *Monarquía indiana* (1975–83), 3:123–24 (bk. 6, chap. 44). See also Perry, *Mexico's Fortress Monasteries,* 41, 55.
16. Similar place-name symbols are displayed on the Christian conventos at Actopan, Ixmiquilpan, Coixtlahuaca, and Malinalco.
17. Besides the decipherable year and day-signs on the Cuilapan plaque are other notations that so far have not been understood. Edmonson, *Book of the Year,* 79, has hypothesized that the two horizontal elements with voluted ends on the bottom of the plaque represent Mixtec month signs. However, on one of these horizontal elements there appears to be a banner raised on some sort of enclosed box and on the other an abraded hand holding a native obsidian-studded sword called a *macana;* these devices depict ceremonial altars on which sacred objects were placed as offerings during the dedication ceremony of the building. See, for instance, similar images for that purpose in the Codex Vindobonensis, fols. 22–21. Edmonson's own proposed conversion of the Mixtec date (May 5–June 5, 1555, and November 15, 1568) does not satisfy the presently accepted correlation method.
18. For an overview of the geography, demography, and distribution of Indian cultures in the Americas, see Coe, Snow, and Benson.
19. For a map indicating the areas in central Mexico where Nahuatl was originally spoken, along with dozens of other native languages, see Gerhard, *Guide to the Historical Geography of New Spain,* 6.
20. The etymology of this word is still uncertain. According to Frances Karttunen, "Chichimec" was not derived from a similar-sounding Nahuatl term for "dog" as is often averred but rather from the Nahuatl word for "suckle" (48).

CHAPTER 1

1. As quoted by Hanke, 175.
2. There's no better witness to this traumatic argument than Michelangelo Buonaroti, whose Sistine Chapel frescoes (the ceiling painted between 1508 and 1512, and the *Last Judgment* between 1534 and 1541) are filled with references to a transcendent and vengeful God who delegates the carrying out of his teleological master plan to earthly prophets anointed not for their charity or moral rectitude but for single-minded ruthlessness.
3. See however Edmundo O'Gorman's careful analysis of Motolinía's treatises, which he claims are incomplete copies after lost originals and were only inscribed by an unknown hand in Spain after 1565 *(Memoriales o libro de las cosas);* Motolinía, *Historia de los indios de la Nueva España* (1969), ix–xix.
4. Motolinía, *Motolinía's History.* Unfortunately, Father Steck did not include a translation of Motolinía's *Memoriales,* containing more details about Indian artisanry. Chapter 60 of the *Memoriales,* for instance, is similar to chapter 13, book 3 of the *Historia* but offers more detail about architecture and painting. On the convoluted history of all Motolinía's writings, including his controversial "letter to Charles V" rebuking Bartolomé de Las Casas for publicly polemicizing about Spanish brutalities in New Spain, even though agreeing that they must be stopped, see Steck's introduction, 1–70, in *Motolinía's History.*
5. More so even than Motolinía, Mendieta stressed the apocalyptic predestination of the missionary enterprise (Mendieta was the inspiration and chief source of Phelan's book), claiming that Cortés had been divinely designated as the second Moses and the King of Spain was God's providential instrument for spreading the Christian faith to the whole world.
6. Ciudad Real, *Tratado curioso,* 2:311–73 (chaps. 141–56).
7. Torquemada's *Monarquía indiana* published in Seville, 1615, is quite dependent on Mendieta's *Historia.* An excellent edition of Torquemada including a chapter by chapter concordance with Mendieta and a magnificent index has been edited by the Seminar for the Study of the Sources for Indigenous Tradition under the direction of Miguel León-Portilla and published by the Universidad Nacional Autónoma de México, Mexico City, 1975.
8. See Motolinía, *Historia de los indios de la Nueva España* (1969), 117–18 (treatise 3, chap. 1); Mendieta, *Historia eclesiástica indiana* (1945), 4:53–57 (bk. 4, chap. 64); Torquemada, *Monarquía indiana* (1975–83), 6:182–89

(bk. 20, chaps. 19–20); also Cuevas, 1:155–77. For a biography of this self-effacing, brilliant teacher, see Ramírez Vásquez.

9. See also the brief but informative article by Kagan discussing the Inquisition.

10. The single Indian was Don Carlos Chichimecatecuhtli, cacique of Texcoco, who was remanded to the secular police and executed in the Mexico City Zocaló on November 30, 1539, for the crime of suborning his native constituents to commit idolatry. As was the custom, he was paraded to the scaffold dressed in a foolscap and yellow cape (called a *sambenito* on which were inscribed his crimes), and there garotted and his body burned; see Greenleaf, *Zumárraga and the Mexican Inquisition,* 68–75. For a Renaissance picture of what this execution may have looked like, see the painting ca. 1495 now in the Prado Museum, Madrid, by Pedro Berruguete entitled *St. Dominic Presides over an Auto da Fé.* Don Carlos's draconian punishment raised such an outcry among both Indians and Spaniards that Bishop Zumárraga, who passed the sentence, was removed from his provisional post as apostolic inquisitor, and no Indian was ever so condemned again. Furthermore, among the hundred or more cases adjudicated during Zumárraga's aborted term as apostolic inquisitor (between 1536 and 1543), only nineteen involved Indians. Although the ritual of the auto-da-fé may have been cruel and unusual as judged by modern standards, it was not so according to the judicial precepts of sixteenth-century Europe. Nor did all autos-da-fé culminate in dramatic executions. The ceremony was actually just a public presentation in which persons found guilty of a socially reprehensible act were made to appear in humiliating dress or pose and perform penance before their neighbors. Judicial punishments by public shaming were not only commonplace in Europe but also among the Indians long before European contact. For more on punishment by humiliation as well as the common forms of judicial torture employed for extracting confessions in late medieval Europe, see Edgerton, *Pictures and Punishment.* It is instructive to compare the small number of Indians punished for religious crimes in Mexico to the much larger number of Europeans sentenced by both Protestants and Catholics during the same period, or to the number of Caucasian witches hanged in seventeenth-century Salem, Massachusetts.

This is not to say the Indians were not harshly treated in many recorded instances by the secular courts and star-chamber proceedings initiated by racist encomenderos; see, for example, the pathetic plea from the Indian officials in Huejotzingo to the King of Spain in 1560, translated in Lockhart, *We People Here,* 288–301.

11. Clendinnen; Timmer.

12. Gante, 15–16; Mendieta, *Historia eclesiástica indiana* (1945), 2:30–35 (bk. 3, chap. 6); Cuevas, 1:158–61.

13. For a good summary of the founding of the Franciscan mission, see Sylvest, 36–37. See also Cervantes de Salazar, *Mexico en 1554,* 50, 112–13.

14. Mendieta, *Historia eclesiástica indiana: A Franciscan's View,* 2:52–53 (bk. 3, chap. 12).

15. As the Franciscans settled in and their original cassocks wore out, they made new ones of coarse native cotton or maguey fibers dyed blue from the juice of the indigenous indigo plant.

16. The *Chronicles* were probably written by a Franciscan friar named Martin de Jesús de Coruña between 1539 and 1541; see Craine and Reindorp, 88; also Thomas, 579.

17. Mendieta, *Historia eclesiástica indiana: A Franciscan's View,* 2:53 (bk. 3, chap. 12); Thomas, 579.

18. Ciudad Real, *Tratado curioso,* 2:221 (chap. 110).

19. Schroeder, 24. See also Mendieta's account of this story in *Historia eclesiástica indiana* (1945), 4:37 (bk. 4, chap. 11). It is puzzling as to just why Fray Martin became so revered by the Indians because, according to both Motolinía and Mendieta, he could never learn to speak Nahuatl.

20. Ciudad Real, *Tratado curioso,* 2:222 (chap. 110); see also Kubler, *Mexican Architecture,* 2:479–80.

21. Kubler, *Mexican Architecture,* 1:116.

22. Mendieta, *Historia eclesiástica indiana* (1945), 3:207–8 (bk. 4, chap. 43); Motolinía, *Motolinía's History,* 90; McAndrew, 33.

23. McAndrew, 33.

24. Duverger, 113; McAndrew, 38.

25. Mendieta, *Historia eclesiástica indiana* (1945), 3:208 (bk. 4, chap. 43); see also Cervantes de Salazar, *Mexico en 1554,* 48–49.

26. Concerning the Augustinian "Americana Thebaida," see Escobar.

27. Ibid; see also Cervantes de Salazar, *Mexico en 1554,* 55–56.

28. For the history of and reasoning behind the peculiar Judeo-Christian belief in the certainty of an apocalyptic second coming of Christ to end the world, see Cohn; also Milhou.

29. Concerning the distress over the sin of avarice at this time in the Western Christian world, see Little.

30. See Watts, "Prophecy and Discovery"; West and Kling.

31. Durán, for instance, believed the Indians were the descendants of the ten tribes of Israel captured by the King of Assyria as described in the Bible (2 Kings 18) and sent to a "remote and distant country" (*The Aztecs,* 3).

32. See the numerous examples in the Codex Vindobonensis, for instance, on obverse fols. 3, 10, 11, 13, 14, 15, 17, and 47.

33. Kubler, citing Fray Alonso da Isla in 1543: "I do believe that it stands with them [the Franciscans] as it did in the primitive church, as we can read in the Acts of the Apostles where it is said, 'And all that believed were together, and had all things common.' It does not seem to be otherwise in these [countries] converted by the twelve apostolic friars" (*Mexican Architecture,* 1:8).

34. Motolinía, *Motolinía's History,* 148–49 (bk. 1, chap. 14):

> There is hardly anything to hinder the Indians from reaching heaven, nothing like the obstacles which hinder us Spaniards and which submerge us. The Indians live in contentment, though what they possess is so little that they have hardly enough to clothe and nourish themselves. Their meal is extremely poor and the same is true of their clothing; for sleep the majority of them have not even a whole mat. They lose no sleep over acquiring and guarding riches, nor do they kill themselves trying to obtain ranks and dignities. They go to bed in their poor blanket and on awakening are immediately ready to serve God; and if they wish to take the discipline, they are neither troubled nor embarrassed with dressing and undressing. They are patient, exceedingly long-suffering, meek as lambs. I do not recall having ever seen them nurturing an injury. They are humble, obedient to all, either of necessity or voluntarily; all they know is to serve and work. They all know how to build a wall and erect a dwelling, to twist a rope, and to engage in such crafts as do not require much skill. Great is their patience and endurance in time of sickness. Their mattress is the hard and bare ground. At most, they have only a ragged mat to sleep on and for a pillow a stone or a piece of wood, while some have no other pillow than the bare earth. Their dwellings are very small, some with a very low roof, others with a roof of straw, while some dwellings resemble the cell of that holy abbot Hilarion, looking more like a grave than a dwelling. The riches that suffice to fill such dwellings show what treasures the Indians have! These Indians live in their little houses—the parents, the children, and the grandchildren. They eat and drink without much noise and talking. They spend their days peacefully and amicably. They seek only what is necessary to sustain life.

35. M. Fernández, *La Jerusalem Indiana.* In his 1579 *Rhetorica Christiana* Franciscan Fray Diego Valadés included an engraving by his own hand showing a schematic Mexican convento patio in the center of which the artist indicated the twelve original Franciscan apostles supporting a palanquin on which sits, as the Latin inscription states, the "first Holy Roman Church in the New World of the Indies" (fig. 2.29). This model is remarkably similar to the idealized image in Martin de Vos's painting. However, the concept of a domed church on a central Greek-cross plan was in high style everywhere in Renaissance Europe during the late sixteenth century. Valadés, who was in Rome during the 1570s, might even have seen the various designs for the completion of Saint Peter's Cathedral exhibited in the Vatican. The wooden model of Antonio da Sangallo's proposed construction is quite similar in appearance to Valadés's imagined edifice.

36. For a good general discussion of the Cisnerian reforms and Spanish humanism in regard to the Franciscan missionaries, see Sylvest, 24–26. See also Castro y Castro, "Lenguas indígenas americanas."

37. See Coe, *Breaking the Maya Code,* for the wondrous and delightful history of the decipherment of Maya hieroglyphics.

38. Mendieta, *Historia eclesiástica indiana* (1945), 4:116–19 (bk. 5, chap. 42).

39. Glass. For an even more thorough examination of this subject including an updating of Glass's catalog of the known surviving examples plus all pertinent bibliography, see Normann; Galarza.

40. For an analysis of Egerton 2898, numbered 813 in her amended catalog, see Normann, 129–65.

41. Ibid., 135–36.

42. Molina, 59 recto, under *momoztlae.*

43. Duverger, 171–75.

44. Mathes, 99; Zavala, "La 'Utopia' de Tomas Moro." Zumárraga's copy of the *Epigrammata* and *Utopia* was the 1518 Basel edition printed by Frobanius. For a philological analysis of Motolinía's writings, demonstrating how he too was closely incorporating Erasmian ideas, see Motolinía, *Memoriales: Libro,* 45–55.

45. Zavala, *Recuerdo de Vasco de Quiroga*; Zavala, "La 'Utopia' de Tomas Moro," 70–76.

46. Concerning Spanish humanism differing from Italian, especially in the Americas, see Bono, *Cultural Diffusion of Spanish Humanism.*

47. See Pagden; F. Rogers.

48. Kemp, 125.

49. For Las Casas's arguments against Sepúlveda, see Las Casas, *In Defense of the Indians;* also Pagden. For a brief but excellent analysis of Las Casas's thought, and how his selective references to Aquinas, Gratian, and Roman law almost seemed to anticipate the philosophers of the Enlightenment, see Tierney, 272–87.

50. For a cogent discussion of the history of natural law and its legal and moral ramifications in Western philosophy, see Passerin d'Entrèves.

CHAPTER 2

1. See, for instance, Toussaint, *Paseos coloniales,* and *Colonial Art in Mexico;* Angulo Iñíguez; Tovar de Teresa, *Renacimiento en México;* Lugo and Manrique; Sartor; Fernández, *La Jerusalem Indiana;* and Sebastián López, Mesa Figueroa, and Gisbert de Mesa.
2. Fray Pedro himself only mentions his skill and desire to teach music and singing in his several letters to Juan de Zumárraga and King Philip II of Spain (see Gante). We know of his interest in the visual arts only through Fray Diego Valadés (see chap. 4), and Fray Geronimo de Mendieta, *Historia eclesiástica indiana* (1945), 4:54 (bk. 5, chap. 8).
3. Concerning how the Augustinians regarded the importance of the Indian school at Tiripetío, see Basalenque, 68; and Escobar, 77–85, 107–27 (chaps. 7, 12–14). One notable "graduate" of the school, and among the few Spanish friars to then have architectural and engineering training, was Diego de Chávez, credited with designing the Augustinian convento at Yuriria, Michoacán, ca. 1550. Like Diego Durán, Chávez had come to the New World as a child, was raised among Indians and apparently trained in the skills of building construction along with Indian apprentices at Tiripetío. Only later in his life did he join the Augustinian order; see Kubler, *Mexican Architecture,* 1:117–18; Saur, 18:357.
4. The school of San José de Naturales and Fray Pedro de Gante's work with the training of Indian youths is described by Mendieta, *Historia eclesiástica indiana* (1945), 4:53–57 (bk. 5, chap. 18); García Icazbalceta, *Bibliografía mexicana,* 93–94; Kubler, *Mexican Architecture,* 1:134–87; and Peterson, *Paradise Garden Murals,* 50–56. See also Cervantes de Salazar, *Mexico en 1554,* 55, 119–20.
5. Motolinía, *Motolinía's History,* 297 (treatise 3, chap. 12):

   > Up to the time we began giving the Indians lessons in Latin or grammar, opinions differed on this point both among the friars and among other persons. Certainly, it was taught them with great difficulty. But we had good success. Time and labor were well spent. Many of the Indians are good grammarians. They compose long and well-written essays and also verses in hexameter and pentameter. What is to be valued most highly is the attention of the students, resembling a group of friar novices. This did not cost their masters much trouble. These students or collegians have a well-ordered college where they receive special instruction. When the friars saw what progress the Indian boys were making in their studies, they moved the boys from the section of San Francisco de Mexico to that of Santiago de Tlaltelolco. Here the boys are now located and two friars are instructing them, assisted by a learned Indian who teaches them grammar.

   Originally, as implied above, the friars planned that the colegio should prepare Indians for the priesthood. That idea, unfortunately, came to naught when the church decided the natives were inherently "unfit"; see Ricard, 20:224–27.
6. For the history and catalog of the library, see Mathes. During the Inquisition years after 1571, many of the books were either proscribed or stolen. Around 1605 what remained of the original contents were removed from the Colegio de Santa Cruz to the nearby Franciscan convento of Santiago de Tlatelolco (Mathes, 27–49). See also Baird, *Drawings of Sahagún's "Primeros Memoriales,"* 21–30. Many of the original books from Tlatelolco as cataloged by Mathes are still preserved in the Adolph Sutro Library, San Francisco, California.
7. These works are cataloged in the Sutro Library as *M. Vitruvius Pollonius, viri suae professionis peritissimi, De architectura libri X . . . /Adiunctis nunc annotationibus in eosdem . . . Argenterati [Strasbourg]: Ex Officina Knoblochiana, per Giorgius Machaeropieum, 1550; Tercero y quarto libro de architectura . . . de Sebastiano Serlio bolones: en los quales se trata de las maneras de como se puedon adornar los edificios: con los exemplos de las antiquedades traduzido de toscano,* Toledo, 1573; *Albrecht Duerer, Pictoris et architecti praestantissimi de uribus, arcibus, castellisque condendis,* Paris (C. Wecheli), 1535; and *L'architettura di Leonbattista Alberti, tradotta in lingua fiorentina da Cosimo Bartoli,* Florence (Torrentino), 1550.

   Concerning Serlio's widespread influence in sixteenth-century Hispanic America, see Sebastián López, "La influencia de los modelos ornamentales"; Sartor, 96. Regarding the influence in Mexico of Alberti's ideas on architecture and urbanism, see Tovar de Teresa, "La Utopia del Virrey de Mendoza." The author notes that Antonio de Mendoza, first viceroy of New Spain (1535–50) and one of the cofounders with Pedro de Gante of the university and library at Tlatelolco, personally owned and annotated a Paris, 1512, Latin edition of Alberti's *De re aedificatoria.* See also Kubler, *Mexican Architecture,* 1:68, 96–102.
8. McAndrew, 491, 603; see also Sebastián López, Mesa Figueroa, and Gisbert de Mesa, 56–91.
9. The documents and history of this building, destroyed in the late eighteenth century, are discussed at length in Kubler, *Mexican Architecture,* 2:330, 466–68. For a late seventeenth-century description, see Vetancurt, *Chronica,* 40–43 (treatise 4, pt. 1, chap. 63).

10. Unfortunately, there is little contemporary documentation of Fray Pedro's architectural contribution, only the curious mention by Mendieta, *Historia eclesiástica indiana* (1945), 4:56 (bk. 5, chap. 18), that "he built more than a hundred churches." For discussion of the few other references to his architectural participation, see McAndrew, 368. See also Kubler, *Mexican Architecture,* 1:118–19.
11. For a discussion of the various nave types employed in the Mexican convento churches, see Kubler, *Mexican Architecture,* 2:283–361.
12. Medieval churches with merlon-studded parapets were not uncommon in Spain, as, for example, the twelfth-century Old Cathedral in Salamanca.
13. Effusively described, although without crediting the Indian craftsman, by Escobar, 351–62 (chap. 45).
14. This anonymous sculptor may also have been an Indian, trained either by or with the Tiripetío-schooled Augustinian Diego de Chávez (see n. 3 this chapter).
15. Escobar, 307–20 (chap. 40); see also Perry, *Blue Lakes and Silver Cities,* 153–56.
16. Interestingly, the builders of the convento dormitories often considered the nature of the Mesoamerican climate. In the cooler highlands, they placed the friaries to the south of the main church; in the more tropical zones, to the north.
17. The idea of a raised-up chapel-like balcony seemed also to have appealed to the contemporaneous missionaries in Peru where several similar structures were originally built in the early churches in and around Cuzco; see Chara Zereceda and Caparó Gíl, 19–24.
18. The presence of so many Zapotec "idols" and artifacts of the "demon" in the vicinity of Teotitlán was duly noted and condemned by Burgoa, *Geográfica descripción,* 2:117–27 (chap. 53).
19. Matos Moctezuma, *The Great Temple of the Aztecs,* 59–85.
20. Concerning the few friars and Spanish artisans in sixteenth-century Mesoamerica who did have some architectural or engineering skills, see Kubler, *Mexican Architecture,* 2:116–33; Sebastián López, Mesa Figueroa, and Gisbert de Mesa, 93–98.
21. McAndrew, 190; Fletcher, 175.
22. On the survival of preconquest masonry techniques in postconquest Mexico, see McAndrew, 190–95.
23. See the Codex Vindobonensis, fol. 22.
24. Vetancurt, 48 (pt. 4, tratado 2, chap. 3).
25. On the Indians' abilities in these skills, see especially Motolinía, *Memoriales de. . . . ,* 184–86.
26. Indian masons, carpenters, other skilled workers, and so on organized into workshops under supervision of a "mastermason"; they probably traveled from site to site like medieval European *Bauhütten;* see Kubler, *Mexican Architecture,* vol. 1, chaps. 3 and 4.
27. Ibid., 1:134–87. For records of some of the abusive treatment suffered by Indian laborers employed by the friars, see Ricard, 20:162–76.
28. Mendieta, *Historia eclesiástica indiana* (1945), 3:82 (bk. 4, chap. 18). Interestingly, there is a long tradition among many Indian cultures in the Americas that regards the sweeping of sacred shrines as a holy act. The Aztecs even celebrated a holiday in September called Ochpaniztli, the Sweeping of the Roads, in honor of the mother-goddess, Toci, whose image showed her holding a broom. On that day "everyone swept his house and properties, the streets and the baths, the four corners of the homes" (Durán, *Book of the Gods,* 229–37). Evidence has also been found, for example, that the ancient "Nazca lines" in Peru were periodically swept by their pre-Inca caretakers, perhaps to "animate" them for special ceremonial purposes. One of the most popular Christian saints among the present-day indigenous Indians of Peru is Saint Martin de Porres, known as the *santo de la escoba* (saint of the broom). Saint Martin, a seventeenth-century mulatto who became a Dominican monk in Lima, was known for his utter humility, signified by his constantly sweeping the floors of his convent. Numerous statues of him may be seen in churches all over Central as well as South America. He is depicted as a Negro in Dominican habit, holding a broom as his attribute. Concerning similar sweeping ceremonies among the present-day Pueblo Indians of New Mexico, see Ortiz, 75.
29. Jarrett, 76; see especially Saint Antonine, vol. 3, tit. 8, cap. 4, col. 308; Las Casas, *In Defense of the Indians.*
30. Motolinía, *Historia de los indios de la Nueva España* (1969), 69 (treatise 1, chap. 33).
31. Fletcher, 259–60. See McAndrew, 231–55, for further discussion on this matter.
32. For a detailed attempt to reconstruct the appearance of San José de los Naturales, see McAndrew, 368. As McAndrew demonstrates, the still-standing (although much-altered) Capilla Real at Cholula, Puebla, may be the closest surviving reflection of the original open chapel. Concerning the latter, see Sebastián López, Mesa Figueroa, and Gisbert de Mesa, 155–59.

    Kubler, *Mexican Architecture,* 2:299–301, mentions that the first cathedral in Mexico City, ca. 1540, was built with three aisles and very high vaults to impress the Indians. Was this also a Moorish inspiration?
33. McAndrew, 237–40.
34. The sacred precinct of Tenochtitlan as postulated by Marquina, 196–97, showing a low crenelated wall known in its time as the *coatepantli* since it was adorned along its base with a continuous serpent motif. See the

similar description of the Aztec temple precinct by Las Casas, *Apologetica Historia,* 345–51 (bk. 3, chaps. 130–32).

35. See Montes Bardo, 63–105, who discusses at length how the architecture of the Franciscan conventos in Mexico deliberately reflected the traditional "cosmovision" of the Christian religion but without acknowledging how similar this was to the traditional Indian worldview.

36. See León-Portilla, 25–62. This same macro- and microcosmic concept is fundamental also to the belief system of the present-day Tz'utujil Maya of Santiago Atitlán, Guatemala (see Christenson, 111–13) and similarly among the Tzotzil Maya of Zinacantan, Chiapas, in Mexico (see Vogt, 58).

37. García Zambrano. See also Bernal-Garcia.

38. Concerning Tenochtitlan as symbolic cosmic template, see Broda, Carasco, and Matos Moctezuma, *The Great Temple of the Aztecs;* Townsend; and Mundy, *The Mapping of New Spain,* xiv–xvii; see also Miller and Taube, 93–96, 166–67.

39. For a more precise analysis of the altepetl and calpolli, see Lockhart, *Nahuas after the Conquest,* 14–59.

40. See Durán, *The Aztecs,* 30–35; Torquemada, *Monarquía indiana* (1975–83), 1:113–22 (bk. 2, chaps. 1–4); also Seler, 5:93. After the conquest, the original four calpolli of Tenochtitlan were renamed after Christian saints as the barrios of San Pablo, San Juan, Santa María in Redondo, and San Sebastián (Durán, *The Aztecs,* 32).

41. Motolinía, *Motolinía's History,* 136–38 (treatise 1, chap. 12). See McAndrew, 236–39, for even more documentary evidence that the Indian ceremonial precinct influenced the concept of the Mexican Christian convento.

42. Concerning the difficulty the friars had in correlating the Aztec solar calendar, divided into eighteen months of twenty days each with five extra bad-luck days, with the Christian seasonal calendar, see Cline; Prem; and Aveni and Calnek.

43. Sahagún, *The Florentine Codex,* 43, 141–55, 176 (bk. 2); Durán, *Book of the Gods,* 457–60. See also Seler, 5:93–99.

44. See Schele and Freidel, 110–11, for a reconstruction of how, in early Preclassic times (ca. 50 B.C.E.), the Maya kings of Cerros, Belize, had their temples built in such a way that they could present themselves to the gods and to their people by ritually tracing the path of the rising and setting sun.

Counterclockwise ritual direction is especially emphasized in the Aztec-Mixtec codices, in particular the Codex Borgia depicting the *tonalpohualli,* or 260-day sacred year, laid out like a ritual procession paying homage to the four cardinal directions. The days are divided into twenty sequences of thirteen days each called *trecenas.* The first trecena progresses toward the east, the next to the north, then west, then south, and so on; see Díaz and Rodgers.

For a description of how the present-day Tz'utujil Maya community of Santiago Atitlán, Guatemala, still conceives itself as a cosmogram defined by the quadrangular course of the sun whose movement through the sky must be continuously fueled by ritual processions of the townspeople following in a precise counterclockwise direction, see Carlsen and Prechtel. In the same regard, Robert Carlsen emailed the following communication to me in April 1998: "A central (almost defining) aspect of cofradía cosmology has been what is called R'kan Sak R'kan Q'ij, Footpath (or foot) of the Dawn, Footpath of the Sun. This concept refers to a belief that cofradía ritual fuels the progression of the sun across the sky. Footpath of the Dawn, Footpath of the Sun manifests itself on the horizon (as seen from the center of the world, Santiago Atitlán) in a counter-clockwise direction. It is helpful to envision the essential operation as a square, each of the four cardinal directions occupying a side. From the winter solstice until the summer solstice, the focus is on the east horizon of the Lake Atitlán basin where the sun rises (moving consistently in a more northward direction along the east). Then from the summer solstice until the winter solstice, the focus shifts to the west horizon and the places where the sun sets (moving consistently toward the south). The focus then shifts back to the east . . . the major axis for the local Mayas is a line running through town from east to west."

For the similar importance of counterclockwise ritual processions among the present-day Tzotzil Maya of Chamula, Chiapas in Mexico, see Gossen.

45. While the similarity of the Panquetzaliztli to Corpus Christi was certainly observed by the friars, they abhorred the human sacrifices that accompanied it; see Motolinía, *Historia de los indios de la Nueva España,* (1980), 39–42 (tratado 1, chap. 6). Dominican Fray Diego Durán writing during the 1580s (*Book of the Gods,* 426), and Franciscan Fray Agustín de Vetancurt, writing a century later (86; pt. 2, treatise 3, chap. 10), both remarked on the parallel between Corpus Christi and the Aztec fifth-month feast of Toxcatl celebrating the god Tezcatlipoca in May, thus closer to the actual time of the Christian celebration. Vetancurt linked the Aztec feast to the worship of Quetzalcoatl, whose image he described was also made of maize dough and carried in procession through Tenochtitlan. He even claimed that the Aztec holiday was a deliberate perversion of the Christian festival on the part of the "demon."

46. Rubin, 267–71.

47. See Very, 106; *Enciclopedia dello Spettacolo,* 3:1502–14; *Enciclopedia Universal Ilustrada,* 15:842–47; *New Catholic Encyclopedia,* 4:347. Miguel de Cervantes even had his hero Don Quixote witness

some of these wild folk dances performed during Corpus Christi; see chaps. 20 and 61, for example.

48. Very, 14. Motolinía, *Memoriales de . . .*, 92–98, describes the processions in the Mexican conventos as likewise being preceded by celebrants strewing flowers, sedge, pine branches, mint, roses, and bulrushes.

49. *New Catholic Encyclopedia,* 4:347. Seventeenth-century Peruvian mestizo artist Diego Quispe Trito painted a remarkable set of sixteen canvases depicting a Corpus Christi procession composed of native Incas carrying symbols overtly referring to preconquest sun worship. The paintings were formerly hung in the Church of Santa Ana, Cuzco, Peru, but are now in the Museo del Arzobispado in the same city.

50. In his 1579 *Rhetorica Christiana,* Fray Diego Valadés noted that Corpus Christi celebrations in Mexican towns were already becoming too elaborate and that they should be contained and controlled within the convento patio; *Retórica Cristiana,* 110, 477 (pt. 4, chap. 23).

51. Motolinía provides a long description of a Corpus Christi celebration performed by the Indians of Tlaxcala in 1538 in *Historia de los indios de la Nueva España* (1969). The abridged version below includes a few word changes from Steck's translation:

> The Holy Day of Corpus Christi having arrived . . . the Tlaxcalans here celebrated the feast with such solemnity that it deserves to be recorded. . . . Although neither jewels nor brocades were in evidence, other fineries were just as attractive, especially the flowers and roses that God cultivated on the trees and in the fields, insomuch that it was a pleasure to rest one's gaze on them and to note how a people, until now regarded as beasts, should know how to arrange such a thing. [Just the year before, in 1537, Pope Paul III had declared in a papal bull that Indians indeed had souls and were therefore "human."]
>
> The Most Holy Sacrament was carried in procession, together with many crosses and with andas bearing the images of Saints. The drapes on the crosses and the trimmings on the andas were of gold and feather-work. The statues on the andas had the same adornments which in Spain, on account of their fine workmanship, would have been more highly prized than brocade. There were many banners of the Saints, among them the Twelve Apostles attired in their insignia. Many of those who took part in the procession carried lighted candles. The entire road was covered with sedge grass and reeds and flowers, while someone kept strewing roses and carnations, and many kinds of dances enlivened the procession. On the road there were chapels with their altars and retables well adorned, for resting during the procession. (Motolinía, Motolina's History, 152–54; tratado 1, chap. 25)

52. A possibility that the Mexican posa and its architectural position in the corner of a walled patio had a European prototype is, however, at least suggested in certain fifteenth-century Flemish paintings of the Virgin Mary, sometimes shown in a walled courtyard with curious buildings of unknown purpose at the corners (see fig. 8.2). Fray Pedro de Gante, perhaps the inventor of the posa idea in the first place, was after all a native Fleming.

53. Concerning the widespread prevalence of this peculiar directional orientation in the positioning of both patio posas and cloister testeras in Mexican conventos, see Kubler, *Mexican Architecture,* 1:338.

54. The Corpus Christi procession in Europe originally followed no particular canonical direction from station to station as it progressed through various cities and towns. However, since the Counter-Reformation and quite possibly due to influence from the Franciscans in Mexico, counterclockwise has become more and more the standard. For example, the annual Corpus Christi procession at Saint Patrick's Cathedral on Fifth Avenue in New York City leaves the church through its south transept entrance on Fiftieth Street, marches east to Madison Avenue, then north to Fifty-first Street, west on the latter, and back south again on Fifth Avenue where it reenters the cathedral.

55. The other three being Mexico City, Tlaxcala, and Texcoco.

56. Sebastián López, "La significacion salomonica del Templo de Huejotzingo."

57. Webster, "Art, Ritual, and Confraternities." Mendieta, *Historia eclesiástica indiana* (1945), 3:84 (bk. 4, chap. 19), mentions similar directional processions for Corpus Christi and other holidays: "From time to time, they [the Indians] make their triumphal arches, and in the four corners where the procession makes the circuit or turn they raise up chapels, very covered and adorned with images and grills of flowers with an altar in every one. . . . Another chapel like these is made at the exit from the patio opposite the door of the church which is the first stop and pausing place of the procession" (3:84).

58. Kubler, *Mexican Architecture,* 2:339.

59. For a description of the activities in Fray Pedro's school, see Valadés, *Retórica Cristiana,* 474–77. The tiny detail of Fray Pedro in the upper left corner of Valadés's engraving shows him actually demonstrating a Christianized form of hieroglyphic script apparently invented by Fray Jacobo de Testera, a fellow Franciscan (fig. 9.5); see Watts, "Hieroglyphs of Conversion"; Normann.

60. Torquemada, *Monarquía indiana* (1975–83), 1:414 (book 3, chap. 26).
61. Fernández, *La Jerusalem Indiana,* 191–96.
62. Codex Vindobonensis, fol. 37.
63. Lafaye.
64. An especially poignant example of Jesus carved in a tree-as-cross can be seen in the Museo Regional Michoacáno in Morelia.
65. Motolinía, *Memoriales o libro de las cosas,* (pt. 1, chap. 60). About forty years later, Mendieta recounted the same story almost verbatim but added that the Indians were at first "afraid" to stand under the new arch after the scaffolding had been removed (Mendieta, *Historia eclesiástica indiana* [1945], 3:61 (bk. 4, chap. 13). Motolinía had said nothing of the Indians having such fear.
66. See Molina, 13 recto, under "Arco toral de edificio."

CHAPTER 3

1. Motolinía, *Memoriales o libro de las cosas,* 242 (pt. 1, chap. 60): "El año de mil y quinientos y veinte y cinco se hizo la iglesia de San Francisco de México. Es iglesia pequeña: la capilla es de bóveda, que se hizo un cantero de Castilla."

   Mendieta, *Historia eclesiástica indiana* (1945), 2:65–66 (bk. 3, chap. 18): "Cubrióse el cuerpo de la iglesia de madera, y la capilla mayor de bóveda."

   Commenting further in 1698, Franciscan Fray Agustín de Vetancurt added that not only was the "first church in all the Indies" vaulted in masonry in 1525 but that it was constructed from "piedras quadradas de los escalones del Templo Mayor de los Indios, donde se derramó tanta sangre humana" (32; pt. 4, treatise 2).

   Kubler, based on other evidence, has corrected the construction date to 1526 (*Mexican Architecture,* 2:295). See also ibid., 1:113, for a list of twenty-one *maestros de obras* or *alarifes,* Spanish-Moorish craft titles we would translate today as "general contractors," who worked in Mexico City between 1521 and 1595. These craftsmen presumably served also as teachers of the Indians in the art of arch and vault construction. See also McAndrew, 397–99, for a ground plan and subsequent fate of San Francisco, its reconstruction in 1590, and its dismantling and reuse as secular government offices in the late nineteenth century. Nothing of the original fabric of this most historic building may be seen today. For a contemporaneous (1554) description of the San Francisco convento in Mexico City, see Cervantes de Salazar, *Life in the Imperial and Loyal City,* 53–55.
2. Motolinía, *Memoriales o libro de las cosas,* 242 (pt. 1, chap. 60).
3. Motolinía, *Historia de los indios de la Nueva España* (1969), 64–65 (treatise 1, chap. 15); Motolinía, *Motolinía's History,* 156.
4. Fray Toribio lived in the Tlaxcala convento between 1537 and June 1539; see Motolinía, *Historia de los indios de la Nueva España* (1969), xxviii.
5. For an analysis of the Rosary Chapel in relation to Motolinía's comment, see McAndrew, 418–43; Artigas, *Capillas abiertas aisladas de Tlaxcala;* chap. 7 of this book.
6. Ricard, 20:77–78.
7. Concerning the position and considerable powers of this lay officer in the Yucatán Maya church, known as *ahcambezah* in the Yucatec language, see Farriss, *Maya Society under Colonial Rule,* 233, 335–36; Restall, 150–51. The ahcambezah seems to have been much more than a mere "master of the choir"; in fact he was the Christian replacement of the preconquest Maya *ahk'in,* or high priest, now in charge not only of church upkeep and parish formalities but also the Christian education of the parish children. His name is often inscribed on the dedicatory plaques posted on the facades of many Yucatán churches, as at Hocaba, Ichmul, and Pixila.
8. Kubler, *Mexican Architecture,* 2:305, 323–25, 341–43; McAndrew, 518–24.
9. Wagner. My special thanks to him for an extraordinary, personal on-site tour in August 1997 of all the Yucatán churches discussed in this chapter.
10. Concerning the preconquest history of the Yucatán Maya, see Roys, *Indian Background of Colonial Yucatán.*
11. Concerning the Maya notion of *kah,* see Restall, 13–41. While Restall spells the word *cah,* I follow Yucatec orthography as in Barrera Vásquez.
12. Roys, *Political Geography of the Yucatan,* 3–10.
13. Many geologists now accept that the Yucatán peninsula was formed by the impact of a giant asteroid that struck the earth about 65 million years ago, forming a vast crater thought to have centered on what was later the town of Chicxulub about fifty kilometers northeast of Mérida. Not only did this collision lead to the formation of the present limestone peninsula but also the monstrous explosion of dust into the atmosphere may have caused a dramatic worldwide climate change.

Some paleontologists now suspect that this event led directly to the extinction of the dinosaurs.

14. A. Miller.

15. See Gerhard, *The Southeast Frontier of New Spain,* 23–30, for a demographic analysis of the Yucatán population between 1492 and 1800. For example, according to statistics cited by Gerhard, the native population of the Yucatán dropped from a high of 1,128,000 in 1511 to a low of only 150,000 in 1600. Concerning Montejo's conquest of the Yucatán, see Castillo Peraza, 103–59.

16. For a good introduction to the history of the Franciscan mission to the Yucatán, see Perry and Perry, 9–65.

17. Bretos, "Yucatan," 399–400.

18. Artigas, *Capillas abiertas aisladas de México,* 158.

19. Ciudad Real, *Fray Alonso de Ponce,* 304, and *Tratado curioso,* 2:314 (chap. 142). Artigas, *Capillas abiertas aisladas de México,* 158, has provided a helpful graph showing the distribution of the friars among these twenty-two conventos during the sixteenth century. While Mérida had ten friars in residence, Izamal, Maní, Tizimin, and Valladolid only had four. All the rest had three or fewer.

20. Roys, "Conquest Sites," 154.

21. Because of the shallow topsoil covering the limestone bedrock of the northern Yucatán peninsula, there are few tall trees to give canopy cover but only thick and brambly low growth that makes moving through this jungle slow and difficult; Roys, *Indian Background of Colonial Yucatan,* 5–6. Curiously, the bleached soils of the peninsula truly do make the unpaved roads look "white."

22. Roys, "Conquest Sites."

23. See ibid., 167–77. For a good word picture of just how many ancient pyramid ruins and preconquest temple structures were still strewn about the Yucatán landscape even as late as the nineteenth century, see Stephens and Catherwood. In *Fray Alonso* and *Tratado curioso* Ciudad Real makes frequent reference to these vestigial pyramids, always remarking that while once the Indians had performed human sacrifices upon them, now they were all surmounted by Christian crosses.

24. See Wagner, 117–82. For a reproduction of Catherwood's engraving, see Stephens and Catherwood, 2:282–83, plate 53.

25. See Clendinnen, 45–129.

26. Roys, "Conquest Sites," 146.

27. Ibid., 180: "Not only are a large number of the towns in northern Yucatán located at their pre-Spanish sites, but the present churches and plazas are situated at the ceremonial centers of the old towns."

28. The notion of building superimposition, of course, hardly began with the Spanish in Mesoamerica. Indeed, it was always the practice; nearly every temple in preconquest Mexico was itself built upon an earlier structure, often in "onion skin" fashion with the more recent masonry layered right over the older.

29. In his comments on the visit he and Commissary General Alonso Ponce made to Calkini, Yucatán, on August 29, 1588, Fray Antonio de Ciudad Real decribed the newly completed convento there as "situated on a *ku* or *mul* of the ancients" (*Fray Alonso de Ponce,* 343; *Tratado curioso,* chap. 127). The Yucatec Maya word *mul* refers more specifically to a man-made hill, that is, a pyramid supporting a temple. On the general use of this term (Hispanicized as *cu,* pl. *cues*) throughout New Spain to denote a preconquest temple, see Cervantes de Salazar, *Crónica de la Nueva España,* 314–16 (chap. 20).

30. Hanson.

31. Roys, *Indian Background of Colonial Yucatan,* 18–19.

32. As quoted in Perry and Perry, 71.

33. "Anagogical" was one of four levels of understanding that medieval churchmen should apply to the exposition of Scripture; the others being the "literal," "tropological" (moral), and "allegorical." See, for example, Saint Antonine, vol. 4, tit. 11, cap. 2, cols. 560–61: "Littera, gesta docet, quod credas Allegoria, Moralis quod agas, quo tendas Anagogia. . . . Lex vetus figura est novae legis; et ipsa nova lex est figura futurae gloria . . . [ille] est sensus anagogicus" (The literal sense teaches the history, the allegorical sense what you should believe, the moral sense what you must do, and the anagogical sense to where you extend [your mind]. . . . The old law is the figure of new law; and the new law is the figure of future glory . . . [and that] is the sense of the anagogical).

Fray Francisco de Toral, Bishop of Yucatán from 1560 to 1571, owned a printed copy of Saint Antonine's *Summa theologica* (originally written in fifteenth-century Florence and published subsequently in numerous European editions), which he brought with him to New Spain in 1541 and donated to the Colegio de Santa Cruz library in Mexico City. (The importance of Saint Antonine's teachings to the friars in Mexico is discussed at length in chap. 4.) Diego Valadés, a native Mexican schooled at the Colegio de Santa Cruz who joined the Franciscan order to become a missionary himself in Mexico, also discussed at length the meaning and significance of anagogica in his famous treatise *Rhetorica Christiana* published in 1579 (*Retórica Cristiana,* 337–51; pt. 3, chaps. 11–12). This treatise is discussed in some detail in chaps. 4 and 9.

34. Simson, 22.

35. Ibid., 109, 134. For a fulsome and lengthy argument, with ample quotations from Saint Augustine, Peter of Celle, Abbot Suger, and others relative to the anagogical

qualities being instilled in vaulted churches during the Middle Ages, especially as they affected the building of Chartres Cathedral, see also ibid., 22, 109, 115, 119–20, 126–27, 134, 194, 196–97.

36. Pendergast, 120, discovered a small clay vessel shaped like a jaguar buried beside the doorway of the first Christian visita at Lamanai. He interpreted this as being a propitiation of some Maya worker to the ancient gods for having defiled the former sacred pagan site with a Christian church. I would argue that it could just as logically have been placed there by an enthusiastic convert in the same spirit of similar Christian offerings in Europe.

37. Christenson, 55. Friars and Indian workers made a similar dedication of precious objects including crosses, gems, and coins, which they sealed into the cornerstone of the convento church at Yanhuitlán, Oaxaca; see Perry, *Mexico's Fortress Monasteries,* 184.

38. Valadés, *Retórica Cristiana,* 406; Valadés, *Rhetorica Christiana,* 147 (xvi); see also Palomera, 364–65. Fray Agustín de Vetancurt, writing as late as 1698, was also convinced that "the Indians were not strangers to vaults because in Texcoco and in other places vaults of admirable architecture are found, and look, they made them no doubt without having seen and then built them" (no estrañarian las bobedas los Indios porque in Texcoco, y in otras partes se hallararon bobedas de admirable arquitectura, y pues ellos las hizieron no ay duda sino que las havian visto, y las havian fabricado) (32; pt. 4, treatise 2).

39. Folan; Bretos, "Yucatan," and *Iglesias de Yucatán;* Artigas, *Capillas abiertas aisladas de México,* 163–70.

40. Bretos, *Iglesias de Yucatán,* 87–89. See the discussion and controversy regarding the dated fragment in Folan, 187–90.

41. Bretos, *Iglesias de Yucatán,* 21–23.

42. Folan, 186.

43. Cogolludo, bk. 8, chap. 3, as cited in Castillo Peraza, 208–9. See also Bretos, "Yucatan," 401; and Perry and Perry, 126–34.

44. See Hanson, 18–19, for archaeological evidence of the earliest examples, as at Tipú and Lamanai in Belize. See also Pendergast, for more on Lamanai, where the ruins of two sixteenth-century churches may be seen. The masonry walls of the later of these still stand with heavy quoins outlining the western entrance indicating that it was once spanned by an impressive keystone arch. Another example not mentioned by Hanson or Pendergast, and with its great arch still intact, can be seen on the property of the Hacienda Chalanté, Sudzal, known locally as the Capilla de Santa Catalina.

45. In the medieval Catholic church it was traditional for the sacristy to the left of the sanctuary to serve secular community functions. Here, marriage and business contracts would be signed, vows taken, and local disputes between parishioners adjudicated, all under the eyes of God, so to speak. The vestry, traditionally to the right of the sanctuary, was supposedly the place where the priest's vestments were stored, but in the Yucatán churches it seems to have been the most convenient place in which to perform the sacrament of baptism. It was also the place where the Indian choir would sit, accompanying the Mass with music and chants.

46. Burns, 37–38:

Well, there in the town of Maní there is a deep well [cenote].
There's a huge box there;
there's a huge rope there, rolled up in the box.
It's a thick rope.
The thing is, the rope lives—it has blood [kuxa'an suum].
There in the middle of the town of Maní it is rolled up. . . .
There at the deep well there in the middle of the center of Maní,
there is water,
because the well is enchanted.
It was made that way by the ancient Makers.
It was spoiled in the old times.
At midday strange things are heard. . . .
There is a big path inside the Deep Well that runs to the town of Ho [Mérida]
There underneath the cathedral the big path comes out.
The road keeps going, it doesn't have an end.
It just keeps going, it doesn't have an end.
Because the path that runs there goes all the way to Jerusalem.

47. Bassie-Sweet, *From the Mouth of the Dark Cave,* and *At the Edge of the World;* Stone; and Brady.

48. The seventeenth-century Indian historian Domingo Francisco Chimalpahin mentioned with admiration that Fray Martin de Valencia lived in a cave called Chalchiumomoztli in the center of Amecameca, later called Sacramonte, and had visions there. Local King Quetzalmacatzin was so impressed, he had the Church of Santo Tomas built there; see Schroeder, 24.

49. Interestingly, the Yucatec Maya word *k'u,* which in preconquest times meant "holy temple" and was commonly used by the Spanish conquistadors to describe the native pyramids, became the common word after the conquest for "church." K'u can also mean the hollowed nest of a squirrel or bird.

50. Schele and Freidel, 239; Schele and Mathews, 29, 40.

51. Folan, 197.

52. Perry and Perry, 161–62.

53. For an interesting description and analysis of the relationship between preconquest "sacred spaces" and the superimposition of Christian shrines, especially at Chalma, see Wagner, 83–97.

54. In the remains of the sixteenth-century Franciscan church at Tipú in Belize, one may still see the stone foundation for such a ramada with its western extended end typically curved; see Hanson, 18–19.

55. Curiously, the "atrio cross," ubiquitous in the conventos of central Mexico, is rarely if ever found in the patios of the Franciscan missions in the Yucatán. In fact, there is really only one arguable example, at Maní. This stone cross, actually a conventional Crucifix, as is never the case in central Mexico, is presently exhibited inside the Maní convento. No one knows where it was originally located. So conditioned to the standard presence of the central Mexican atrio cross was John McAndrew, that he had one erroneously included in his drawing of the convento at Izamal (242).

56. On the political and ethnic struggles of colonial Yucatán society leading to the terrible Caste Wars of the mid-nineteenth century, see Rugeley.

57. Bretos, "Yucatan," 405. Sea-level Yucatán, unlike the Pacific-rim cordillera region of the Americas, is little troubled by earthquakes, thus posing no danger to arcuated buildings.

58. Another popular addition to seventeenth- and eighteenth-century Yucatán churches was the *camerín* (little room), appended behind the sanctuary. This is a masonry-enclosed cell with an opening through the sanctuary wall above the altar. Here resided the cult image of the patron santo of the parish, which could be moved in and out of the sanctuary proper through the conjoining window. During the day, the santo was passed through the window and exposed to the congregation in a niche in the retablo. At night, the image was returned to the camerín and the conjoining window closed. A prominent camerín can be visited at Izamal, which houses the famous cult image of the Virgin, moved back and forth on a special set of tracks. Remains of a similar camerín are behind the open chapel at Pixila/Cuauhtémoc. The idea certainly derived from the great Extremadura shrine of Guadalupe, Spain, where the fourteenth-century wooden image of the Virgin is still lodged in an extraordinarily sumptuous camerín.

59. The traditional Maya love of bright colors has never diminished, of course, in their woven cotton textiles. It is also significant that the Maya still consider bright colors, especially green and blue, as appropriate to the decoration of their village cemeteries. An especially vivid and charming example may be visited near the town of Hoctun, just off Highway 180 about forty kilometers east of Mérida.

60. Published in Stephens and Catherwood.

CHAPTER 4

Note that the epigraph, which is from the *Memoriales* of about 1550, differs in several important details from a similar paragraph he wrote some ten years earlier in his *Historia,* as translated by Steck in Motolinía, *Historia de los indios de la Nueva España* (1969), 212 (bk. 3, chap. 13):

In the mechanical arts the Indians have made great progress, both in those which they cultivated previously and in those which they learned from the Spaniards. After the arrival of the Flemish and Italian models and paintings which the Spaniards brought, excellent artists developed among the Indians. Some very valuable pieces of painting have come to this land. Everything comes to where there is gold and silver, and this helps especially the painters of Mexico, as anything of value that comes to this land ends up in this city. Formerly the Indians knew only how to paint a flower or a bird or design. If they painted a man or a man on horseback, the proportions were poorly done. But now they paint well. (212)

Motolinía's comments here were more or less copied and expanded upon by Fray Geronimo de Mendieta in his 1595 *Historia eclesiástica indiana* (see Mendieta, *Historia eclesiástica indiana* (1945), 3:54–59 (bk. 4, chap. 12) and then copied and modified further by Fray Juan de Torquemada in his 1615 *Monarquía indiana* (see Torquemada, *Monarquía indiana* (1975–83), 4:253–57 (bk. 13, chap. 34).

1. This chapter addresses only the matter of convento mural painting and not the rich and much more thoroughly studied subject of postconquest manuscript illumination. For a review of literature about the latter, see Baird, *Drawings of Sahagún's "Primeros Memoriales,"* 13–20.

2. Kubler, *Mexican Architecture,* 2:361–417, devoted a long chapter to the subject, although in general treating it only as a rather clumsy effort at imitating current styles in provincial Spain.

3. A happy exception to this trend is Ellen Baird; see Baird, *Drawings of Sahagún's "Primeros Memoriales,"* and "Adaptation and Accommodation."

4. For the iconography and attributes of Saint Catherine of Siena as depicted in Dominican churches and monasteries, see Jameson, *Legends of the Monastic Orders,* 420–35.

5. For an analysis of the iconography and style of the Tetela del Volcán murals, see Martínez Marín, 85–111; and Phillips, 446–58. Martínez Marín dates the cloister paintings between 1562 and the end of the century and detects various hands at work, all under the one chief master who painted the Saint Catherine and whose style he observed as "*completamente occidental*." The only painter at the site he unequivocally identifies as an Indian was the artist who painted a mural in an upper story chapel dedicated to a local miracle of the Virgin of the Rosary, including a scene of hell filled with "*formas indigenas*" (107). On this latter image, see chaps. 6 and 8 of this book.
6. This argument is also quite apparent in Gruzinski's, *La Guerra de las imágenes*, 71–102, and *L'Aigle et la sibylle*, 29, neither as yet translated into English.
7. Concerning how pre-Columbian American artifacts also influenced many avant-garde European artists, see Braun.
8. On this see especially Gablik.
9. Pastor, 4.1:567, 4.2:92–93, 536.
10. Mendieta, *Historia eclesiástica indiana* (1945), 4:97 (bk. 5, chap. 34); later copied by Torquemada, *Monarquía indiana* (1975–83), 6:245 (bk. 20, chap. 34).
11. See the extensive references to Saint Antonine listed in the index to Torquemada, *Monarquía indiana* (1975–83), 7:575.
12. For the iconography of Saint Antonine as imaged in Dominican monasteries and churches in general, see Jameson, *Legends of the Monastic Orders*, 435–40.
13. Cataloged in Sutro as *Quarta pars totius summe maioris Beati Antonini. . . . Incipit probemium in quartem partem summe Domini Antonini Archiepicopi Fiorenntis ordinis predicatorum*, Lyons (Johan Cleyn), 1500; see Mathes, 51. The present bound volume, lacking books 1 and 2, still bears the stamp of the Convento de Santiago Tlatelolco (all remaining books in the original library were transferred to this nearby convento in 1605; see Mathes, 43), and also the signature of the Franciscan friar Francisco de Toral, who came to Mexico in 1542, probably bringing along this tome and several other books which he then donated to the library (Mathes, 89). In 1565 Toral was appointed bishop of the Yucatán in the wake of the controversial auto-da-fé persecutions of Indian "heretics" by Diego de Landa. Interestingly, the Jesuit missionaries to India during the early seventeenth century also furnished the Mohammedan Mughal emperor Akbar with a European library including a printed volume of Saint Antonine's writings, which was translated by Akbar's scribes; see Bailey, "Indian Conquest of Catholic Art."
14. Saint Antonine, vol. 4, tit. 11, cap. 2, cols. 560–65.
15. Ibid., tit. 16, cap. 1. For further information concerning the significance of this passage in relation to fifteenth-century Renaissance religious imagery, see Edgerton, "*Mensurare temporalia facit Geometria spiritualis.*"
16. Saint Antonine, vol. 3, tit. 11, cap. 10. This passage has been analyzed in relation to the popular early quattrocento international Gothic-style painting in Italy by Gilbert. Interestingly, Fray Ortiz de Hinojosa, vicar general of the Archdiocese of Mexico, presented somewhat the same warning to the Third Council of the Franciscan order in 1580, remarking that "religious art should not depict demons or animals . . . because the Indians were thus tempted to fall back into idolatry"; see Poole, *Pedro Moya de Contreras*, 142.
17. For a more technical explanation of Albertian perspective and the full texts of Alberti's treatise in this regard, see Edgerton, *Renaissance Rediscovery of Linear Perspective*.
18. See ibid., 16–32; Edgerton, *The Heritage of Giotto's Geometry*, 288–91; Baird, "Adaptation and Accommodation," 46–49.
19. Fray Pedro makes no mention of this in his few surviving letters nor are there any other confirming documents. Nonetheless, we do know from his first letter to Juan de Zumárraga that he left Flanders in April 1522, arriving in Spain on July 22 (Gante, 15), where Cardinal Adrian (born Adrian Florenszoon Boeyens) was already resident as grand inquisitor of Castille. It is not unlikely, therefore, that Fray Pedro went to Spain in the first place to join in the celebration of Cardinal Adrian's election to the papacy that previous January and to travel with the new Pope to Rome for the official coronation on the coming August 31. In any case, Fray Pedro was back in Spain by May 1, 1523, when he sailed from there to Mexico.
20. See especially book 3 of Alberti, *Leon Battista Alberti on Painting*, 94–108. Concerning the increasing influence of Raphael's decorous style on early sixteenth-century Flemish painting, see Ainsworth and Christiansen, 39–63; 319–28.
21. Plato, lines 19b–22e.
22. *De pictura libri II*, Basel, 1540; editions also printed in both Nuremberg and Venice in 1547; again in Nuremberg, 1558; Monte Regale (Italy), 1565; twice in Venice in 1568; and Basel, 1582. These numerous printings, after the treatise on painting had languished in manuscript for more than a century (originally written in 1435–36), surely indicate a revived popularity of Alberti's ideas, no doubt because of (and exacerbating) a rising reaction against the vagaries of mannerist art in the context of the Council of Trent. See Schlosser Magnino, 127–29.
23. Tovar de Teresa, "La Utopia del Virrey de Mendoza,"

17–41. A Spanish translation of Alberti's treatise on architecture was published in 1582.

24. The standard biography of Valadés is by Palomera; see also Alejos-Grau. Concerning Valadés's artistic training and influences, see Maza, 15–44. Valadés's alleged native mestizo birth, of which Palomera and other Mexican writers have made so much, has been challenged by Vásquez Janeiro.

25. Valadés, *Retórica Cristiana* and *Rhetorica Christiana.*

26. Valadés, *Retórica Cristiana,* 211, and *Rhetorica Christiana,* 478 (pt. 4, chap. 23). A copy of this engraving was used by Fray Juan de Torquemada as the frontispiece for his *Monarquía Indiana,* (1975–83).

27. Valadés, *Rhetorica Christiana,* 110–12 *[sic]* (pt. 4, chap. 23). The correct page numbers are 210–12. After page 204, a typographical error occurs, and all subsequent pages are numbered again in the 100s.

28. Interestingly, Motolinía also mentions that the Indians brought pictures with them to confession; see Motolinía, *Historia de los indios de la Nueva España* (1969), 95 (treatise 2, chap. 6).

29. Valadés, *Retórica Cristiana,* 93–96, 233–39 (pt. 2, chap. 27). Actually, printed pictures with alphabetic letter symbols referring to accompanying explanatory text, just as in his own book, were becoming a standard convention in post-Gutenberg Europe. Nevertheless, the Franciscans may indeed have been the first to employ pictures for missionary instruction (although the Dominicans were just as interested), and Fray Diego's book may even have inspired the far more famous *Evangelicae historiae imagines* of Hieronymus Nadal. This great work, illustrated with 150 engravings by well-known Flemish artists, was labored over for many years by the Jesuit Nadal and finally published posthumously in 1593. It quickly became the standard proselytization "field manual" of the post-Tridentine Counter-Reformation. For full discussion of this work and especially its impact in China and on Chinese art, see Edgerton, *The Heritage of Giotto's Geometry,* 254–88.

30. The same tactic in this regard was apparently also followed by the Jesuits in China during the early seventeenth century. While the Indians of Mesoamerica were obviously fascinated by bloodied images of Jesus and the martyred saints, the Chinese were quite offended. Hence, the Jesuits evangelizing in China deliberately played down the Passion and emphasized instead Jesus' "holy family," which particularly appealed to traditional Confucian and Buddhist values; see Edgerton, *The Heritage of Giotto's Geometry,* 254–88.

31. Christian, *Local Religion in Sixteenth-Century Spain.*

32. Valadés, *Retórica Cristiana,* 110, 476–77 (pt. 2, chap. 27).

33. Curiously, while the Classic Maya had developed an almost Greek-like foreshortening of the human figure in profile (for example, in their painting and relief-carving of persons sitting cross-legged), this technique was never adopted in the succeeding arts of central Mexico during the Postclassic period. By the time of the Spanish arrival, figures both in painting and sculptural relief tended to be rendered in flattened profile with little or no modeling. Furthermore, neither Maya nor western Mexican artists ever attempted to depict figures in an illusionistic three-dimensional space. In preconquest art, depicted backgrounds behind figures are always spatially neutral, indicating neither illusionistic depth nor any sense of illumination from a directional light source. Time and place were indicated only by symbolic props, never by atmospheric ambiance.

34. Valadés, *Retórica Cristiana,* 236–37, and *Rhetorica Christiana,* 94–95.

35. Valadés, *Retórica Cristiana,* 5 and 10, 57, 67 (pt. 1, chap. 2).

36. Ibid., 6, 59 (pt. 1, chap. 2).

37. Concerning the resistance of Spanish painters to the use of complex geometric perspective during the sixteenth century, see Cabezas Gelabert, "La 'perspectiva angular'" and "La teoria de la perspectiva"; Garriga.

38. Valadés, *Retórica Cristiana,* 6, 59 (pt. 1, chap. 2). Fray Diego's insistence in his engraving of depicting a geometrical sphere as the special symbol of his disdain for worldliness could also have been provoked by another recent and popular treatise he may have examined during his sojourn in Rome: Daniele Barbaro's *Pratica della perspettiva,* published in Venice in several editions between 1567 and 1569, contained perspective diagrams of reticulated spheres with raised protuberances as exercises for teaching art students how to draw cast shadows. Galileo no doubt studied this very book and was able to apply its geometrical principles in 1609 when he discovered by looking through his telescope that the dark spots on the moon were in fact cast shadows caused by raised protuberances (mountains) on the spherical lunar surface; see Edgerton, *The Heritage of Giotto's Geometry,* 223–53.

39. See the Codex Borgia, and Díaz and Rodgers.

40. Landa, 169.

41. Valadés, *Retórica Cristiana,* 95, 237–39 (pt. 2, chap. 27). For further interpretation of Valades's ideas on this matter, see Pagden, 188–89.

42. Valadés, *Retórica Cristiana,* 11, 69 (pt. 1, chap. 2): *Speculum talis est naturae, quod imaginem quam recipit, statim ostendit: nescir enim aliquid celare.*

43. Mendieta, *Historia eclesiástica indiana* (1945), 1:102 (bk. 2, chap. 13).

44. Motolinía, *Memoriales o libro de las cosas,* 240 (chap. 60).

45. Illustration from the Codex Borgia, fol. 56. Fray Pedro's opinion about such images from this is implicit from this comment in his first letter to Juan de Zumárraga, dated June 27, 1529:

> For the demons of this land who are reputed to be gods were so many and varied that the [Indians] were ignorant of the number. They believed that every single thing had a god, that one ruled this, another that. There was a god of fire, another of air, another of earth: one they called a snake, another the wife of the snake, another six snakes, and another five rabbits, and so on to infinity. . . . To some of these they sacrificed human hearts, to others human blood . . . conforming to the diverse rites and ceremonies that the demons demand, and according to the various qualities of the gods. For some were painted black, others yellow, and other colors. (Gante 13)

Alberti, *Leon Battista Alberti on Painting,* 84–85.

46. McAndrew, 386; Peterson, *Paradise Garden Murals,* 51–56.

47. Alberti, *Leon Battista Alberti on Painting,* 86–87.

48. Manuel Toussaint, *Paseos coloniales,* maintained that only after 1576 do Mexican convento murals take on more vivid coloration.

49. It is noteworthy that even artists in Spain and Italy were responding to a similar "dark manner" in apparent emulation of Leonardo da Vinci who in fact was reflecting Alberti. This new puritanic style was especially countenanced by the Catholic reformers at the Council of Trent. About 1555, for example, the Florentine painter Agnolo Bronzino was ordered by his patroness, the Spanish-born and arch-Catholic grand duchess of Tuscany, Eleanora of Toledo, to redo in muted grisaille a large wall-painting of the lamentation of Christ that he originally painted in bright colors for her private chapel in the Florentine Palazzo Vecchio. Such an association of black and white with images of moral tragedy may even have been an archetype in the mind of Spanish-born Pablo Picasso when in 1937 he painted his *Guernica,* likewise in grisaille, to commemorate the infamous bombing of an innocent town during the Spanish civil war.

The most widely consulted authority on the proper role that the visual arts should play in the service of the church after the Council of Trent was Gabriele Paleotti, Bishop of Bologna, whose *Discorso intorno alle imagini sacre e profane* of 1582 and Latin edition of 1584 discussed pretty much the same artistic program as advocated by Diego Valadés and other native artists trained after Pedro de Gante. I have found no evidence that his treatise was directly consulted, nor is any copy of it in the Sutro Library, San Francisco, which does contain a large number of religious tracts once in the Mexican convento libraries. Nonetheless, on the general contents and influence of this work and its apparent similarity to the Mexican experience, see Jones.

50. Robertson, 191. See also Manrique. However, in an elegant study of map-making by Indian artists in colonial Mexico, Barbara Mundy, without offering documents to counter Robertson, argues that the natives were trained in this art in the convento schools and were even granted unusual license to employ many of their preconquest map-making conventions, including bright colors and human figures *tan fieros* (*The Mapping of New Spain,* 61–90). I suspect she is correct insofar as the friars would have probably considered map-making a more secular specialty and thus appreciated the continuing use of native symbols in order that the maps be more communicable to the Indians. In a subsequent article the same author argues, again correctly in my opinion, that the famous map of the city of Tenochtitlan that Cortés sent to Emperor Charles V in 1521, which was then printed as a woodcut in Nuremberg in 1524, was originally drawn by an Indian showing the sacred Templo Mayor precinct in the center, probably deliberately so in order to evoke a correspondence in the eyes of European viewers with the popular "T-and-O" Christian *mappamundi,* which shows the world with Jerusalem in the center ("Mapping the Aztec Capital"). Here is an interesting reverse application of my theory of expedient selection, now applied to convince the Holy Roman Emperor to accept Cortés's claim that the Aztec empire was just as advanced a civilization as that of Christian Europe.

51. *Trattato della Perfezione,* ca. 1350; see abridged edition in Levasti, 273.

CHAPTER 5

1. Concerning the few professional Spanish and (mostly) Flemish artists who arrived in Mexico during the later sixteenth century, see Kubler and Soria, *Art and Architecture,* 306–7; Tovar de Teresa, *Renacimiento en México,* 110–11. Simon Pereyns, who came to the New World from Antwerp in 1566, and Andrés de la Concha from Seville a year later mostly painted retablos, large multipaneled altarpieces framed in gilded wood that became popular attractions in Mexican churches at the end of the 1500s. There is no evidence that the above two masters ever taught Indian apprentices or painted murals in the missionary conventos.

2. I do not know if the obviously Catholic Carvajal family in Cáceres was related to the famous *converso* branch of

the Carvajals in Mexico, descended from Portuguese Jews but becoming Catholics and serving the Spanish Crown with distinction in the Province of Nuevo Léon. The bitter story of their persecution and execution as crypto-*Judaizantes* by the Holy Office of the Inquisition during the 1580s is described in Greenleaf, *The Mexican Inquisition,* 169–71.

3. Garrido and Pison, 44–47. The Convento of Santa Inés in Seville contains similarly crude sixteenth-century murals; illustrated in Peterson, *Paradise Garden Murals,* plate 8.
4. See the long discussion in Kubler, *Mexican Architecture,* 2:361–417; see also Kubler and Soria, *Art and Architecture,* 164.
5. For a comprehensive discussion of the training and status of native artists in sixteenth-century Mexico, see Peterson, *Paradise Garden Murals,* 29–83. For a brief but instructive overview of the kind of art that was being imported to the Americas and being taught to the Indians during the sixteenth century, see Manrique.
6. Alberti, *Leon Battista Alberti on Painting,* 82–83.
7. For a brief overview of this problem, see Manrique; also the interesting comments on the Actopan artists' use of perspective by Donald Robertson in Edmonson, *Sixteenth-Century Mexico,* 151–65. For an excellent and beautifully illustrated survey of Flemish painting and its impact on Christian Europe during the fifteenth and sixteenth centuries, see Ainsworth and Christiansen. Among the most appreciative patrons of Flemish painting at this time were of course Ferdinand and Isabella of Spain.
8. Sebastián López, *Iconografia e iconologia del arte novohispano,* 66; Perry, *Mexico's Fortress Monasteries,* 61.
9. Perry, *Mexico's Fortress Monasteries,* 55. Grijalva, 300 (bk. 3, chap. 22), notes that Fray Andrés de Mata "built the two famous conventos of Actopan and Ixmiquilpan, for which merit only his fame should be eternal" but says nothing of his earlier artistic or architectural training.
10. See Mora, Mora, and Philippot, 83, and plate 89. The authors, however, have misidentified their photograph of the Actopan murals as being in Acolman. In classic Renaissance Italian fresco technique, the final plaster surface to be painted *(intonaco)* is laid up in irregular patches called *giornate,* each covering as much space as can be painted before the plaster dries (roughly a day), always starting at the top of the wall and working downward one level of giornate at a time. The authors note, however, that in other techniques, as at Actopan, the day-work, which they prefer to call *puntate,* was laid up in broad horizontal bands stretching across the entire breadth of each register, with its sutures only detectable in the borders at top and bottom.
11. According to Mora, Mora, and Philippot, sixteenth-century Mexican mural painters also used an indigenous preconquest technique similar to that of ancient Rome, that is, to exploit the natural calcite properties of plaster and clay wall surfaces by burnishing them into a high polish.
12. García Icazbalceta, *Bibliografia mexicana,* 279 item no. 82(71); Beristain de Souza, 1:334, 384. Alciati's book was the seventy-first volume published by the Mexican press. Only one copy of this book is extant, in bad condition and lacking forty-one pages, in the library of the British Museum, London.
13. See, for instance, the discussion in Sebastián Lopéz, Mesa Figueroa and Gisbert de Mesa, 46–56, of the diffusion of Renaissance book illustrations in the New World as sources for convento mural painting.
14. During the early seventeenth century, Chinese artists were commissioned to copy the woodcuts and engraved illustrations from a number of sixteenth-century European treatises on technology. Because the copyists did not know or even recognize the European illusionistic conventions, they naively translated the Western images into the traditional Chinese style in such a way that the technological information in the original pictures was completely misrepresented; see Edgerton, *The Heritage of Giotto's Geometry,* 254–88.
15. Grijalva, 113 (bk. 1, chap. 30).
16. The architectural term "testera" has nothing to do with the name of the sixteenth-century Franciscan Fray Jacobo de Testera, who supposedly invented "Testerian hieroglyphics."
17. Manuel Toussaint called the Epazoyucán murals the most important of their genre in all Mexico. Furthermore, he attributed them to Juan Gerson (*Colonial Art in Mexico,* 92). Kubler, *Mexican Architecture,* 2:367, made the same attribution, yet neither at the time were aware that Juan Gerson was an Indian. It appears likely that both Toussaint and Kubler thought the murals too sophisticated to have been done by any other than a European master. See also Gruzinski, *L'Aigle et la sibylle,* 10–28.
18. Concerning Alberti's instructions for drawing figures, see his *Leon Battista Alberti on Painting,* 73–87.
19. Castillo Negrete; see also Moyssén, "Pinturas murales en Epazoyucán."
20. That the Cuilapan murals were painted by Indian artists is attested to by Fray Francisco de Burgoa, Dominican chronicler of the Oaxacan missions in 1670; see Burgoa, *Geográfica descripción,* 1:402 (chap. 38).
21. Regarding the illusionistic effects of the Assisi frescoes, see Edgerton, *The Heritage of Giotto's Geometry,* 47–88. Concerning the peculiar and variable "period eye" of different civilizations and historical times (especially during the European Middle Ages and Renaissance) and how cultural and ideological indoctri-

nation affect the way people "see reality" in pictorial representation, see Baxandall; and Shearman.

22. See Lindberg.

23. Brunelleschi's original linear perspective painting has unfortunately been lost since the fifteenth century. For a full explanation and analysis of Brunelleschi's as well as Alberti's achievement, see Edgerton, *Renaissance Rediscovery of Linear Perspective.*

24. For more details of this interesting cross-cultural artistic confrontation, see Bailey, *Art on the Jesuit Missions,* 90–91. See also Spence; Dunne; Edgerton, *The Heritage of Giotto's Geometry,* 254–87; and Belting, 312–14, 485–86.

25. Elia, 2:123 n. 5.

26. Bailey, "Indian Conquest of Catholic Art."

27. See Gruzinski's comments on this in *La Guerra de las imágenes,* 82–90.

28. In spite of the increasing popularity of Alberti's theories during the sixteenth century, Flemish and Spanish painters also consulted Jean Pélerin Viator's *De artificiali perspectiva,* Toul, 1505 and 1509. In fact, a number of printed treatises on perspective were circulating in Europe during the early sixteenth century, many even written by professional mathematicians with complex diagrams and illustrations offering a variety of geometric alternatives; see Schlosser Magnino, 259–89.

29. Concerning this "mirror" effect of sixteenth-century Spanish, especially Catalan, perspective painting, see Garriga, 42.

30. Kubler, *Mexican Architecture,* 2:375–76, 392–96, first noticed the similarity of the Calpan relief sculpture to a version of the popular woodcut published in Pedro de la Vega's *Flos sanctorum,* Zaragoza, 1521 (depicted also in Lyell, 136). The ultimate source of this Crucifixion grouping, hence its wide international popularity, was a woodcut that appeared in Hartmann Schedel's great *Weltchronik* (Nuremberg chronicle) of 1493 (fol. 265v). A variation was then reprinted in Venice in several broadsheet versions after 1510, and again in nine editions of the Spanish tract *Flos sanctorum* in Spain after 1521. At least one if not several copies of *Flos sanctorum* were recorded in the Colegio de Santa Cruz library (Mathes, 4–5, 19, 35). It would seem, however, that the Calpan sculptor did not base his relief on the *Flos santorum* print per se but had either another source (perhaps the Venice variant) or simply improvised from the former. In any case, the Latin inscription was not in the print sources and was added by the sculptor. It reads: *Intercede Virgo Sacra ora pro nobis* (Intercede O Sacred Virgin and pray for us) to the left, and *Dedit illi Dominus omne iudicio* (The Lord judges all of them) at right. Below the figure of Christ, the inscription reads, *Surgite mortui venite ad iudicium* (Let the dead arise and come to judgment).

31. A few exceptions are worth noting. Writing in 1615, Fray Juan de Torquemada twice lauds a certain Indian working on the grand retable in Santiago de Tlatelolco named "Miguel Mauricio," renowned as both painter and sculptor, whose sculptural art in particular surpassed that of any Spaniard of his time; see Torquemada, *Monarquía indiana* (1975–83), 4:255 (bk. 13, chap. 34); and 5:314 (bk. 17, chap. 1). Torquemada was also involved, this time less pleasantly, with another Indian painter named Agustín Garcia who denounced the friar before the *audiencia* for having beaten and whipped him during an argument; see Torquemada, *Monarquía indiana* (1975–83), 7:37.

Fray Agustín de Vetancurt, writing in 1698, mentions in two places a certain "Balthazar Cháves el viejo," referring to an artist who painted lienzos in the cloister of the Convento de San Francisco in Mexico City during the early sixteenth century; see Vetancurt, 33, 39 (pt. 4, treatise 2, chap. 3). Vetancurt does not identify him as an Indian, but another contemporaneous Mexican Indian painter called Gaspar Cháves, whose name also sounds suspiciously Christianized—perhaps a brother or son of Balthazar—is recorded in Saur, 18:357. No works by these artists are known today.

32. Díaz del Castillo, 170, 581. I have translated Díaz del Castillo's word *entalladores* as "carvers." It is not clear whether he meant sculptors of stone, or engravers of prints, or both, since the word can be used for either.

33. Toussaint, *Colonial Art in Mexico,* 40; see also McAndrew, 386–87. The altarpiece is apparently represented in a drawing in the Codex Aubin for the year 1564.

34. In 1556 a hearing was held in Mexico City in which the recent successor to Juan de Zumárraga as Archbishop of Mexico, Dominican Fray Alonso de Montúfar, charged that the Franciscans had wronged him regarding his support for a shrine to the Virgin Mary on the nearby Tepeyac hill now called Guadalupe. Franciscan Fray Francisco de Bustamente then bitterly attacked Montúfar's policy in a public sermon in which he claimed that the image of the Virgin had only been painted for the shrine by an Indian named Marcos and that the local Indian population was worshipping it like a preconquest pagan idol. For the full documentation of this dispute in context, see García Icazbalceta, *Nueva colección de documentos,* 122–36. My book is not the place to detail the long and complex history of the painted image of the Virgin of Guadalupe, claimed to have been divinely imprinted on the cloak of a poor Indian convert named Juan Diego in 1531. He is said to have seen a vision of the Virgin on a hill near Mexico City that had once been sacred to the Aztec mother deity, Tonantzin.

For an excellent analysis of all the known documents concerning this apparition and the history of the image (from a quite skeptical viewpoint), see Poole, *Our Lady of Guadalupe,* 1–68.

35. In any case, the image has been extensively restored if not completely repainted several times since the seventeenth century; see Torre Villar and Novarro; and Poole, *Our Lady of Guadalupe.*
36. Mathes, 54, 77, 98.
37. Moyssén, "Tecamachalco y el pintor indigena Juan Gerson"; Landa Abrego; Fernández, *La Jerusalem Indiana,* 119–39; Gruzinski, *Painting the Conquest,* 178; and especially Gruzinski, *L'Aigle et la sibylle,* 91–132.
38. I am following the spelling of this and all other Nahuatl words used in this book according to Karttunen. On what little further is known about native tlahcuiloqueh, see Kubler, *Mexican Architecture,* 2:367.
39. Phillips, 227, and Peterson, *Paradise Garden Murals,* have both noticed that many tequitqui designs derive from tapestries, as were commonly hung out windows and over balconies during feast days.
40. Robertson, 15–23, 59–67; Peterson, *Paradise Garden Murals,* 34.
41. Gibson, *Perception of the Visual World.*
42. See, for instance, Claire Farago, "'Vision Itself Has Its History,'" for an informative review of the historiography of Renaissance art history as taught in the Western world since the nineteenth century, especially under the impact of increased multicultural awareness, and how interpretations have changed concerning the very meaning of "visual reality" since Jacob Burckhardt first hypothesized that the Italian Renaissance signaled the beginning of the modern nation-state and the age of scientific rationalism. Burckhardt's thoroughly Eurocentric view, which also implied that Renaissance perspective defined absolute visual truth, is now giving way to a new revisionism that seeks, as Farago states, "to develop a theory of representation on a relativistic epistemological foundation that treats the social circumstances in which visual images circulate" (87). In other words, deemphasizing the singular scientific basis for Renaissance art and "reconceptualizing" it as but one among many "international multicultural phenomena."
43. See Hagen and Johnson; Hagen and Jones.
44. Concerning the universality of human visual perception, see the work of psychologists James J. and Eleanor Gibson, and their many students. I am following here especially the arguments of James J. Gibson, *Perception of the Visual World* and *The Senses Considered as Perceptual Systems;* Margaret A. Hagen, *The Perception of Picture;* and Michael Kubovy.
45. Perceptual psychologist Margaret Hagen has provided a particularly vivid example of this persistent Western academic muddle-headedness (since Margaret Meade?) in its relentless quest for a "pure" expressive art in the cultures of non-Western peoples, uncontaminated by Renaissance-style "realism." Below, she remarks on certain studies of native Eskimo art by psychologists Helga Eng and Louise Maitland:

    I think there is no other issue in the psychology of art subject to more prejudice and less thought than the question of development in culture and in individuals. . . . Helga Eng [1931], after observing that Eskimo art is the product of highly practiced artists who use a multiple station point [perspective] system, presents a study by Louise Maitland on the art of Eskimo children. Maitland writes, "Everything in these drawings is full of life and motion. At the same time, we find the mistakes characteristic of children's drawings, mixed profiles, confusion of plan and elevation, transparency and turning over . . . ." I cannot understand how it could have escaped anyone's attention that these observations apply equally well to the skilled artists of that culture. By Maitland's criteria, as the children grow more proficient in the creation of the art of the culture, they will grow even more childlike. (Varieties of Realism, 287)

46. See Burke; McAndrew, 386.
47. Interestingly enough, the Dominican convento at Tetela del Volcán was originally dedicated to Saint Antonine. In 1578, however, it was rededicated to Saint John the Baptist; see Phillips, 601.

CHAPTER 6

1. See, for example, the extensive remarks by Thomas Gage, an English Dominican who traveled through Hispanic America for twelve years (1625–37). He was particularly bothered by the elaborate "popish" processions and ceremonies being performed by the Indians at the behest of the Spanish missionaries. Because of this and the hypocritical and lascivious lifestyle of the Spanish clerics he claimed to have observed, Gage renounced Catholicism and joined Oliver Cromwell's Puritan cause when he returned to England.
2. "Theater" was a common title for printed and illustrated books on various didactic subjects in all Western

countries during the sixteenth and seventeenth centuries, such as *Theatrum musicum* (Italy, 1571), *Théatre des instruments mathématiques . . .* (France, 1578), *Theatrum crudelitatum hereticorum nostri temporis* (Flanders, 1588), *Theatrum Botanicum* (England, 1640), Fray Agustín de Vetancurt's *Teatro Mexico* of 1698, and perhaps most famously, *Theatrum orbis terrarum* (Flanders, 1570).

3. For interesting thoughts on this notion, see Burkhart, "Pious Performances," and especially Harris.

4. Fray Pedro de Gante, for instance, had this to say in his fifth letter to King Philip II, June 23, 1558: "And as I saw . . . that all their songs were dedicated to their gods, I composed a very solemn song concerning the law of god and of the Faith . . . and also I gave them liberty to paint on their garments in which they danced, just as they were used to doing; thus in keeping with the [kinds of] dances and songs they once sang, they now clothed themselves with joy or sorrow or victory" (García Icazbalceta, *Nueva colección de documentos,* 2:231–232; Gante, 46).

5. This famous "fall of man" neixcuitilli in Tlaxcala, was apparently also witnessed by Bartolomé de Las Casas, *Apologetica Historia,* 1:163 (chap. 64), later it was recorded by Torquemada, *Monarquía indiana* (1975–83), 5:342–43 (bk. 17, chap. 9). Among these authors there is some confusion as to the exact year. Las Casas implies 1538, while Motolinía, the eyewitness supplying the most detailed account, is unclear as to whether he meant 1538 or 1539. Torquemada, writing many years later and certainly deriving his story from the earlier chroniclers, was probably in error when he gave the date as 1536. Modern historians are still unsure. Horcasitas, 175, says 1538, while Edmundo O'Gorman (Motolinía, *Historia de los indios de la Nueva España* [1969], 65) insists on 1539. I support 1538. Note that Motolinía mentions that the elaborate setting the Indians prepared contained "everything that is characteristic of April and May." In 1538 Easter Sunday occurred on April 21, two weeks later than in 1539, and the play was actually produced on the following Wednesday, thus close to the first of May.

6. As Angel García Zambrano has stated: "Such a place [any site of an Indian community] had to recall the mythical moment when the earth was created: an aquatic universe framed by four mountains with a fifth elevation in the middle of the water. The mountain at the core had to be dotted with caves and springs, and sometimes surrounded by smaller hills. A setting like this duplicated and forever would freeze, the primordial scene when the waters and sky separated and the earth sprouted upwards" (218). See also Bernal-Garcia.

7. See the remarkable lesson on this subject in Dominican Fray Pedro de Cordoba's *Doctrina larga,* written as a catechism for Indians and printed in Mexico in 1544. Fray Pedro, who must have known some of the indigenous myths of Indian creation, rather freely reworded the story of Genesis so that it seemed to conflate with the native version:

> And you must know that before God created this man and this woman, He created all these things that we see in the world. And He created in the best part of the world a very pleasant place that He filled with all the good things there are in this world—all the fruits, roses, flowers, trees, and beautiful savory, fragrant, and attractive things—the best that there are in all the world. He also created there a very large spring from which issues forth very powerful rivers, with which that place was watered; and it was very large. . . . This spot is very delightful and surrounded by very high walls. It was called earthly paradise, which means flower garden or garden of pleasures. . . . After God placed our first parents, Adam and Eve, in the earthly paradise, . . . [He] said to Adam and to Eve. . . . only you shall not eat of the tree of knowledge of good and evil, which is placed in the middle of Paradise. (Cordoba, 66–74)

Concerning the traditional Nahua notion of a primordial paradise, see Burkhart, "Flowery Heaven."

8. Sahagún, *The Florentine Codex,* 47–48, 298 (bk. 3); Furst, 23–32.

9. Graulich; see also Mace, 56, 62.

10. This translation by Francis Borgia Steck was originally published in Motolinía, *Motolinía's History of the Indians of New Spain,* 157–59, edited by Steck; it is reprinted here courtesy of the Academy of American Franciscan History, Washington, D.C. For the original Spanish text, see Motolinía, *Historia de los indios de la Nueva España* (1969), 65–67 (treatise 1, chap. 15). I have generally followed Father Steck's word choice but have changed a few words for greater clarity and relevance. For an interesting analysis of this text in relation to other European and Nahuatl theatrical examples of this favorite medieval Christian subject, see Horcasitas, 175–85, and Arróniz, 56–61.

11. Motolinía, *Motolinía's History,* 160.

12. Horcasitas, 507–8; Gibson, *Perception of the Visual World,* chap. 3. See also the delightful analysis of this remarkable spectacle in relation to Bakhtinian theory of subversion of the ruling class by the carnivalesque antics of the "Other" in Harris, 88–94.

13. See Motolinía, *Historia de los indios de la Nueva España* (1969), 67–74 (treatise 1, chap. 15), and Motolinía, *Motolinía's History,* 152–67; see also Ricard's discussion of this play, 20:196–98; Horcasitas, 505–9, and especially Harris, 82–92.

14. See also Weckmann, 535–49.

15. See Webster, *Art and Ritual*. The most spectacular of these paso processions was and still is performed annually during Semana Santa (Holy Week) in Seville. The chief attraction is the paso carrying the Macarena, the lifelike effigy of the Virgin Mary richly garbed in taffeta and with a highly illusionistic glass tear on her porcelain cheek.
16. See Burkhart, *Holy Wednesday*, 14–48. Perhaps the ultimate spectacle of this sort was what came to be known as the *sacromonte* [holy mountain], after the place near the town of Varallo in northern Italy where the first example was constructed in the late fifteenth century. Sacromontes consisted of several stagelike chapels grouped on hilltops to which the public was invited to make pilgrimages. When viewers looked inside the chapels, they would behold life-size effigies posed in realistic settings representing various Old and New Testament events. Each sacromonte vied with the next in astonishing its audience with new tricks of verisimilitude, with effigies of polychrome wax even wearing wigs and beards of human hair; see Nova. For a thorough explanation of this uniquely Western Christian phenomenon in terms of the psychology of "image power," see Freedberg, 192–245.
17. Durán, *Book of the Gods;* Sahagún, *The Florentine Codex*.
18. Interestingly, the Panquetzaliztli marked the fifteenth month of the Aztec calendar, thus falling between November and December in the Christian calendar. To the newly converted Indians this coincidence suggested an association with Christmas, a dual homage that is observed in parts of indigenous Mexico to this day.
19. In his third letter to Emperor Charles V, Cortés described how, during the siege of Tenochtitlan in 1521, he had built a catapult and placed it on a raised platform in the middle of the Tlatelolco market plaza, which was like "a kind of stage *[teatro]*, . . . built of masonry, rectangular, about [four meters] high and some thirty paces from corner to corner. Here they used to hold celebrations and games on their feast days, so the participants could be seen by all the people in the square, and also by all those under and on top of the arcades [*portales*]" (256–57)
20. In using this word, which today has a more pejorative meaning than in the sixteenth century, Durán might have wished merely to make a distinction between a Christian *auto* and a non-Christian play, which he chose here to call a farsia, a common Spanish expression at the time for secular theater.
21. Durán, *Book of the Gods*, 134–35.
22. Horcasitas, 81–89.
23. For a fascinating analysis of how Christian participants, especially citizens of Seville, Spain, similarly react even today during the great public processions of Semana Santa (Holy Week), see Webster, *Art and Ritual*, 164–88.
24. Burkhart, *Holy Wednesday*, 42–48; Duverger, 47–88.
25. Recorded by the Indian historian Francisco de San Antón Chimalpahín in 1620, as cited in Arróniz, 19. Fray Agustín de Vetancurt, writing in 1698, claimed without citing a date that the earliest *auto* in Mexico was performed at San José de los Naturales (41; pt. 4, treatise 2, 41). For differing arguments concerning this "first" Indian neixcuitilli, see Horcasitas, 561–67; and Arróniz, 19–21.
26. Horcasitas; see also Arróniz, and Argudín. For briefer overviews in English, see Burkhart, *Holy Wednesday*, 14–48; McAndrew, 216–19.
27. Burkhart, *Holy Wednesday*.
28. On this see also Lockhart, *Nahuas after the Conquest*, 402–4.
29. Notwithstanding, see Grijalva, 160–65 (bk. 2, chaps. 6–7), for brief descriptions of colorful processions that the Indians under Augustinian tutelage performed in the convento patios during Sundays and festivals, with flowers and images and accompanied by music and singing.
30. Sleight, 126–31.
31. Burgoa, *Geográfica descripción*, 1:396 (chap. 37). The fiesta of Santiago Matamoros at Cuilápan continues to this day, performed every July 25. The Dominicans of Cuilapan also prepared a complete libretto for the Indians to perform "Dance of the Conquest," the sixteenth-century manuscript of which still exists; see Sleight, 128–31; Perry, *Mexico's Fortress Monasteries*, 172.
32. Pierce, "Identification of the Warriors in the Frescoes" and "Sixteenth-Century Nave Frescoes."
33. Grijalva, 300 (bk. 3, chap. 22); see also Carrillo y Gariel; Reyes-Valerio, "Los tlaquilos y tlaquicuic de Ixmiquilpan"; Gerlero, "El friso monumental de Itzmiquilpan"; Pierce, "Sixteenth-Century Nave Frescoes," 1–8.
34. Pierce, "Sixteenth-Century Nave Frescoes," 32–40.
35. Concerning the style and iconography of the Cacaxtla murals, see Baird, "Stars and War at Cacaxtla."
36. Furst, 177.
37. Pierce, "Identification of the Warriors in the Frescoes," 7; Carrillo y Gariel; Gerlero, "El friso monumental de Itzmiquilpan."
38. Powell, *Soldiers, Indians, and Silver*, 105–8.
39. Pierce, "Sixteenth-Century Nave Frescoes," 9–19.
40. That the Ixmiquilpan murals may have been associated with a native Otomí dance procession has also been suggested by Gruzinski, *L'Aigle et la sibylle*, 52–90. See also Guerrero Guerrero et al. for a summation of other pinions regarding the iconographic sources of the

Ixmiquilpan murals. The authors, however, either ignored or were quite unaware of Pierce's interpretation. For a completely different analysis arguing that the murals disguise covert references to the preconquest Aztec "paradise of fallen warriors" and that the Christian patron saint of Ixmiquilpan, San Miguel, actually disguises the pagan deity Tezcatlipoca, see Albernoz Bueno.

CHAPTER 7

1. The tower depicted to the left of the colonnaded building represents the actual Torre del Popolo, which does indeed stand beside Santa Maria Sopra Minerva in Assisi to this day. However, it was not built until a half century after Saint Francis's death, further indication that the fresco depicts a reenactment of the story contemporaneous with the painting not with the historical event.
2. Edgerton, *The Heritage of Giotto's Geometry,* 47–88.
3. The argument over whether Giotto had anything to do with the Assisi frescoes is one of the most perplexing in all art history. Most Italian scholars claim he was the master designer of the entire Saint Francis cycle. Most American scholars tend to doubt his presence at all. In any case, at least six separate hands have been traced in the twenty-eight scenes. I have advanced the theory that if Giotto were present, he would most likely have been the master who prepared the entire cycle by measuring and painting the surrounding perspective frames. This is the first "Renaissance" example of perspective based on on-site empirical observation not just copied from some earlier conventionalized model; see Edgerton, *The Heritage of Giotto's Geometry,* 47–88.
4. Vitruvius, 1:26–27, and 2:70–71, as quoted and discussed in Edgerton, *Renaissance Rediscovery of Linear Perspective,* 71. Interestingly, a manuscript of Vitruvius is known to have been in the eighth-century C.E. library of the Benedictine Abbey of Sankt Gallen in Switzerland where one of the earliest forms of religious drama (called *Quem quaeretis?* "The Three Maries at the Tomb of Jesus") may have also been performed; see Horcasitas, 60.
5. Parkhurst.
6. See Ainsworth and Christiansen, 216–19; Panofsky, *Early Netherlandish Painting,* 1:259.
7. This observation has also been made by Peterson, *Paradise Garden Murals,* 77–82; and Phillips, 227.
8. Valadés, *Rhetorica Christiana,* 227 (pt. 4, chap. 25), and *Retórica Cristiana,* 228.
9. See Horcasitas, 243–47.
10. Horcasitas, 107–16. Two-story wooden stages with raised balconies for presentation of special effects were also common in Spanish secular theaters of the sixteenth century, very similar to the Shakespearean theaters (for example, the Globe) in England; see Allen. Dominican Fray Bartolomé de Las Casas also witnessed the same spectacles in Tlaxcala recorded by Motolinía during 1538–39 (see chap. 6 epigraph). His brief description of the *autos* are concealed in long excursuses on the ingenuity, talents, and Christian devotion of Indian musicians, singers, and actors even as they spoke and sang in their own language. Nonetheless, his accounts hint at the use also of clever stage machinery, such as mechanical means for lowering Gabriel down from an upper level to speak to the Virgin Mary in an *auto* of the Annunciation, and conversely to raise the Virgin (always impersonated by a male) on a cloud into the sky in a similar neixcuitilli of the Assumption. These plays, he noted, were staged on tablados in the patio of the church of Saint John the Baptist and witnessed by eighty thousand Indians; see Las Casas, *Apologetica Historia,* 165 (chap. 64); also Horcasitas, 440–43.
11. Agustín Estrada Monroy, 168–74, recounts a theatrical spectacle by the K'ekchi' Maya of Guatemala in celebration of the founding of their new Christian community of San Juan Chamelco on the fiesta of Saint John the Baptist, June 24, 1543. The Indians built a stage in two levels under a thatched ramada. On the upper level, actors dressed as the mythical Maya Hero Twins, Hun Ahpu and Xbalanque, danced and then descended through a trap door to the lower level, which represented the Maya underworld called Xbalba where they battled the Lords of the Night to reincarnate their sacrificed father, Hun Hun Ahpu the Young Maize God (see Tedlock, 91–141). So impressed with the Indians' theatrics was Dominican Fray Luis Cáncer that he recast the play on the same stage but changed the Hero Twins into the Devil and Lucifer, Xbalba into hell, and the reincarnation of the Young Maize God into the Resurrection of Jesus Christ.
12. M. Rogers, 225–30.
13. Shoemaker, chapter 3, describes the medieval Spanish multiple stage as divided not only vertically but also often horizontally, with as many as five separate but adjoined settings called "mansions" (presumably framed by decorative pilasters and cornices) and each presenting a sequential scene of a holy narrative.
14. Horcasitas, 440; see also, 130, in regard to the painted *Last Judgment* in the lower cloister corridor at Acolman. See also Bailey, "The Lahore Mirat Al-Quds," for a

fascinating account of how Christian theatrical spectacles sponsored by the Jesuits evangelizing in Mughal, India, during the late sixteenth century, in turn influenced the style and subject matter of native Mughal painting.

15. For a sample of the variety of open chapel plans in Mexico, see Artigas, *Capillas abiertas aisladas de Tlaxcala.*
16. Concerning the rising power of the secular clergy in Mexico, see Schwaller.
17. McAndrew, 352.
18. For example, Valadés, *Retórica Cristiana,* 474–77; see also Fray Agustín Vetancurt's comment that because Bishop Juan de Zumárraga had forbidden "indecent dancing" during the feast of Corpus Christi, so when this occurred again after his death, rain should suddenly fall on the procession as if sent as a message from the bishop's soul in heaven (62).
19. Horcasitas, 116–25.
20. Ciudad Real, *Fray Alonso de Ponce,* 321, 353, and *Tratado curioso,* 2:326 (chap. 144), 2:366 (chap. 154).
21. See Hammond, 115–253; Weil.
22. For a lengthy discussion of all the possibilities, see McAndrew, 418–43; Artigas, *Capillas abiertas aisladas de Tlaxcala;* Perry, *Mexico's Fortress Monasteries,* 129–30.
23. For the original Spanish text, see Motolinía, *Historia de los indios de la Nueva España* (1969), 62–63 (treatise 1, chap. 15). I have generally here followed the translation of Francis Steck (Motolinía, *Motolinía's History,* 156) but again changed a few words for greater clarity and relevance.
24. See Horcasitas, 125–26.
25. Dávila Padilla, 256 (chap. 81); Burgoa, *Geográfica descripción,* 1:42–43 (chap. 4).
26. Described and illustrated in Martínez Marín, 103–6. This somewhat awkwardly painted mural was certainly not done by the same artist as the beautiful image of Saint Catherine of Siena discussed in chap. 4. See also Perry, *Mexico's Fortress Monasteries,* 163.
27. Dávila Padilla, 255–59 (chap. 81).
28. Mullen, *Architecture and Sculpture of Oaxaca,* 108–16. See also McAndrew, 545–55. Burgoa, *Palestra historial de virtudes y examplares,* 85–87 (chap. 10), mentioned that it was the (presumably Franciscan) Bishop of Tlaxcala who granted the Dominicans permission to build conventos in the Mixteca Alta and that Fray Francisco Marin was one of the first to heed the latter's call.
29. Kiracofe, 160–63.
30. Other open chapels framed with proscenium-like arches and with extending diagonal side walls just like Teposcolula, such as Tlalmanalco, were observed by Kubler as functioning like "theater stages"; see Kubler and Soria, *Art and Architecture,* 70.
31. For a full discussion of the Convento of San Pedro de Teposcolula, including the kinds of religious spectacles that might have been performed in the great open chapel, see Kiracofe; see also Arróniz. For pictures and contemporaneous descriptions of stage machinery actually built and used in fifteenth- and sixteenth-century Italy, especially for dramatic theatrical presentations of the Annunciation and ascension of Christ into heaven, see Fabri et al., 55.
32. Vetancurt, 42 (pt. 4, treatise 2).
33. Ciudad Real, *Tratado curioso,* 2:100–102 (chap. 79).
34. See Horcasitas, 511–12. The Codex Aubin barely hints that the Indian actors made fictive ships, but Las Casas does give details of a similar mock naval battle he witnessed in Mexico City in 1539, for which the Indians "built grand ships with sails which they navigated through the plaza as if on water" (*Apologetica Historia,* 1:165 [chap. 64]).
35. Codex Aubin, 47, 83, and 135 (fols. 58r and 19v); ee Horcasitas, 499–504; also Kubler, *Mexican Architecture,* 2:466–67, who refers to this document as "anales de Ramirez."
36. Robertson, 38.
37. Mullen, 95–107; see also McAndrew, 486–93.
38. McAndrew, 489–90.
39. Concerning the notion of Tollan in Indian mythology and its importance as a divinely destined goal of Indian migrations, see Schele and Mathews. For the Mixtec version of this legend, see Byland and Pohl, 143–49.
40. Byland and Pohl, 148–50; also the Codex Zouche-Nuttall, fol. 52.
41. M. Smith, 245, fig. 46; see also 65–66, 80, and 245, fig. 45a.
42. See, for instance, McAndrew, 490.
43. M. Smith, 65.
44. Between the entwined feathered snakes in each pair, tiny birds that should be pelicans are also shown, piercing their left sides (oddly, not the canonical right) with their beaks. This is an ancient Christian bestiary analog to the sacrifice of Christ. The pelican, like Christ, offers its own blood to "nourish" its children, that is, the human race. Curiously, the proverbial Christian pelican, certainly a bird as familiar as any in Mesoamerica, was carved here to look like the likewise native crested eagle-hawk. For whatever reason, this peculiar ornithological switch between pelican and eagle, which the missionary friars seem to have tolerated, became somewhat common in sixteenth-century Indo-Christian iconography. It occurs again at Malinalco (Peterson, *Paradise Garden Murals,* 161–62) and even in Chiantla, Guatemala.

45. Burgoa, *Geográfica descripción,* 1:338, 2:151 (chap. 29, chap. 57); see also Byland and Pohl, 200.
46. See especially Burgoa's account of the mammoth cave at Juxtlahuaca in *Geográfica descripción,* 1:359–62 (chap. 31). Motolinía made a similar observation: "The principal idols together with their insignia and ornaments and the vestments of the demons were concealed by the Indians sometimes under the ground, at other times in caves and on mountains. After the Indians were converted and baptized, they uncovered many of these" (Motolinía, *Motolinía's History,* 335 [treatise 3, chap 20).
47. Concerning Last Judgment imagery and *autos* in Mexico, see Fernández, *La Jerusalem Indiana,* 119–37.
48. Concerning the architectural history of Tlalmanalco, see Kubler, *Mexican Architecture,* 2:479–80; and McAndrew, 535–43.
49. Kubler, *Mexican Architecture,* 2:479.
50. Ibid., 2:402: "the skill of ornamental execution suggests European work."
51. For references to indigenous influence see, Angulo Iñíguez, 1:341–44, and Toussaint, *Colonial Art in Mexico,* 55–57. Reyes-Valerio, *Arte Indocristiano,* 192–97.
52. Kubler and Soria, *Art and Architecture,* 70, 166; McAndrew, 536–37.
53. Curiel; on 95: *"El programa es cristiana en su totalidad."*
54. Mendieta, *Historia eclesiástica indiana* (1945), 4:97–98 (bk. 5, chap. 34); later recited in the same words by Torquemada, *Monarquía indiana* (1975–83), 6:245 (bk. 20, chap. 39).
55. Horcasitas, 566; Arróniz, 19.
56. Angulo Iñíguez (1945), 1:338.
57. Ciudad Real, *Fray Alonso de Ponce,* 351.

CHAPTER 8

1. Ainsworth and Christiansen, 112–13. Concerning the relationship between the hortus conclusus and the Virgin's Annunciation, see Robb; the article "Verkündigung" in *Lexikon der christlichen Ikonographie,* 4:435–438; Panofsky, *Early Netherlandish Painting,* 1:132–134; Edgerton, *"Mensurare temporalia facit Geometria spiritualis";* also Jameson, *Legends of the Madonna,* 55–56.
2. Fernández, *La Jerusalem Indiana,* 18–19.
3. Adams, 84, 96.
4. Phillips, 131–262.
5. Many medieval conventos in Spain likewise have testeras in the corners of their cloisters, but they were never arranged in consistent counterclockwise directional order.
6. Phillips.
7. Motolinía, *Motolinía's History,* 141, (treatise 1, chap. 13). On the Indians' native interest in flowers as symbols of heaven and the divine, and its easy conflation with Christian concepts, see Burkhart, "Flowery Heaven."
8. Peterson, *Paradise Garden Murals,* and "Synthesis and Survival." Peterson also notes that the muralists began to carry the "garden" theme into the convento church (*Paradise Garden Murals,* 158–60). It remains unclear, however, how much of the wall space was covered, whether the iconography of the cloister murals was continued into the church, and whether the church murals were done at the same time.
9. Comparison of the Malinalco murals to European tapestry styles has been made by Gerlero, "Malinalco," and Peterson, *Paradise Garden Murals.*
10. McAndrew, 570–72.
11. A brand new patio cross, copied from a sixteenth-century prototype derived from an old convento near Mexico City, has been "reinstalled" on the original Malinalco pedestal.
12. Gerlero, "Malinalco"; Fernández, *La Jerusalem Indiana,* 139–157; Peterson, *Paradise Garden Murals.*
13. Peterson, *Paradise Garden Murals,* 146–49. She also acknowledged the connection of the Malinalco imagery to that of the "live" flora and fauna setting described by Motolinía for the Tlaxcala "fall of man" spectacle in 1538 (ibid., 146), observing further that the early seventeenth-century Augustinian friar-chronicler Juan de Grijalva likewise mentioned admiringly such trompe l'oeil simulations of nature constructed by Indians in celebration of Corpus Christi and Easter (Grijalva, 163–67 [bk. 2, chap. 7]). For more concerning native attitudes regarding the gardens as symbolic "paradise," see Sahagún, "The Aztec-Spanish Dialogues of 1524," lines 950–92; Brundage (1983), 45–49; Graulich; and Burkhart, "Flowery Heaven."
14. Peterson, *Paradise Garden Murals,* 167. As she further stated: "The frescoes depicting the terrestrial paradise, then, could be seen by the general and nonprofessed populace through the open doorways and passageways, but were experienced in their totality only by the friars and those natives received into their confidence" (161). See also 169–70.

15. The term derived from the desert wilderness of upper Egypt near the ancient city of Thebes where, according to legend, the hermetic tradition of Christian monasticism was first conceived. The early fifteenth-century Italian artist-monk Fra Lippo Lippi painted one well-known example, a now much-abraded fresco depicting "the founding of the Carmelite Order" in the Church of Santa Maria del Carmine, Florence; see Ruda, 49.
16. Peterson, *Paradise Garden Murals,* 165. The eighteenth-century Augustinian friar-chronicler Fray Matías de Escobar even entitled his history of the order in Mexico *Americana Thebaida.*
17. Motolinía, *Motolinía's History,* 159.
18. García Zambrano, 219, as quoted by the author from the *Titulos de San Matias Cuixingo (1532),* fols. 76–79, in the National Archives, Mexico City.
19. Ibid.
20. The enclosed cloister garden at Malinalco has been discovered to have had a stone duct that once carried water from an outside spring to a well in the middle, thus fortifying its association with the Song of Solomon's "fountain of gardens, a well of living waters" (4:15); see Fernández, *La Jerusalem Indiana,* 149.
21. After Eve sinned, according to this fundamental Christian (and Augustinian) doctrine, an angry God turned the terrestrial paradise (Garden of Eden) into a disordered *natura naturans* (nature naturing), growing wildly without restraint. Only with the redemptive coming of Christ was divine order, *natura naturata* (nature natured), restored in the world. A good European illustration of this Christian duality is found in the Scrovegni Chapel at Padua, Italy, where the early fourteenth-century painter Giotto depicted opposing images of Justice and Injustice. The latter is shown as a devilish male seated in an old and crumbling archway behind an untended landscape where trees grow helter-skelter even blocking the archway entrance, while Justice, personified as the Virgin Mary, is seated in a well-constructed "modern" portico commanding a scene in which all nature—animal, vegetable, and human—lives together in controlled harmony; see Reiss; see also Edgerton, *Pictures and Punishment,* 128 n. 2. A similar painting overtly contrasting a wild, untamed garden and a well-ordered "church" before which Mary receives the Angel Gabriel is the *Friedsam Annunciation,* ca. 1430, now attributed to the Flemish painter Petrus Christus, in the Metropolitan Museum of Art, New York.

    Preachers in late medieval Europe often played punningly upon a rearrangement of the three letters of Eve's Latinate name, Eva. First, Eva who sinned, then vae, the Latin word for "woe," and finally Ave, the salutation to Mary and promise of Christ's salvation. This contrast between old and new dispensation was widespread all over late medieval Europe, as noted by Erwin Panofsky, *Early Netherlandish Painting,* 1:132–37.
22. García Zambrano.
23. Peterson, *Paradise Garden Murals,* 47–50.
24. Codex Borbonicus, fol. 4, reproduced in Peterson, *Paradise Garden Murals,* 48, fig. 29.
25. Concerning the attributes and qualities of Huehuecoyotl, see Nicholson, 418; Miller and Taube, 92; Wirth, 5.
26. For a succinct account of how the Aztec ritual calendar worked, see Codex Telleriano-Remensis, 132.
27. For instance, the Codex Mendoza, 2:47.
28. Peterson, *Paradise Garden Murals,* 49–50.
29. The sapote or sapodilla tree is also the source of chicle, the milky sap from which chewing gum is made. Its hard wood is very resistant to rot and was often used by the ancient Maya as lintels and reinforcement of their masonry corbel arches. The Spanish colonists treasured both the cacao and sapote trees; see Torquemada, *Monarquía indiana* (1975–83) 4:428 (bk. 14, chap. 42).
30. Grapes, surprisingly, were indigenous to the Americas before Europeans arrived but were not of the wine variety. The Indians treasured only the leaves, from which they made a medicine for skin rashes; see Peterson, *Paradise Garden Murals,* 96.
31. For the typological and tropological iconography of all these plants and animals (roses, pomegranates, monkeys, snakes, and birds) in relation to the Virgin Mary, see Jameson, *Legends of the Madonna,* 55–57. For more on the species of flowers and plants favored in Aztec representations of heavenly paradise, see Burkhart, "Flowery Heaven."
32. Torquemada, *Monarquía indiana* (1975–83), 3:196 (bk. 8, chap. 3), similarly discusses the theological primacy of east, citing Saint Antonine of Florence as his source.
33. For more on the sacredness of the direction east to Christian theology, especially in relation to the Virgin's Annunciation, see Edgerton, *"Mensurare temporalia facit Geometria spiritualis,"* 118–19; and Steinberg and Edgerton. Regarding its cartographic importance, see Edgerton, *Pictures and Punishment.*
34. Peterson, *Paradise Garden Murals,* 96. As she points out, a certain species of grape unsuited for wine was native to the Americas before Europeans arrived, but the presence of grape vines in the imagery of all four walls of the Malinalco cloister was surely intended to glorify the recently imported European wine grape and especially to emphasize its sacramental importance.
35. Ibid., 107, fig. 97, 131. For an excellent analysis of the tree and animal symbols associated with the Garden of Eden, see Panofsky, *Albrecht Dürer,* 1:84–87, regarding Dürer's 1504 engraving *Fall of Man,* a print well known

in sixteenth-century Mexico, by the way, through many reproductions and copies.

36. Peterson, *Paradise Garden Murals,* 104–5, 131–32.

37. Panofsky, *Early Netherlandish Painting,* 1:133. Concerning monkey iconography in Christian art, see also Janson; Jameson, *Legends of the Madonna,* 59. In the Franciscan convento in Cuzco, Peru, there is a large oil painting of the Last Supper by seventeenth-century mestizo artist Diego de Ribera showing Christ and the apostles dining on a meal of roast meat, which appears to be a carcass composed of a lamb's hind quarters fused to the foreparts of a monkey!

38. Fray Pedro's hand is also detected in the very similar Codex Vaticanus B, filled also with Spanish-language comments that essentially relate the same comparisons between preconquest Nahua mythology and the biblical Genesis.

39. Codex Telleriano-Remensis, 113–32.

40. For more on this, see Lafaye.

41. Codex Telleriano-Remensis, 24–25 (fols. 10v and 11r).

42. Ibid., 259–60.

43. Ibid., 260.

44. Ibid.

45. Redated this time to July 23, but still not a One Flower date according to the Caso correlation (Codex Telleriano-Remensis, 239).

46. Caso. Caso's system has been generally accepted as the basis for establishing any Nahua-Christian date correlation, past or present, and has been adapted to most computerized calculation programs (see Voorburg). Caso's system is based on the recorded fall of Tenochtitlan as simultaneously reported by the Spanish on August 13, 1521 (Julian), and by the Aztecs on the Aztec day One Serpent in the year Three House. Thus, according to Caso, the Aztec "new year" 1562 should have begun
on January 14, with day One Flower commencing on September 22. While July 27 was crossed out and thus regarded as wrong by the Codex Telleriano-Remensis commentator, on folio 49r he states as follows: "This year of Five Rabbit on the day One Flower they had a feast; and this year of 1562 the feast was on the 23rd of July. There was an omen that on that day One Flower in the province of the Huasteca [vicinity of Veracruz] a flower appeared in the land, which was called by this very precious name" (276). For a critique of Caso's correlation and an attempt to explain the above discrepancies in the Codex Telleriano-Remensis, see Cline.

47. On the upper facade of the Franciscan convento church at Huaquechula, Puebla, for instance the Nahua glyph Six Flint is carved, no doubt indicating the year 1576 when the structure was completed (Perry, *Mexico's Fortress Monasteries,* 115). Similar Nahua calendric glyphs dating the completion of convento buildings are preserved at Tecali and Tecamachalco, also in Puebla.

48. Return to chapter 2 and look at fig. 2.26, the *Founding of Tenochtitlan* in the Aztec Codex Mendoza. Note that the third glyph from the right in the bottom row is also the year sign Two Reed, here emphasized by another symbol just above depicting a smoking drill, signifying the date of the "New Fire" ceremony in 1351 and the beginning of the second fifty-two year cycle, twenty-six years after the city's founding in Two House. For more on the meaning of these dates in Aztec history, see Read.

49. Sahagún, *The Florentine Codex,* 21–22 (bk. 7, pt. 8, chap. 7). See also León-Portilla, 54–55; Read, 92–93.

50. Graulich. Note also the comments included with the article arguing that this legend too may have been only a postconquest construct by the friars. See also Burkhart, "Flowery Heaven."

51. Codex Telleriano-Remensis, 276.

52. The reason for emphasis on the numbers eight and five had originally to do with the astronomical fact that the planet Venus as morning and evening star only returns to its same cardinal position relative to the zodiac constellations once every five of its own planetary cycles, which take exactly eight solar years to complete. Since ancient times in Mesoamerica, especially among the Maya, Venus was observed to complete its cycle as morning and evening star every 584 days (now referred to as its sidereal cycle). The Indians then calculated that five times Venus's sidereal cycle exactly equaled eight solar years, or 2,920 days, and then Venus returned to its original position in relation to the sun; see Aveni, 83–86; Codex Dresden, fols. 46–50; Seler, 3:265. Apparently the eight-year Venus cycle established a cosmic imprimatur for scheduling other important feasts in the Aztec religious calendar even though the astronomical timing may not have been exactly adhered to. For instance, the ceremony known as Atamalcualiztli [the eating of the water tamales] was also celebrated every eight years on the day One Flower regardless of Venus, although only during Flint-knife years instead of Rabbit years; see Sahagún, *Primeros memoriales,* 67–69, 140–46 (chap. 1, para. 2b, fols. 253v, 277v–280r); Codex Telleriano-Remensis, 238, 276.

53. Graulich.

54. Even though Venus and the sun will arrive by arithmetical day-count at exactly the same positions relative to each other once every eight solar years, that event could only synchronize with the same day in the Nahua ritual calendar once every 104 solar years or two complete calendar rounds. Since according to Graulich the legend apparently originated in eastern Mesoamerica, in the land of the Maya-speaking Huasteca, there may possibly have been a much earlier Venus heliacal rising coinciding with the slightly offset Maya calendar.

55. Codex Telleriano-Remensis, 228–29. Because of a severe famine in the land and the sudden appearance of a comet in the sky during 1506, the newly crowned Emperor Motecuhzoma had good reason to believe that his reign during the following fifty-two-year cycle would be inauspicious. The famous comet of 1506 that supposedly so disturbed Motecuhzoma is not depicted among the other comets in the Codex Telleriano-Remensis but is indeed recorded in many contemporaneous chronicles in both Europe and Asia, appearing on July 31, 1506, and remaining bright in the sky for more than two weeks; see Ho, 208, no. 540; Hasegawa, 84, no. 868; and Kronck, 164–65.

56. Motolinía described the living plants and flowers the Indians used to decorate their staged Garden of Eden as representative of "April and May," thus indicating that the play was performed, at the very earliest, late in April. He also talked specifically of the Corpus Christi and Saint John the Baptist's Day celebrations of 1538, mentioning particularly that the latter fell on a Monday just after Corpus Christi, which would have happened on the previous Thursday (Motolinía, *Motolinía's History,* 151–55). For this reason, the date given for Easter 1538 in Edmonson as March 17 must be wrong (*Book of the Year,* 69). Since Saint John the Baptist's day is fixed on June 24, and in 1538 that was a Monday, then Corpus Christi, usually the first Thursday following Trinity Sunday, would have occurred on June 20 since Trinity Sunday would have been June 16. The latter feast day in turn always ends the week in which Pentecost is celebrated, and Pentecost always comes on Monday just fifty days after Easter. Therefore Easter Sunday 1538 could only have occurred on April 21. Edmund O'Gorman assumed the Tlaxcala *auto* occurred in 1539, but he wrongly computed the date for Easter Sunday in that year as April 13, when in fact it fell on April 6, thus probably too early to agree with Motolinía's description. See, however, O'Gorman's otherwise interesting discussion of the Tlaxcala *auto* in his footnotes to Motolinía, *Historia de los indios de la Nueva España* (1969), 63–65. All Easter dates have here been verified in Simon Kershaw, "Easter Day."

57. It was during this same Pascua Florida week in 1513, six days after Easter Sunday on Saturday, April 2, that Ponce de León discovered a land he mistakenly thought to be an island, which he named, in honor of the holiday, La Florida; see Morison, *European Discovery of America: The Southern Voyages,* 506–7.

58. Peterson, *Paradise Garden Murals,* 112–13; Klein, *The Face of the Earth,* 126–30.

59. See Martínez Marín, 104; Perry, *Mexico's Fortress Monasteries,* 162–63. This mural is hardly by the same hand that executed the beautiful *Saint Catherine of Siena* discussed in chap. 4. The fact that it depicts the salvation of a sinful Indian "Eve" by the miraculous agency of the rosary does indicate however that the chapel was surely intended for Indian worshipers even though it is in the upper corridor of the cloister at Tetela del Volcán, adding further evidence to Richard Phillips's argument that cloisters were indeed accessible to the native population.

60. See Sahagún, *The Florentine Codex,* 23–25 (bk. 4, chap. 7). See also Codex Telleriano-Remensis, 168; León-Portilla: "He who is born on [the day named One Flower], whether a noble or not, became a lover of songs, an entertainer, an actor, an artist" (169).

61. Thomas, 175.

62. See Mendieta, *Historia eclesiástica indiana* (1945), 1:98–100 (bk. 2, chap. 10), 2:11–16; (bk. 3, chap. 1). See also Phelan, 29–41.

63. See Anthony Pagden's discussion of the source of this legend and how Sahagún, *The Florentine Codex,* 11–13 (bk. 12, chap. 4) may have manipulated it for Christian advantage.

64. Peterson, *Paradise Garden Murals,* 139; Grijalva, 15 (chap. 1).

65. Peterson, *Paradise Garden Murals,* 22–24.

66. Ibid., 52–53.

67. Codex Telleriano-Remensis 239 (fol. 49r). The commentator first wrote "February 24," then crossed out the "24."

68. See Cline, 20–24, for a complex dissection of this matter. Motolinía, *Historia de los indios de la Nueva España* (1969), 29 (treatise 1, chap. 25) and Cervantes de Salazar, *Crónica de la Nueva España,* 50 (bk. 1, chap. 27), both writing circa 1550, stated unequivocally that the Indians celebrated the beginning of the new year in early March. On the other hand, Torquemada, *Monarquía indiana* (1975–83), 3:93 (bk. 6, chap. 28), 3:364 (bk. 10, chap. 10), and the Christian Aztec chronicler of the Codex Chimalpahin, 2:119–27, both writing in the early seventeenth century after the Gregorian calendar reform of 1582, were in disagreement about the Nahua new year. (Torquemada set it in late January, with the nemontemi following in early February.) All this confusion would seem to underscore the likelihood that the native dating system, perhaps once uniform under Aztec imperial authority, was more and more breaking down into local variations, a process perhaps benevolently encouraged by the friar missionaries in order to have it better correlated with Christian liturgy.

69. See Peterson, *Paradise Garden Murals,* chap. nine on this; also 171–78. She cites the eighteenth-century Augustinian friar-chronicler, Fray Matías de Escobar, 358–59 (chap. 45), commenting on the convento at

Cuitzeo: "In the testeras of the upper and lower cloisters they [now] put lienzos executed in beautiful brushwork. . . . Everything was painted, the convento having been whitewashed" (171). And earlier in reference to the main altarpiece: "Then [in the sixteenth century] it was considered a marvel; today with the new works, it no longer appears so much so" (171).

CHAPTER 9

1. McHenry, 32–33.
2. Taylor, 50–51.
3. Currently in the Adolph Sutro Library, San Francisco, California; cataloged as *M. Fabii Quintiliani oratoriarum institutionum libri 12: una cum novendecim sive eiusdem, sive, Alterius declamationibus subtillissimis ad severae antiquitatis limam reconditis,* Paris (Nicolas Sauetier), 1527, and bearing the seal of the Convento de Santiago Tlatelolco; see Mathes, 55. Concerning the art of memory and the importance of Quintilian's treatise in relation to it, see Yates, 21–25. It is noteworthy that the Sutro Library, whose rare books mainly come from colonial conventos in Mexico, possesses no less than three early sixteenth-century printings of Quintilian's work plus one edition of *Ad Herennium* (*Rhetoricorum ad C. Herennium,* Paris, Simon Colines, 1545). The latter was the most famous and popular of all ancient art of memory treatises and the one on which Quintilian's and all subsequent medieval and Renaissance art of memory tracts were based.
4. See Loerke, 41.
5. Yates, 92–95.
6. See Taylor, 51.
7. Valadés, *Retórica Cristiana,* 87–125, 222–301 (pt. 2, chaps. 24–29). Concerning Fray Diego's sources, see Taylor; Watts, "Hieroglyphs of Conversion."
8. Valadés, *Retórica Cristiana,* 89–90, 224–27 (pt. 2, chap. 25).
9. On Valadés's interpretation of Horapollon, see Watts, "Hieroglyphs of Conversion," 419–20.
10. On the influence of Lullism upon Franciscans in the late sixteenth century, see Yates, 173–98.
11. Valadés, *Retórica Cristiana,* 248 (after second 100; see chap. 4 n. 27 [pt. 2, chap. 28]); see Watts, "Hieroglyphs of Conversion," 426.
12. Rosenthal, *"Plus ultra, non plus ultra"* and "Invention of the Columnar Device."
13. Watts, "Hieroglyphs of Conversion," 426–27.
14. Valadés, *Retórica Cristiana,* 103–24, 257–301 (pt. 2, chap. 29). See the very good and concise description of Valadés's system here in Watts, "Hieroglyphs of Conversion," 429–33.
15. Spence.
16. Letter from Viglius Zuichemus to Erasmus dated 1532, as translated and quoted in Yates, 130–31.
17. Interestingly, Valadés was writing his *Rhetorica* during a time of much discussion about the errors in the Julian solar year that reached its culmination in 1582 with the establishment of the Gregorian calendar. A year later, Scaliger published his famous *De emendatione temporum* (On the improvement of time) in which he offered his own judgment on the newly accepted reform, bolstering his argument with extraordinarily erudite examination of all the other known calendric systems of the world including a brief (and somewhat erroneous) commentary on the Aztec calendar, which he may very well have derived from Valadés.

CHAPTER 10

1. Kubler, *Mexican Architecture,* 1:19–21. The competition between the newly founded Jesuits and the old, established Franciscan and Dominican orders quickly led to back-stabbing. The mendicants never forgave the Jesuits for challenging their autonomy in the Americas and in revenge began to undermine the Jesuits who in the meantime had embarked on their own great campaign to convert the millions of "heathens" in China. The Franciscans, Dominicans, and especially the Jansenists finally convinced the Pope in 1743 to ban the special "rites" enjoyed by the Jesuits in the Far East and so probably provoked the collapse of the whole Catholic mission in China, inadvertently leading to the demise of Western influence until the present day; see Edgerton, *The Heritage of Giotto's Geometry,* 365n; Dunne, 367–70; and Hay (1956).
2. Mendieta, *Historia eclesiástica indiana* (1945), 3:159–93, 218–27 (bk. 4, chaps. 33–39, 46). See also Phelan, 81–129.

3. An abridged Spanish and English reprint of the Laws of the Indies has been published in Lejeune, 18–34.
4. Concerning the Chichimec wars and the efforts of the friars to ameliorate these recalcitrant Indians, see Powell, *Soldiers, Indians, and Silver.* As the northern frontier of New Spain (properly Nueva Vizcaya, as the frontier region between central Mexico and present-day New Mexico was then called) became more pacified by the mid-seventeenth century, a number of churches were built under the auspices of both Franciscan and Jesuit missionaries. Some of these bear stylistic elements similar to the New Mexican pueblo prototype, most famously the Church of the Virgin of Guadalupe in Ciudad Juárez, twin-city to El Paso, Texas, just across the Rio Grande. Built in the 1660s, this fine example was mercifully spared destruction during the 1680 Pueblo Revolt and still possesses its original timber-supported roof and transverse clerestory window. For more on these northern Mexican structures, their similarity to the New Mexican pueblo style with possibly even Moorish mudéjar derivations, see Olvera, 123–34.
5. For a study of the Spanish settlement of Florida in the sixteenth century, see Milanich, especially 131–37, concerning what little survives of the mission architecture. Since so few traces are extant, it is curious for the author to claim as he does unequivocally that "the missions of La Florida bore little resemblance to the seventeenth-century adobe missions of the southwest United States or the eighteenth-century Franciscan missions of California" (137). See also Fontana, *Entrada,* which gives brief but insightful background on the various U.S. National Parks and Monuments where the scant remains of these settlements are preserved.
6. Kubler, *Religious Architecture of New Mexico,* 137–41.
7. Cabeza de Vaca. Cabeza de Vaca's personal recounting of his adventures was originally published in 1542 as *La relación* in Zamora, Spain, followed by a second edition retitled *Naufragios. . . .* in 1555, printed in Valladolid.
8. For the legends of Antilia, see Morison, *European Discovery of America: The Northern Voyages,* 97–102.
9. For an excellent "swashbuckling" account of Coronado's adventure, see Bolton.
10. Weber, 46.
11. As quoted in Bolton, 28.
12. See Rodack.
13. Ibid., 35–36.
14. Ibid., 49. Fray Marcos was apparently referring to the American bison.
15. On the origin of the meaning of this strange word that, like Cíbola, so attracted the gold-seeking Spaniards, see Simmons, 156.
16. These were ordained priest Fray Juan de Padilla, lay brothers Fray Luis de Escalona and Juan de la Cruz, and two converted Indians named Lucas and Sebastian. Mendieta, writing in 1585, makes several mentions of Fray Marcos de Niza and Coronado's adventure, referring to the lands they discovered as collectively called "Cibola" (*Historia eclesiástica indiana* [1945], 3:49, 51, 202 (bk. 4, chaps. 10–11, 42), 4:126–30 (bk. 5, chap. 45).
17. Among these ordinances was Philip's famous decree that all colonial towns have their house plots and streets laid out on an "Albertian" grid; see Zavala, "La 'Utopia' de Tomas Moro."
18. Lejeune, 19.
19. These various expeditions are well discussed in Weber, 60–92, and Fontana, *Entrada,* 9–71.
20. The story of Oñate's expedition is well summarized in Fontana, *Entrada,* 58–63.
21. Simmons, 106.
22. For details of this trial and punishment, see Minge, 11–16, and Simmons, 133–46.
23. As quoted in Fontana, *Entrada,* 61.
24. For an excellent explanation of the many Indian communities of the American Southwest, including northern Mexico, their customs, language differences, and relations with one another and with the Spanish and later Anglos, see Spicer. See also Fontana, *Guide to Contemporary Southwest Indians.*
25. Murphy, 57–60.
26. Vivian, 1.
27. Torquemada, *Monarquía indiana* (1975–83), 2:454 (bk. 5, chap. 39).
28. Scholes and Bloom, 71.
29. Benavides, *The Memorial of Fray Alonso de Benavides,* 42–43; Scholes and Bloom.
30. James Ivey, personal communication, September 1999; see also Kubler, *Religious Architecture of New Mexico,* 118–27. Vetancurt in his *Teatro Mexicano* of 1698, 100–103 (part 4, treatise 3, 37–61) names and briefly describes only twenty-five missions active in the Province of New Mexico before the 1690 revolt: Zandia; Santo Domingo; Santa Fe; Tezuqui; Nambe; San Ildefonso; Santa Clara; San Juan de Caballeros; Pecuris; Taos; Acoma; Jemez; Halona; Aguico; Awatowi; Xongopabi; Oraibi; Cochiti; Galisto; Pecos; San Marcos; Chilili; Quarai; Tajique; and Abo.
31. According to Ivey, "*Un Templo Grandioso,*" 23–24, archaeological evidence indicates that early convento remains from the years 1600 to about 1626 reveal living quarters for only one friar each. After 1626 the conventos seem to have been planned for about three friars each, yet historical records indicate that, in actuality, that hoped-for number of residents was rarely reached.

In fact, after 1631 the number of friars in all New Mexico decreased. Only in the 1650s did the missionary population pick up again, along with a momentary burst in church and convento expansion.

32. Knaut, 76–77.
33. For instance, Weber, 114–15, and Knaut, 53–88.
34. Ironically, just as the Jesuits had been sent to Mexico to curb the often unorthodox conversion methods of the mendicant orders, so by the middle of the seventeenth century, the Jesuits were under attack for the same sins by the now more-orthodox mendicants (especially influenced by the French Jansenists; see Hay).
35. As at Abó, where garbage from the convento kitchen was thrown into the kiva sometime after the second church was built in 1630; see Ivey, *In the Midst of a Loneliness*, 415–21, and "Convento Kivas in the Missions of New Mexico," 121–52.
36. See Scholes; Scholes and Bloom, 320–23.
37. For a good account of the Pueblo Rebellion, see Knaut. See also Weber, 133–41. Vetancurt in his 1698 *Teatro Mexicano* likewise took notice of the revolt, 103–4 (pt. 4, titulus 3).
38. Kubler, *Religious Architecture of New Mexico*, 118–27.
39. Montoya, 9.

CHAPTER 11

1. For a good sense of how the Indians of the Southwest, particularly the Navajo, still regard their extraordinary natural landscape, read any of the many mystery novels by Tony Hillerman; *Coyote Waits*, *Skinwalkers*, *Listening Woman*, and *Thief of Time* are but a few of his provocatively titled books published since 1970.
2. For forensic evidence that such practices did occur among the Indians of this region, see Turner and Turner.
3. For just what and when distinguishes a true kiva, see W. Smith, *When Is a Kiva?* Regarding its architectural form and ideology, see Nabokov and Easton, 348–409.
4. Nabokov and Easton, 378.
5. Torquemada, *Monarquía indiana* (1975–83), 2:457 (bk. 5, chap. 40).
6. Among many Pueblo peoples, the fifth or central direction actually includes both up and down; see Nabokov and Easton, 376–78.
7. This sad and embarrassing story in Hopi history is given balanced review in Spicer, 190–92. For a worst-case version based on recently discovered forensic evidence by physical anthropologist Christy Turner, see Douglas Preston, "Cannibals in the Canyon," *New Yorker*, November 30, 1998, 76–89. See also the Special Reports issue of *Discovering Archaeology*, May–June 1999, 42–66.
8. Montgomery, Smith, and Brew; W. Smith, *Prehistoric Kivas of Antelope Mesa*.
9. W. Smith, *Prehistoric Kivas of Antelope Mesa*, 64.
10. Ivey, "Convento Kivas in the Missions of New Mexico"; see also Ivey, *In the Midst of a Loneliness*, 415–23.
11. Ivey, *In the Midst of a Loneliness*, 415–21, and "Convento Kivas in the Missions of New Mexico," 121–52.
12. As to the meaning and etymology of the Old English word, see under "garth" in the *Oxford English Dictionary*.
13. Toulouse, 11–13: "The one exotic feature of the [Abó] mission is the kiva. . . . In the West Court patio, slightly off center, is a kiva which appears to have been constructed during the building of the church, as there are no other signs of Indian occupation underlying the church in this neighborhood, except refuse under the main altars. Ashes filled the firepit and the ashpit, but no traces of the roof were found. The kiva had been used as a disposal pit for refuse from the mission kitchen. . . . Beneath the patio, walls of an earlier and underlying courtyard, with the kiva in its center, were traced on the east and south sides. . . . No sipapu was found. The roof [of the kiva] was supported by four posts placed in an east-west and north-south line. The ventilator was on the east."
14. Personal conversation with James Ivey at Pecos, August 4, 1999. Because the cloister-patio at Pecos rests on bedrock, the kiva there was positioned in the corral just outside to the east. Since there are a number of clay sources in the vicinity of Pecos from which the natives made their mortar, the fact that the peculiar red clay mortar used to cement the bricks in both church and kiva came from the same source is further evidence of simultaneous building. Alden Hayes, however, maintained that this kiva was but another example of "superposition," at the same time observing the curious fact that when finally abandoned altogether, this kiva too—just as at Awatovi—was covered with "remarkably clean sand. . . . The impression was that it was deliberately back-filled" (34).
15. As first proposed by Ivey, *In the Midst of a Loneliness*, 141.
16. Valadés, *Rhetorica Christiana*, 146–49 (pt. 3, chap. 12),

and *Retórica Cristiana,* 345–51. In these pages, the Franciscan discussed at length this method of Christian exposition, citing from a number of Patristic sources including Ezekiel, the Epistles of Paul, Saint Euquerius, Saint Augustine, and Saint Jerome.

17. The settlement of San Gabriel no longer exists, but ruins of adobe walls that may once have been part of the convento may still be seen near Highway 285 just north of the town of Española, New Mexico, and have sometimes been touted as the "oldest building erected by Europeans in North America" (Forrest, 39). That honor, however, belongs to the Spanish remains in Saint Augustine, Florida. For an archaeological reconstruction of the San Gabriel, New Mexico site, see Agoyo and Brown, 10–39.
18. Ivey, "The Architectural Background of the New Mexican Missions."
19. Ivey, *In the Midst of a Loneliness,* 35–55.
20. Ibid., 67. See also, 39–40, for the inventory of materials that each friar brought with him from Mexico City for the building of his church. This consisted not only of the usual carpenters' tools such as hammers and saws but also iron hardware such as nails, hinges, and locks. No measuring equipment or architectural drawings are listed, however.
21. Vetancurt.
22. McAndrew, 397–98.
23. See Mathes, 27–49, concerning the fate of the library during the Inquisition years after 1571, when many of the books were either proscribed or stolen. What remained of the original contents were removed from the Colegio de Santa Cruz to the convento of Santiago de Tlatelolco around 1605 when Torquemada was resident there.
24. The Franciscans, equally active in South America during the sixteenth century, had established already in 1535 their first "model convento" in Quito, Ecuador, which, like San Francisco in Mexico City, served to set the standard for church-building throughout that region; see Kubler and Soria, *Art and Architecture,* 87–89.
25. Torquemada remained as Guardian of Santiago de Tlatelolco from 1603 until his death, supposedly in 1624. There is some confusion about the latter since the single document that gives the date states: "1624, year 5-Reed. At that time our beloved Fray Juan de Torquemada died on Tuesday, [in the morning of] the first day of the month of January" (*Anales coloniales de Tlatelolco, 1519–1633,* Biblioteca, Museo Nacional de México).

    This statement must be in error. Unless there had been some major, as yet unrecorded, Aztec calendar change in Tlatelolco, January 1, 1624, could not have occurred in Nahua year Five Reed, but rather in One Reed. (Five Reed should correlate with 1627–28.) Furthermore, January 1, 1624, should have fallen on Monday, if, as we must assume, Mexico City in 1624 was following the recently established Gregorian calendar reform. For Fray Juan's biography in brief, see Torquemada, *Monarquía indiana* (1964), vii–xliii; see also Phelan, 111–18.
26. Torquemada's books were heavily derivative from Mendieta's unpublished *Historia,* although carefully edited so that he left out the latter's criticisms of Philip II. Like Mendieta, Torquemada believed the Franciscans were mandated by God to convert the Indians, but he did not share Mendieta's universal apocalyptic vision of the "Indian republic" as the antiworld "City of God." Rather, he was more in favor of Hispanicizing the Indians and joining them to the this-world hegemony of the universal Hapsburg monarchial empire.
27. Torquemada, *Monarquía indiana* (1975–83), 2:449–56 (bk. 5, chaps. 37–40): *Cartas de Relacíon,* from Fray Juan de Escalona, Custodian of the New Mexican mission to the Franciscan Provincial in Mexico City, October 1, 1601; and from Fray Francisco de San Miguel to the Franciscan Provincial of Michoacán, February 29, 1602.
28. Torquemada, *Monarquía indiana* (1975–83), 3:184–249 (bk. 8). Much of Torquemada's material in book 8 was derived from Las Casas, *Apologetica Historia,* bk. 3, chaps. 128–33.
29. Kubler, *Religious Architecture of New Mexico,* 59–61, first called attention to the Gesù as possible model for the New Mexican pueblo churches; for further on the Gesù's influence, see Ackerman, 15–28, and Wittkower, 15–16.
30. Weil.
31. Ivey, *In the Midst of a Loneliness,* 40.
32. Fray Alonso de Benavides boasted of converting "sixty thousand" Pueblo Indians, a number larger than the entire native population of New Mexico; see Spicer, 158.
33. Torquemada, *Monarquía indiana* (1975–83), 2:456 (bk. 5, chap. 39).
34. Kubler, *Religious Architecture of New Mexico,* 75–76.
35. The inspiration for this architectural adjustment may possibly have come all the way from Peru where during the last quarter of the sixteenth century in Cuzco and vicinity the Franciscans built several churches with similar raised porches above the main portals; see Kubler and Soria, *Art and Architecture,* 89.
36. Ivey, *In the Midst of a Loneliness,* 39.
37. Ackerman, 19–20.
38. For a good description of adobe and the various building materials available to the Pueblo Indians, see Bunting, 17–52.

39. Hayes, 41.
40. Nevertheless, the size of the church at Ácoma pales in comparison to the first church at Pecos. Reduced at present to mere stubble wall, this once huge edifice was twice as large in overall size and was originally spanned by vigas more than sixty feet in length.
41. Vetancurt, 77–78.
42. Kubler, *Religious Architecture of New Mexico,* 92–94; Minge, 20–21. Concerning the ingenious engineering that was necessary to cut and set these huge beams, see Ivey, *In the Midst of a Loneliness,* 49–50; 55. It is also worth considering that the idea of massively heavy building materials being carried on the backs of native laborers for very long distances was hardly unusual in pre-Columbian America. Indeed, the "ratio" between weight and size of materials, distance to be hauled, and height of temple on which the materials were to be hoisted had some special and profound spiritual significance for indigenous peoples: witness the colossal Olmec heads cut from basalt boulders dragged from quarries more than a hundred kilometers distant or the gigantic granite blocks used in the construction of Inca Ollantaytambo and Sacsahuaman, some of which weighed more than three hundred tons and were dragged from remote mountain quarries.
43. Lavin, 1:33. There is even evidence of this in some of the ruins of Hadrian's garden villa at Tivoli.
44. Treib, 41. Kubler, *Religious Architecture of New Mexico,* 67, and *Mexican Architecture,* 2:273–74, also wrestled with the problem of sources for the transverse clerestory window.
45. Ivey, "The Architectural Background of the New Mexican Missions."
46. For a review of the edicts of the Council of Trent issued after 1563 regarding the visual arts, see Wittkower, 1–9.
47. Ivey, "*Un Templo Grandioso.*"
48. Ivey, *In the Midst of a Loneliness,* 83. See also Florence Hawley Ellis's archaeological reconstruction of the ruins of Oñate's original capital at San Gabriel, in Agoyo and Brown, 10–38, with a putative plan of what she claims was the convento church on p. 51. The plan is curiously oriented with its supposed altar end at the northwest. While true that several later New Mexican churches also were aligned altar to the north, they did so for reasons having to do with illuminating the altar from special directions by means of the transverse clerestory window. If Ellis is right and this San Gabriel structure is the ruin of the first permanent church in New Mexico, did it then also have the first transverse clerestory window?
49. On the other hand, Torquemada in his book 8 on architecture conservatively insisted (again drawing on the authority of Saint Antonine of Florence) that churches be built with their "shoulders" *(espaldas)* to the east and entrances to the west. However, he also observed that at the Last Judgment Jesus will descend from heaven from the east "in the same manner as a [light] ray," thus concluding that the "head *[cabeza]* of the temple or church ought to be looking toward the east" (*Monarquía indiana,* [1975-83] 3:194–96 [bk. 8, chap. 3]).
50. Ivey, personal communication, September 1999; see also Kubler, *Religious Architecture of New Mexico,* 23. Noteworthy is the fact that only a very few churches were ever built in New Mexico facing the canonical west (the second, eighteenth-century Pecos church is a rare example), and none at all are known to have been planned with their entrance-facades facing north.
51. Ivey, *In the Midst of a Loneliness,* 213–14.
52. Concerning Pueblo winter solstice ceremonies, see Ortiz, and Williamson, 79–84. A famous example of signaling winter solstice by the ancient Anasazi Indians of Chaco Canyon, New Mexico, has been claimed for certain petroglyphs on the Fajada Butte; see Carlson and Judge, 43–71.
53. Lavin, 1:33–36.
54. Kubler, *Religious Architecture of New Mexico,* 62–71.
55. Ivey, *In the Midst of a Loneliness,* 41–42.
56. Such a parallel has also been mentioned by Treib; see his plate 16.
57. Ivey, *In the Midst of a Loneliness,* 210. For further information and documentation about the installation of retablos, see ibid., 209–13.
58. Kubler, *Religious Architecture of New Mexico,* 135; M. Elliot, 21.
59. Wroth, 69.
60. See Storey on the iconography and persistence of this subject in Hispanic America.
61. See Wroth; Steele; Pierce et al.

BIBLIOGRAPHY

Ackerman, James S. "The Gesù in the Light of Contemporary Church Design." In *Baroque Art: The Jesuit Contribution*, ed. Rudolf Wittkower and Irma B. Jaffe, 15–29. New York: Fordham University Press, 1972.

Actas del II Congreso Internacional sobre los Franciscanos en el Nuevo Mundo: Siglo XVI, La Rábida, 21–26 septiembre 1987. Madrid: Editorial Deimos, 1988.

Agoyo, Herman, and Lynnwood Brown, eds. *When Cultures Meet: Remembering San Gabriel del Yunge Oweenge: Papers from the October 20, 1984, Conference Held at San Juan Pueblo, New Mexico*. Santa Fe: Sunstone Press, 1987.

Ainsworth, Maryan W., and Keith Christiansen, eds. *From Van Eyck to Bruegel: Early Netherlandish Painting in the Metropolitan Museum of Art*. New York: Harry N. Abrams, 1998.

Albernoz Bueno, Alicia. *La Memoria del Olvido: El Lenguaje del Tlacuilo; Glifos y Murales de la Iglesia de San Miguel Arcángel, Ixmiquilpan, Hidalgo Teopan Dedicado a Tezcatlipoca*. Pachuca: Universidad Autónoma del Estado de Hidalgo, 1994.

Alberti, Leon Battista. *De pictura praestantissima et nunquam satis laudata arte tres absolutissimi Leonis Baptistae de Albertis. . . .* Basel: Th. Venatorius, 1540.

———. *Leon Battista Alberti on Painting and on Sculpture: The Latin Texts of "De Pictura" and "De Statua."* Ed. and trans. Cecil Grayson. New York and London: Phaidon, 1972.

Adams, James Noel. *The Latin Sexual Vocabulary*. Baltimore: Johns Hopkins University Press, 1982.

Alejos-Grau, Carmen José. *Diego Valadés, educador de Nueva España: Ideas pedagógicas de la Rhetorica christiana (1579)*. Pamplona, Spain: Ediciones Eunate, 1994.

Allen, John S. *El Corral del Principe*. Gainesville: University of Florida Press, 1983.

Almaráz, Felix D., Jr. "Transplanting 'Deep, Living Roots': Franciscan Missionaries and the Colonization of New Mexico—the Fledgling Years, 1598–1616." In *Seeds of Struggle: Harvest of Hate; Papers of the Archdiocese of Santa Fe Catholic Cuarto Centennial Conference: The History of the Catholic Church in New Mexico*, ed. Thomas J. Steele, Paul Rhetts, and Barbe Anwalt. Albuquerque: LPD Press, 1998.

Angulo Iñiguez, Diego. *Historia del arte hispanoamericano*. 3 vols. Barcelona and Buenos Aires: Salvat Editores, 1945.

Antonine, Saint. *Sancti Antonini Summa theologica*. 4 vols. 1740. Reprint, Graz: Akademische Druck- und Verlagsanstalt, 1959.

Argudín, Yolanda. *Historia del teatro in México: Desde los rituales prehispánicos hasta el arte dramático de nuestras días*. Mexico City: Panorama, 1985.

Arias Martínez, Manuel, and Luis Luna. *Museo Nacional de Escultura [Valladolid]*. Madrid: Ministerio de Cultura, 1995.

Arróniz, Othón. *Teatro de evangelización en Nueva España*. Mexico City: Universidad Nacional Autónoma de México, 1979.

Artigas, Juan B. *Capillas abiertas aisladas de México*. Mexico City: Universidad Nacional Autónoma de México, 1992.

———. *Capillas abiertas aisladas de Tlaxcala*. Mexico City: Universidad Nacional Autónoma de México, 1985.

Aveni, Anthony F. *Skywatchers of Ancient Mexico*. Austin: University of Texas Press, 1980.

Aveni, Anthony F., and Edward E. Calnek. "Astronomical Considerations in the Aztec Expression of History, Eclipse Data." *Ancient Mesoamerica* 10.1 (1999):87–98.

Bailey, Gauvin A. *Art on the Jesuit Missions in Asia and Latin America, 1542–1773*. Toronto: University of Toronto Press, 1999.

———. "The Indian Conquest of Catholic Art: The Mughals, the Jesuits, and Imperial Mural Painting." *Art Journal* 57.1 (1998):24–30.

———. *The Jesuits and the Grand Mogul: Renaissance Art at the Imperial Court of India, 1580–1630*. Vol. 2. Washington, D.C.: Freer Gallery of Art, Arthur M. Sackler Gallery, Smithsonian Institution Press, 1998.

———. "The Lahore Mirat Al-Quds and the Impact of Jesuit Theatre on Mughal Painting." *South Asian Studies* 13 (1997):31–44.

Baird, Ellen T. "Adaptation and Accommodation: The Transportation of the Pictorial Texts in Sahagún's Manuscripts." *Native Artists and Patrons in Colonial America*, ed. Emily Umberger and Tom Cummins. *Phoebus* 7 (1995):36–52.

———. *The Drawings of Sahagún's "Primeros Memoriales": Structure and Style*. Norman: University of Oklahoma Press, 1993.

———. "Stars and War at Cacaxtla." In *Mesoamerica after the Decline of Teotihuacan*, ed. Richard A. Diehl and Janet Catherine Berlo, 105–22. Washington, D.C.: Dumbarton Oaks, 1989.

Barrera Vásquez, Alfredo, ed. *Diccionario Maya Cordemex: Maya-Español, Español-Maya*. Mérida, Yucatán: Ediciones Cordemex, 1980.

Basalenque, Padre Diego. *Historia de la Provincia de San Nicolás de Tolentino de Michoacán, del Orden de N.P.S. Augustín* 1673. Reprint, Mexico City: Editorial Jus, 1963.

Bassie-Sweet, Karen. *At the Edge of the World: Caves and Late Classic Maya World View*. Norman: University of Oklahoma Press, 1996.

———. *From the Mouth of the Dark Cave: Commemorative Sculpture of the Late Classic Maya*. Norman: University of Oklahoma Press, 1991.

Baudot, Georges. *Utopia and History in Mexico: The First Chronicles of Mexican Civilization, 1520–1569*. Trans. Bernard R. and Thelma Ortiz de Montellano. Niwot, Colo.: University Press of Colorado, 1995.

Baxandall, Michael. *Painting and Experience in Fifteenth-Century Italy: A Primer in the Social History of Pictorial Style*. Oxford: Oxford University Press, 1972.

Bede, the Venerable, Saint. *A History of the English Church and People*. Baltimore: Penguin, 1968.

Belting, Hans. *Likeness and Presence: A History of the Image before the Era of Art*. Chicago and London: University of Chicago Press, 1994.

Benavides, Fray Alonso de. *Fray Alonso de Benavides's Revised Memorial of 1634*. Trans. and ed. Frederick W. Hodge, George P. Hammond, and Agapito Rey. Albuquerque: University of New Mexico Press, 1945.

———. *The Memorial of Fray Alonso de Benavides, 1630*. Trans. Mrs. Edward E. Ayer; annot. Frederick Webb Hodge and Charles Fletcher Lummis. 1916. Reprint, Albuquerque: Horn and Wallace, 1965.

Beristain de Souza, José Mariano. *Biblioteca hispano americano septentrional; . . . .* 5 vols. in 2. Mexico City: Editorial Fuente Cultural, 1947.

Bernal-Garcia, Maria Elena. "Carving Mountains in a Blue Bowl: Mythological Urban Planning in Mesoamerica." Ph.D. dissertation, University of Texas, Austin, 1993.

Bjurström, Per. "Baroque Theater and the Jesuits." In *Baroque Art: The Jesuit Contribution*, ed. Rudolf Wittkower and Irma B. Jaffe. New York: Fordham University Press, 1972.

Bolton, Herbert E. *Coronado, Knight of Pueblos and Plains*. Albuquerque: University of New Mexico Press, 1949.

Bono, Dianne M. *Cultural Diffusion of Spanish Humanism in New Spain: Francisco Cervantes de Salazar's "Diálogo de la dignidad del hombre."* New York: Peter Lang, 1991.

Boxer, C. R. *The Church Militant and Iberian Expansion, 1440–1770*. Baltimore: Johns Hopkins University Press, 1978.

Brady, James E. "Settlement Configuration and Cosmology: The Role of Caves at Dos Pilas." *American Anthropology* 99.3 (1997):602–18.

Braun, Barbara. *Pre-Columbian Art and the Post-Columbian world: Ancient American Sources of Modern Art*. New York: Harry N. Abrams, 1993.

Bray, Warwick, ed. *The Meeting of Two Worlds: Europe and the Americas, 1492–1650*. Oxford: Oxford University Press, 1993.

Bretos, Miguel A. *Arquitectura y arte sacro de Yucatán, 1545-1823*. Mérida, Yucatán, México: Producción Editorial Dante, 1987.

———. *Iglesias de Yucatán*. Mérida, Yucatán, México: Producción Editorial Dante, 1992.

———. "Yucatan: Franciscan Architecture and the Spiritual Conquest." In *Franciscan Presence in the Americas: Essays on the Activities of the Franciscan Friars in the Americas, 1492–1900*, ed. Francisco Morales, 393–420. Potomac, Md.: Academy of American Franciscan History, 1983.

Bricker, Victoria Reifler. *The Indian Christ, the Indian King: The Historical Substrate of Maya Myth and Ritual*. Austin: University of Texas Press, 1981.

Broda, Johanna, Davíd Carrasco, and Eduardo Matos Moctezuma. *The Great Temple of Tenochtitlan: Center and Periphery of the Aztec World*. Berkeley: University of California Press, 1987.

Brown, Jonathan. "Spain in the Age of Exploration: Crossroads of Artistic Cultures." In *Circa 1492: Art in the Age of Exploration*, ed. Jay A. Levinson, 41–49. Washington, D.C.: National Gallery of Art; New Haven, Conn.: Yale University Press, 1991.

Brown, Peter. *The Cult of the Saints: Its Rise and Function in Latin Christianity*. Chicago: University of Chicago Press, 1981.

Brundage, Burr Cartwright. *The Fifth Sun: Aztec Gods, Aztec World*. Austin: University of Texas Press, 1983.

Bunting, Bainbridge. *Early Architecture of New Mexico*. Albuquerque: University of New Mexico Press, 1976.

Burgoa, Fray Francisco de. *Geográfica descripción de la parte septentrional del Polo Artico de la América y nueva iglesia de las Indias Occidentales, y sitio astronómico de esta Provincia de Predicatores de Antequera, Valle de Oaxaca*. 2 vols. 1674. Reprint, Mexico City: Editorial Porrúa, 1989.

———. *Palestra historial de virtudes y exemplares apostolicos. Fundada del zelo de insignes heroes de la sagrada Orden de predicatores en este nuevo mundo de America en las Indias Occidentales*. 1670. Reprint, Mexico City: Editorial Porrúa, 1989.

Burke, Marcus. "Mexican Painting of the Renaissance and Counter-Reformation." In *Mexico: Splendors of Thirty Centuries, An Exhibition of Art, October 10, 1990–January 13, 1991*, 286–88. New York: Metropolitan Museum of Art and Bulfinch Press, 1990.

Burkhart, Louise M. "Flowery Heaven: The Aesthetic of Paradise in Nahuatl Devotional Literature." *RES* 21 (spring 1992):88–110.

———. *Holy Wednesday: A Nahua Drama from Early Colonial Mexico*. Philadelphia: University of Pennsylvania Press, 1996.

———. "Pious Performances: Christian Pageantry and Native Identity in Early Colonial Mexico." In *Native Traditions in the Postconquest World*, ed. Elizabeth H. Boone and Tom Cummins. Washington, D.C.: Dumbarton Oaks, 1998.

———. *The Slippery Earth: Nahua-Christian Moral Dialogue in Sixteenth-Century Mexico*. Tucson: University of Arizona Press, 1989.

Burns, Allan F. *An Epoch of Miracles: Oral Literature of the Yucatec Maya.* Austin: University of Texas Press, 1983.

Butzer, Karl F., ed. "The Americas before and after 1492: Current Geographical Research." *Annals of the Association of American Geographers* 82.3 (1992).

Byland, Bruce E., and John M. D. Pohl. *In the Realm of Eight Deer: The Archaeology of the Mixtec Codices.* Norman: University of Oklahoma Press, 1994.

Cabeza de Vaca, Álvar Núñez. *Adventures in the Unknown Interior of America.* Trans. and annot. Cyclone Covey. Albuquerque: University of New Mexico Press, 1983.

Cabezas Gelabert, Lino. "La 'perspectiva angular' y la introducción de la perspectiva artistica en la España del siglo XVI." *D'art: Barcelona* 15 (1989):167–81.

———. "La teoria de la perspectiva en la España del siglo XVI." In *La prospettiva: Fondamenti teorici ed esperienze figurative dall'antichità al mondo moderno: Atti del Convegno Internazionale di Studi, Istituto Svizzero di Roma, 11–14 settembre 1995,* ed. Rocco Sinisgalli, 103–20. Florence: Edizione Cadmo, 1998.

Camille, Michael. *Images on the Edge: The Margins of Medieval Art.* Cambridge, Mass.: Harvard University Press, 1992.

Carlsen, Robert. *The War for the Heart and Soul of a Highland Maya Town.* Austin: University of Texas Press, 1997.

Carlsen, Robert, and Martin Prechtel. "Weaving the Cosmos amongst the Tzutujil Maya." *RES* 15 (1988).

Carlson, John B., and W. James Judge, eds. *Astronomy and Ceremony in the Prehistoric Southwest.* Albuquerque: Maxwell Museum of Anthropology, 1987.

Carrillo y Gariel, Abelardo. *Ixmiquilpan.* Mexico City: INAH, 1961.

Caso, Alfonso. "Calendrical Systems of Central Mexico." *Handbook of Middle American Indians: Archaeology of Northern Mesoamerica.* Austin: University of Texas Press, 1971, 10:333–48.

Castañeda, Daniel, and Vicente T. Mendoza. *Instrumental Precortesiano.* Vol. 1, *Instrumentos de percusión.* Mexico City: Museo Nacional de Arqueologica y Etnografia, 1933.

Castillo Negrete, Manuel del. "Las Pinturas Murales en el Convento de Epazoyucán." *Boletin INAH* 16 (1964):1–4.

Castillo Peraza, Carlos, ed. *Historia de Yucatán: Antología.* 2d ed. Mérida, Yucatán, México: Producción Editorial Dante, 1987.

Castro y Castro, Manuel, OFM. "Lenguas indígenas americanas transmitidas por los franciscanos del siglo XVI." In *Actas del II Congreso Internacional sobre los Franciscanos en el Nuevo Mundo: Siglo XVI, La Rábida, 21–26 septiembre 1987,* 485–573. Madrid: Editorial Deimos, 1988.

Cather, Willa. *Death Comes for the Archbishop.* New York: Knopf, 1927.

Cervantes, Fernando. *The Devil in the New World: The Impact of Diabolism in New Spain.* New Haven, Conn.: Yale University Press, 1994.

Cervantes de Salazar, Francisco. *Crónica de la Nueva España.* Ca. 1558. Reprint, Mexico City: Editorial Porrúa, 1985.

———. *Life in the Imperial and Loyal City of Mexico in New Spain and the Royal and Pontifical University of Mexico. . . .* Trans. Minnie Lee Barrett Shepard. Austin: University of Texas Press, 1953. Reprint, Westport, Conn.: Greenwood Press, 1970.

———. *Mexico en 1554 y Tumulo Imperial.* Ed. Edmundo O'Gorman. Mexico City: Editorial Porrúa, 1972.

Chara Zereceda, Oscar, and Viviana Caparó Gil. *Iglesias del Cusco: Historia y arquitectura.* Cusco: Editorial Universitaria UNSAAC, 1998.

Christenson, Allen J. "Scaling the Mountain of the Ancients: The Altarpiece of Santiago Atitlán, Guatemala." Ph.D. dissertation, University of Texas, Austin, 1998.

Christian, William A., Jr. *Apparitions in Late Medieval and Renaissance Spain.* Princeton, N.J.: Princeton University Press, 1981.

———. *Local Religion in Sixteenth-Century Spain.* Princeton, N.J.: Princeton University Press, 1981.

Ciudad Real, Fray Antonio de. *Fray Alonso de Ponce in Yucatan, 1588.* Trans. Ernest Noyes. New Orleans: Middle American Research Institute, Tulane University, 1932.

———. *Tratado curioso y docto de las grandezas de la Nueva España. . . .* 2 vols. Ca. 1590. Reprint, Mexico City: Universidad Nacional Autónoma de México, 1993.

Clendinnen, Inga. *Ambivalent Conquests: Maya and Spaniard in Yucatan, 1517–1570.* Cambridge: Cambridge University Press, 1987.

Cline, Howard F. "The Chronology of the Conquest: Synchronologies in Codex Telleriano-Remensis and Sahagún." *Journal de la Société des Américanistes* 62, (1973):9–33.

Codex Aubin. *Geschichte der Azteken: Codex Aubin und verwandte Dokumente.* Ed. and trans. Walter Lehmann and Gerdt Kutscher. Berlin: Gebr. Mann, 1981.

Codex Borbonicus. *El Libro del Ciuacoatl, Homenaje para el año del Fuego Nuevo: libro explicativo del llamado Códice Borbónico.* Ed. Ferdinand Anders, Maarten Jansen, and Luis Reyes García. Mexico City: Fondo de la Cultura Económica, 1991.

Codex Borgia. *Los Templos del Cielo y de la Oscuridad Oráculos y Liturgia: libro explicativo del llamado Códice Borgia.* Ed. Ferdinand Anders, Maarten Jansen, and Luis Reyes García. Mexico City: Fondo de la Cultura Económica, 1993.

Codex Chimalpahin. *Society and Politics in Mexico Tenochtitlan, Tlatelolco, Texcoco, Culhuacan, and other Nahua Altepetl in Central Mexico.* Ed. Arthur J. O. Anderson and Susan Schroeder. 2 vols. Norman: University of Oklahoma Press, 1997.

Codex Dresden. *Un Comentario al Codice de Dresden, Libro de jeroglifos mayas.* Ed. J. Eric S. Thompson. Mexico City: Fondo de la Cultura Económica, 1993.

Codex Mendoza. *Codex Mendoza the Mexican Manuscript known as the Collection of Mendoza and Preserved at the Bodleian Library.* Ed. and trans. James Cooper Clark. 3 vols. Oxford, London: Waterlow and Sons, 1938.

Codex Telleriano-Remensis. *Ritual, Divination, and History in an Aztec Manuscript.* Ed. and trans. Eloise Quiñones Keber. Austin: University of Texas Press, 1995.

Codex Vindobonensis. *Origen e Historia de los Reyes Mixtecos: Libro explicativo del llamado Códice Vindobonensis.* Ed. Ferdinand Anders, Maarten Jansen, and Luis Reyes García. Mexico City: Fondo de Cultura Económica, 1992.

Codex Zouche-Nuttall. *Crónica Mixteca: El Rey 8 Venado, Garra de Jaguar, y la dinastia de Teozacualco-Zaachila: Libro explicativo del llamado Códice Zouche-Nuttall.* Ed. Ferdinand Anders, Maarten Jansen, and Luis Reyes García. Mexico City: Fondo de Cultura Económica, 1992.

Coe, Michael D. "The Aztec Empire: Realm of the Smoking Mirror." In *Circa 1492: Art in the Age of Exploration,* ed. Jay A. Levinson, 499–505. Washington, D.C.: National Gallery of Art; New Haven, Conn.: Yale University Press, 1991.

———. *Breaking the Maya Code.* New York: Thames and Hudson, 1992.

Coe, Michael, Dean Snow, and Elizabeth Benson. *Atlas of Ancient America.* New York: Facts on File Publications, 1986.

Cogolludo, Fray Diego López de. *Los tres siglos de la dominación española en Yucatán, o sea historia de esta provincia.* 2 vols. 1688. Reprint, Graz: Akademische Druck- und Verlagsanstalt, 1971.

Cohn, Norman. *The Pursuit of the Millennium: Revolutionary Millenarians and Mystical Anarchists of the Middle Ages.* New York and London: Oxford University Press, 1961.

Cordoba, Pedro de. *Christian Doctrine: For the Instruction and Information of the Indians.* Trans. and ed. Sterling A. Stoudemire. Coral Gables, Fla.: University of Miami Press, 1970.

Cortés, Hernán. *Hernán Cortés: Letters from Mexico.* Ed. and trans. Anthony Pagden. New Haven, Conn.: Yale University Press, 1986.

Craine, Eugene R., and Reginald C. Reindorp, eds. and trans. *The Chronicles of Michoacán.* Norman: University of Oklahoma Press, 1970.

Cuevas, Mariano, S.J. *Historia de la iglesia en mexico.* Vol. 1, *Origenes de la iglesia en Nueva España, 1511–1548.* 6th ed. Mexico City: Editorial Porrúa, S.A., 1992.

Cummins, Tom. "From Lies to Truth: Colonial Ekphrasis and the Act of Cross-cultural Translation." In *Reframing the Renaissance: Visual Culture in Europe and Latin America, 1450–1650,* ed. Claire Farago, 152–75. New Haven, Conn.: Yale University Press, 1995.

Curiel, Gustavo. *Tlalmanalco: Historia e iconología del conjunto conventual.* Mexico City: Universidad Nacional Autónoma de México, 1988.

Dávila Padilla, Fray Augustín. *Historia de la fundación y discorso de la provincia de Santiago de México, de la Orden de Predicatores.* 1596. Reprint, Mexico City: Editorial Academia Literaria, 1955.

Dean, Carolyn S. "Who's Naughty and Nice: Childish Behavior in the Paintings of Cuzco's Corpus Christi Procession." *Native Artists and Patrons in Colonial America,* ed. Emily Umberger and Tom Cummins. *Phoebus* 7 (1995):107–26.

Deneven, William M., ed. *The Native Population of the Americas in 1492.* 2d ed. Madison: University of Wisconsin Press, 1992.

Díaz, Gisele, and Alan Rodgers. *The Codex Borgia: A Full-Color Restoration of the Ancient Mexican Manuscript.* New York: Dover, 1993.

Díaz del Castillo, Bernal. *Historia Verdadura de la Conquista de la Nueva España.* Ed. Joaquin Ramirez Cabaña. Mexico City: Porrúa, 1972.

Donovan, Richard B. *The Liturgical Drama in Medieval Spain.* Toronto: Pontifical Institute of Medieval Studies, 1958.

Drain, Thomas A. *A Sense of Mission: Historic Churches of the Southwest.* San Francisco: Chronicle Books, 1994.

Dunne, George H., S.J. *Generation of Giants: The Story of the Jesuits in China in the Last Decades of the Ming Dynasty.* Notre Dame, Ind.: University of Notre Dame Press, 1962.

Durán, Fray Diego. *The Aztecs: The History of the Indies of New Spain.* Trans. Doris Heyden and Fernando Horcasitas. New York: Orion Press, 1964.

———. *Book of the Gods and Rites and the Ancient Calendar.* Trans. Fernando Horcasitas and Doris Heyden. Norman: University of Oklahoma Press, 1971.

Duverger, Christian. *La conversión de los indios de Nueva España.* 1564. Reprint, Mexico City: Fondo de Cultura Económica, 1996.

Edgerton, Samuel Y. "From Mental Matrix to *Mappamundi* to Christian Empire." In *Art and Cartography: Six Essays,* ed. David Woodward. Chicago: University of Chicago Press, 1987.

———. *The Heritage of Giotto's Geometry: Art and Science on the Eve of the Scientific Revolution.* Ithaca, N.Y.: Cornell University Press, 1991.

———. "Leon Battista Alberti *vs.* Quetzalcoatl: Renaissance Art Theory in the Service of the Christian Mission to Mexico, 1523–1600." In *La prospettiva: Fondamenti teorici ed esperienze figurative dall'antichità al mondo moderno: Atti del Convegno Internazionale di Studi, Istituto Svizzero di Roma, 11–14 settembre 1995*, ed. Rocco Sinisgalli, 103–20. Florence: Edizione Cadmo, 1998.

———. "*Mensurare temporalia facit Geometria spiritualis*: Some Fifteenth-Century Italian Notions about When and Where the Annunciation Happened." In *Studies in Late Medieval and Renaissance Painting in Honor of Millard Meiss*, ed. I. Lavin and J. Plummer, 115–31. New York: New York University Press, 1977.

———. *Pictures and Punishment: Art and Criminal Prosecution during the Florentine Renaissance.* Ithaca, N.Y.: Cornell University Press, 1985.

———. *The Renaissance Rediscovery of Linear Perspective.* New York: Basic Books, 1975.

Edmonson, Munro S. *The Book of the Year: Middle American Calendrical Systems.* Salt Lake City: University of Utah Press, 1988.

———. *Sixteenth-Century Mexico: The Work of Sahagún.* Albuquerque: University of New Mexico, 1974.

Elia, Pasquale M. d', S.I., ed. *Fonti Ricciane: documenti originali concernenti Matteo Ricci e la storia delle prime relazioni tra l'Europa e la Cina (1579–1615).* Rome: Libreria dello Stato, 1942–49.

Elliott, J. H. *Spain and Its World, 1500–1700.* New Haven, Conn.: Yale University Press, 1989.

Elliott, Michael L. "New Mexico State Monument: Jémez." Santa Fe: Museum of New Mexico, 1993.

Enciclopedia dello Spettacolo. Rome: Le Maschere, 1956.

Enciclopedia universal ilustrada. Madrid: Espasa-Calpe S.A., 1958.

Escobar, Matías de. *Americana Thebaida: Vitas Patrum de los religiosos hermitaños de N.P. San Augustín de la Provincia de San Nicolás Tolentino de Michoacán.* 1729. Reprint, Morelia, Mexico: Balsal Editores, 1970.

Espinosa, Carlos. "Colonial Visions: Drama, Art, and Legitimation in Peru and Ecuador." *Native Artists and Patrons in Colonial America*, ed. Emily Umberger and Tom Cummins. *Phoebus* 7 (1995):84–107.

Estrada de Gerlero, Elena. "El friso monumental de Itzmiquilpan." In *Actes du XLIIe Congrès international des américanistes: Congres du centenaire.* Vol. 10. Paris: Société des américanistes, 1976.

———. "El programa pasionario en el convento franciscano de Huejotzingo." *Jahrbuch für Geschichte von Staat, Wirtschaft, und Gesellschaft Lateinamerikas* 20 (1983):643–62.

———. "Malinalco: Origines de su traza, convento y capillas." In *Malinalco: Imágenes de un destino*, Luis Mario Schneider, Elena Isabel E. de Gerlero, and Eduardo Matos Moctezuma. Mexico City: Banca Cremi, Soceidad Nacional de Crédito, 1989.

Estrada Monroy, Augustín. *El Mundo K'ekchi' de la Vera-Paz.* Guatemala City: Editorial del Ejercito, 1979.

Fabri, Mario, Elvira Garbero Zorzi, and Anna Maria Petrioli Tofani, eds. *Il Luogo teatrale a Firenze: Brunelleschi, Vasari, Buontalenti, Parigi.* Exhibition catalog, *Spettacolo e musica nella Firenze Medicea.* Florence: Electra, 1975.

Fane, Diana, ed. *Converging Cultures: Art and Identity in Spanish America.* New York: Harry N. Abrams, 1996.

Farago, Claire. "'Vision Itself Has Its History': 'Race' Nation, and Renaissance Art History." In *Reframing the Renaissance: Visual Culture in Europe and Latin America, 1450–1650*, ed. Claire Farago, 67–89. New Haven, Conn.: Yale University Press, 1995.

———, ed. *Reframing the Renaissance: Visual Culture in Europe and Latin America, 1450–1650.* New Haven, Conn.: Yale University Press, 1995.

Farriss, Nancy M. *Maya Society under Colonial Rule: The Collective Enterprise of Survival.* Princeton, N.J.: Princeton University Press, 1984.

———. "Sacred Power in Colonial Mexico: The Case of Sixteenth-Century Yucatán." In *The Meeting of Two Worlds: Europe and the Americas, 1492–1650*, ed. Warwick Bray, 145–63. Oxford: Oxford University Press, 1993.

Fernandez, Justino, ed. *Catálogo de construcciones religiosas del estado de Yucatan.* 2 vols. Mexico City: Secretaria de Hacienda y Crédito Público Dirección General de Bienes Naciónáles/Talleres Graficos de la Nación, 1945.

Fernández, Miguel Angel. *La Jerusalem Indiana: Los conventos-fortaleza mexicanos del siglo XVI.* Mexico City: Privately pub. by Smurfit Carton y Papel de Mexico, SA de CV, 1992.

Fletcher, Banister, Sir. *A History of Architecture on the Comparative Method.* 17th ed. New York: Charles Scribner, 1967.

Folan, George M. *The Open Chapel of Dzibilchaltun, Yucatan.* New Orleans: Middle American Research Institute, Tulane University, 1961.

Fontana, Bernard L. *Entrada: The Legacy of Spain and Mexico in the United States.* Tucson: Southwest Parks and Monuments Assoc., 1994.

———. *A Guide to Contemporary Southwest Indians.* Tucson: Southwest Parks and Monuments Assoc., 1999.

Forrest, Earle R. *Missions and Pueblos of the Old Southwest, Their Myths, Legends, Fiestas, and Ceremonies, with Some Accounts of the Indian Tribes and their Dances, and of the "Penitentes."* Glorieta, N.Mex.: Rio Grande Press, 1979.

Fraser, Valerie. *The Architecture of Conquest: Building in the Viceroyalty of Peru, 1535–1635*. Cambridge: Cambridge University Press, 1990.

Freedburg, David. *The Power of Images: Studies in the History and Theory of Response*. Chicago: University of Chicago Press, 1989.

Freidel, David, Linda Schele, and Joy Parker. *Maya Cosmos: Three Thousand Years on the Shaman's Path*. New York: Morrow, 1993.

Furst, Jill Leslie McKeever. *The Natural History of the Soul in Ancient Mexico*. New Haven, Conn.: Yale University Press, 1995.

Gablik, Suzi. *Progress in Art*. New York: Rizzoli, 1977.

Gage, Thomas. *Thomas Gage's Travels in the New World*. Ed. J. Eric S. Thompson. 1648. Reprint, Westport, Conn.: Greenwood Press, 1930.

Galarza, Joaquin. *Estudios de escritura indigena tradicional*. Mexico City: Archivo General de la Nación-Mexico, 1980.

Gante, Fray Pedro de. *Cartas de Fr. Pedro de Gante, O.F.M.* Ed. Fidel de J. Chauvet, O.F.M. Mexico City: Talleres "Fr. Junipero Serra," 1951.

García, Sebastián, O.F.M. *La Rábida, pórtico del nuevo mundo: Síntesis histórico-artística*. La Rábida, Spain: Communidad Franciscana del Convento de Santa Maria de La Rábida, 1992.

García Icazbalceta, Joaquin, ed. *Bibliografia mexicana del siglo XVI: Catálogo razonado de libros impresos en México de 1539 á 1600. Con biografias de autores y otras ilustraciones*. 1886. Reprint, Mexico City: Fondo de Cultura Económica, 1954.

———. *Colección de documentos para la historia de México*. 5 vols. 1858. Reprint, Mexico City: Editorial Porrúa, 1980.

———. *Investigacion historica y documental sobre la aparicion de la Virgen de Nueva colección de documentos Guadalupe de Mexico*. Mexico City: Ediciones Fuente Cultural, 1896.

———. *Nueva colección de documentos para la historia de México*. 5 vols. Mexico City: Andrade y Morales, 1889–92.

García Zambrano, Angel J. "Early Colonial Evidence of Pre-Columbian Rituals of Foundation." In *Seventh Palenque Round Table, 1989*, ed. Merle Greene Robertson and Virginia M. Fields, 217–27. San Francisco: Pre-Columbian Art Research Institute, 1994.

Garrido, Luis, and Angel Pison. *El Real Convento de Santa Clara y su Museo*. Salamanca: Hergar, 1994.

Garriga, Joachim. "Images amb 'punt': El primer ressò de la perspectiva lineal en la pintura catalana vers 1490–1500." *D'art: Barcelona*, 16 (1990):59–81.

Gasparini, Graziano. "The Spanish-American Grid Plan, an Urban Bureaucratic Form." University of Miami School of Architecture, Miami, Fla. *The New City: Foundations* (fall 1991):6–18.

Gerhard, Peter. *A Guide to the Historical Geography of New Spain*. Rev. ed. Norman: University of Oklahoma Press, 1993.

———. *The Southeast Frontier of New Spain*. Rev. ed. Norman: University of Oklahoma Press, 1993.

Gibson, Charles. *The Aztecs under Spanish Rule: A History of the Indians in the Valley of Mexico, 1519–1810*. Stanford, Calif.: Stanford University Press, 1964.

———. *Tlaxcala in the Sixteenth Century*. New Haven, Conn.: Yale University Press, 1952.

Gibson, James J. *The Perception of the Visual World*. Boston: Houghton Mifflin, 1950.

———. *The Senses Considered as Perceptual Systems*. Boston: Houghton Mifflin, 1966.

Gilbert, Creighton. "The Archbishop and the Painters of Florence." *Art Bulletin* 41 (1959):75–89.

Glass, John B. "A Census of Middle American Testerian Manuscripts." In *Guide to Ethnohistorical Sources*. Vol. 14 of *Handbook of Middle American Indians*. Austin: University of Texas Press, 1975.

Gombrich, E. H. *Art and Illusion: A Study in the Psychology of Pictorial Perception*. Princeton, N.J.: Princeton University Press, 1960.

Gossen, Gary. "Temporal and Spatial Equivalents in Chamula Ritual Symbolism." In *Reader in Comparative Religion: An Anthropological Approach*, ed. William A. Lessa and Evon Z. Vogt. New York: Harper and Row, 1979.

Graulich, Michael. "Myths of Paradise Lost in Pre-Hispanic Central Mexico." *Current Anthropology* 24.5 (1983):575–88.

Greenleaf, Richard E. "The Inquisition and the Indians of New Spain: A Study of Jurisdictional Confusion." *Americas* 22 (1965):138–66.

———. *The Mexican Inquisition of the Sixteenth Century*. Albuquerque: University of New Mexico Press, 1969.

———. *Zumárraga and the Mexican Inquisition, 1536–1543*. Washington D.C.: Academy of American Franciscan History, 1961.

Grijalva, Juan de. *Crónica de la Orden de N P S Agustín en las provincias de la Nueva España en cuatro edades desde el año de 1533 hasta el de 1592*. Mexico City: Editorial Porrúa, 1985.

Gruzinski, Serge. *El águila y la sibila: Frescos indios de México*. Barcelona: Moleiro Editor, S.A., 1994.

———. *L'Aigle et la sibylle: Fresques indiennes du mexique*. Paris: Imprimerie Nationale, 1994.

———. *The Conquest of Mexico: The Incorporation of Indian Societies into the Western World, Sixteenth–Eighteenth Centuries*. Trans. Eileen Corrigan. Cambridge, Eng.: Polity Press, 1993.

———. *La Guerra de las imágenes de Cristóbal Colón a "Blade Runner": 1492–2019*. Mexico City: Fondo de Cultura Económica, 1994.

———. *Painting the Conquest: The Mexican Indians and the European Renaissance.* Trans. Deke Dusinberre. Paris: UNESCO, Flammarion, 1992.

Guerrero Guerrero, Raúl, et al. *Murales de Ixmiquilpan.* Pachuca, Hidalgo, México: Gobierno de Estado Hidalgo, 1992.

Gutiérrez Solana, Nelly. *Códices de México: Historia e interpretación de los grandes libros pintados prehispánicos.* Mexico City: Panorama Editorial, 1992.

Hagen, Margaret A. *The Perception of Pictures.* 2 vols. New York: Academic Press, 1980.

———. *Varieties of Realism: Geometries of Representational Art.* Cambridge: Cambridge University Press, 1986.

Hagen, Margaret A., and Margaret M. Johnson. "Hudson Pictorial Depth Perception Test: Cultural Content and Question with a Western Sample." *Journal of Social Psychology* 101 (1977):3–11.

Hagen, Margaret A., and Rebecca K. Jones. "Cultural Effects on Pictorial Perception: How Many Words Is One Picture Really Worth?" *Plenum* (1978):171–212.

Hammond, Frederick. *Music and Spectacle in Baroque Rome: Barberini Patronage under Urban VIII.* New Haven, Conn.: Yale University Press, 1994.

Handbook of North American Indians. Vol. 9, *Southwest.* Ed. Alfonso Ortiz. Washington D.C.: Smithsonian Institution Press, 1979.

Hanke, Lewis. *The Spanish Struggle for Justice in the Conquest of America.* Philadelphia: University of Pennsylvania Press, 1949.

Hanson, Craig A. "The Hispanic Horizon in Yucatan: A Model of Franciscan Missionization." *Ancient Mesoamerica* 6.1 (1995):15–28.

Harris, Max. *The Dialogical Theatre: Dramatization of the Conquest of Mexico and the Question of the Other.* New York: St. Martin's Press, 1993.

Hasegawa, Ichiro. "Catalogue of Ancient and Naked-Eye Comets." In *Vistas in Astronomy,* ed. A. Beer, 24:59–102. New York: Pergamon, 1980.

Hay, Malcolm. *Failure in the Far East: Why and How the Breach between the Western World and China First Began.* Wetteren, Belgium: Scaldis, 1956.

Hayes, Alden C. *The Four Churches of Pecos.* Albuquerque: University of New Mexico Press, 1974.

Hecht, Johanna. "Mexican Architecture and Sculpture in Renaissance Modes." In *Mexico: Splendors of Thirty Centuries, An Exhibition of Art, October 10, 1990–January 13, 1991,* 280–86. New York: Metropolitan Museum of Art and Bulfinch Press, 1990.

Hill, Robert M. *Colonial Cakchiquels: Highland Maya Adaptations to Spanish Rule, 1600–1700.* New York: Harcourt Brace Jovanovich, 1992.

Hills, Paul. *The Light of Early Italian Painting.* New Haven, Conn.: Yale University Press, 1987.

Historia del arte mexicano. Vol. 4, *Arte colonial.* Mexico City: SEP: Salvat, 1986.

Ho, Peng Yoke. "Ancient and Medieval Observations of Comets and Novae in Chinese Sources." In *Vistas in Astronomy,* ed. A. Beer, 5:127–225. New York: Pergamon, 1962.

Horcasitas, Fernando. *El teatro Nahuatl: Epocas novohispana y moderna.* Part 1. Mexico City: Universidad Nacional Autónoma de México, 1974.

Ivey, James E. "The Architectural Background of the New Mexican Missions." In *Seeds of Struggle/Harvest of Hate: Papers of the Archdiocese of Santa Fe Catholic Cuarto Centennial Conference: The History of the Catholic Church in New Mexico,* ed. Thomas J. Steele, Paul Rhetts, and Barbe Anwalt. Albuquerque: LPD Press, 1998.

———. "Convento Kivas in the Missions of New Mexico." *New Mexico Historical Review* 73.2 (1998):121–52.

———. *In the Midst of a Loneliness: The Architectural History of the Salinas Missions.* Santa Fe, N.Mex.: National Park Service, 1988.

———. "*Un Templo Grandioso*: A Structural Assessment of the Mission Church at Jemez State Monument, New Mexico." Typescript, 1999.

Jameson, Mrs. (Anna). *Legends of the Madonna as Represented in the Fine Arts.* Boston and New York: Riverside Press, 1895.

———. *Legends of the Monastic Orders as Represented in the Fine Arts, Forming the Second Series of Sacred and Legendary Art.* Boston: Ticknor and Fields, 1866.

Janson, H. W. *Apes and Ape-Lore in the Middle Ages and the Renaissance.* London: Warburg Institute, 1952.

Jarrett, Bede, O.P. *S. Antonino and Medieval Economics.* Saint Louis and London: B. Herder and Manresa Press, 1914.

Jones, Pamela M. "Art Theory as Ideology: Gabriele Paleotti's Hierarchical Notion of Painting's Universality and Reception." In *Reframing the Renaissance: Visual Culture in Europe and Latin America, 1450–1650,* ed. Claire Farago, 127–39. New Haven, Conn.: Yale University Press, 1995.

Kagan, Richard L. "The Spain of Ferdinand and Isabella." In *Circa 1492: Art in the Age of Exploration,* ed. Jay A. Levinson, 55–61. Washington, D.C.: National Gallery of Art; New Haven, Conn.: Yale University Press, 1991.

Karttunen, Frances. *An Analytical Dictionary of Nahuatl.* Norman: University of Oklahoma Press, 1983.

Kaufmann, Thomas Dacosta. "Italian Sculptors and Sculpture Outside of Italy (Chiefly in Central Europe): Problems of Approach, Possibilities of Reception." In *Reframing the Renaissance: Visual Culture in Europe and Latin America, 1450–1650,* ed. Claire Farago, 47–67. New Haven, Conn.: Yale University Press, 1995.

Keen, Benjamin. *The Aztec Image in Western Thought.* New Brunswick, N.J.: Rutgers University Press, 1990.

Keleman, Pál. *Medieval American Art.* 2 vols. New York: Macmillan, 1944.

Kemp, Martin. *Leonardo da Vinci: The Marvelous Works of Nature and of Man.* Cambridge, Mass.: Harvard University Press, 1981.

Kershaw, Simon. "Easter Day." http://www.ely.anglican.org/cgi-bin/easter.

Kiracofe, James Bartholomay. "Architectural Fusion and Indigenous Ideology in Early Colonial Mexico: A Case Study of Teposcolula, Oaxaca, 1535–1580, Demonstrating Cultural Transmission through Negotiation and Consent in Planning a New Urban Settlement." Ph.D. dissertation, Virginia Polytechnic Institute and State University, Blacksburg, Va., 1996.

Klein, Cecelia F. "Editor's Statement: Depictions of the Dispossessed." *Art Journal* 49.2 (1990):106–9.

———. *The Face of the Earth: Frontality in Two-Dimensional Mesoamerican Art.* New York: Garland Press, 1976.

Klor de Alva, J. Jorge. "The Aztec-Spanish Dialogues of 1524." *Alcheringa: Ethnopoetics* 4.2 (1980):56–194.

———. "Spiritual Conflict and Accommodation in New Spain: Toward a Typology of Aztec Responses to Christianity." *Inca and Aztec States, 1400–1800.* Ed. George A. Collier, Renato I. Rosaldo, John D. Wirth. New York: Academic Press, 1982.

Knaut, Andrew L. *The Pueblo Revolt of 1680: Conquest and Resistance in Seventeenth-Century New Mexico.* Norman: University of Oklahoma Press, 1995.

Kögelgen Kropfinger, Helga von. "Europaische Buch export von Seville nach Neuspanien im Jahre 1586." In *Europaische Bücher in Neuspanien zu Ende des 16. Jahrhunderts,* 5–105. Wiesbaden: Steiner, 1973.

Kronck, Gary W. *Cometography: A Catalogue of Comets.* Vol. 1, *Ancient–1799.* Cambridge: Cambridge University Press, 1999.

Kubler, George. *Mexican Architecture of the Sixteenth Century.* 2 vols. New Haven, Conn.: Yale University Press, 1948.

———. "On the Colonial Extinction of the Motifs of Pre-Columbian Art." In *Essays in Pre-Columbian Art and Archaeology,* ed. Samuel K. Lothrop, 14–34. Cambridge, Mass.: Harvard University Press, 1961.

———. *The Religious Architecture of New Mexico in the Colonial Period and since the American Occupation.* Colorado Springs, Colo.: Taylor Museum, 1940.

———. *The Shape of Time: Remarks on the History of Things.* New Haven, Conn.: Yale University Press, 1962.

Kubler, George, and Martin Soria. *Art and Architecture in Spain and Portugal and their American Dominions.* Baltimore: Penguin Books, 1959.

Kubovy, Michael. *The Psychology of Perspective and Renaissance Art.* Cambridge: Cambridge University Press, 1986.

Lafaye, Jacques. *Quetzalcoatl and Guadalupe: The Formation of Mexican National Consciousness, 1531–1813.* Trans. Benjamin Keen. Chicago: University of Chicago Press, 1976.

Lamb, Susan. *Pueblo and Mission: Cultural Roots of the Southwest.* Flagstaff, Ariz.: Northland, 1997.

Landa, Fray Diego de. *Landa's Relación de las Cosas de Yucatan: A Translation.* Ed. and trans. Alfred M. Tozzer. Vol. 18, Harvard University, Peabody Museum of American Archeology and Ethnology, Papers. Cambridge, Mass.: The Museum, 1941.

Landa Abrego, María Elena. *Juan Gerson, Tlacuilo.* Puebla, México: Gobierno del Estado de Puebla, 1992.

Landis, Dennis Channing, ed. *The Literature of the Encounter: A Selection of Books from European Americana: Catalogue of an Exhibition.* Providence, R.I.: John Carter Brown Library, 1991.

Lara, Jaime. "Conversion by Theater: The Drama of the Church in Colonial Latin America." *Yale Latin American Review* (spring 1999):49–52.

Las Casas, Bartolomé de. *Apologetica Historia de las Indias I.* Ed. M. Serrano y Sanz. Vol. 1 of *Historiadores de Indias.* Madrid: Bailly, Bailliére y Hijos, 1909.

———. *In Defense of the Indians: The Defense of the Most Reverend Lord, Fray Bartolomé de las Casas, of the Order of Preachers, Late Bishop of Chiapas, against the Persecutors and Slanderers of the Peoples of the New World Discovered across the Seas.* Ed. and trans. Stafford Poole. Dekalb: Northern Illinois University Press, 1974.

Lavin, Irving. *Bernini and the Unity of the Visual Arts.* 2 vols. New York and London: Pierpont Morgan Library and Oxford University Press, 1980.

Lejeune, Jean-François, ed. *The New City.* Coral Gables: University of Miami School of Architecture (fall 1991).

León-Portilla, Miguel. *Aztec Thought and Culture: A Study of the Ancient Nahuatl Mind.* Trans. Jack Emory Davis. Norman: University of Oklahoma Press, 1963.

Levasti, Arrigo, ed. *Mistici del duecento e del trecento.* Milan: Rizzoli, 1935.

Levinson, Jay. A., ed. *Circa 1492: Art in the Age of Exploration.* Washington, D.C.: National Gallery of Art; New Haven, Conn.: Yale University Press, 1991.

Lexikon der christlichen Ikonographie. Ed. Engelbert Kirschbaum, S.J., et al. 8 vols. Rome and Freiburg: Herder, 1972.

Lindberg, David. *Theories of Vision from Al-Kindi to Kepler.* Chicago: University of Chicago Press, 1976.

Little, Lester K. "Pride Goes before Avarice: Social Change and the Vices in Latin Christendom." *American Historical Review* 76 (1971):16–50.

Lockhart, James. *The Nahuas after the Conquest: A Social and Cultural History of the Indians of Central Mexico, Sixteenth through Eighteenth Centuries.* Stanford, Calif.: Stanford University Press, 1992.

———. *Nahuas and Spaniards: Postconquest Central Mexican History and Philology.* Stanford, Calif.: Stanford University Press, 1991.

———, ed. and trans. *We People Here: Nahuatl Accounts of the Conquest of Mexico.* Vol. 1. Berkeley: University of California Press, 1993.

Loerke, William. "'Real Presence' in Early Christian Art." In *Monasticism and the Arts,* ed. Timothy G. Verdon, 29–53. Syracuse, N.Y.: Syracuse University Press, 1984.

Lyell, James P. R. *Early Book Illustration in Spain.* London: Grafton, 1926.

Mace, Carroll Edward. *Two Spanish-Quiché Dance-Dramas of Rabinal.* New Orleans: Tulane University, 1970.

Mâle, Émile. *L'art religieux de la fin du XVIe siécle, du XVIIe siécle et du XVIIIe siécle: Étude sur iconographie aprés le Concile de Trente, Italie–France–Espagne–Flandres.* Paris: Librairie Armand Colin, 1951.

Manrique, Jorge Alberto. "The Progress of Art in New Spain." In *Mexico: Splendors of Thirty Centuries, An Exhibition of Art, October 10, 1990–January 13, 1991,* 237–42. New York: Metropolitan Museum of Art and Bulfinch Press, 1990.

Markman, Sidney David. *Colonial Architecture of Antigua, Guatemala.* Philadelphia: American Philosophical Society, 1966.

Marquina, Ignacio. *Arquitectura prehispanica.* Mexico City: INAH, 1951.

Martínez Marín, Carlos. *Tetela del Volcán: Su historia y su convento.* Mexico City: Universidad Nacional Autónoma de México, 1984.

Mathes, W. Michael. *The America's First Academic Library, Santa Cruz de Tlatelolco.* Sacramento: California State Library Foundation, 1985.

Matos Moctezuma, Eduardo. "The Aztec Main Pyramid: Ritual Architecture at Tenochtitlan." In *The Ancient Americas: Art from Sacred Landscapes,* ed. Richard Townsend, 187–97. Exhibition catalog, Chicago Art Institute, Chicago, October 10, 1992–January 3, 1993.

———. *The Great Temple of the Aztecs, Treasures of Tenochtitlan.* Trans. Doris Heyden. New York: Thames and Hudson, 1988.

Maza, Francisco de la. *Fray Diego Valades: Escritor y grabador franciscano del siglo XVI.* Mexico City: Anales del instituto de investigaciones esteticas nr. 13, 1945.

McAndrew, John. *The Open-Air Churches of Sixteenth-Century Mexico: Atrios, Posas, Open Chapels, and Other Studies.* Cambridge, Mass.: Harvard University Press, 1965.

McHenry, Lawrence C. *Garrison's History of Neurology: Revised and Enlarged with a Bibliography of Classical, Original, and Standard Works in Neurology.* Springfield, Ill.: Charles C. Thomas, 1969.

Mendieta, Fray Gerónimo de. *Historia eclesiástica indiana.* Ed. Fray Joan de Domayquia. 4 vols. Mexico City: Editorial Salvador Chavez Hayhoe, 1945.

———. *Historia eclesiástica indiana: A Franciscan's View of the Spanish Conquest of Mexico.* Lewiston, N.Y.: Edwin Mellen Press, 1997.

Mexico: Splendors of Thirty Centuries, An Exhibition of Art, October 10, 1990–January 13, 1991. New York: Metropolitan Museum of Art and Bulfinch Press, 1990.

Mignolo, Walter D. *The Darker Side of the Renaissance: Literacy, Territoriality, and Colonization.* Ann Arbor: University of Michigan Press, 1995.

Milanich, Jerald T. *Laboring in the Fields of the Lord: Spanish Missions and Southeastern Indians.* Washington, D.C.: Smithsonian Institution Press, 1999.

Milhou, Alain. "El concepto de 'destrucción' en el evangelismo milenario franciscano." In *Actas del II Congreso Internacional sobre los Franciscanos en el Nuevo Mundo: Siglo XVI, La Rábida, 21–26 de septiembre de 1987.* Madrid: Editorial Deimos, 1988.

Millares Carlo, Augustín. "Apuntes para un estudio bibliografico del humanisto Francisco Cervantes de Salazar." In *Cuatro estudios biobibliográficos mexicanos,* 17–159. Mexico City, 1986.

———. *Cuatro estudios biobibliográficos mexicanos: Francisco Cervantes de Salazar, Fray Agustín Dávila Padilla, Juan José De Eguiara y Eguren, José Mariano Beristáin de Souza.* Mexico City: Fondo de Cultura Económica, 1986.

Miller, Arthur G. "The Iconography of the Painting in the Temple of the Diving God, Tulum, Quintana Roo, Mexico: The Twisted Cords." In *Mesoamerican Archaeology: New Approaches: Proceedings of a Symposium on Mesoamerican Archaeology held by the University of Cambridge Centre of Latin American Studies, August 1972,* ed. Norman Hammond, 167–86. Austin: University of Texas Press, 1974.

Miller, Mary, and Karl Taube. *The Gods and Symbols of Ancient Mexico and the Maya: An Illustrated Dictionary of Mesoamerican Religion.* New York: Thames and Hudson, 1993.

Miller, Robert Ryal. *Mexico: A History.* Norman: University of Oklahoma Press, 1985.

Minge, Ward Alan. *Ácoma, Pueblo in the Sky.* Albuquerque: University of New Mexico Press, 1991.

Molina, Fray Alonso de. *Vocabulario del Lengua Castellana y Mexicana.* Mexico City: Casa de Antonio de Spinosa, 1571.

Montes Bardo, Joaquín. *Arte y espiritualidad franciscana en Nueva España, siglo XVI: Iconología en la provincia del Santo Evangelio.* Jaén, Spain: Universidad de Jaén, 1998.

Montgomery, Ross G., Watson Smith, and John Otis Brew. *Franciscan Awatovi: The Excavation and Conjectural Reconstruction of a Seventeenth-Century Spanish Mission Establishment at a Hopi Indian Town in Northeastern Arizona.* Cambridge, Mass.: [Peabody] Museum, 1949.

Montoya, Joe L. *Isleta Pueblo and the Church of St. Augustine.* Isleta, N.Mex.: Saint Augustine Church, Isleta, 1986.

Mora, Paola, Laura Mora, and Paul Philippot. *Conservation of Wall Paintings.* London: Butterworths, 1984.

Morison, Samuel Eliot. *The European Discovery of America: The Northern Voyages,* A.D. *500–1600.* New York: Oxford University Press, 1971.

———. *The European Discovery of America: The Southern Voyages,* A.D. *1492–1616.* New York: Oxford University Press, 1974.

Motolinía, Fray Toribio de Benavente. *Historia de los indios de la Nueva España.* In *Colección de documentos para la historia de México,* ed. Joaquin Garcia Icazbalceta. 1858. Reprint, Mexico City: Editorial Porrúa, 1980.

———. *Historia de los indios de la Nueva España: Relación de los ritos antiguos, idolatrías y sacrificios de los indios de la Nueva España, y de la maravillosa conversión que Dios en ellos ha obrado.* Ed. and annot. Edmundo O'Gorman, Mexico City: Editorial Porrúa, 1969.

———. *Memoriales de. . . .* Mexico City: Casa del Editor, 1903.

———. *Memoriales: Libro de oro,* MS JGI *31.* Ed. and annot. Nancy Joe Dyer. Mexico City: Centro de Estudios Linguísticos y Literarios, El Colegio de México, 1996.

———. *Memoriales o libro de las cosas de la Nuevo España y de los naturales de ella.* Ed. and annot. Edmundo O'Gorman, Mexico City: Instituto de Investigaciones Históricas, Universidad Nacional Autónoma de México, 1971.

———. *Motolinía's History of the Indians of New Spain.* Trans. and annot. Francis Borgia Steck, O.F.M. Washington, D.C.: Academy of American Franciscan History, 1951.

Moyssén, Xavier. "Pinturas murales en Epazoyucan." *Boletin* INAH 22 (1965):20–27.

———. "Tecamachalco y el pintor indigena Juan Gerson." *Anales del Instituto de Investigaciones Estéticas* 33 (1964):23–40.

Mullen, Robert J. *Architecture and Its Sculpture in Viceregal Mexico.* Austin: University of Texas Press, 1997.

———. *Architecture and Sculpture of Oaxaca, 1530s–1980s.* Tempe: Center for Latin American Studies, Arizona State University, 1995.

———. *Dominican Architecture in Sixteenth-Century Oaxaca.* Tempe: Center for Latin American Studies, Arizona State University, 1975.

Mundy, Barbara E. *The Mapping of New Spain: Indigenous Cartography and the Maps of the "Relaciones Geográficas."* Chicago: University of Chicago Press, 1996.

———. "Mapping the Aztec Capital: The 1524 Nuremberg Map of Tenochtitlan, Its Sources and Meanings." *Imago Mundi* 50 (1998):11–33.

Murphy, Dan. *Salinas Pueblo Missions: Abó, Quarai, and Gran Quivira.* Tucson: Southwest Parks and Monuments Assoc., 1993.

Nabokov, Peter. *Architecture of Acoma Pueblo: The 1934 Historic American Buildings Survey Project.* Santa Fe, N.Mex.: Ancient City Press, 1986.

Nabokov, Peter, and Robert Easton. *Native American Architecture.* New York: Oxford University Press, 1989.

Neumeyer, Alfred. "The Indian Contribution to Architectural Decoration in Spanish Colonial America." *Art Bulletin* 30.1 (1948):104–21.

New Catholic Encyclopedia. Washington, D.C.: Catholic University of America, 1967.

Nicholson, Henry B. "Religion in Pre-Hispanic Central America." In *Archaeology of Northern Mesoamerica,* 395–445. Vol. 10 of *Handbook of Middle American Indians.* Austin: University of Texas Press, 1971.

Normann, Anne Whited. "Testerian Codices: Hieroglyphic Catechisms for Native Conversion in New Spain." Ph.D. dissertation, Tulane University, 1985. UMI no. 8515175, Ann Arbor, Mich.

Nova, Alessandro. "'Popular' Art in Renaissance Italy: Early Response to the Holy Mountain at Varallo." In *Reframing the Renaissance: Visual Culture in Europe and Latin America, 1450–1650,* ed. Claire Farago, 113–27. New Haven, Conn.: Yale University Press, 1995.

Nutini, Hugo G., and Betty Bell. *Ritual Kinship: The Structure and Historical Development of the Compadrazgo System in Rural Tlaxcala.* 2 vols. Princeton, N.J.: Princeton University Press, 1980.

Oakley, Francis. *The Western Church in the Later Middle Ages.* Ithaca, N.Y.: Cornell University Press, 1979.

Olvera, H. Jorge. *Finding Father Kino: The Discovery of the Remains of Father Eusebio Francisco Kino, S.J., 1965–1966.* Tucson: Southwestern Mission Research Center, 1998.

Ortiz, Alfonso. *The Tewa World: Space, Time, Being, and Becoming in a Pueblo Society.* Chicago: University of Chicago Press, 1969.

Padden, R. C. *The Hummingbird and the Hawk: Conquest and Sovereignty in the Valley of Mexico.* Columbus: Ohio University Press, 1967.

Pagden, Anthony. *The Fall of Natural Man: The American Indian and the Origins of Comparative Ethnology.* Cambridge: Cambridge University Press, 1982.

Palomera, Esteban J., S.J. *Fray Diego Valadés, o.f.m.: Evangelizador humanista de la Nueva Espana: El hombre, su época y su obra.* Mexico City: Universidad Iberoamericana, 1988.

Panofsky, Erwin. *Albrecht Dürer.* 2 vols. Princeton, N.J.: Princeton University Press, 1948.

———. *Early Netherlandish Painting: Its Origins and Character.* 2 vols. Cambridge, Mass.: Harvard University Press, 1958.

Parkhurst, Charles. "Giotto's Arena Chapel Frescoes and Religious Theater in His Time." Paper delivered at the College Art Association Annual Convention, San Francisco, January 1989.

Passerin d'Entrèves, A. *Natural Law: An Introduction to Legal Philosophy.* London: Hutchinson University Library, 1963.

Pastor, Lodovico [Ludwig] von. *Storia dei Papi dalla fine del Medio Evo.* Rome: Desclée and C. Editori Pontifici, 1926–42.

Pasztory, Esther. *Aztec Art.* New York: Harry N. Abrams, 1983.

Payne, Stanley G. *Spanish Catholicism: An Historical Overview.* Madison: University of Wisconsin Press, 1984.

Pendergast, David M. "Worlds in Collision: The Maya/Spanish Encounter in Sixteenth and Seventeenth Century Belize." In *The Meeting of Two Worlds: Europe and the Americas, 1492–1650,* ed. Warwick Bray, 105–45. Oxford: Oxford University Press, 1993.

Perry, Richard D. *Blue Lakes and Silver Cities: The Colonial Arts and Architecture of West Mexico.* Santa Barbara, Calif.: Espadaña Press, 1997.

———. *Mexico's Fortress Monasteries.* Santa Barbara, Calif.: Espadaña Press, 1992.

———. *More Maya Missions: Exploring Colonial Chiapas.* Santa Barbara, Calif.: Espadaña Press, 1994.

Perry, Richard D., and Rosalind Perry. *Maya Missions: Exploring the Spanish Colonial Churches of Yucatan.* Santa Barbara, Calif.: Espadaña Press, 1988.

Peterson, Jeanette Favrot. *The Paradise Garden Murals of Malinalco: Utopia and Empire in Sixteenth-Century Mexico.* Austin: University of Texas Press, 1993.

———. "Synthesis and Survival: The Native Presence in Sixteenth-Century Murals of New Spain." *Native Artists and Patrons in Colonial America,* ed. Emily Umberger and Tom Cummins. *Phoebus* 7 (1995):14–36.

Phelan, John Leddy. *The Millennial Kingdom of the Franciscans in the New World.* 2d rev. ed. Berkeley: University of California Press, 1970.

Phillips, Richard E. "Processions through Paradise: A Liturgical and Social Interpretation of the Ritual Function and Symbolic Signification of the Cloister in the Sixteenth-Century Mendicant Monasteries of Central Mexico." Ph.D. dissertation, University of Texas, Austin, 1993.

Pierce, Donna L. "From New Spain to New Mexico." In *Converging Cultures: Art and Identity in Spanish America,* ed. Diana Fane et al., 59–69. Exhibition catalog, Brooklyn Museum of Art, Brooklyn, N.Y., March 1–July 14, 1996.

———. "Identification of the Warriors in the Frescoes of Ixmiquilpan." *Research Center for the Arts Review* 4.4 (October 1981):1–8.

———. "The Mission: Evangelical Utopianism in the New World, 1523–1600." In *Mexico: Splendors of Thirty Centuries, An Exhibition of Art, October 10, 1990–January 13, 1991,* 243–69. New York: Metropolitan Museum of Art and Bulfinch Press, 1990.

———. "The Sixteenth-Century Nave Frescoes in the Augustinian Mission Church at Ixquimilpan, Hidalgo, Mexico." Ph.D. dissertation, University of New Mexico, Albuquerque, 1987.

Pierce, Donna, et al. *Transforming Images: Locating New Mexican Santos in between Worlds.* Boulder: University Press of Colorado, forthcoming.

Plato. *Philebus.* Ed. and trans. Robin Waterfield. Hammondsworth, Eng.: Penguin, 1982.

Ponce, Fray Alonso. See Ciudad Real, Fray Antonio de.

Poole, Stafford, C. M. "The Declining Image of the Indian among Churchmen in Sixteenth-Century New Spain." In *Indian-Religious Relations in Colonial Spanish America,* ed. Susan R. Ramírez, 11–19. Syracuse, N.Y.: Maxwell School of Citizenship and Public Affairs, Syracuse University, 1989.

———. *Our Lady of Guadalupe: The Origin and Sources of a Mexican National Symbol.* Tucson: University of Arizona Press, 1995.

———. *Pedro Moya de Contreras: Catholic Reform and Royal Power in New Spain, 1571–1591.* Berkeley: University of California Press, 1987.

Powell, Philip Wayne. "Franciscans on the Silver Frontier of Old Mexico." In *Spanish Borderlands Sourcebook,* ed. David Hurst Thomas, 2:15–31. 1947. Reprint, New York: Garland, 1991.

———. *Soldiers, Indians, and Silver: The Northward Advance of New Spain, 1550–1600.* Berkeley: University of California Press, 1969.

———. *Tree of Hate: Propaganda and Prejudice Affecting United States Relations with the Hispanic World.* New York: Basic Books, 1971.

Prem, Hanns J. "Calendrical Traditions in the Writings of Sahagun." In *The Work of Bernardino de Sahagun, Pioneer Ethnographer of Sixteenth-Century Aztec Mexico,* ed. J. Jorge Klor de Alva, H. B. Nicholson, and Eloise Quiñones Keber, 2:135–49. Institute for Mesoamerican Studies, University at Albany, State University of New York; Austin: Distributed by University of Texas Press, 1977.

Proskouriakoff, Tatiana. *An Album of Maya Architecture.* Norman: University of Oklahoma Press, 1977.

Ramírez Vázquez, Pedro. *Fray Pedro de Gante: El primero y mas grande maestro de la Nueva España.* Mexico City: Editorial Porrúa, 1995.

Read, Kay Almere. *Time and Sacrifice in the Aztec Cosmos.* Bloomington: University of Indiana Press, 1998.

Reiss, Jonathan B. "Justice and the Common Good in Giotto's Arena Chapel Frescoes." *Ars cristiana* 42.701 (1984).

Restall, Matthew. *The Maya World: Yucatec Culture and Society, 1550–1850.* Stanford, Calif.: Stanford University Press, 1997.

Reyes-Valerio, Constantino. *Arte Indocristiano: Escultura del siglo XVI en México.* Mexico City: SEP-INAH, 1978.

———. "Los tlaquilos y tlaquicuic de Ixmiquilpan." *Boletin INAH* 42 (December 1970):9–13.

Reyes-Valerio, Constantino, Gabriela García Lascuráin, Eduardo del Rio, and Mariella Paullada. "El origen de una pintura de Metztitlán." *Antropologia: Boletin Oficial del Instituto Nacional de Antropologia e Historia,* n.s., 9 (1986): 17–18.

Ricard, Robert. *The Spiritual Conquest of Mexico: An Essay on the Apostolate and the Evangelizing Methods of the Mendicant Orders in New Spain, 1523–1572.* Trans. Lesley Byrd Simpson. Vol. 20. Berkeley: University of California Press, 1966.

Robb, David M. "The Iconography of the Annunciation in the Fourteenth and Fifteenth Centuries." *Art Bulletin* 18 (1936):480–526.

Robertson, Donald. *Mexican Manuscript Painting of the Early Colonial Period.* 1959. Reprint, Norman: University of Oklahoma Press, 1994.

Rodack, Madeleine. "Cibola Revisited." In *Southwestern Culture History: Papers Collected in Honor of Albert H. Schroeder,* ed. Charles H. Lange. Santa Fe: Published for the Archaeological Society of New Mexico by Ancient City Press, 1985.

Rogers, Francis M. *The Quest for Eastern Christians: Travels and Rumors in the Age of Discovery.* Minneapolis: University of Minnesota Press, 1962.

Rogers, Mark Christopher. "Art and Public Festival in Renaissance Florence: Studies in Relationships." Ph.D. dissertation, University of Texas, Austin, 1996.

Rosenthal, Earl E. "The Invention of the Columnar Device of Charles V at the Court of Flanders, 1516." *Journal of the Warburg and Courtauld Institutes* 36 (1973):198–230.

———. "*Plus ultra, non plus ultra,* and the Columnar Device of Charles V." *Journal of the Warburg and Courtauld Institutes* 34 (1971).

Roys, Ralph L. "Conquest Sites and the Subsequent Destruction of Maya Architecture in the Interior of Northern Yucatan." In *Contributions to American Anthropology.* Vol. 11, no. 54. Washington D.C.: Carnegie Institution of Washington, 1952.

———. *The Indian Background of Colonial Yucatan.* Washington, D.C.: Carnegie Institution of Washington, 1943.

———. *The Political Geography of the Yucatan Maya.* Washington, D.C.: Carnegie Institution of Washington, 1957.

Rubin, Miri. *Corpus Christi: The Eucharist in Late Medieval Culture.* Cambridge: Cambridge University Press, 1991.

Ruda, Jeffrey. *Fra Lippo Lippi: Life and Works with a Complete Catalogue.* New York: Harry N. Abrams, 1993.

Rugeley, Terry. *Yucatan's Maya Peasantry and the Origins of the Caste War.* Austin: University of Texas Press, 1996.

Sahagún, Fray Bernardino de. "The Aztec-Spanish Dialogues of 1524." Trans. J. Jorge Klor de Alva. *Alcheringa* 4.2 (1980):56–194.

———. *The Florentine Codex: General History of the Things of New Spain.* Trans. Arthur O. J. Anderson and Charles E. Dibble. 2d rev. ed. Santa Fe, N.Mex.: School of American Research, 1981.

———. *Primeros memoriales.* Norman: University of Oklahoma Press, 1997.

Sartor, Mario. *Arquitectura y urbanismo en Nueva Espana: Siglo XVI.* Mexico City: Grupo Azabache, 1992.

Saur, K. G., ed. *Allgemeines Künstlerlexikon: Die bildenden Künstler aller Zeiten und Völker.* 19 vols. Munich and Leipzig: K. G. Saur, 1998.

Schele, Linda, and David Freidel. *A Forest of Kings: The Untold Story of the Ancient Maya.* New York: William Morrow, 1990.

Schele, Linda, and Peter Mathews. *The Code of Kings: The Language of Seven Sacred Maya Temples and Tombs.* New York: Scribner, 1998.

Schlosser, Julius, Ritter von. *La letteratura artistica: Manuale delle fonti della storia dell'arte moderna.* 3d ed. Florence and Vienna: La Nuova Italia, 1964.

Scholes, France V. "Troublous Times in New Mexico, 1659–1670." *New Mexico Historical Review* 12 (1937); 13 (1938); 15 (1940); 16 (1941).

Scholes, France V., and Lansing B. Bloom. "Friar Personnel and Mission Chronology, 1598–1629." *New Mexico Historical Review* 19 (1944):319–36; 20 (1945):58–82.

Schroeder, Susan. "Chimalpahin's View of Spanish Ecclesiastics in Colonial Mexico." In *Indian-Religious Relations in Colonial Spanish America,* ed. Susan R. Ramírez, 21–38. Syracuse, N.Y.: Maxwell School of Citizenship and Public Affairs, Syracuse University, 1989.

Schwaller, John Frederick. *The Church and Clergy in Sixteenth-Century Mexico.* Albuquerque: University of New Mexico Press, 1987.

Sebastián López, Santiago. *Iconografia e iconologia del arte novohispano.* Mexico City: Grupo Azabache, 1992.

———. "La influencia de los modelos ornamentales de Serlio en Hispanoamerica." *Boletin del Centro de Investigaciones Historicas y Esteticas* 7 (1967):30–36.

———. "La significacion salomonica del Templo de Huejotzingo: Mejico." *Traz y baza* 2 (1973):77–88.

Sebastián López, Santiago, José de Mesa Figueroa, and Teresa Gisbert de Mesa. "Arte iberoamericano desde la colonización a la independencia: prima parte." In *Summa artis: Historia general del arte.* Vol. 28. 4th ed. Madrid: Espasa-Calpe, 1992.

Seler, Eduard. *Collected Works in Mesoamerican Linguistics and Archaeology.* 6 vols. Ed. J. Eric S. Thompson and Francis R. Richardson. Lancaster, Calif.: Labyrinthos Press, 1990–98.

Shearman, John. *Only Connect—: Art and the Spectator in the Italian Renaissance.* Princeton, N.J.: Princeton University Press, 1992.

Sheridan, Thomas E., ed. *The Franciscan Missions of Northern Mexico.* New York: Garland Press, 1991.

Shoemaker, William. *The Multiple Stage in Spain during the Fifteenth and Sixteenth Centuries.* Princeton, N.J.: Princeton University Press, 1935.

Simmons, Marc. *The Last Conquistador: Juan de Oñate and the Settling of the Far Southwest.* Norman: University of Oklahoma Press, 1991.

Simson, Otto von. *The Gothic Cathedral: The Origins of Gothic Architecture and the Medieval Concept of Order.* London: Rutledge and Kegan Paul, 1956.

Sleight, Eleanor Friend. *The Many Faces of Cuilapan.* Orlando, Fla.: Pueblo Press, 1988.

Smith, Mary Elizabeth. *Picture Writing from Ancient Southern Mexico: Mixtec Place Signs and Maps.* Norman: University of Oklahoma Press, 1973.

Smith, Watson. *Prehistoric Kivas of Antelope Mesa, Northeastern Arizona.* Cambridge, Mass.: Peabody Museum of Archaeology and Ethnology, Harvard University, 1972.

———. *When Is a Kiva? And Other Questions about Southwestern Archaeology.* Ed. Raymond H. Thompson. Tucson: University of Arizona Press, 1990.

Spence, Jonathan D. *The Memory Palace of Matteo Ricci.* New York: Viking, 1984.

Spicer, Edward H. *Cycles of Conquest: The Impact of Spain, Mexico, and the United States on the Indians of the Southwest, 1533–1960.* Tucson: University of Arizona Press, 1962.

Steele, Thomas J., S.J. *Santos and Saints: The Religious Folk Art of Hispanic New Mexico.* Santa Fe, N.Mex.: Ancient City Press, 1994.

Steinberg, Leo, and Samuel Y. Edgerton. "How Shall This Be? Reflections on Filippo Lippi's *Annunciation* in London." *Artibus et Historiae* 16 (1987):25–55.

Stephens, John Lloyd, and Frederick Catherwood. *Incidents of Travel in Yucatan.* 2 vols. 1843. Reprint, Norman: Oklahoma University Press, 1962.

Stevenson, Robert. *Music in Aztec and Inca Territory.* Berkeley: University of California Press, 1968.

Stoichita, Victor I. *Visionary Experience in the Golden Age of Spanish Art.* London: Reaktion Books, 1995.

Stone, Andrea J. *Images from the Underworld: Naj Tunich and the Tradition of Maya Cave Painting.* Austin: University of Texas Press, 1995.

Storey, Ann Elizabeth. "The Identical 'Synthronos' Trinity: Representation, Ritual, and Power in the Spanish Americas." Ph.D. dissertation, University of Washington, Seattle, 1997.

Sylvest, Edwin Edward, Jr. *Motifs of Franciscan Mission Theory in Sixteenth-Century New Spain, Province of the Holy Gospel.* Washington, D.C.: Academy of American Franciscan History, 1975.

Taylor, René. "El arte de la memoria en la Nuevo Mundo." *44th International Conference of Americanists, Manchester, UK, 1987,* 45–76. Mexico City: Instituto de Investigaciones Esteticas, Universidad Nacional Autónoma de México, 1987.

Taube, Karl Andreas. *The Major Gods of Ancient Yucatan.* Washington, D.C.: Dumbarton Oaks, 1992.

Tedlock, Dennis, ed. and trans. *Popol Vuh: The Definitive Edition of the Mayan Book of the Dawn of Life and Glories of Gods and Kings.* New York: Simon and Schuster, 1996.

Thomas, Hugh. *Conquest: Montezuma, Cortes, and the Fall of Old Mexico.* New York: Simon and Schuster, 1993.

Tierney, Brian. *The Idea of Natural Rights: Studies on Natural Rights, Natural Law, and Church Law, 1150–1625.* Atlanta: Scholars Press, 1997.

Timmer, David. "Providence and Perdition: Fray Diego de Landa Justifies His Inquisition against the Yucatan Maya." *Church History* 66.3 (1997):477–88.

Torquemada, Fray Juan de. *Monarquía indiana.* Ed. Miguel León-Portilla. 7 vols. 1615. Reprint, Mexico City: Instituto de Investigaciones Históricas, Universidad Nacional Autónoma de México, 1975–83.

———. *Monarquía indiana: Selección, introducción, y notas.* Ed. Miguel Léon-Portilla. Mexico City: Universidad Nacional Autónoma de México, 1964.

Torre Villar, Ernesto de la, and Ramiro Novarro. *Testimonios históricos guadalupanos.* Mexico City: Fondo de Cultura Económica, 1982.

Toulouse, Joseph H., Jr. *The Mission of San Gregorio de Abó: A Report on the Excavation and Repair of a Seventeenth-Century New Mexico Mission.* Albuquerque: University of New Mexico Press, 1949.

Toussaint, Manuel. *Colonial Art in Mexico.* Ed. and trans. Elizabeth Wilder Weismann. Austin: University of Texas Press, 1967.

———. *Paseos coloniales.* Mexico City: Imprenta universitaria, 1939.

Tovar de Teresa, Guillermo. "La Utopia del Virrey de Mendoza." In *La Utopia mexicana del siglo XVI: Lo bello, lo verdadero y lo bueno,* ed. G. Tovar de Teresa, M. Léon-Portilla, and S. Zavala, 17–41. Mexico City: Grupo Azabache, 1992.

———. *Renacimiento en México: Artistas y retablos.* Mexico City: Sahop, 1982.

Townsend, Richard. *State and Cosmos in the Art of Tenochtitlan.* Washington, D.C.: Dumbarton Oaks, 1979.

Treib, Marc. *Sanctuaries of Spanish New Mexico.* Berkeley: University of California Press, 1993.

Turner, Christy W., II, and Jacqueline A. Turner. *Man Corn: Cannibalism and Violence in the Prehistoric American Southwest.* Salt Lake City: University of Utah Press, 1999.

Umberger, Emily, and Tom Cummins, eds. "*The Monarchia Indiana* in Seventeenth-Century New Spain." In *Converging Cultures: Art and Identity in Spanish America,* ed. Diana Fane et al., 46–59. Exhibition catalog, Brooklyn Museum of Art, Brooklyn, N.Y., March 1–July 14, 1996.

———. *Native Artists and Patrons in Colonial Latin America. Phoebus* 7 (1995).

Valadés, Fray Diego. *Retórica Cristiana.* Facsimile of the 1579 Latin *Rhetorica Christiana* with facing-page Spanish translation by Tarsicio Herrera Zapien. Mexico City: Universidad Nacional Autónoma de México, Fondo de Cultura Económica, 1989.

———. *Rhetorica Christiana, ad concionandi, et orandi usum accommodata virisque facultatis exemplis suo loco insertis: Quae quidem ex indorum maxime deprompta sunt historijs. Unde, praeter doctrinam summa quoque delectatio comparabitur . . . R. admodum P. F. Didaco Valadés totius ordinis Fratrum Minorum Regularis Observantia olim Procuratore Generali.* Perugia, 1579.

Vásquez Janeiro, Isaac, OFM. "Fray Diego de Valadés, nueva aproximación a su biografía." In *Actas del II Congreso Internacional sobre Los Franciscanos en el Nuevo Mundo: Siglo XVI, La Rábida, 21–26 de septiembre de 1987.* Madrid: Editorial Deimos, 1988.

Very, Francis George. *The Spanish Corpus Christi Procession: A Literary and Folkloric Study.* Valencia, Spain: Tipografia Moderna, 1962.

Vetancurt, Agustín de. *Teatro mexicano, descripción breve de los sucesos ejemplares, históricos y religiosos del Nuevo Mundo de las Indias: Crónica de la Provincia del Santo Evangelico de Mexico. . . .* Mexico City: Editorial Porrúa, 1982.

Vijil, Ralph H. "Bartolomé de Las Casas, Judge Alonso de Zorita, and the Franciscans: A Collaborative Effort for the Spiritual Conquest of the Borderlands." In *Spanish Borderlands Sourcebook,* ed. David Hurst Thomas, 20:1–15. 1981. Reprint, New York: Garland, 1991.

Vitruvius, Marcus Pollio. *Vitruvius on Architecture: De architectura libri decem.* Ed. and trans. Frank Granger. 2 vols. London: W. Heinemann, 1934.

Vivian, Gordon. *Excavations in a Seventeenth-Century Jumano Pueblo: Gran Quivira, with a Chapter on Artifacts from Gran Quivira.* Tucson: Southwest Parks and Monuments Assoc., 1979.

Vogt, Evon Z. *Tortillas for the Gods: A Symbolic Analysis of Zinacanteco Rituals.* Norman: University of Oklahoma Press, 1993.

Voorburg, René. "The Aztec Calendar." http://www.aztec calendar.com.

Wagner, Eugene Logan. "Open Space as a Tool of : The Syncretism of Sacred Courts and Plazas in Post-Conquest Mexico." Ph.D. dissertation, University of Texas, Austin, 1997.

Watts, Pauline Moffitt. "Hieroglyphs of Conversion: Alien Discourses in Diego Valades's *Rhetorica Christiana.*" *Memorie Domenicane,* n.s., 22 (1991):405–33.

———. "Languages of Gesture in Sixteenth-Century Mexico: Some Antecedents and Transmutations." In *Reframing the Renaissance: Visual Culture in Europe and Latin America, 1450–1650,* ed. Claire Farago, 140–52. New Haven, Conn.: Yale University Press, 1995.

———. "Prophecy and Discovery: On the Spiritual Origins of Christopher Columbus's 'Enterprise of the Indies.'" *American Historical Review* 90.1 (1985):73–102.

Weber, David J. *The Spanish Frontier in North America.* New Haven, Conn.: Yale University Press, 1992.

Webster, Susan Verdi. *Art and Ritual in Golden Age Spain: Sevillian Confraternities and the Processional Sculpture of Holy Week.* Princeton, N.J.: Princeton University Press, 1998.

———. "Art, Ritual, and Confraternities in Sixteenth-Century New Spain: Penitential Imagery at the Monastery of San Miguel, Huejotzingo." *Anales del Instituto de Investigaciones Esteticas* 70 (1997b):5–43.

———. "The Descent from the Cross in Sixteenth-Century New Spain." *Early Drama, Art, and Music Review* 19.2 (spring 1997a):69–85.

Weckmann, Luis. *The Medieval Heritage of Mexico.* Trans. Frances M. López-Morillas. New York: Fordham University Press, 1992.

Weil, Mark. "The Devotion of the Forty Hours and Roman Baroque Illusion." *Journal of the Warburg and Courtauld Institutes* 37 (1974):218–49.

Weismann, Elizabeth Wilder. *Art and Time in Mexico: Architecture and Sculpture in Colonial Mexico.* New York: Harper and Row, 1985.

———. *Mexico in Sculpture, 1521–1821*. Cambridge, Mass.: Harvard University Press, 1950. Reprint, Greenwood Press, Westport, Conn., 1971.

West, Delno C., and August Kling, eds. and trans. *The Libro de las profecías of Christopher Columbus*. Gainesville: University of Florida Press, 1991.

Whitecotton, Joseph. *Zapotecs: Princes, Priests, and Peasants*. Norman: University of Oklahoma Press, 1977.

Williams, Ronald Boal. *The Staging of Plays in the Spanish Peninsula prior to 1555*. Iowa City: University of Iowa Press, 1935.

Williamson, Roy A. *Living the Sky: The Cosmos of the American Indian*. Norman: University of Oklahoma Press, 1984–87.

Wirth, Diane E. *A Comprehensive Guide to the Gods of Ancient Mexico*. Longmont, Colo.: Privately published, 1996.

Wittkower, Rudolph. *Art and Architecture in Italy, 1600–1750*. Baltimore: Penguin Books, 1958.

Wright, Ronald. Review of *The Devil in the New World: The Impact of Diabolism in New Spain* by Fernando Cervantes. *London Times Literary Supplement*, February 17, 1995, 25.

Wroth, William. *Christian Images in Hispanic New Mexico: The Taylor Museum Collection of Santos*. Colorado Springs: Taylor Museum, 1982.

Yates, Frances A. *The Art of Memory*. Chicago: University of Chicago Press, 1966.

Zavala, Silvio. "La 'Utopia' de Tomas Moro en la Nueva España." In *La Utopia mexicana del siglo XVI: Lo bello, lo verdadero y lo bueno*, G. Tovar de Teresa, M. Léon-Portilla, and S. Zavala, 67–95. Mexico City: Grupo Azabache, 1992.

———. *Recuerdo de Vasco de Quiroga*. Mexico City: Editorial Porrúa, 1987.

Zimmermann, Günter. *Die Relationen Chimalpahin's zur Geschichte México's. Vol. 1, Die Zeit bis zur Conquista, 1521*. Vol. 2, Das Jahrhundert nach der Conquista, 1522–1615. Hamburg: Cram, Degruyter, 1963–65.

INDEX

(Page numbers for photos and illustrations are in italics.)